RECENT ISSUES IN THE THEORY
OF FLEXIBLE EXCHANGE RATES

Studies in
Monetary Economics

Editor

KARL BRUNNER

Associate Editors

RUDIGER DORNBUSCH
PIETER KORTEWEG
THOMAS MAYER

Volume 8

NORTH-HOLLAND PUBLISHING COMPANY – AMSTERDAM • NEW YORK • OXFORD

Recent Issues in the Theory of Flexible Exchange Rates

FIFTH PARIS–DAUPHINE CONFERENCE ON
MONEY AND INTERNATIONAL MONETARY PROBLEMS
JUNE 15–17, 1981

Edited by

E. CLAASSEN

Université Paris–Dauphine and INSEAD

P. SALIN

Université Paris–Dauphine

1983

NORTH-HOLLAND PUBLISHING COMPANY–AMSTERDAM · NEW YORK · OXFORD

ISBN: 0 444 86389 3

Publishers

NORTH-HOLLAND PUBLISHING COMPANY
AMSTERDAM · NEW YORK · OXFORD

Sole Distributors for the U.S.A. and Canada

ELSEVIER SCIENCE PUBLISHING COMPANY, INC.
52 VANDERBILT AVENUE
NEW YORK, N.Y. 10017

Library of Congress Cataloging in Publication Data

Paris-Dauphine Conference on Money and International
    Monetary Problems (5th : 1981 : University of
    Paris-Dauphine)
    Recent issues in the theory of flexible exchange
rates.

    (Studies in monetary economics ; v. 8)
    1. Foreign exchange–Congresses. I. Claassen,
Emil Maria, 1934-   .   II. Salin, Pascal
III. Université de Paris IX: Dauphine.   IV. Title.
V. Series.
HG205 1981   332.4'56   82-14315
ISBN 0-444-86389-3 (U.S.)

PRINTED IN THE NETHERLANDS

INTRODUCTION TO THE SERIES

This new series will publish books of interest to students and researchers working in the fields of macroeconomics, monetary theory and policy, banking and the operation of financial markets. It is intended that works of empirical emphasis will be included in the series along with theoretical contributions. Publications will include research monographs and the proceedings of significant conferences. The editor welcomes submissions of manuscripts for inclusion in the series.

IN MEMORY OF

HARRY G. JOHNSON

CONTENTS

PREFACE

This is the third North-Holland publication of the Paris—Dauphine Conferences on Money and International Monetary Problems. The first one was *Stabilization Policies in Interdependent Economies* published in 1972 and the second one *Recent Issues in International Monetary Economics* appeared in 1976.

This conference has been made possible by the generous help of the Thyssen Stiftung. For additional financial help we are grateful to the Crédit Commercial de France, to the Délégation Générale à la Recherche Scientifique et Technique, to the German Marshall Fund, to the US Embassy in Paris, to the Association pour la Liberté Economique et le Progrès Social (ALEPS) and especially to the University of Paris—Dauphine at which the conference was held. The rapid publication of the conference volume at a relatively low price has been made possible by a subsidy granted by the French Government at the beginning of July 1981 though her agency, the Commissariat Général du Plan.

The conference volume has been dedicated to the memory of Harry G. Johnson. He participated at all other Paris—Dauphine Conferences. There is no doubt that without his intellectual and moral encouragement these conference would not have taken place.

Emil CLAASSEN
Pascal SALIN

LIST OF PARTICIPANTS

FLORIN AFTALION, Ecole des Sciences Sociales, Economiques et Commerciales, Cergy, France
VICTOR ARGY, OECD, Paris, France
GIORGIO BASEVI, Università di Bologna, Bologna, Italy
JEAN-CLAUDE CHOURAQUI, OECD, Paris, France
MAX CORDON, Nuffield College, Oxford, England
EMIL-MARIA CLAASSEN, Université Paris–Dauphine, Paris, France and European Institute of Business Administration, Fontainebleau, France
MICHAEL CONNOLLY, University of South Carolina, Columbia, South Carolina, USA
STANLEY FISCHER, Massachussets Institute of Technology, Cambridge, USA
JACOB A. FRENKEL, University of Chicago, Chicago, USA
HELMUT FRISCH, Technische Universität, Vienna, Austria
ROBERT GORDON, Northwestern University, Evanston, Illinois, USA
PAUL DE GRAUWE, Université Catholique de Louvain, Louvain, Belgium
ABDESSATAR GRISSA, Institut Supérieur de Gestion, Université de Tunis, Le Bardo, Tunisia
ARMIN GUTOWSKI, HWWA-Institut für Wirtschaftsforschung, Hamburg, Germany
RONALD W. JONES, Rochester University, Rochester, New York, USA
SERGE-CHRISTOPHE KOLM, Ecole Nationale des Pont et Chaussées, Paris, France
PENTTI J.K. KOURI, New York University, New York, USA and Helsinki University, Helsinki, Finland
DAVID LAIDLER, University of Western Ontario, London, Canada
HERWIG LANGOHR, European Institut of Business Administration, Fontainebleau, France
FRITZ MACHLUP, Princeton University, Princeton, USA
JOHN MARTIN, OECD, Paris, France
JACQUES MELITZ, Institut National de la Statistique et des Etude Economiques, Paris, France
ROBERT A. MUNDELL, Columbia University, New York, USA
DOUGLAS D. PURVIS, Queen's University, Kingston, Canada
JEFFREY SACHS, Harvard University, Cambridge and National Bureau of Economic Research, USA
NASSER SAÏDI, Institut Universitaire des Hautes Etudes Internationales, Geneva, Switzerland and University of Chicago, Chicago, USA
PASCAL SALIN, Université Paris–Dauphine, Paris, France
JÜRGEN SCHRÖDER, Universität Mannheim, Germany
FRANCO SPINELLI, Instituto di Economia Università Cattolica, Milan, Italy
ALEXANDER SWOBODA, Institut Universitaire des Hautes Etudes Internationales, Geneva, Switzerland
HENRI TEZENAS DU MONTCEL, Université Paris–Dauphine, Paris, France
HENRY C. WALLICH, Board of Governors of the Federal Reserve System, Washington, USA
CHARLES WYPLOSZ, European Institute of Business Administration, Fontainebleau, France

INTRODUCTION

Emil-Maria CLAASSEN and Pascal SALIN

We are pleased to present a new volume of studies on international monetary economics. The papers presented at the Fifth Paris-Dauphine Conference on Money and International Monetary Problems[1] help to give a better understanding of the working of floating exchange rate systems. In fact, the generalization of floating rates, mainly since 1973, has given to the observer a great choice of practical experiences which allow a better empirical analysis of exchange rate models. Meanwhile, the theoretical debate has been greatly deepened during that period so that it is not excessive to say that there is now a traditional — although recent — approach to the functioning of the system of flexible exchange rates.

The following papers draw on this conventional corpus of theory. In particular they accept the purchasing power parity doctrine as the basic factor in the long-run determination of the exchange rate. But they prefer to focus on short-run aspects, especially because it appears, from the actual working of floating rates in the seventies, that the variability of some important variables — for instance, nominal and real exchange rates, trade balances, interest rates — was higher than had been expected. The contributions to the present volume offer several new and important ideas to explain these phenomena. Moreover, some of them try to define principles for the determination of optimal policies in an environment of imperfect information.

The volatility of nominal exchange rates in the present floating exchange rate system is often described as "erratic". Moreover, it corresponds to a significant volatility of real exchange rates which means that exchange rate changes and/or relative national monetary policies are not neutral, at least in the short run. The three papers in the first part of the book, *Nominal and Real Exchange Rates*, give different and not incompatible explanations for these phenomena.

As *Saïdi/Swoboda* show in their contribution "Nominal and Real Exchange Rates: Issues and Some Evidence", based on empirical research of a series of countries, there is:

---

[1] The proceedings of some of the former Paris-Dauphine Conferences have been published as *Stabilization Policies in Interdependent Economies* (North-Holland, 1972), *Recent Issues in International Monetary Economics* (North-Holland, 1976) and *Exchange Rate Regimes and Currency Areas (Zeitschrift für Wirtschafts- und Sozialwissenschaften*, 1979, Duncker & Humblot, Berlin).

— a high degree of variability in the real exchange rate;
— a strong positive correlation between changes in the nominal and real exchange rates;
— a correlation between changes in the real exchange rate and deviations in real output from its trend value.

The explanation of these phenomena is contained in their stochastic model which represents an extension of the standard open-economy IS—LM model. The high variability of the nominal and real exchange rate is produced by general disturbances to the economy which may affect the supply-side or the demand-side. Supply-side shocks produce a negative correlation of nominal and real exchange rates. Demand-side shocks involve the opposite case. One type of demand-side shock refers to monetary disturbances and, in particular, to monetary policy. Only the unanticipated portion of monetary policy — the "news" component — affects the real exchange rate. Because their model includes the hypothesis of the natural unemployment rate with rational expectations, both a Phillips-curve type relationship between inflation and output and a relationship between the real exchange rate and output emerge only from unexpected movements in aggregate demand.

In their paper "International Differences in Response to Common External Shocks: The Role of Purchasing Power Parity", *Jones/Purvis* propose another explanation for the variability of real exchange rates. This explanation does not rely on lags or on an index problem, but on differences in the way countries react to a common external shock (an increase in the world price of a commodity). The authors assume that the commodity imported from the rest of the world by two small countries is not directly consumed, but is a middle product. The law of one price is realized at all times for the middle product, which is also produced in the two small countries. However, the answer of these countries is not similar to an increase in the world price with respect to the value-added and, therefore, to the general price level. In fact, the world increase in the price of the middle product induces reallocations of labor. With full employment and perfect adjustment of wages, according to differences in techniques, the value-added does not change in the same proportion in both countries. Under *fixed exchange rates*, the effect of the increase in the world price of the middle product (implying a decrease in real income) depends on monetary policy. If, for instance, the quantity of money in a small country does not increase, there is a transitory discrepancy between income and consumption and a corresponding trade balance surplus which influences the reallocation of factors. Moreover, the precise change in the general price level depends on the "flexibility" of the economy (for instance, the technological flexibility). Therefore, there are real exchange rate changes, although the law of one price is effective at any time. Under *flexible exchange rates* the differences in wages (when there is a common external real shock) are absorbed by the exchange rate and national prices reflect differences in the dependence on imports. Jones and Purvis claim that their model explains long-run discrepancies of the nominal exchange rate from the PPP-rate without having to have recourse to relative price changes. However, their conclusions stem from the assumption that one part of the price of the final product — the national value-added — is not submitted to the law of one price. This part of the product is not tradable. In that sense it can be considered that the explanation of real exchange rate changes given by Jones and Purvis belongs to the broader class of relative price changes, the relevant prices being here the price of the input and the price of the value-added. Instead of assuming, as in traditional models, that there are tradable goods and non-tradable goods, it is assumed here that goods have a tradable component and a non-tradable component.

The paper by *Claassen* brings another explanation for the changes in real exchange rates. Using a simple two-country quantity-theoretical model, he extends the (now) usual analysis to a two-country case with an explicit real exchange rate. An expansionary monetary policy of the inside type, i.e. without any wealth effect, has an effect on the interest rate. Applying the Mundell analysis of the effect of inflation on capital formation, he analyses the change in the stock of real capital and in the stock of foreign assets due to the interest rate effect in the home country and their influences on the real exchange rate. Monetary creation implies a depreciation of the real exchange rate and a corresponding trade imbalance. This effect is a long-run one and it lasts until a steady state has been reached. In the steady state interest payments between countries create a slight real exchange rate effect.

The second part of the book broadens the issue of floating rates to the examination of the *Macroeconomics of Flexible Exchange Rates.*

What does happen to the exchange rate, to employment and to the price level of a small and thus very open economy when there is an external shock in the form of a higher real interest rate in the international economy? This is the basic question *Kouri* asks in his paper "Macroeconomic Adjustment to Interest Rate Disturbances: Real and Monetary Aspects". The short-run effects are rather known in the literature. An increase in the world interest rate causes a shift from domestic towards foreign assets and thus leads to an immediate depreciation. The domestic interest rate begins to adjust to the international one. There is a fall in the demand for money because of the rise in the interest rate and in order to equilibrate the money market for a given money supply, the domestic output increases in a Keynesian model and the domestic price level rises in a quantity-theoretical model. Furthermore, in general, both frameworks imply a surplus in the current account provided that the economy was initially in a stationary full-stock equilibrium. As it is also known from the literature, in the new long-run stock equilibrium where the current account will be again in balance, there will be an appreciation of the real exchange rate because the increase in foreign interest earnings has to be matched by a trade account deficit. It is at this moment in the sequence of events where Kouri's proper analysis starts. With capital market integration, the domestic economy has to adjust to changes in the world interest rate in the same way that it has to adjust to changes in the terms of trade, in the relative price of traded and non-traded goods or in the relative prices of raw materials. An interesting aspect of the Kouri paper concerns his discussion of the welfare implications of capital controls. Capital market integration improves efficiency of intertemporal resource allocation and increases domestic welfare even though it exposes the domestic economy to fluctuations of the world interest rate.

Connolly's paper on "Exchange Rates, Real Economic Activity and the Balance of Payments: Evidence from the 1960s" deals with the question of the effects of a change in the exchange rate (in most cases the effects of a devaluation) on the real growth rate on the one hand and on the balance of payments on the other hand. This subject, even though it does not refer properly to the regime of flexible exchange rates, gives nevertheless some information on the main effects of a change in the exchange rate, still relevant for many countries having an adjustable peg today, or for the effects of a permanent change in the rate of exchange under floating exchange rates. The first evidence from a series of devaluations in the 1960s concerns a rather weak relationship between the magnitude of devaluation and the positive effect on the growth rate. Changes in growth appear to be related more to the magnitude of the previous slump existing before the devaluation so that any additional growth may reflect recovery from a recession rather than the expansionary effects of a devaluation *per se* on aggregate demand and/or aggregate supply. As *Schröder* points out in his comment, one possible interpretation of this result is the fact that the devaluation-induced increase in nominal wages may have been moderate because of the previous slump so that there was little negative effect — or even a positive one — on domestic activity via aggregate supply. The other empirical relationship concerns the effect of devaluation on the balance of payments. It is shown that the extent of improvement in the balance of payments is weakly related to the rate of devaluation, but rigidly linked to the domestic credit policy carried out for one or two years after the devaluation. This evidence certainly gives support to the monetary approach of the balance of payments.

The contribution by *Sachs* on the "Aspects of the Current Account Behaviour of OECD Economies" represents a rather non-orthodox approach of explaining current account imbalances, on the one hand, and of establishing a possible link between current account imbalances and the behaviour of the nominal and real exchange rate, on the other hand. As far as the first aspect is concerned, Sachs starts from the accounting identity for which the current account imbalance is equal to the difference between savings and investment (by neglecting the government sector). Whereas he considers saving shifts as rather irrelevant for current account deficits or surpluses (even though the oil shocks could have worked temporarily on savings through the drop in real income leading only much later to a reduction in absorption when the fall in real income was felt as a permanent one), he attaches the dominant role to the behaviour of investment. With respect to the second aspect, the link between the current account and the exchange rate, he presents a by far richer model based on intertemporal choices than those models which exist in recent literature. The wealth effect of current account imbalance which leads to the exchange rate movements comprises not only changes in financial assets but also changes in human capital and in the value of fixed capital. Even though he gives some empirical support to the recent theory that current account surpluses (deficits) are accompanied by the appreciation (depreciation) of the nominal and real exchange rate at least for large countries, on a theoretical level he does not find any clear-cut relationship. Because current account imbalances are mainly related to shifts in investment where the latter constitutes a large part relative to financial assets, a high rate of investment may cause a current account deficit, but a strong wealth effect of investment may appreciate the exchange rate. In the traditional models, a current account deficit implies declining wealth and thus depreciation. By explicitly considering investment, a current account deficit may be accompanied by rising wealth and thus by appreciation, in particular if the deficit reflects an investment boom.

The paper by *Laidler, Bentley, Johnson* and *Johnson*, "A Small Macroeconomic Model of an Open Economy: The Case of Canada", is an extension and adaptation to the case of a small economy in a system of flexible exchange rates of a former model which had been tested for the United Kingdom and Italy. The model is used to study the relationships between the exchange rate, the balance of payments, inflation, output and the monetary and fiscal policy variables. It is first shown that the model, when it is applied to the case of Canada, only works by assuming that Canada behaves "as if" the exchange rate was fixed or, at least, was exogenous (the changes in the exchange rate being exogenous in relation to the variables of the model). The modified model considers a complete independence of the inflation expectations on the exchange rate in the years of a flexible exchange rate. There are rational expectations with respect to the exchange rate. Moreover, in order to take account of the fact that there is dirty floating, the model includes the variable "exchange market pressure", which is the sum of the change in the log of reserves and the change in the log of the exchange rate. However, the introduction of this variable does not make possible the description of a policy reaction function. In conformity with the theory, it appears that inflation is proxied by lagged world inflation under fixed exchange rates and by lagged domestic inflation under flexible rates. The fact that the exchange rate does not play a role in the determination of expected inflation could imply that there is no vicious circle. In both exchange rate systems the real income is influenced by fiscal and monetary policies and by the level of national prices in relation with world prices. Excess demand and inflation expectations explain actual inflation.

The phenomenon that the exchange rate overshoots its long-run equilibrium value during the adjustment process towards an overall equilibrium situation has been observed and much analysed in the contemporary literature. In his "Exchange Rate Oscillations and Catastrophe Theory", *De Grauwe* starts from this literature and tries to explain a continuous overshooting around the long-run equilibrium value of the exchange rate where these oscillations are characterized furthermore by jumps (a "catastrophe") of the exchange rate. His basic assumption is that of the well-known hypothesis about the different speed of adjustment in the financial assets markets and in the goods markets when there is a disequilibrium in both of them. The "fast" variable is the exchange rate (and the interest rate) and the "slow" variables are the price level and real output. His basic framework is that of the interest rate parity. Using extrapolative expectations for the exchange rate when the latter is near to the long-run equilibrium level *and* (non-linear) regressive expectations for the opposite situation, De Grauwe obtains the phenomenon of oscillations of the exchange rate in the neighbourhood of the equilibrium exchange rate.

The third part of the book is concerned with the *Behaviour of Monetary Authorities under Floating Exchange Rates.* Frenkel/Aizenman and Melitz in their respective papers discuss the choice of instruments, whereas Grissa tries to draw lessons from the behaviour of the authorities during a specific period of floating rates – that of France in the 1920s.

The paper by *Frenkel* and *Aizenman* "Aspects of the Optimal Management of Exchange Rates" is an effort to go beyond the traditional discussion about fixed vs. flexible exchange rates, as is expressed for instance in the literature on optimum currency areas. Frenkel/Aizenman determine a coefficient of optimal managed float taking into account the existence of three sorts of shocks (monetary, real and foreign ones). As was found by Fischer, the desirability of fixed rates is greater when the variance of real shocks is high. Similarly, if there were only monetary shocks it would be optimal that exchange rate changes correct them and the desirability of flexibility is increased by a high speed of adjustment to asset disequilibrium. If the variance of real shocks is great, the fluctuations in the trade balance play a compensating role. Therefore, in order to minimize the fluctuations in the transitory income, central banks have to intervene and it is optimal that they have larger reserves. However, a part of the real shock can be absorbed by the capital market if people hold part of their transitory income in the form of securities so that the need for official reserves is lower. The desirability of flexibility is reduced by a low openness of the country (characterized by a high relative proportion of non-tradable goods), especially if the elasticities of demand and supply are low. In fact, in such a case, a greater part of the adjustment to a monetary shock takes place through relative price changes which make exchange rate changes less desirable. In the reverse case, in a completely open economy, adjustment cannot take place via relative price changes. In other words, the internal price flexibility due to the existence of non-tradables is a substitute to external flexibility. Therefore, Frenkel/Aizenman's analysis leads to an important conclusion: contrary to traditional wisdom according to which a small country ought to choose fixity for considerations related to the liquidity of money, a high degree of openness may create a justification for flexibility. As the authors underline in their conclusion, their prescriptions rely on the implicit assumption that shocks come from the private sector and not from government intervention. The government is assumed to have more information, although the index of optimal intervention they define is not intended to be perfectly precise and is rather a sort of qualitative guide for the choice of exchange rate management.

The role of information is also crucial in the paper by *Melitz*. The optimal choice of instruments, generally speaking, depends on the model, on the value of the coefficients of the model and on the characteristics of the random variables. Melitz also assumes that the authorities have a good knowledge of the underlying macroeconomic model (and, implicitly, he further assumes that his own model represents a correct specification). Therefore the policy prescriptions only depend on the value of the coefficients and the characteristics of the random variables. Four variables can play the role of instruments in the model: the interest rate, the quantity of money, the exchange rate and the level of reserves. From the structure of the model, two variables can be instruments. However, not all pairings are possible (for instance, it is not consistent to have an interest rate policy and a quantity of money policy). Moreover, it is also assumed that, for instance, the exchange rate and the quantity of money are not inconsistent in the long run with the monetary policy of other countries. The past literature on the policy-mix had made clear that there would not be any problem of choice of instruments if there was perfect information on the working of the macroeconomic system.[2] The approach of Melitz is similar: given some general knowledge on the *relative* value of different coefficients and the relative importance of different shocks, is it possible to recommend efficient policy mixes in order to minimize a loss function, which is a combination of the variances of prices and income? The choice of instruments may vary according to the relative importance of price targets and income targets. However, it appears generally that, when there is intervention on the exchange market, it is preferable to have control of the quantity of money than of the interest rate. When the authorities have adopted a policy of monetary control, it is not clear whether one has to choose a reserve policy or an exchange rate policy.

The paper by *Grissa*, "The French Monetary and Exchange-Rate Experience in the 1920s", sheds some light on an important experience of floating rates. Following the opinion of Nurkse, it is usually considered that this experience is one of inherent instability of floating rates, where the persistent depreciation of the franc was self-aggravating because of its effects on the quantity of money (anticipations made the renewing of short-run treasury bills more difficult, causing a higher monetary creation). Grissa shows that there was not an automatic vicious circle. In fact, the savers no longer desired to re-buy pegged Treasury bills, and they bought non-pegged bonds. The increase in the money supply was mainly due to the direct financing of the government by the Banque de France and to the budget deficit. In turn, the depreciation of the franc resulted from the change in the equilibrium rate and not from destabilizing speculation. The instability of the franc became tremendous when there had been a considerable political instability (from October 1925 to July 1926) and uncertainties about the future monetary and fiscal policies. The return to stability of the exchange rate occurred, without any central bank intervention, when the government succeeded in controlling the quantity of money and the budget deficit.

---

[2] See, for instance, A.K. Swoboda, "On Limited Information and the Assignment Problem", in: E.M. Claassen and P. Salin (eds.), *Stabilization Policies in Interdependent Economies* (Amsterdam, North-Holland, 1972).

PART I

NOMINAL AND REAL EXCHANGE RATES

Recent Issues in the Theory of Flexible Exchange Rates, edited by E. Claassen and P. Salin
© *North-Holland Publishing Company, 1983*

Chapter 1.1

NOMINAL AND REAL EXCHANGE RATES: ISSUES AND SOME EVIDENCE

Nasser SAÏDI and Alexander SWOBODA*

1. Introduction

Recent literature has paid a great deal of attention to changes in the "real exchange rate", its determinants and implications. The real exchange rate is usually defined as the ratio of a broadly based index of "the" foreign price level expressed in domestic currency units (through multiplication by the exchange rate) to a similar index of the domestic price level. A change in the real exchange rate then reflects a discrepancy between the rate of change of the nominal exchange rate and the difference between domestic and foreign price level inflation. Though wide use of the "real exchange rate" terminology is relatively new, the issues and interpretations are not. There are at least three analytical contexts within which variations in the real exchange rate play a crucial role, though they go, or went, by another name.

The first of these is of course the purchasing power parity (PPP) doctrine. There, changes in the real exchange rate are called deviations from PPP and are taken to reflect either temporary disequilibria of monetary origin that will be corrected by exchange rate or price level changes, or more long-lasting changes in a variety of real conditions, or, finally, measurement error. In the absence of these last two factors, the maintenance of PPP over the medium to long run is a consequence of either the law of one price, or of homogeneity of degree zero in money and prices, or both.[1]

A second tradition focuses on changes in the terms of trade as a source of real exchange rate variations or as a consequence of nominal exchange rate changes. At the extreme, it is assumed that countries produce and export different products whose domestic currency price is fixed; a given percentage change in the nominal exchange

* Support from research grant No. 4.367.079.09 of the Swiss National Science Foundation is gratefully acknowledged.
[1] In the presence of non-traded goods, the law of one price is not sufficient to insure PPP even when no changes in real factors are at work. On the other hand, even if all economies were "homogeneous" there must be at least one traded good (or asset) whose price is equalized internationally to provide a link between price levels and the exchange rate.

rate then produces an equivalent change in the terms of trade, and on the assumption of specialization in production and no purely domestic goods, in the real exchange rate. In that view, or model, which underlies much of the work in open-economy macro-economics in the Keynesian (with or without money) tradition, the nominal exchange rate is thus a powerful instrument to affect the real exchange rate, the terms of trade, the trade balance, and unemployment.

Third, more recent analysis has emphasized the role of the relative price of traded and non-traded goods, especially in the short run. With the law of one price holding for traded goods and no change in the terms of trade occurring, changes in the real exchange rate must reflect, barring measurement error and weighting problems, changes in the price of non-traded relative to traded goods. An increase in the real exchange rate (a nominal depreciation of the home currency in excess of the difference between home and foreign inflation) is interpreted as a gain in competitiveness (a "real depreciation") which is associated with an increase in the relative price of non-traded goods abroad and/or a decrease in the relative price of non-traded goods at home. A change in the nominal exchange rate is seen as changing the real exchange rate if the price of non-traded goods is not immediately brought into line with that of traded goods. For instance, a devaluation may at first depress the *relative* price of non-traded goods at home, raising the real exchange rate in the process, and yielding an improvement in the trade balance and a positive output effect.

The real exchange rate thus has become a seemingly convenient, though somewhat confusing, variable on which to focus attention, both analytically and for policy purposes. This tendency has been reinforced by the observation of a number of stylized facts. First, although purchasing power parity seems to hold in the long run, the real exchange rate has proved highly variable in the short run, suggesting that it is influenced by cyclical, or highly volatile, monetary variables in addition to longer-term real forces. Second, short-run movements in real exchange rates tend to be dominated by nominal exchange rate rather than by relative price level variations. Third, movements in levels of real exchange rates are highly auto-correlated; they persist over significant periods of time. Fourth, they seem to some extent to be correlated with changes in real economic activity in a manner which, the models sketched above would suggest, is consistent with their being of monetary origin.

These observations together with analytical considerations, not to mention more popular beliefs, have suggested that variations in the real exchange rate are one means by which monetary policy can affect the domestic economy in addition to playing a crucial role in the international transmission of economic disturbances. This paper examines this view critically.

We proceed by reviewing briefly some empirical evidence on the behavior of real exchange rates and explanations for that behavior in the next section, paying particular attention to the role of monetary disturbances and to the connection between nominal and real exchange rate changes. We conclude that traditional explanations all rely on either money illusion (including wage rigidity) of some kind or on the existence of disequilibrium (including non-equilibrium expectations) to explain the stylized facts referred to above, in particular the association between money, the real exchange rate, and real economic activity.

Section 3 presents a simple rational expectations model capable of accounting for this association. The model is in the Mundell–Fleming tradition but incorporates a natural rate of unemployment and rational expectations. The inclusion of these features yields implications that are broadly compatible with the observed behavior of nominal and real exchange rates but carry non-traditional policy conclusions. The most noteworthy implications are as follows: (1) the correlation between nominal and real variables arises from their response to common underlying disturbances; (2) the sign of the contemporaneous correlation between the nominal and real exchange rate depends on the source of the disturbance (supply *versus* demand); (3) output variations are correlated with both nominal and real exchange rate changes; (4) monetary policy exerts systematic effects on the nominal exchange rate but, just as the output–inflation trade-off is not exploitable by monetary policy, neither is the output–real exchange rate trade-off; (5) the model does yield positively serially correlated movements in the real exchange rate, but these serially correlated movements do not imply a role for monetary policy.

2. Real exchange rate changes: Evidence and explanations

2.1. *Empirical regularities*

Three characteristics of the recent behavior of real exchange rates are especially relevant in the present context: (1) real exchange rates appear to exhibit near constancy, or mild trends, only over the long run (PPP holds approximately in the long run); (2) real exchange rates are highly variable in the short run; (3) deviations of the real exchange rate from trend exhibit strong positive serial correlation – in other words, deviations from PPP are persistent. In addition, a number of associations between changes in real exchange rates and in other variables appear to characterize their behavior. Two of these are of particular interest here: (i) changes in nominal and real exchange rates exhibit a strong correlation in the short run: movements in nominal rates seem to "dominate" movements in real exchange rates; (ii) movements in real exchange rates in turn appear to be correlated with deviations of output from trend. We review briefly some of the evidence for these characteristics and associations below.

The tendency for PPP to hold over longer time periods is well documented in either time series or cross-section studies. For instance, Gailliot (1970) presents supporting evidence on a time series basis over a more than sixty-year period. In a recent paper, Saïdi and Swoboda (1981) use data for 44 countries over 1960–1979 to test, on a cross-section basis, a number of long-run neutrality propositions. The evidence strongly supports these propositions a few of which are particularly relevant here. It turns out that a given change in the difference between two countries' rates of monetary expansion elicits an equal change (a) in the difference in their rates of price inflation and (b) in the rate of exchange-rate depreciation. It follows that a given change in the inflation differential between two countries is associated with an equal change in the rate of exchange-rate depreciation, i.e. the "real exchange rate" is constant over the long run or, if you prefer, relative PPP holds over that run. In addition, it turns out that across these countries and over the long run, changes in nominal exchange-rate depreciation are independent of the rate of change of the real exchange rate.[2]

Turning to the short-run variability of real exchange rates, the evidence overwhelmingly points to large deviations from PPP. For instance, Frenkel (1981), based on monthly observations, concludes that purchasing power parity, even in its relative version, has thoroughly collapsed as a short-run relationship between inflation differentials and rates of change of exchange rates in the 1970s. This is confirmed in Saïdi and Swoboda (1981) who argue, in addition, that PPP hardly held better, as a short-run relationship in the 1920s than in the 1970s. The variability of real exchange rates is also illustrated in table 1.1 which presents summary statistics on the mean and standard deviations of the quarterly rates of change of spot and real exchange rates for six industrial countries over the period 1974 I to 1980 III.[3] With the exception of Canada, there is a tendency for real appreciation over the period *vis-à-vis* the United States, relative to which all statistics are calculated, casting doubt on the constancy of the real dollar exchange rate over that particular period. More relevant here are the large standard deviations of changes in real exchange rates relative to their mean (note also the variance of the real exchange rate is of the same order of magnitude as that of the nominal rate). These

Table 1.1
Summary statistics.[a]

	Means			Standard deviations		
	(1) Ds	(2) Dq (CPI)	(3) Dq (WPI)	(4) Ds	(5) Dq (CPI)	(6) Dq (WPI)
United Kingdom	−0.000044	−0.01561	−0.0149	0.0454	0.0456	0.0478
Italy	0.0133	−0.00411	−0.00355	0.0404	0.0355	0.0299
Germany	−0.01339	−0.00272	−0.00139	0.0389	0.0404	0.0432
Japan	−0.00821	−0.00832	−0.00203	0.0492	0.0497	0.0454
Canada	0.00546	0.00504	0.00362	0.0164	0.0164	0.0172
Switzerland	−0.0241	−0.0108	−0.0040	0.0484	0.0499	0.0490

Data are quarterly and extend from 1974 I to 1980 III (except for Canada where the last observation is 1980 II).
Source: IFS tapes.
[a] Ds denotes the rate of change of the bilateral (period average) exchange rate with the U.S. dollar; Dq the corresponding rate of change of the real exchange rate, defined as SP^*/P, where P^* is the U.S. price index (CPI or WPI).

[2] Saïdi and Swoboda (1981) also provide some times series evidence on the longer-run near-constancy of real exchange rates, both in the 1920s and 1970s. For a review of stylized facts about nominal exchange rates, see Mussa (1979).
[3] With the exception of Canada, where the sample period extends only to 1980 II.

deviations are clearly inconsistent with short-run constancy of real exchange rates.

Movements of real exchange rates around their long-term mean, furthermore, exhibit high positive serial correlation. This correlation appears quite clearly if one plots the residuals of regressions of real exchange rates on a constant and time trend and from the Durbin–Watson statistics of such regressions.[4] The persistence of deviations raises a number of questions as to the stochastic process generating them. Table 1.2 helps gain some insight into the time series behavior of real exchange rates. It presents the results of autoregressions of real exchange rates for the six countries mentioned above, using quarterly data over the period 1974–1980. To focus on non-systematic movements of the real exchange rate, we prefiltered the time series data by a preliminary regression of (the log of) the level of the real exchange rate on a constant, time trend, and seasonal dummies. Autoregressions of the filtered data, including three lags, were calculated for three different measures of the real exchange rate using, respectively, CPIs, WPIs, and GDP or GNP deflators as price indices.

The results suggest that levels of real exchange rates tend to follow a low-order autoregressive process. Most countries in the sample exhibit a first-order autoregression (in some cases the possibility of a random walk cannot be excluded) or a second-order process. This implies that shocks to the level of real exchange rates tend to have substantial "persistence". In addition, once corrections for constant terms and time trend have been made, the real exchange rate process is highly similar for WPI- and CPI-based measures of q. The standard error of the regressions (S.E. in table 1.2) are virtually identical.[5] The GNP- or GDP-based regressions are broadly similar to those based on other price indices but have higher standard errors as a result of the higher variance of the q-series based on these deflators.

These results are quite similar to those obtained by Saïdi and Swoboda (1981) for the time series behavior of monthly observations of the real exchange value of the Swiss franc in terms of four other currencies (the RM-DM, \$, £, and FF) for both the 1920s and 1970s. Autoregressions including up to six lags were calculated for (prefiltered) series based on WPIs for the 1920s and on both WPIs and CPIs for the 1970s. Of the twelve resulting autoregressions, five appear to follow a second-order regression, the majority (the remaining seven) a first-order scheme with an autoregression parameter close to unity (close to a random walk for the level deviations). In all cases the autocorrelation coefficients fall off very rapidly towards zero. The first common statistical regularity is again that a low-order autoregression fits the data. A second regularity is that, for each currency, essentially the same autoregressive scheme fits real exchange rate changes in both the 1920s and 1970s. Third, the 1970s autoregressions of deviations based on monthly wholesale prices indices are again virtually identical to those based on CPIs.

---

[4]   See Swoboda (1981) for such regressions and plots, using quarterly data for the five countries mentioned in the preceding footnote plus Switzerland and the United States. The value of the D.W. statistic ranges from 0.062 to 0.375.

[5]   It seems, though, that a_1 tends to be somewhat higher for the CPI than for the WPI regressions with the reverse pattern holding for a_2.

Table 1.2
Autoregressions of real exchange rates: Quarterly data, 1974 II – 1980 IV. Estimates of: $q_t = \sum_{i=1}^{3} a_i q_{t-i} + u_t$.[a] (Standard errors in parentheses)

	United Kingdom			Italy			Germany			Japan			Canada			Switzerland	
	CPI	WPI	PGDP	CPI	WPI	PGDP	CPI	WPI	PGNP	CPI	WPI	PGNP	CPI	WPI	PGNP	CPI	WPI
a_1	0.89 (0.20)	0.76 (0.20)	1.04 (0.20)	1.01 (0.20)	0.91 (0.21)	1.05 (0.20)	0.65 (0.21)	0.60 (0.20)	0.70 (0.21)	1.31 (0.20)	1.05 (0.20)	1.19 (0.19)	1.12 (0.21)	0.91 (0.20)	1.29 (0.22)	0.95 (0.21)	0.83 (0.21)
a_2	−0.02 (0.27)	0.01 (0.25)	−0.09 (0.29)	−0.07 (0.29)	−0.13 (0.29)	−0.13 (0.29)	0.05 (0.25)	−0.05 (0.24)	−0.007 (0.26)	−0.39 (0.33)	−0.29 (0.29)	−0.15 (0.31)	−0.20 (0.34)	−0.02 (0.28)	−0.43 (0.34)	−0.12 (0.30)	−0.09 (0.27)
a_3	0.02 (0.20)	0.07 (0.20)	−0.05 (0.20)	−0.16 (0.20)	−0.03 (0.21)	−0.10 (0.20)	0.06 (0.19)	0.19 (0.19)	0.06 (0.19)	−0.15 (0.21)	−0.07 (0.20)	−0.30 (0.20)	−0.11 (0.22)	−0.18 (0.19)	−0.06 (0.20)	−0.17 (0.22)	−0.05 (0.21)
R^2	0.728	0.651	0.805	0.745	0.627	0.764	0.454	0.392	0.485	0.847	0.690	0.844	0.787	0.648	0.823	0.617	0.510
D.W	1.77	1.69	1.79	1.73	1.76	1.67	1.47	1.46	1.49	2.08	2.04	2.04	1.96	2.00	1.93	1.75	1.69
S.E	0.0455	0.0455	0.0488	0.0335	0.0314	0.0354	0.0408	0.0408	0.0411	0.0409	0.0404	0.0408	0.0154	0.0157	0.0182	0.0497	0.0498

Source: IFS tapes.
[a] q_t is obtained from the residuals of a regression of log $(SP*/P)$ on a constant, time trend, and seasonal dummies. Column headings identify the price indexes, $P*$ and P, used in calculating q.
The exchange rate, S, is the quarterly average of the domestic price of the U.S. dollar. Price indices are quarterly averages. For Canada, the sample extends from 1974 II to 1980 III.

Thus, movements in real exchange rates, once correction is made for systematic components, seem to share similar time series properties across countries, time periods, and alternative price indices. As we note in Saïdi and Swoboda (1981), they share these common properties with a large number of other macroeconomic time series, the behavior of which is investigated, for instance, by Nelson and Plosser (1980). This suggests to us the important implication that movements in real exchange rates cannot be explained solely by deterministic models. Rather, an interpretation is likely to emerge from the type of stochastic model also capable of explaining the time series behavior of a large number of macroeconomic variables.

Turning to associations between movements in real exchange rates and other economic variables, we begin by noting that, though the association between the quantity of money and the nominal rate of exchange is very close in the long run, it is far from exact in the short run.[6] On the other hand, the relationship between nominal and real exchange rate changes appears strong in the short run but vanishes in the long run (see above). The short run is illustrated in table 1.3. As the bottom part of the table shows, simple correlations between quarterly changes in nominal and real exchange rates are quite strong. Another measure of the strength of the association is given by the coefficient of determination (R^2) of regressions of the real on one future, current, and lagged values of the nominal exchange rate (top part of table 1.3) and of the reverse regressions (middle part of table 1.3).[7] Two features of the results are worth noting here. First, the R^2's are uniformly high for these first-differenced distributed lags, whether one includes real or nominal exchange rates as right-hand-side variables. Second, for any given country, the strength of the association is roughly similar whether a CPI, WPI, or GNP deflator is used to define the real exchange rate.[8]

Both the extent of the correlation between Δq and ΔS (bottom part of table 1.3) and an examination of individual coefficients of the regressions underlying the R^2's reported in table 1.3 indicate that the relationship between Δq and ΔS is largely contemporaneous. As a tentative conclusion, changes in real and nominal exchange rates appear to be jointly determined by underlying disturbances.

Whether the short-run association between nominal and real exchange rates is exploitable by policy is another matter. The tentative conclusion that movements in both variables may be jointly generated by an underlying stochastic process casts doubts on this possibility. Nevertheless, and contrary to the neutrality results in Saïdi and Swoboda (1981), it has been suggested that over medium-time spans (say 4 to 5 years), a somewhat loose but nevertheless significant relationship does exist between nominal and real exchange rates. For instance, taking a sample of fifteen industrialized countries and regressing the change in the real exchange rate over the period March 1973 to

---

[6] On the long-run relationship, see the neutrality propositions tested in Saïdi and Swoboda (1981).
[7] We have not reported individual regression coefficients here since (likely) correlation of the error term with the independent variable leads to inconsistent estimates. Instead we concentrate on measures of association.
[8] The association appears slightly weaker for the WPI.

Table 1.3
Real, nominal exchange rate associations: Quarterly.

		U.K.	Italy	Germany	Japan	Canada	Switzerland
R^2 for regressions:[a] $\Delta q_t = a_0 + \sum_{i=-1}^{+3} b_i \Delta S_{t-i} + u_t$	CPI	0.889 (0.0173)	0.933 (0.0100)	0.973 (0.0072)	0.951 (0.0130)	0.835 (0.0070)	0.979 (0.0085)
	WPI	0.890 (0.0181)	0.750 (0.0170)	0.941 (0.0113)	0.934 (0.0139)	0.800 (0.0084)	0.961 (0.0111)
(real on nominal)	PGNP PGDP	0.930 (0.0148)	0.917 (0.0121)	0.980 (0.0060)	0.974 (0.0096)	0.926 (0.0065)	n.a.
R^2 for regressions: $\Delta S_t = a'_0 + \sum_{i=-1}^{+3} b'_i \Delta q_{t-i} + v_t$	CPI	0.881 (0.0180)	0.948 (0.0102)	0.966 (0.0076)	0.945 (0.0133)	0.825 (0.0075)	0.979 (0.0082)
	WPI	0.875 (0.0185)	0.848 (0.0176)	0.933 (0.0106)	0.945 (0.0137)	0.825 (0.0068)	0.929 (0.0111)
(nominal on real)	PGNP PGDP	0.924 (0.0144)	0.936 (0.0114)	0.980 (0.0058)	0.973 (0.0093)	0.923 (0.0050)	n.a.
Correlations of Δq and ΔS	CPI	0.925	0.942	0.980	0.931	0.917	0.988
	WPI	0.907	0.703	0.960	0.833	0.872	0.965

Definition of variables and source: see table 1.2.
[a] The standard error of the regression is given in parentheses.

December 1978 on the change in the nominal effective rate, Dornbusch finds that it takes, on average, a five percent nominal depreciation to "induce" a one percent depreciation (increase) of the real exchange rate.[9] As Swoboda (1981) points out, however, the relationship is very unstable: it loses significance and the parameters change for only slight changes in the estimation period.

In short, the relationship between nominal and real exchange rates, though strong in the very short run, disappears in the long run, and is highly unstable in the medium run. This suggests, on the one hand, that the dynamics of any model attempting to explain movements in the real exchange rate should be able to generate a statistical association between nominal and real rates of exchange. It suggests, on the other hand, that the relationship, though stable over short periods of time, is unstable over longer periods and may not be systematically exploitable by policy. The implications are very similar to those attached to the statistical association between inflation and unemployment rates — the inflation–output trade-off. The existence of a relationship between nominal and real exchange rates in the short run does not imply that it is exploitable by policy since the very attempt to do so will tend to change the coefficient relating the real to the nominal exchange rate.

Interest in variations in real exchange rates arises partly from a presumption that such changes are associated with changes in real activity as measured by output or the trade balance. Table 1.4 reports the contemporaneous correlations between first-differences of exchange rates (nominal and real) and output. The results suggest the following observations. In contrast to the high, positive correlation between nominal and real exchange rates, the correlation between these two variables and output movements are weak, though the correlation between real exchange rate changes and output movements may, on the whole, be somewhat stronger. Correlations of changes in output with leads and lags in nominal and real exchange rates (not shown here) tend to be weaker than the contemporaneous correlations and exhibit a variety of patterns. This

Table 1.4
Changes in output, nominal, and real exchange rates: Contemporaneous correlations.

Correlation of Δy with: [a]	U.K.	Italy	Germany	Japan	Switzerland	Canada
ΔS	0.17	0.24	0.24	−0.07	0.39	−0.07
Δq (CPI)	0.24	0.22	0.23	0.10	0.44	−0.22
Δq (WPI)	0.24	0.09	0.24	0.17	0.37	−0.12

Definitions and source: see table 1.2.
Quarterly data for 1974 I to 1980 IV (1980 III for Canada).
[a] Δy is a change in GNP (Germany, Japan, Canada), GDP (Italy, United Kingdom), or industrial production (Switzerland).

[9] See Swoboda (1981) for reference to this finding and discussion thereof.

loose association of exchange rates and output, together with the fact that, though most of the contemporaneous correlations are positive, some are negative, suggests that the association is the result of common underlying disturbances, and that the nature of the association may well depend on the sources of the disturbances (monetary *versus* real shocks, or demand *versus* supply disturbances). Hence, one avenue for future research is to investigate the dynamic response of exchange rates (nominal and real) and output to the occurrence of alternative disturbances. Further, it may be the case that exchange rate movements are more closely associated with changes in the composition of economic activity (e.g. exportables *versus* importables, traded *versus* nontraded) rather than with measures of aggregate economic activity.

Finally, one additional feature of the relationship between real exchange rates and real output may be mentioned here. Preliminary results obtained by Nasser Saïdi on the German and Swiss cases shed some light on the relation between unexpected movements in real exchange rates and deviations of output growth from trend. Using annual data for the postwar period, he finds a positive correlation between real output and contemporaneous and lagged values of innovations in the real exchange rate; a one-period lead of the real exchange rate is also significant. As similar results obtain for the association between current changes in the real exchange rates and current, past, and future values of real output growth deviations, one may tentatively conclude that causation runs both ways. The pattern of coefficients is remarkably similar for the German and Swiss cases.

2.2. *Explaining real exchange rate changes*

Traditional explanations for changes in the real exchange rate ("deviations from PPP") can, for convenience, be regrouped under four broad headings: (1) failure of the law of one price; (2) measurement error; (3) real explanations; (4) monetary explanations. The same models often underlie explanations that fall under the third and fourth heading. We comment briefly on each of these categories below.

(1) *Failure of the law of one price.*   The observation that domestic currency equivalents of fairly narrow SITC categories of goods tend to differ and vary at different rates across countries has led to the expression of doubts as to the validity of the law of one price as a maintained hypothesis in international economic analysis. Relying on an asserted, or observed, failure of the law of one price as an explanation for real exchange rate changes is, however, thoroughly unsatisfactory until one explains *why* the law of one price fails. The existence of transport cost or impediments to trade (of whatever form) is not sufficient to explain divergences in terms of rates of price change, even if it can explain differences in levels. The same is true of monopolistic practices or product differentiation beyond the very short run. This is not to deny that search and information considerations lead one to expect price distributions for the same product across as well as within countries. But an analysis of real exchange-rate changes that systematically builds on this insight is a far cry from a simple appeal to the failure

of markets. In fact, most of the explanations usually given for the apparent failure of the law of one price basically appeal to one form of measurement error or another.

(2) *Measurement error.*   A large part of recorded long-run as well as short-run variations in real exchange rates may be due to measurement problems. Most of these are well known and only the most obvious are listed here with little comment.[10] First, since price indices are averages of individual prices, they will tend, by virtue of the law of large numbers, to be less variable than the exchange rate (which is the price of one particular "good"), making for high variability of the real exchange rate. Second, differences in the timing of data collection (or of administered price changes), differences in the tax treatment (including trade barriers) of individual items, differences in the seasonal pattern of price fluctuations among countries, all make for measured, and possibly persistent systematic deviations from PPP. Third, different weights (in national price indices) for different commodity groups, whether traded or non-traded, induce deviations from PPP when relative prices change; these deviations will be persistent as long as relative price changes persist.[11]

It should be noted that though the various reasons given above can potentially explain a substantial portion of the systematic elements in deviations from PPP, they fail, in and of themselves, to provide an account of the time series behavior of real exchange rates. An explanation related to measurement error has been recently provided by Magee (1977). He shows that, if domestic and foreign goods prices are fixed at contract time in terms of the expected exchange rate, deviations from the law of one price will be generated by forecast errors in the exchange rate, even though PPP always holds on an *ex ante* basis. For individual goods, the variance of measured deviations from PPP can be shown (on the assumption of a random walk for the exchange rate) to increase with contract length. Furthermore, if there is a distribution of contract lengths, an aggregated price index of traded goods will show persistent deviations from PPP. In fact, the "real exchange rate" will follow a moving average process with monotonically declining weights and mean zero, if the nominal exchange rate follows a random walk. The degree of serial correlation in deviations from PPP depends on the frequency distribution of contract lengths. Magee's model thus possesses several attractive features and is consistent with part at least of real exchange rate behavior. A number of questions, however, remain. The model is highly sensitive to the assumed nature of the contract (which, given the foreign price at t_0, fixes the actual future delivery domestic currency price at $t_0 + j$ to domestic buyers on the basis of the exchange rate expected to prevail at $t_0 + j$ as of t_0); the coexistence of different spot and contract prices requires explanation; relative price changes between traded and non-traded goods should be allowed an influence; and one would wish to see the contract-length insight imbedded in a more general model capable of generating both exchange rate and price movements from underlying real and monetary shocks.

---

[10]   See, for instance, Saïdi and Swoboda (1981) for further comments.
[11]   See Appendix A for an illustration of the role of different weighting schemes and on the relation between relative price changes and the real exchange rate.

(3) *Changes in underlying real variables*.   Changes in technology and tastes may lead to changes in relative prices (both in terms of trade and/or the relative price of non-traded goods) and these in turn to changes in the real exchange rate. Stockman (1980), for instance, shows that exogenous changes in the terms of trade induce systematic deviations from purchasing power parity and a correlation between the exchange rate and the terms of trade, a correlation which, however, cannot be exploited by monetary policy. The model used to reach these conclusions is an equilibrium model which incorporates rational expectations and relies heavily on wealth effects.

The most popular "real" explanation for variations in the real exchange rate is the Balassa—Samuelson hypothesis on the secular variation of the price of traded relative to non-traded goods. Fast growing economies at an early stage of development may experience a more rapid growth in the relative price of non-traded goods than more mature and more slowly growing economies, and hence a fall in their real exchange rate (whether one calls this a "measurement" problem or not is to a large extent a moot question).

Though such changes in the underlying structure of tastes and technology can play an important role in explaining measured longer-term changes in real exchange rates, it is doubtful that they can explain the cyclical pattern of real exchange rate changes and their short-term association with nominal exchange rate changes. To explain the latter, the literature has, on the whole, focused on the role of monetary disturbances.

(4) *Monetary disturbances*.   Monetary disturbances can have an effect on the real exchange rate in standard versions of both the exportables/importables and traded/non-traded goods models. These effects usually rely on the existence of some form of money illusion (or lagged adjustment) and/or static expectations. Under flexible exchange rates an increase in the domestic money supply depreciates the domestic currency, worsens the terms of trade and, provided marginal propensities to import sum to less than unity, leads to a fall in the real exchange rate, provided domestic currency prices are rigid.[12] More interestingly, money supply shocks can have systematic short-run effects on the real exchange rate in the traded/non-traded goods model, apparently without drawing on money illusion in the fixed exchange rate case. An increase in the home money stock results in an increase in the relative price of non-traded goods (provided that market adjusts instantaneously), and a temporary fall in the real exchange rate, *provided* that it takes time for the initial deficit in the balance of payments to resorb itself. The process thus relies on slow adjustment in the traded goods or asset markets, which is not unlikely if the shock to the money supply is unexpected and price expectations are static, but much less so otherwise. Under flexible rates, the traded/non-traded goods model provides a channel for monetary effects on the nominal and real exchange rate (and a positive association between the two) on the reverse assumption that the traded goods market clears instantaneously but that non-traded goods prices are sticky. A monetary expansion induces a rise in the price of foreign exchange, a decrease in the relative price of non-traded goods (an increase in the real exchange rate) and an excess demand for the home good which may be associated with transistory positive output

[12]   See Appendix A.

effects. These effects disappear with full price and wage flexibility and are most relevant, again, to the case of unexpected changes in the money stock and static expectations.

Models that combine differential speeds of adjustment in different markets with some explanation for the stickiness in prices and wages have recently become popular to explain the association between the nominal exchange rate, the real rate, and output changes. For instance, Dornbusch (1980a, chapter 9) presents a traded/non-traded goods model under variable exchange rates in which there are overlapping wage contracts which generate persistence of price disturbances. Such models have the advantage of producing time series behavior of nominal rates, real exchange rates and output that are somewhat consistent with the stylized facts reviewed above. They have, however, a number of serious disadvantages. They assume, first, that the structure of wage contracts is independent of the economic environment. Second, to the extent that wage contracts are industry wide but are entered at different points of time, these models would imply that business cycles are industry-specific and out of phase with each other, an implication that does not seem to be borne out empirically. Third, they imply that there are systematic differences at one point in time in the rewards to the same factor of production depending on the time of contracting. It may be possible to justify such differences by appeal to the existence of imperfect information, but one would like to have the nature of the imperfection spelled out and incorporated, together with the expectations formation process, in the specification of the model and of the wage contracting process.

In brief, standard models of the relationship between monetary disturbances, exchange rate changes and prices do provide elements in the explanation of real exchange rate changes. They do, however, suffer from a number of defects from our point of view. First, they tend to rely on either money illusion or non-equilibrium expectations to generate real effects of nominal exchange rate changes. Second, they fail to provide a convincing explanation for the time series cyclical behavior (and cross correlations) between the nominal exchange rate, the real exchange rate, and real output. Third, they are most relevant to unexpected changes in money and fail to give much insight into the effects (or lack of such) of systematic components of monetary policy on real variables in a framework in which economic agents are assumed to make the best use of the information at their disposal.

3. Real exchange rates and expectations in a stochastic model

This section discusses some of the issues raised above in the context of an illustrative model. Specifically, we address the following questions. First, what factors determine the high correlation between movements in nominal and real exchange rates? Do underlying real disturbances imply a different cross-correlation pattern than financial or monetary disturbances? Further, what underlies the temporal dependence of the process generating movements in real exchange rates? Second, what is the nature of the association between movements in real exchange rates and measures of economic activity such as aggregate output or unemployment? Third, given the existence of a structural relationship between movements in real exchange rates and aggregate activity, what determines the dynamic relationship between exchange rates and real activity? Further, what role do expectations play in the dynamic process? Fourth, given the presence of a systematic impact of monetary and financial variables on the time path of nominal exchange rates, what are the implications for the conduct of monetary policy? In particular, does the presence of a relationship between monetary variables and real exchange rates, and a relationship between real exchange rates and aggregate activity imply scope for monetary policy as a device for the stabilization of economic activity? Is there an "exploitable" relationship between nominal exchange rate movements and aggregate activity?

To suggest some answers, we have harnessed a version of the standard Mundell–Fleming open economy aggregative model. There are obvious limitations to working within an *ad hoc* framework. Our strategy is to inquire whether a parsimonious modification of the standard workhorse is capable of yielding predictions that are consistent with "stylized facts" about real and nominal exchange rates. An additional concern is whether our version of the standard aggregative model supports some commonly accepted policy prescriptions.

Our stochastic version of the open-economy IS–LM model under flexible exchange rates is contained in eqs. (1)–(6). We interpret this linearized model as applying to cyclical movements in the included variables and abstract from systematic growth and long-run structural changes.

$$y_t = a_0 + a_1 (p_t - p_t^e) + a_2 y_{t-1} + u_t, \qquad a_1 > 0, \quad 0 < a_2 < 1, \tag{1}$$

$$m_t = p_t + c_0 + c_1 y_t - c_2 i_t + v_t, \qquad c_1, c_2 > 0, \tag{2}$$

$$y_t = b_0 - b_1 [p_t - (p_{t+1}^e - i_t)] - b_2 (p_t - s_t - p_t^*) + \epsilon_t, \qquad b_1, b_2 > 0, \tag{3}$$

$$i_t = i_t^* + s_{t+1}^e - s_t, \tag{4}$$

$$i_t^* = r_t^* + (p_{t+1}^{*e} - p_t^*), \tag{5}$$

$$x_{t+j}^e = E(x_{t+j} | \Omega_{t-1}), \qquad j \geq 0, \quad x \equiv p, p^*, s. \tag{6}$$

Equation (1) is an aggregate supply schedule for the domestic good incorporating the natural rate hypothesis. It is consistent with the existence of one-period wage contracting,[13] with an unexpected increase in the price of final output reducing the real wage and implying an increase in output. The lagged output term appearing above can be justified by appeal to the existence of costs of adjustment penalizing rapid changes

---

[13] See Appendix B.

in production. As will be seen below, this dynamic element is important in explaining temporal dependence of the real exchange rate. As an aside, note that the specification in (1) constrains the transmission of foreign disturbances to domestic output to operate via the channel of current and/or lagged price prediction errors. This is an obvious limitation if the intent is to discuss the transmission of supply shocks. One remedy is to allow a richer specification of production technology to include trade in intermediate inputs or capital. But that is the subject of another and different paper.

Equation (2) is a standard portfolio balance schedule. We assume that domestic and foreign one-period bonds differ only with respect to currency denomination. With perfect capital markets, (4) says that the equilibrium nominal rate of interest i_t can differ from the exogenous foreign rate i_t^* only by the expected rate of change of the exchange rate. Equation (5) says that the foreign rate is determined by movements in the real rate and in expected foreign inflation.[14]

Aggregate demand for domestic output (3) is inversely related to the real rate of interest and to the relative price of domestic to foreign output, $(p_t - s_t - p_t^*)$, the inverse of the "real exchange rate" $(s_t + p_t^* - p_t)$ in this model. Domestic and foreign goods are imperfect substitutes, so that an increase in home output faces a downward sloping demand schedule. Note that commodity arbitrage implies that the (log of) domestic price of the foreign good is $(s_t + p_t^*)$. The aggregate demand schedule is shifted by the random term ϵ_t, which is assumed to incorporate both domestic and foreign (export) shocks.[15] Finally and for simplicity, we assume that wealth effects are negligible so that, for example, no real balance terms appear in (3).

Equations (1)–(5) determine the equilibrium values of p_t, s_t, and y_t as a function of the time paths of exogenous and predetermined variables, the random shocks, u_t, v_t, ϵ_t, and the expectations. To close the model we impose rationality so that the expectations appearing in (1)–(5) are linear least-squares forecasts conditioned on information available up to the beginning of period t, Ω_{t-1}, as in (6). For notational simplicity we use the notation $E_{t-1} x_{t+j}, j \geqslant 0$, to refer to the projection of x_{t+j} on the information set Ω_{t-1}.

To determine the equilibrium paths of p, s and y, solve (1)–(5) for the values of p_t and s_t that clear the output and asset markets.[16] These reduced forms are:[17]

$$p_t = \gamma_0 + \gamma_1 E_{t-1} p_t + \gamma_2 E_{t-1} p_{t+1} + \gamma_3 p_t^* + \gamma_4 m_t + \gamma_5 (i_t^* + E_{t-1} s_{t+1})$$

$$+ \gamma_6 y_{t-1} + \gamma_7 v_t + \gamma_8 u_t + \gamma_9 \epsilon_t, \tag{7}$$

---

[14] Foreign variables are exogenous in this version. However, the home country faces a downward-sloping demand curve for its exports.

[15] For simplicity, the dependence of aggregate demand on foreign expenditure is suppressed. The effects of unexpected foreign demand shifts is captured by the composite error term ϵ_t. Below, it is seen that the latter generate unanticipated price movements and lead to fluctuations in domestic output.

[16] See Appendix B for additional discussion.

[17] It can be easily checked that the following coefficients are positive: $\gamma_1, \gamma_2, \gamma_3, \gamma_4, \gamma_5, \gamma_9$, ϕ_4, ϕ_5. The other coefficients of the reduced form (apart from constant terms) are negative.

where

$$\gamma_1 = -a_1 \gamma_8, \quad \gamma_2 = b_1 \gamma_9, \quad \gamma_3 = \gamma_5 = b_2 \gamma_9, \quad \gamma_4 = (b_1 + b_2) k^{-1},$$

$$\gamma_6 = a_2 \gamma_8, \quad \gamma_7 = -\gamma_4, \quad \gamma_8 = -[c_2 + c_1(b_1 + b_2)] k^{-1},$$

$$\gamma_9 = c_2 k^{-1}, \quad k = a_1 c_2 + (1 + a_1 c_1 + c_2)(b_1 + b_2).$$

$$s_t = \phi_0 + \phi_1 E_{t-1} p_t + \phi_2 E_{t-1} p_{t+1} + \phi_3 p_t^* + \phi_4 m_t + \phi_5 (i_t^* + E_{t-1} s_{t+1})$$

$$+ \phi_6 y_{t-1} + \phi_7 v_t + \phi_8 u_t + \phi_9 \epsilon_t, \tag{8}$$

where

$$\phi_1 = a_2 \phi_8, \quad \phi_2 = b_1 \phi_9, \quad \phi_3 = b_2 \phi_9, \quad \phi_4 = -\phi_7,$$

$$\phi_5 = [c_2(a_1 + b_1 + b_2) + b_1(1 + a_1 c_1)] k^{-1}, \quad \phi_6 = a_2 \phi_8,$$

$$\phi_7 = -(a_1 + b_1 + b_2) k^{-1}, \quad \phi_8 = -[c_1(b_1 + b_2) - 1] k^{-1},$$

$$\phi_9 = -(1 + a_1 c_1) k^{-1}.$$

Several features of these reduced forms deserve comment. First, s_t and p_t are jointly determined variables responding to the same set of underlying variables, although their dynamic time paths need not be identical. Second, s_t and p_t depend on the time paths, current and expected, of domestic and foreign variables. To see this, take the expectations operator through on both sides of (7). Repeated substitution yields:

$$E_{t-1} p_t = \frac{\gamma_3}{1 - \gamma_1} \sum_{j=0}^{\infty} \left(\frac{\gamma_2}{1 - \gamma_1} \right)^j E_{t-1} p_{t+j}^* + \frac{\gamma_4}{1 - \gamma_1} \sum_{j=0}^{\infty} \left(\frac{\gamma_2}{1 - \gamma_1} \right)^j E_{t-1} m_{t+j}$$

$$+ \frac{\gamma_5}{1 - \gamma_1} \sum_{j=0}^{\infty} \left(\frac{\gamma_2}{1 - \gamma_1} \right)^j E_{t-1} (i_{t+j}^* + s_{t+j+1})$$

$$+ \frac{\gamma_6}{1 - \gamma_1} \sum_{j=0}^{\infty} \left(\frac{\gamma_2}{1 - \gamma_1} \right)^j E_{t-1} y_{t+j-1},$$

where we assume that v_t, u_t, ϵ_t are all serially independent processes. Note that this expression for $E_{t-1} p_t$ is not complete since it depends on $E_{t-1} s_{t+j}$, $j \geq 1$, to be obtained from (8), and on $E_{t-1} y_{t+j-1}$, $j \geq 0$. The important point is that the forward-looking rational expectations solution of (7) and (8) implies that p_t and s_t depend on the whole future time paths of the exogenous variables, the money supply, foreign prices and interest rates as well as random shocks. Hence, the rational expectations version of the standard open-economy model incorporates the main features of the "asset approach" to exchange rate determination.[18]

[18] To see this, update (8) and repeatedly substitute for terms in $E_{t-1} p_{t+j}$, $E_{t-1} s_{t+j}$ and $E_{t-1} y_{t+j}$.

To obtain an explicit solution for p_t, s_t, y_t, we need to specify the process generating the exogenous variables. For illustrative purposes, it is convenient to adopt the simple specifications:

$$\Delta p_t^* = \bar{p}^* + \eta_t^*, \quad \Delta m_t = \bar{m} + \lambda y_{t-1} + \eta_t, \quad \lambda < 0, \quad r_t^* = \bar{r}^*, \tag{9}$$

and $\eta_t, u_t, v_t, \epsilon_t, \eta_t^*$ are serially and mutually independent processes with zero means and finite variances, so that $E_{t-1} x_{t+j} = 0, j > 0$ ($x = \eta, u, v, \epsilon, \eta^*$). According to (9) the foreign inflation rate is random with a mean of $\bar{p}^*$. Monetary policy follows a countercyclical feedback rule, while η_t is an unavoidable random shock to the money supply process. Finally, the foreign real rate is deterministic, equal to a constant. Equation (9) implies that $E_{t-1} p_{t+j}^* = p_{t-1}^* + (j+1)\bar{p}^*$, and $E_{t-1} m_{t+1} = m_{t-1} + 2\bar{m} + \lambda y_{t-1} + \lambda E_{t-1} y_t$, where $E_{t-1} y_t = a_0 + a_2 y_{t-1}$, using (1). Movements in output lead to "persistence" in the money supply process.

To solve the model, we use the by now familiar method of undetermined coefficients, with the details relegated to Appendix B. Briefly, one writes p, s and y as time invariant functions[19] which are linear in the underlying state variables. The market clearing conditions (7) and (8) thus yield the cross equation restrictions implied by rationality. Neglecting the constant terms, the explicit solutions for the price level, nominal exchange rate and output are:

$$p_t = m_{t-1} - \left[1 - \frac{\lambda}{a_2}(1 + c_2)\right] a_2 y_{t-1} + \gamma_4(\eta_t - v_t) + \gamma_8 u_t + \gamma_9 \epsilon_t,$$

$$s_t = m_{t-1} - \left[1 - \frac{\lambda}{a_2}(1 + c_2) - \frac{1}{(1 + a_1)b_2}\right] a_2 y_{t-1} - p_t^*$$

$$+ \phi_4(\eta_t - v_t) + \phi_8 u_t + \phi_9 \epsilon_t, \tag{10}$$

$$y_t = a_1[\gamma_4(\eta_t - v_t) + \gamma_8 u_t + \gamma_9 \epsilon_t] + a_2 y_{t-1} + u_t.$$

Prior to discussing the character of this solution, consider the implied solution for the "real exchange rate" or the term $q_t = (s_t + p_t^* - p_t)$. From (10):

$$q_t = [(1 + a_1)b_2]^{-1} a_2 y_{t-1} + a_1 k^{-1}(\eta_t - v_t) + (1 + c_2)k^{-1} u_t$$

$$- (1 + a_1 + c_2)k^{-1} \epsilon_t, \tag{11}$$

so that the real exchange rate can be written as a function of y_{t-1} and of unanticipated random shocks.[20]

---

[19] Since the structure of the model (behavioral functions, stochastic processes, nature of information) is not expected — correctly — to change over time.

[20] Note that additional lags of y would appear in (11) in the presence of higher-order costs of adjustment. Further, in an extended two-country model, lags of foreign output would appear.

We are now in a position to provide some answers to the questions posed at the beginning of this section.

Consider first the association between nominal and real exchange rates. As is clear from (10), s_t responds to both anticipated and unanticipated movements in real and monetary variables. However, the real exchange rate does not respond to the anticipated portion of the domestic money supply. In this framework, the contemporaneous correlation of s_t with q_t arises from a common response to lagged output, as well as the occurrence of random serially uncorrelated shocks. Consider the contemporaneous correlation of s with q each relative to its prior predicted value. From (10) and (11):

$$E(s_t - Es_t)(q_t - Eq_t) = a_1 \phi_4 k^{-1} (\sigma_\eta^2 + \sigma_v^2) + \phi_8 (1 + c_2) k^{-1} \sigma_u^2$$
$$- \phi_9 (1 + a_1 + c_2) k^{-1} \sigma_\epsilon^2,$$

where $\sigma_x^2 (x = \eta, v, u, \epsilon)$ denotes the variances of the error terms. Note that while the covariance is positive for aggregate demand shocks ϵ, the random portion of monetary policy η and the portfolio balance disturbance v, it is negative in the case of real aggregate supply disturbances. More generally, movements in y_{t-1} or a contemporaneous aggregate supply shock induce negatively correlated movements in s_t and q_t. Consider a positive occurrence of u_t. This implies an unexpected rightward shift in aggregate supply, leading to an unexpected decline in the price of output. Although there is an appreciation of the nominal rate (s_t decreases), we require a decline in the relative price of the home good ($p_t - s_t - p_t^*$) or a rise in the real exchange rate to clear the home goods market. By contrast, an unexpected monetary shock, $\eta_t > 0$ say, leads to a shift in aggregate demand, an unexpected rise in the domestic price level and a rise in aggregate output. There is a depreciation of the nominal exchange rate (s_t increases), but we also require a relative price change, a real exchange rate depreciation to clear the output market. As an empirical proposition, we obtain the hypothesis that the contemporaneous correlation between nominal and real exchange rates depends on the source of the underlying disturbance. Periods or countries in which supply-side disturbances predominate will, *ceteris paribus*, tend to display negative contemporaneous covariation of nominal and real exchange rates, while a positive covariance is likely if monetary and/or aggregate demand disturbances are predominant.[21]

Second, monetary policy has a systematic impact on the nominal exchange rate, but only the random, unanticipated portion of monetary policy affects the real exchange rate. Specifically, the policy feedback parameter, λ, appears in the nominal exchange rate solution, but does not enter the expression for q_t. The reason is that the systematic attempt at countercyclical stabilization policy leads to anticipated movements in the money supply (since $E_{t-1} m_t = \bar{m} + m_{t-1} + \lambda y_{t-1}$), which affect the actual and anticipated price level and nominal exchange rate in the same, one-to-one proportion. The result is that the time path of the nominal exchange rate is affected, but

---

[21]   Note that q_t will be correlated with lagged and future values of s_t, since the presence of costs of adjustment leads to a persistence of shocks.

the distribution of q_t is invariant to the monetary feedback rule. Hence, although it is true that monetary policy can and does affect the contemporaneous covariance of s and q by affecting the time path of the nominal rate, this has no impact on the distribution of the real exchange rate. It should be clear that this result does not depend on the specific form of the feedback rule. For instance, suppose that instead of (10), the feedback rule included a response to either (lagged) nominal or real exchange rates, a policy of "leaning against the wind". To the extent that such a policy were systematic and known by private agents, it would again alter current and anticipated future nominal exchange rates, but would not affect the time path of the real exchange rate.

Third, the model is also characterized by the Lucas (1973)–Sargent and Wallace (1975), LSW, proposition, that the distribution of y_t is invariant to the systematic portion of monetary policy. The result, as is well known, depends on the absence of an informational absolute advantage for the monetary authorities and the joint natural rate/rational expectations hypothesis. An additional remark is in order: in contrast to the traditional literature, this open-economy LSW proposition is independent of the degree of capital mobility. Within our framework, the presence or absence of capital movements affects the time paths of nominal variables such as the rate of interest, as well as the nature of the transmission of foreign disturbances, but not the proposition that the monetary authorities cannot induce systematic expectational errors. Further, note that the solutions for q_t and y_t imply that output and the real exchange rate are correlated. The sign of the correlation depends on the source of the underlying shock, and the magnitude is a function of the structural parameters. This suggests that the bivariate system (q_t, y_t) will – in general – exhibit two way causality, or feedback. More generally, the dynamic relationship between the real exchange rate and output emerges from the interaction of production technology and unexpected movements in aggregate demand. The important point to be stressed is that though q and y are dynamically related, this observation does not imply an exploitable relationship for monetary policy. In sum, the standard model with a natural rate/rational expectations modification yields both a Phillips-curve type relationship between inflation and output, and a relationship between the real exchange rate and output, neither of which is "exploitable" through the use of monetary policy. We are not, of course, saying that no policy can have an impact on the real exchange rate; it would be easy to construct cases in which commercial policy and/or fiscal policy matter.

Fourth, there is "persistence" in movements of the real exchange rate. To see this, consider the correlation of q_t with q_{t-1}. Rewrite the expression for q_t as: $q_t = \beta_1 y_{t-1} + \beta_2 (\eta_t - v_t) + \beta_3 u_t + \beta_4 \epsilon_t$. Multiply by q_{t-1} and take expected values on both sides to obtain:

$$
\begin{aligned}
\mathrm{E}(q_t q_{t-1}) &= \beta_1 \mathrm{E}(y_{t-1} q_{t-1}) \\
&= \beta_1 \{ a_2 \beta_1 \sigma_y^2 + \gamma_4 a_1 \beta_2 (\sigma_\eta^2 + \sigma_v^2) \\
&\quad + \beta_3 (1 + a_1 \gamma_8) \sigma_u^2 + \gamma_9 a_1 \beta_4 \sigma_\epsilon^2 \}
\end{aligned}
$$

where we have used the fact that the random shocks are independent, so that $E(\eta_t q_{t-1})$ = 0 etc., and where σ_y^2 is the variance of output. The first-order lagged covariance is positive, and one can show that the covariance declines geometrically with increasing lag – this requires the y_t process to be stable or that $a_2 < 1$. The persistence of real exchange rate movements in this setup derives directly from the persistence of output and employment. With the presence of the lagged output term in (1), past price prediction errors have persistent effects on the current level of output. Given the contemporaneous realizations of shocks, movements in y_{t-1} imply proportional movements in y_t and consequently require changes in the real exchange rate, q_t. Hence, in this model, the existence of real costs of adjustment transforms serially uncorrelated shocks to aggregate demand and supply into a serially correlated process for the real exchange rate. In particular, serially uncorrelated monetary "surprises" will have a distributed lag effect on real exchange rates. One issue for future research is to investigate the dynamic response of real exchange rates to monetary and real disturbances. It is likely that the simple model developed here is not rich enough to characterize the data. For example, we suspect that the relationship between q_t and unanticipated monetary/ financial variables will prove to be "hump-shaped", i.e. with a lagged peak effect. To generate such a pattern, we would need a richer description of production technology, including higher order costs of adjustment and/or time delays between production inputs and resulting output.

Finally, the setup here has an "unrealistic" feature in that foreign permanent price disturbances even though unexpected do not lead to unexpected aggregate demand movements. As a result they are not transmitted to domestic output. The reason for the lack of transmission of foreign price shocks is that in the absence of a signal extraction problem and of differential information, the nominal exchange rate adjusts, one-to-one, to movements in p_t^*.[22] The exchange rate moves to insulate the economy from foreign price disturbances. Note that this does not mean that the domestic economy is immune to the occurrence of foreign disturbances in this model. As mentioned above, the ϵ_t disturbance to aggregate demand incorporates foreign demand shifts, and these do induce serially correlated movements in y_t and q_t. In addition, it is easily shown that random variations in the foreign real rate r_t^* – which was assumed constant above – would be transmitted to the domestic economy. To see this, allow the foreign real rate to fluctuate randomly about a non-stochastic mean: $R_t^* = \bar{R}^* + \epsilon_t^*$, with ϵ^* serially independent and orthogonal to all other shocks. Here ϵ^* would represent transitory variations in the real rate, and it is easily shown that these imply positively associated movements in s_t and q_t as well as in p_t.

We conclude this section with some remarks on the nature of the framework and some tentative conclusions. The Mundell–Fleming open-economy aggregative model has been and continues to be (*vide* Dornbusch 1980) the standard workhorse for discussions of monetary and fiscal policy under alternative exchange rate regimes. The

---

[22]   See Saïdi (1980) for a model in which the exchange rate acts as a "noisy" signal about underlying disturbances.

standard model and variations on it have well-known advantages as well as limitations; these are reviewed in Mussa (1979). We have merely developed a stochastic version with some simple dynamics; both these elements seem necessary to account for the nature of the "stylized facts" that emerge from the discussion in section 2. However, the major cutting₁edge of the analysis derives from the imposition of the joint natural rate/rational expectations hypothesis. More specifically, we would like — in guise of conclusion — to stress two ideas that have implications for monetary policy.

First, observed cross-correlations between real and nominal exchange rates can be fruitfully analyzed as emerging from the realization of a stochastic equilibrium process (see Stockman (1980) for a specific example). It follows that uncertainty, imperfect information and the process of expectations formation are likely to play a crucial role in both theoretical and empirical analysis of the real/nominal exchange rate association. More specifically, the distinction between anticipated and unanticipated changes in monetary policy leads to the conclusion that while anticipated movements can affect the time paths of the nominal exchange rate and the dynamic cross-correlation with the real exchange rate, the distribution of the real exchange rate is only affected by the unanticipated component of monetary policy. Hence, the relationship does not allow for systematic "exploitability". As was mentioned previously, there is a direct analogy to unemployment—inflation trade-offs. This prompts us to advance an additional (unproven but testable) proposition, which is the analogue of the Lucas (1973) hypothesis: the slope of nominal—real exchange rate "trade-offs" will become steeper the more volatile are nominal aggregate demand shocks.

Second, observed cross-relations between measures of real activity and real exchange rates arise from the dynamic interaction of production technology and changes in both aggregate and relative demand. Hence, the cyclical associations can be viewed as common responses to underlying shocks. It is a task for future research to characterize the nature of the time series process and provide an explanation in terms of structural parameters. From the viewpoint of monetary policy the issue hinges on whether this relationship is exploitable through a systematic impact of monetary policy on the nominal exchange rate. To the extent that the monetary authorities cannot induce systematic expectational errors, the scope for systematic countercyclical monetary policy operating on nominal exchange rates, may be severely limited.

Appendix A

The influence of different weighting schemes on the decomposition of real exchange rate changes can be illustrated as follows. Suppose that the home price index is a weighted average of import prices (M), export prices (X), and home (non-traded) good prices (H), and similarly abroad (foreign variables are identified by an asterisk), thus:

$$P = M^{(\lambda-\theta)} X^{\theta} H^{(1-\lambda)} \tag{A.1}$$

$$P^* = M^{*(\lambda^* - \theta^*)} X^{*\theta^*} H^{*(1-\lambda^*)}. \tag{A.2}$$

Assuming the law of one price to hold, that is, assuming that the domestic price of imports is equal to their foreign price times the exchange rate, E (i.e. $M = EX^*$), and similarly for the other traded good, the percentage change (denoted by a "hat") of the real exchange rate, R, is given by:

$$\hat{R} = [1 - \lambda^*] \hat{E} + [\lambda^* - \theta^* - \theta] \hat{X} + [\theta^* + \theta - \lambda] \hat{M} + [1 - \lambda^*] \hat{H}^* - [1 - \lambda] \hat{H}. \tag{A.3}$$

Equation (A.3) makes it immediately obvious that the effect of a change in relative prices depends, among other things, on possible differences in the weight of the same good in the home and foreign price index.

A number of propositions can be derived from the above expression: (1) If there are no changes in relative prices ($\hat{H} = \hat{M} = \hat{X}$ and $\hat{H}^* = \hat{M}^* = \hat{X}^*$), the real exchange rate should remain constant. However, changes in weights can spuriously change the real exchange rate even if relative prices remain constant. (2) Equal changes in the relative price of non-traded goods across countries (e.g. $\hat{H} = \hat{H}^* \neq \hat{M} = \hat{X} = \hat{M}^* = \hat{X}^*$) would cause systematic changes in the real exchange rate if weighting schemes differ across countries, an instance of measurement error by common-sense criteria. (3) Turning to the special case where there are no non-traded goods, it is easy to show that $\hat{R} = [\theta^* + \theta - 1](\hat{M} - \hat{X})$. This is equivalent to stating that a worsening in the terms of trade of the home country raises or lowers the real exchange rate depending on whether the sum of the expenditure shares of imports in the two countries is smaller or larger than one. With unit income elasticities of demand, this is reminiscent of the classical transfer criterion. (4) In the special "Keynesian" case where each country's supply of its export good is infinitely elastic with respect to its domestic currency price, $\hat{X} = 0, \hat{M} = \hat{E}$, and $\hat{R} = [\theta^* + \theta - 1]\hat{E}$. A devaluation (and the associated equal worsening in the terms of trade) has an ambiguous effect on the *real* exchange rate, the outcome depending again on the above "transfer criterion". In other words, a change in the terms of trade need have no effect on the real exchange rate.[23] (5) If there are no changes in the terms of trade, imports and exports can be lumped into a single traded commodity with price T. The real exchange-rate formula becomes:

$$\hat{R} = (1 - \lambda)(\hat{T} - \hat{H}) + (1 - \lambda^*)(\hat{H}^* - \hat{T}^*). \tag{A.4}$$

Changes in the real exchange rate depend only on the relative price of traded and non-traded goods at home and abroad.

---

[23]   The only reason for which this result is at variance with some statements in the literature is the careless use of terminology which identifies the real exchange rate with a number of different concepts. See the introductory section of this paper.

Appendix B

This Appendix develops some of the algebra underlying the results in section 3. We assume that the current level of output, y_t, varies directly with its lagged level and inversely with the real wage rate $(w_t - p_t)$ as in:

$$y_t = \alpha_0 - \alpha_1 (w_t - p_t) + \alpha_2 y_{t-1} + u_t, \tag{B.1}$$

where u_t is a contemporaneous disturbance term and the α's are positive constants.

A one-period contract sets the nominal wage rate as in (B.2):

$$w_t = \beta_0 + E_{t-1} p_t + \beta_1 E_{t-1} y_t, \qquad \beta_0, \beta_1 > 0, \tag{B.2}$$

so that the nominal wage rate is indexed to the price level expected to prevail in the current period. The real wage is equal to β_0 plus an anticipated productivity effect as captured by the term $\beta_1 E_{t-1} y_t$. Substituting for w_t from (B.2) yields:

$$y_t = (\alpha_0 - \alpha_1 \beta_0)(1 + \alpha_1 \beta_1)^{-1} + \alpha_1 (p_t - E_{t-1} p_t)$$
$$+ \alpha_2 (1 + \alpha_1 \beta_1)^{-1} y_{t-1} + u_t, \tag{B.3}$$

which is equivalent to eq. (1) in the text.

To proceed, substitute for i_t from eq. (4) into (2) and solve for the exchange rate that yields portfolio equilibrium:

$$c_2 s_t = m_t - p_t - c_0 - c_1 y_t + c_2 (i_t^* + E_{t-1} s_{t+1}) - v_t \tag{B.4}$$

To obtain the expressions for p_t and s_t appearing in the text, equate aggregate demand and supply, eqs. (1) and (3). This operation yields an expression for p_t that includes s_t. Simple algebra then permits us to express p_t and s_t as functions of expectations of prices and exchange rates, the set of exogenous and predetermined variables of the model $(m_t, y_{t-1}, p_t^*, i_t^*)$ and the various disturbances. The joint contemporaneous determination of p_t and s_t is obvious from (7) and (8). To see this, consider the effects of an unexpected disturbance to aggregate supply, say $u_t > 0$. Recall that although the u_t process is serially independent, such disturbances "persist" due to the appearance of lagged output in (1). At the initial domestic price level and exchange rate we have a situation of excess supply of the home good and excess demand for real balances. In the absence of any monetary accomodation (either contemporaneous or in the future), restoration of equilibrium requires a fall in the price level and an appreciation of the nominal exchange rate (a fall in s_t) so that ϕ_8 [in eq. (8)] is negative (a condition for stability). In addition, we also require a relative price change, a decline in the relative price of the domestic good, so that $(p_t - s_t - p_t^*)$ falls.

To obtain an explicit solution for p_t, s_t and y_t in terms of exogenous and predetermined variables, we consider writing p_t and s_t as unknown functions of the state variables:

$$p_t = \pi_{10} + \pi_{11} m_{t-1} + \pi_{12} a_2 y_{t-1} + \pi_{13} p^*_{t-1} + \pi_{14} \eta_t + \pi_{15} u_t + \pi_{16} v_t$$
$$+ \pi_{17} \epsilon_t + \pi_{18} \eta^*_t,$$

$$s_t = \pi_{20} + \pi_{21} m_{t-1} + \pi_{22} a_2 y_{t-1} + \pi_{23} p^*_{t-1} + \pi_{24} \eta_t + \pi_{25} u_t + \pi_{26} v_t$$
$$+ \pi_{27} \epsilon_t + \pi_{28} \eta^*_t. \tag{B.5}$$

This trial solution makes use of the fact that we are operating within a linear, time-invariant structure and of the stochastic specification in eq. (9). Given (B.5) it is trivial to calculate the expressions for $E_{t-1} p_t$, $E_{t-1} p_{t+1}$ and $E_{t-1} s_{t+1}$ which appear in the market clearing conditions, in eqs. (7) and (8). If the trial solution in (B.5) is an equilibrium, then substituting from (B.5) and for expectations into (7) and (8) must yield identities in the state variables. The resulting identities are (neglecting constants):

$$(1 - \gamma_1 - \gamma_2) \pi_{11} = \gamma_4 + \gamma_5 \pi_{21}, \quad (1 - \phi_5) \pi_{21} = \phi_4 + (\phi_1 + \phi_2) \pi_{11},$$

$$(1 - \gamma_1 - \gamma_2) \pi_{12} = (\gamma_2 + \gamma_4 + \gamma_5) \lambda + \gamma_6 + \gamma_5 \pi_{22},$$

$$(1 - \phi_5) \pi_{22} = (\phi_2 + \phi_4 + \phi_5) \lambda + \phi_6 + (\phi_1 + \phi_2) \pi_{12},$$

$$(1 - \gamma_1 - \gamma_2) \pi_{13} = \gamma_3 + \gamma_5 \pi_{23}, \tag{B.6}$$

$$(1 - \phi_5) \pi_{23} = \phi_3 + (\phi_1 + \phi_2) \pi_{13},$$

$$\pi_{14} = \gamma_4, \quad \pi_{24} = \phi_4, \quad \pi_{15} = \gamma_8, \quad \pi_{25} = \phi_8,$$

$$\pi_{16} = \gamma_7, \quad \pi_{26} = \phi_7, \quad \pi_{17} = \gamma_9, \quad \pi_{27} = \phi_9,$$

$$\pi_{18} = \gamma_3 - \gamma_5, \quad \pi_{28} = \phi_3 - \phi_5.$$

Solving the linear equations in (B.6) for the π_{ij} $(i = 1, 2, j = 1, ..., 9)$ yields

$$\pi_{11} = \pi_{21} = 1, \quad \pi_{12} = -1 + (1 + c_2) \frac{\lambda}{a_2}, \quad \pi_{22} = \pi_{12} + [(1 + a_1) d_2]^{-1},$$

$$\pi_{13} = \pi_{18} = 0, \quad \pi_{23} = \pi_{28} = -1.$$

The remaining coefficients are as in (B.6). Substituting back into (B.6) yields the expressions for p_t and s_t appearing in eq. (10).

To obtain the solution for output, simply note that from eq. (1) we have:

$$y_t = a_0 + a_2 y_{t-1} + a_1 (p_t - E_{t-1} p_t) + u_t$$

$$= a_0 + a_2 y_{t-1} + a_1 (\pi_{14} \eta_t + \pi_{15} u_t + \pi_{16} v_t + \pi_{17} \epsilon_t) + u_t.$$

In the above (and in the text) we have assumed the income elasticity of demand for real balances, $c_1 = 1$. This involves no loss in generality.

References and selected bibliography

Dornbusch, R., 1980a, Open economy macroeconomics (Basic Books, New York).

Dornbusch, R., 1980b, Exchange rate economics: Where do we stand?, Brookings Papers on Economic Activity, no. 1.

Findlay, R. and A. Rodriguez, 1977, Intermediate imports and macroeconomic policy under flexible exchange rates, Canadian Journal of Economics.

Frenkel, J., 1978, Purchasing power parity: Doctrinal perspective and evidence from the 1920s, Journal of International Economics 8.

Frenkel, J., 1981, The collapse of purchasing power parities during the 1970s, European Economic Review 14.

Gailliot, H.H., 1970, Purchasing power parity as an explanation of long-term changes in exchange rates, Journal of Money, Credit and Banking 2.

Genberg, H., 1978, Purchasing power parity under fixed and flexible exchange rates, Journal of International Economics 8.

Hodrick, R.J. and E. Prescott, 1980, Post-war U.S. business cycles: An empirical investigation, Working Paper, Carnegie-Mellon University.

Lucas, R.E. Jr., 1976, Econometric policy evaluation: a critique, in: K. Brunner and A.H. Meltzer, eds., The Phillips curve and labor markets Carnegie-Rochester Conferences on Public Policy 1 (North-Holland, Amsterdam).

Lucas, R.E., Jr., 1973, Some international evidence on output–inflation tradeoffs, American Economic Review 63.

Magee, S., 1977, Traded-goods prices and exchange rates, mimeo, January.

McCallum, Bennett, 1978, Price level adjustment and the rational expectations approach to macroeconomic stabilization policy, Journal of Money, Credit and Banking 10.

Mundell, R., 1968, International economics (Macmillan, New York).

Mussa, M., 1976, Macroeconomic interdependence and the exchange rate, in: R. Dornbusch and J. Frenkel, eds., International economic policy: Theory and evidence (Johns Hopkins University Press, Baltimore).

Mussa, M., 1979, Empirical regularities in the behavior of exchange rates and theories of the foreign exchange market, in: Policies for employment, prices and exchange rates, Carnegie-Rochester Conferences on Public Policy 11 (North-Holland, Amsterdam).

Nelson, C. and C. Plosser, 1980, Trends and random walks in macroeconomic time series, University of Rochester, Center for Research in Government Policy and Business, Working Paper, no. GPB 80-11, August.

Sachs, J., 1980, Wages, flexible exchange rates and macroeconomic policy, Quarterly Journal of Economics 94.

Saïdi, N., 1980, Fluctuating exchange rates and the international transmission of economic disturbances, Journal of Money, Credit and Banking 12.

Saïdi, N. and A. Swoboda, 1981, Exchange rates, prices and money, with reference to Switzerland in the 1920s and 1970s, Graduate Institute of International Studies, Geneva, mimeo, April.

Sargent, T.J., 1979, Macroeconomic Theory (Academic Press, New York).

Sargent, T.J. and N. Wallace, 1975, Rational expectations, the optimal monetary instrument, and the optimal supply rule, Journal of Political Economy 83.

Sargent, T.J. and N. Wallace, 1976, Rational expectations and the theory of economic policy, Journal of Monetary Economics 2.

Stockman, A., 1980, A theory of exchange rate determination, Journal of Political Economy 88.

Swoboda, A., 1981, Exchange-rate flexibility in practice: A selective survey of experience from 1973 to 1979 in: H. Giersch, ed., Macroeconomic policies for growth and stability: A European perspective (Mohr, Tübingen).

Recent Issues in the Theory of Flexible Exchange Rates, edited by E. Claassen and P. Salin
© *North-Holland Publishing Company, 1983*

COMMENT ON SAÏDI AND SWOBODA

John P. MARTIN

This paper aims to examine critically the hypothesis that monetary policy can exert systematic influence on real output and employment through engineering changes in the real exchange rate. It represents a simple extension to the open economy of the long-running debate of the late 1960s and early 1970s as to whether or not the output—inflation trade-off was exploitable by policy makers. Indeed, the paper is very much in the tradition of the new classical macroeconomics with its emphasis on rational expectations and the so-called Lucas—Phelps "surprise" aggregate supply schedule. That being so, I venture to suggest that no-one will be greatly surprised by the substantive results of the paper. I will return to this point in my concluding remarks.

The paper begins with a brief discussion of the concept of the "real exchange rate" which plays a major role in recent theoretical and empirical work. Since there is some confusion about this concept in the literature, I found this discussion helpful. Saïdi and Swoboda point out that the real exchange rate plays a crucial role in three different analytical approaches:

(1) purchasing power parity (PPP) — where changes in the real exchange rate are simply deviations from PPP;
(2) changes in the terms of trade as a source of real exchange rate variations; and
(3) the so-called Salter—Swan dependent economy model where the real exchange rate is simply the relative price of non-traded goods.[1]

The second section of the paper reviews some empirical evidence on the behaviour of real exchange rates in the 1970s. It also briefly examines explanations for the observed variation of real exchange rates, concentrating on factors which can account for the observed correlations between nominal and real exchange rates and real output.

1. Empirical regularities

Several of the points they highlight are in line with conventional wisdom. First, real exchange rates exhibit a great deal of short-run variability (PPP does not hold). Second,

---

[1] If the nominal price of non-traded goods is given, changes in the price ratio can only come about through changes in the price of traded goods. Assuming that the law of one price holds for traded goods, the exchange rate has to adjust.

real exchange rates appear to exhibit little or no long-run trend (PPP holds in the long-run). Third, short-run movements in real exchange rates are not random but instead are serially correlated. Fourth, there is a strong positive correlation between nominal and real exchange rates in the short-run but it disappears in the long-run. Finally, variations in the real exchange rate are correlated with deviations in real output from trend.

Very little evidence in support of these empirical propositions is provided in the paper. Instead we are referred to another paper by the authors — Saïdi and Swoboda (1981) — for the detailed results.

There is one point on which the empirical propositions in this paper are not in agreement with the recent literature. While it is true that studies of the last decade universely reject PPP in the short-run, it has become part of the conventional wisdom, *grâce à* Jacob Frenkel[2] that PPP held reasonably well in the short-run during the previous period of flexible exchange rates in the 1920s. However, Saïdi and Swoboda do not accept this verdict. They claim, once again referring the reader to their previous paper, that PPP hardly worked better in the 1920s than in recent years.

Their evidence is based on an analysis of the experience of the Swiss franc/dollar, the Swiss franc/pound, the Swiss franc/French franc and the Swiss franc/DM exchange rates. Their econometric results for the relative version of PPP using wholesale prices suggest that the coefficients are very unstable. They argue that Frenkel's equations are misspecified and speculate that, if appropriate account were taken of specification error, his results would be much less favourable to PPP.

Speaking as a bystander it seems to me not unreasonable to ask the protagonists to come to some agreement about the role of PPP in the 1920s. Perhaps another conference or a journal supplement is in order here. I had the slight, and clearly unworthy, suspicion of a conspiracy between Jacob and the authors to continue this debate which we had all imagined to be settled!

2. Causes of variation in real exchange rates

The paper briefly reviews four common explanations:

(1) failure of the law of one price;
(2) measurement errors;
(3) shifts in the price ratio between traded and non-traded goods; and
(4) monetary disturbances.

Each of these hypotheses is judged against the criterion of whether they can account for the observed time series behaviour of real exchange rates. On the whole the authors lean to the view that monetary shocks are the main factor.

An alternative hypothesis might argue, however, that differential speeds of adjustment in commodity and asset markets combined with some rigidity in prices and wages

---

[2]   See, for example, Frenkel (1978, 1980, 1981).

can account very well for the stylised facts of the association between real exchange rates and real output. Saïdi and Swoboda acknowledge this point but are unhappy about the price rigidity assumption. However, plausible models have been developed with multi-period wage and price contracts *and* rational expectations to account for sticky prices.[3] Saïdi and Swoboda object that such multi-period labour market contracts are independent of the economic environment and thus may be inconsistent if public sector agents change their behaviour. This criticism ignores the fact that legal and institutional constraints exist which restrict the opportunities of private sector agents to convert multi-period contracts into contingent forward contracts.

Before discussing their model I would like to draw attention to another theme of the new classical macroeconomics which is strongly emphasised in the paper. This is the stress laid on the time series cyclical behaviour of real and nominal variables. The authors stress the need for models which can satisfactorily mimic not only cyclical movements but also account for cross correlations between the nominal and real magnitudes. This emphasis on methods of time series analysis, once the data have been pre-filtered to ensure stationarity, is very evident in several recent articles on macro-modelling.[4]

3. The stochastic model

In the final section of the paper the authors directly confront the policy neutrality issue. The question at issue is whether given (1) a relationship between monetary policy and the real exchange rates and (2) a relationship between the real exchange rate and real output, there is any role for monetary policy to systematically influence real output via the real exchange rate.

In order to answer this question, they rely on an extended version of the standard open-economy IS–LM model. The model is presented in eqs. (1–6). It is a very familiar one within the new classical approach. The aggregate supply schedule for domestic output is the well-known "surprise" supply function. Since this is a one-good model, foreign shocks are constrained to affect domestic output only via price prediction errors. This, as the authors readily admit, is a weakness of the present specification. However, to relax it would require a much richer production structure.

Perfect capital markets are assumed and there is no role for non-traded assets. Aggregate demand simply depends on the real interest rate and the real exchange rate. There are no wealth effects and no government sector so there is no role for fiscal policy. Random error terms are added to the aggregate demand and supply schedules and also to the money demand schedule to give the model a very simple stochastic structure. Finally, the model is closed with the assumption of rational expectations.

What are the results? Are any of them novel? As to the first question, I would high-

---

[3]   For example see Fischer (1977) or Buiter and Jewitt (1981).
[4]   For example Sargent (1981) or Sims (1980).

light four results. First, the direction of the correlation between the nominal and real exchange rate depends on the source of the underlying shock. If supply-side shocks are dominant, the model suggests negative covariance of nominal and real exchange rates; *vice versa* for demand-side or monetary disturbances. Second, fully anticipated monetary policy affects the nominal exchange rate but only unanticipated actions by the monetary authorities – the "news" component – affect the real exchange rate. Third, fully anticipated monetary policy cannot affect the association between real output and real exchange rates. Finally, movements in the real exchange rate are not random but exhibit positive serial correlation in line with the persistence of movements in real output. This in turn reflects the existence of adjustment costs in production so that price surprises have persistent effects on real output.

However, none of these results is very surprising given the model specification. The net outcome is an additional wrinkle to the policy neutrality theorem of the new classical school. The wrinkle comes from the observation that movements in nominal and real exchange rates are highly correlated and that there is a relationship between real output and the real exchange rate. However, the combination of the "surprise" supply function *and* rational expectations effectively rules out any possibility for monetary policy to systematically exploit these relationships in such a simple model which gives no consideration to real capital formation nor to the impact of wealth effects on aggregate demand.

Thus, I find the substance of the paper disappointing since it really adds nothing to our knowledge on the policy neutrality debate beyond pinning down a small wrinkle associated with the real exchange rate. However, I would like to compliment the authors on the clarity of their exposition. It is not a trait I normally associate with the literature on rational expectations where algebraic fog is generally the order of the day!

References

Buiter, Willem H. and Ian Jewitt, 1981, Staggered wage setting with real wage relativities: Variations on a theme of Taylor, Manchester School of Economics and Social Studies 47, 211–228.

Fisher, Stanley, 1977, Long-term contracts, rational expectations and the optimal money supply rule, Journal of Political Economy 85, 169–191.

Frenkel, Jacob A., 1978, Purchasing power parity: Doctrinal perspective and evidence from the 1920s, Journal of International Economics 8, 169–191.

Frenkel, Jacob A., 1980, Exchange rates, prices, and money: Lessons from the 1920s, American Economic Review 70, 235–242.

Frenkel, Jacob A., 1981, The collapse of purchasing power parities during the 1970s, European Economic Review 16, 145–165.

Saïdi, Nasser and Alexander Swoboda, 1981, Exchange rates, prices and money: Switzerland in the 1920s and 1970s, Graduate Institute of International Studies, Geneva, mimeo.

Sargent, Thomas J., 1981, Interpreting economic time series, Journal of Political Economy 89, 213–248.

Sims, Christopher A., 1980, Macroeconomics and reality, Econometrica 48, 1–48.

Recent Issues in the Theory of Flexible Exchange Rates, edited by E. Claassen and P. Salin
© *North-Holland Publishing Company, 1983*

Chapter 2

INTERNATIONAL DIFFERENCES IN RESPONSE TO COMMON EXTERNAL SHOCKS: THE ROLE OF PURCHASING POWER PARITY

Ronald W. JONES and Douglas D. PURVIS

"... readers of Keynes from 1915 to 1930 generally held simultaneously the view that PPP was a trivial truism of arbitrage *and* besides was quite untrue." [Samuelson (1964)]

1. Introduction

The 1970s witnessed a return to flexible exchange rates by most industrialized nations. The behavior of this system has revealed a number of surprises and has stimulated a large volume of theoretical and empirical research on the nature of exchange rate determination. One of the puzzles that has emerged from the experience of the 1970s is the large variability of nominal exchange rates, variability in excess of that ex-plained by developments in commonly-held "fundamental determinants". In particu-lar, many bilateral exchange rates displayed a variability far in excess of that of the respective national price levels, leading to what Frenkel (1980) described as "The Collapse of Purchasing Power Parities During the 1970s". Frenkel summarizes the facts in stating that "During the 1970's short-run changes in exchange rates bore little relationship to short-run differentials in national inflation rates, and frequently, divergences from purchasing power parities have been cumulative".

Our surprise at these events is not that "PPP has collapsed" but rather that others have been surprised by the collapse. PPP is, after all, nothing but the open economy implication of money neutrality − if the absolute level of *all* prices in one country changes proportionately without affecting *any* price ratios or real magnitudes, these changes will be accompanied by a proportionate change in the exchange rate. During the 1970s exchange rates were buffeted by real forces which could not be expected to conform to the "neutral money" condition required by PPP. This last statement, we feel, is neither controversial nor novel. Nevertheless, we believe it still to be pertinent in light of the prevalence and persistence of PPP-oriented views about current levels of exchange rates. These "PPP views" are perhaps suggested most strongly by the prominence of the terms "over-valued" and "under-valued" to describe currencies for which the actual exchange rate is, respectively, below or above its PPP value. Our contention is that these PPP views are highly misleading.

It is not grossly inaccurate to characterize prevailing conventional wisdom about PPP in the following two propositions:

(1) PPP does *not* hold in the short run.
(2) There are strong tendencies towards PPP so that it does hold in the long run.

The force of the second of these is its implication that one should expect actual exchange rates to converge towards their PPP values, and hence that comparing relative national price levels is a useful guide to the formation of exchange rate expectations.[1]

While it should be obvious that there is no reason to expect arbitrage activity to cause price *indexes* to be equal when measured in a common currency[2] – this being the implication of PPP – there is nevertheless a tendency to treat discrepancies from PPP "as if" they are due to arbitrage failures, and the long-run tendency to PPP is viewed as the long-run operation of the "law of one price".

This paper presents a framework in which the "law of one price" obtains at all times, yet national price levels are determined in a manner that involves factors other than those reflected in nominal exchange rates. In much of the paper we abstract from the index number issue by assuming that there is only one good consumed in each country.

The key to the separation of developments in national price levels from those in exchange rates is the specification that goods which enter into international trade are not directly consumed. Traded goods require the application of domestic value-added prior to being consumed so that, in any particular country, final goods are produced using internationally traded "middle products" plus domestic labor.[3] Arbitrage in traded middle products is perfect so that the law of one price applies to any individual such middle product.

In applying this model, we hope to identify one set of factors which can lead to systematic and persistent deviations from PPP as well as to identify situations where actual and PPP exchange rates might move in opposite directions.

In order to fix ideas prior to the development of the details of the model, it is worth examining the basic framework more explicitly. Consider two countries, each small in relation to the rest of the world, facing a common disturbance in the form of an exogenous increase in the "world price" of a particular middle product, good A. The law of one price ensures that in each country the change in the respective internal

---

[1] Of course, even if PPP were a valid long-run theory, it alone would not be sufficient to determine what variables adjust to establish PPP in the long run.

[2] The index number issue has led to most explanations of PPP failures being cast in terms of relative price changes either in terms of the external (import–export) or internal (traded–nontraded) terms of trade. See, e.g. Balassa (1964), Frenkel (1980), or Usher (1967).

[3] The term "middle products" and the analytical framework on the real side used throughout this paper were first introduced in Sanyal and Jones (1982).

price of A (p_A and p_A^*) equals the sum of the change in the respective nominal exchange rate (E and E^*) in terms of a third currency plus the (common) change in the world price of A measured in terms of this same third currency ($\bar{p}_A$).[4] Hence

$$(\hat{p}_A - \hat{p}_A^*) = (\hat{E} - \hat{E}^*) \equiv \hat{e} \tag{1}$$

where e is the bilateral exchange rate between the two countries and a "ˆ" indicates a percentage change.

In each country, the change in the price of its *final* product ($\hat{p}_O$ and $\hat{p}_O^*$) will reflect both the change in the own-price of the middle product *and* the change in the price of domestic value-added. If the structures of the two economies differ such that the changes in own-prices of domestic value-added differ, then p_O/p_A will change relative to p_O^*/p_A^*. Hence, using eq. (1), ($\hat{p}_O - \hat{p}_O^*$) will differ from $\hat{e}$. The former, being a comparison of national price levels, is what might be termed the change in the PPP exchange rate; that is, it is the change in the exchange rate that would be expected if PPP were to be maintained. The approach taken in this paper focuses on structural aspects of the economy which cause the equilibrium exchange rate[5] to change relative to the PPP rate. The change in the relationship between the PPP and equilibrium exchange rates is captured by the variable μ defined as $(E/p_O)/(E^*/p_O^*)$, so that

$$\hat{\mu} \equiv \hat{e} - (\hat{p}_O - \hat{p}_O^*) \tag{2}$$

The term $\hat{\mu}$ is derived in the context of a model in which labor is used to produce middle products in the "input tier" of the economy and to produce final products in the "output tier" of the economy. International trade allows the composition of middle products produced in the input tier to differ from that of the middle products used as factors of production in the output tier, although if trade is balanced, the aggregate value of each bundle is the same. Labor is allocated between tiers to ensure full employment at a common wage rate. The model provides a solution for domestic wages and the exchange rate; unit costs then determine domestic prices.

The focus of the analysis is on structural, or real, characteristics of the economy; behind the scenes there is a monetary equilibrium implied. The behavior of the monetary sector is downplayed since disturbances arising from that sector, or accommodation occurring in that sector, give rise in the long run to price changes which of course do conform to PPP. Our focus is on disturbances which involve the possibility of relative price changes.[6]

---

[4] Variables that refer to the foreign country will have an asterisk while those that refer to the rest of the world will have a bar over them.

[5] And the actual exchange rate since ours is an equilibrium model.

[6] Monetary factors may of course influence relative prices and hence "distort PPP in the short run". We discuss this explicitly in the context of fixed-exchange rates in the next section. Our formal analysis of flexible exchange rates is restricted to long-run solutions, but the approach could readily be extended to allow for short-run phenomena of the type emphasized, for example, by Dornbusch (1976), or Buiter and Purvis (1980).

The plan of the paper is as follows. In sections 2 and 3 we examine a particularly simple version of the model in which only one good is produced in each tier of the economy. Trade is important because the middle product used in the output tier in the production of final consumption goods is different from the middle product produced in the input tier. In section 2 this model is analyzed for fixed exchange rates while section 3 deals with the flexible exchange rate case. The next two sections are used to explore the implications of elaborating the model to allow for the production of more than one good in the respective tiers. In section 4 the analysis incorporates production of the import-competing middle product so that not all middle-product inputs used in the output tier need to be imported. In section 5 an additional activity is introduced into the output tier; only at this stage, with the introduction of a second consumption good, does the conventional "index number" aspect of the PPP theory arise. Finally, some brief conclusions are offered in section 6.

2. Fixed exchange rates

In this section we examine two small economies, each linked via fixed exchange rates to a large outside world. These two economies have sufficiently similar production structures that in the input tier of each economy a single production process produces a commodity, x_B, with the input of a fixed amount of resource V_B (V_B^* abroad) and labor L_I (L_I^* abroad). In each country the entire volume of output of B is assumed to be exported to the rest of the world in exchange for imports of a product, A, not locally produced. Prices of both middle products in terms of the world currency ($\bar{p}_A$ and $\bar{p}_B$) are assumed to be exogenous.

In the output tier of each economy A is combined with labor to produce quantity x_O (x_O^* abroad) of a single, final, consumption item. Both economies are assumed to respond to the same external shock: a rise in the world price of A, with the world price of middle product B assumed constant. Given fixed exchange rates and the law of one price, $\hat{\bar{p}}_A = \hat{p}_A = \hat{p}_A^*$.

The deterioration in the terms of trade is absorbed in each country by a cutback in real consumption and a reallocation of labor between the input and output tiers of the economy. In the home country,

$$L_I + L_O = L,$$

where L is the total supply of labor and L_O is the allocation of labor to the output tier. Continued full employment requires:

$$\lambda_{LI}\hat{L}_I + \lambda_{LO}\hat{L}_O = 0, \tag{3}$$

where λ_{LI} is the fraction of the home country's labor force allocated to the input tier (to produce x_B). The demand for labor in the input tier is related to the wage rate in B units, w/p_B, by a downward sloping schedule showing labor's marginal product. Letting γ_I express the elasticity of this schedule (defined so as to be positive),

$$\hat{L}_I = -\gamma_I(\hat{w} - \hat{p}_B). \tag{4}$$

In the output tier the demand for labor depends upon the intensity with which it is used per unit output, a_{LO}, and the scale of output of the final consumable, x_O. The relative change in the demand for L_O is thus:

$$\hat{L}_O = \hat{a}_{LO} + \hat{x}_O. \tag{5}$$

Further, a_{LO} will fall if the wage rate rises relative to the price of the other input used to produce the consumption good, p_A. Indeed, if θ_{AO} denotes the share of final output required as payments to obtain A on world markets and σ_O is the elasticity of substitution in the output tier,[7]

$$\hat{a}_{LO} = -\theta_{AO}\sigma_O(\hat{w} - \hat{p}_A). \tag{6}$$

2.1. Accommodating monetary policy

In this subsection we assume that in each country the quantity of money is adjusted to keep current spending levels equal to the level of income. Thus the change in real consumption at home, $\hat{x}_O$, equals the deterioration in home real income, $\hat{y}$. That deterioration is given by the fraction of national income devoted to imports of A, θ_{AO} times the rise in p_A, so we have

$$\hat{x}_O = -\theta_{AO}\hat{p}_A. \tag{7}$$

At a constant wage, the rise in $\bar{p}_A$ creates two opposing forces on the demand for labour in the output tier. Equation (6) shows the increase in L_O resulting from the substitution away from the more expensive input A while eq. (7) shows the reduction in L_O resulting from the contraction in output of final goods in response to the decline in real income. The demand for labor in the output tier may rise or fall at the initial wage depending upon which effect dominates. In equilibrium the fixed labor force reallocates itself between the two tiers; this determines the response of the home wage rate to the change in the world price of A:

$$\frac{\hat{w}}{\hat{p}_A} = \frac{\lambda_{LO}\theta_{AO}(\sigma_O - 1)}{\lambda_{LI}\gamma_I + \lambda_{LO}\theta_{AO}\sigma_O} = \frac{\alpha_1}{\omega_1}. \tag{8}$$

---

[7] Equation (6) is obtained by solving the unit-cost minimization condition, $\theta_{LO}\hat{a}_{LO} + \theta_{AO}\hat{a}_{AO} = 0$, and the definition of σ_O as $(\hat{a}_{AO} - \hat{a}_{LO})$ divided by $(\hat{w} - \hat{p}_A)$.

The numerator of eq. (8), α_1, is positive if σ_O is greater than one, thus indicating that the substitution effect outweighs the income effect. In that case the increase in p_A creates an excess demand for labor in the output tier at the initial wage, and the wage rate rises in the new equilibrium. If σ_O were less than one, the negative income effect dominates and the wage rate would fall. The denominator in eq. (8), ω_1, reveals the two ways in which the demand for labor would rise if the wage rate were to fall by one percent; γ_I shows the increased demand in the input tier and $\theta_{AO}\sigma_O$ the greater reliance on labor in the output tier.[8] A "flexible" economy, meaning one with large elasticities and hence a large ω, will have damped wage responses relative to a "rigid" economy with low elasticities γ_1 and σ_O. A low enough value for σ_O (i.e. $\sigma_O < 1$) will lead to $\hat{w}$ less than zero.

From eq. (8) it can be seen that should the wage rate rise, it would rise by proportionately less than the world price of middle product A since α_1 is less than ω_1. Indeed, the *real* wage, a comparison of w with final output price p_O, must fall. By the competitive profit conditions in the output tier,

$$\hat{p}_O = \theta_{LO}\hat{w} + \theta_{AO}\hat{p}_A, \tag{9}$$

so that with $\hat{w}$ less than $\hat{p}_A$, $\hat{w}$ must also be less than $\hat{p}_O$, a weighted average of $\hat{w}$ and $\hat{p}_A$. These relationships are shown in eq. (10) and fig. 2.1.

$$\frac{\hat{p}_O}{\hat{p}_A} = \left\{ \theta_{LO}\frac{\alpha_1}{\omega_1} + \theta_{AO} \right\}. \tag{10}$$

An elasticity of substitution less than one would cause the wage rate to fall. As illustrated by point E in fig. 2.1, a small enough value for σ_O might even cause an actual reduction in the price level, p_O. The critical value for σ_O at E is given by:

$$\sigma_O = \theta_{LO} - \frac{\lambda_{LI}\gamma_I}{\lambda_{LO}} < 1.$$

Sufficient flexibility in the input tier, reflected in a high value for γ_I, could make this critical value negative, ruling out a fall in p_O. But lack of technological flexibility in both tiers, in the form of low values for γ_I and σ_O, could cause the increase in world p_A to prove "deflationary".

Suppose both the home and foreign countries are importers of A, and that each requires the same value of A per dollar's worth of output (so that θ_{AO} equals θ_{AO}^* and θ_{LO} equals θ_{LO}^*). Nonetheless, differences in technology could require the two countries' price levels to react differently in the face of a common external shock. Indeed, a value of σ_O exceeding unity and σ_O^* falling short of unity would mean that

---

[8] Subscripts have been attached to the α and ω terms because subsequent variations introduced in this model cause slight alterations in these expressions.

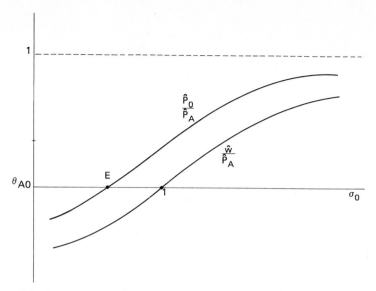

Figure 2.1. Domestic wage and output price responses with monetary accommodation.

the increase in world $\bar{p}_A$ leads to a higher wage rate at home but a lower wage abroad. If σ_O^* were small enough, the foreign country's price level could fall in response to the same shock that caused the domestic price level to rise.

2.2. No monetary accommodation

In fig. 2.1 the determinants of the change in wages and prices all reflect real characteristics of the supply side of the economy. With fixed exchange rates, monetary forces can create a violation of the equality between spending and income if the domestic money supply is initially kept fixed in the face of the rise in the world price of imported input, A. Let Z denote the value of current expenditures, $p_C x_O$, as distinct from the monetary value of final income produced, Y. Assume that individuals attempt over the long run to maintain a level of money wealth proportional to the value of income, Y. If from an initial full equilibrium and a given monetary value of wealth the money value of income should rise, we assume that

$$\hat{Z} = \xi \hat{Y} \text{ where } 0 < \xi < 1. \tag{11}$$

That is, the monetary value of expenditures would rise, but not by much as nominal income does; some hoarding takes place in an effort to increase the value of wealth towards the higher level appropriate to the higher value of Y.[9]

[9] This procedure follows the analysis in Noman and Jones (1980).

The change in nominal income, Y, can be broken down into two components, $\hat{p}_O$ and $\hat{y}$. The change in real income, $\hat{y}$, is once again given by the degree of trade dependence and the deterioration in the terms of trade,

$$\hat{y} = -\theta_{AO}\hat{p}_A.$$

The change in the price level is shown by eq. (9). Combining the real and price level changes in the national income reveals that $\hat{p}_A$ cancels so that

$$\hat{Y} = \theta_{LO}\hat{w}. \tag{12}$$

Thus nominal income rises if and only if the wage rate rises. Nominal spending also changes directly with the wage rate, as

$$\hat{x}_O + \hat{p}_O = \xi\theta_{LO}\hat{w}.$$

Substitution for the price level change reveals that

$$\hat{x}_O = -\{\theta_{AO}\hat{p}_A + (1-\xi)\theta_{LO}\hat{w}\}. \tag{13}$$

That is, if the wage rate rises there is a "monetary drag" revealed in a trade surplus that causes x_O to fall further than shown in eq. (7) when spending was equal to income. With this different solution for changes in consumption of final goods, the market-clearing change in the wage rate becomes

$$\frac{\hat{w}}{\hat{p}_A} = \frac{\lambda_{LO}\theta_{AO}(\sigma_O - 1)}{\lambda_{LI}\gamma_I + \lambda_{LO}[\theta_{AO}\sigma_O + \theta_{LO}(1-\xi)]} = \frac{\alpha_1}{\omega_2}. \tag{14}$$

The new denominator, ω_2, exceeds ω_1 in eq. (8), as a reflection of endogenous trade surpluses (if w rises) or deficits (if w falls).

Figure 2.2 adds two new relationships to those illustrated in fig. 2.1. The dashed curves show how once again unity is the critical value for the elasticity of substitution in the output tier that just balances income and substitution effects to leave wage rates unaltered. If σ_O exceeds unity, w rises. Since nominal income also rises a trade surplus develops as spending is cut below income in an attempt to accumulate wealth. This serves to dampen the wage increase. By contrast, for low values of σ_O the wage rate falls. But in this case current wealth levels exceed desired holdings (since Y has fallen), and import deficits help maintain current consumption, thus limiting the retreat of labor to the input tier of the economy.

As fig. 2.2 reveals, with monetary effects cushioning the decline of real consumption should the wage rate fall, it becomes less likely that the rise in the price of imported A on world markets could actually cause the home price level to fall.[10] Further-

---

[10]   In fig. 2.2 the value of E' is given by $\xi\theta_{LO} - (\lambda_{LI}\gamma_I/\lambda_{LO})$, less than the critical value E of fig. 2.2.

more, differences in the rate at which home and foreign residents wish to obtain a new wealth equilibrium (as captured by ξ and ξ^*) join technological differences between the two countries as possible explanations of divergent national price responses to the similar external shock of terms of trade deterioration under a regime of fixed exchange rates.

3. Flexible exchange rates

In the previous section we showed how in our model national price levels could diverge even under fixed exchange rates and while maintaining the law of one price. The explanation for this lay in the movement of domestic wages, the response of which has shown to be conditioned by monetary factors and their interaction with the current account. In this section we extend the analysis to allow for flexible exchange rates. It is clear that divergent movements in national price levels measured in terms of their home currencies would not be so surprising with flexible exchange rates. We focus instead on factors which give rise to divergent movements in *exchange-rate* adjusted price levels; that is, to equilibrium divergences from PPP.

Movements in domestic wages again play an important role, and it is clear that monetary factors as reflected in the current account balance could influence the results. For simplicity, and in order to emphasize the possibility of equilibrium divergences from PPP, we focus on a simple, long-run view of the exchange rate: it adjusts

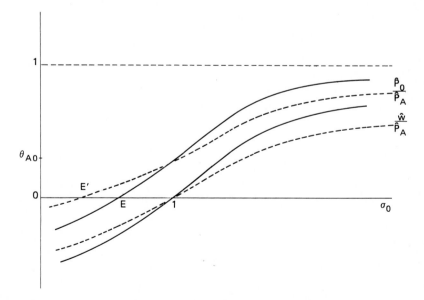

Figure 2.2. Domestic wage and output price response with no monetary accommodation.

to keep the current account in balance. It is well-known that short-run factors such as deviations from the law of one price and the ability to finance current account imbalances through the capital account might lead to temporary divergences from PPP. Our general framework is readily adaptable to these short-run issues, but we restrict our attention to situations of long-run equilibrium.

Given our assumptions concerning domestic expenditure, in order to balance the current account the exchange rate must adjust so that nominal income is constant.

3.1. Common real external disturbances

Such a role for the exchange rate has strong implications for a nation's price level when it is shocked by a rise in the price of imported middle product, A. As before, $\bar{p}_A$ and $\bar{p}_B$ represent world currency units so that local p_A and p_B are given by $E\bar{p}_A$ and $E\bar{p}_B$ respectively. A rise in $\bar{p}_A$ with $\bar{p}_B$ constant lowers real income by

$$\hat{y} = -\theta_{AO}\hat{\bar{p}}_A, \tag{15}$$

independent of any change in the exchange rate. Since the change in nominal income, $\hat{Y}$, is the sum of $\hat{y}$ and the change in the price level, $\hat{p}_O$, the exchange rate must adjust so that the price level rises:

$$\hat{p}_O = \theta_{AO}\hat{\bar{p}}_A. \tag{16}$$

This is a strong result, for it implies that despite any differences in technology between two countries importing (and not producing) middle product A, if the share of income devoted to imports is the same, so will be the consequent rise in the national price level. The direction and extent of the change in the exchange rate, however, does depend on further details of the technology.

The change in the price of final output depends upon costs:

$$\hat{p}_O = \theta_{LO}\hat{w} + \theta_{AO}(\hat{E} + \hat{\bar{p}}_A). \tag{17}$$

Subtraction of eq. (16) from (17) reveals that:

$$\theta_{LO}\hat{w} + \theta_{AO}\hat{E} = 0. \tag{18}$$

The inverse relationship between the wage rate and the exchange rate implied by eq. (18) is illustrated by the downward sloping curve YY in fig. 2.3. Suppose equilibrium is initially at point G and that the rise in the world price of A would, at a constant exchange rate, raise the wage rate as shown by point H. If local money supplies are kept constant, such an increase in w would, as we argued in the last section, lead to a current account surplus to reflect the attempt to hoard to accumulate reserves. Under

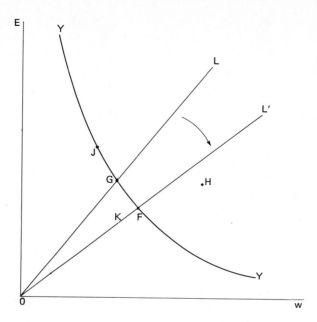

Figure 2.3. Wage and exchange rate determination.

flexible exchange rates the currency appreciates to cut off the incipient trade surplus, the induced fall in p_O restoring nominal income.

Details of the technological relationships in the input and output tiers of the economy also bear upon the behavior of wages when the terms of trade deteriorate. As before, eq. (3) gives the condition for labor market clearing. The demand for labour in the input tier now depends upon the exchange rate as well as the wage rate since the crucial product wage is $(w/E\overline{p}_B)$. With world $\overline{p}_B$ constant,

$$\hat{L}_I = -\gamma_I(\hat{w} - \hat{E}).$$

Similarly, in the output tier,

$$\hat{L}_O = -\theta_{AO}\sigma_O(\hat{w} - \hat{E} - \hat{\overline{p}}_A) + \hat{x}_O.$$

Real consumption is lowered by the same amount as real income, $-\theta_{AO}\hat{p}_A$, so by the condition of the labor market clearing,

$$\hat{w} = \hat{E} + \frac{\alpha_1}{\omega_1}\hat{\overline{p}}_A, \tag{19}$$

where α_1 and ω_1 are as defined in eq. (8).

In fig. 2.3, the proportional relationship between the wage rate and the exchange rate, given the world price of A, that is implied by eq. (19) is shown as the ray OL. A rise in $\bar{p}_A$ causes the ray to rotate, clockwise if the elasticity of substitution in the output tier exceeds unity ($\alpha_1 > 0$) and counterclockwise if it is less than unity. If $(\sigma_O - 1)$ is positive, labor is drawn into the output tier, wages rise, and the rise in nominal income calls forth a currency appreciation (as shown by the new equilibrium at F in fig. 2.3). If $(\sigma_O - 1)$ is negative, labor is sent into the input tier, wages fall, and the currency depreciates to restore the value of money income (as shown by point J in fig. 2.3).

Suppose home and foreign countries differ sufficiently in the flexibility of technology in the output tier. Specifically, let σ_O exceed unity (so that $\alpha_1 > 0$) and σ_O^* fall short of unity (so that $\alpha_1^* < 0$). The domestic price levels, and hence the PPP rate (p_O/p_O^*), depend only upon the extent of trade dependence, so that

$$\hat{p}_O - \hat{p}_O^* = (\theta_{AO} - \theta_{AO}^*)\hat{\bar{p}}_A. \tag{20}$$

Thus if the fraction of national income represented by imports (and demand) for A is comparable in the home and foreign country, both price levels are driven up by the same relative amount and the PPP rate would remain fixed.

However, the exchange rate between countries, $(\hat{E} - \hat{E}^*)$, would not be fixed. In each country eq. (18) and (19) can be solved for the change in the local price of world currency ($\hat{E}$ and $\hat{E}^*$). Such solutions reveal that:

$$(\hat{E} - \hat{E}^*) = -\left\{ \theta_{LO}\frac{\alpha_1}{\omega_1} - \theta_{LO}^*\frac{\alpha_1^*}{\omega_1^*} \right\}\hat{\bar{p}}_A = \hat{e} \tag{21}$$

If, as supposed in this example, α_1 is positive (reflecting $\sigma_O > 1$) and α_1^* is negative (with $\sigma_O^* < 1$), the home country's currency could appreciate sharply relative to the foreign currency. That is, even with the respective price levels responding similarly to the common external shock (thus keeping the PPP exchange rate constant), the country whose technology allows a stronger measure of substitution between own labor and higher-priced middle product A will find its wage rate driven up and currency appreciated relative to the other country. In fig. 2.3 if both countries start at G, the deterioration in the terms of trade of each country with the rest of the world sends the home country to F and the foreign country to J.

3.2. Comparison with fixed exchange rates

It is interesting to compare these results with those that were derived in section 2 for fixed exchange rates. The total discrepancy, $\hat{\mu}$, between changes in the actual exchange rate and the PPP rate, as defined by eq. (2), is the same in this case as in the fixed exchange rate case with monetary accommodation such that spending equals income. This discrepancy is produced by real differences in the two economies. But the share of the discrepancy born by the PPP rate, on the one hand, and the exchange rate, on the other, differs in the two cases. If exchange rates are free to fluctuate, they absorb the different wage experience in each country, leaving the national price levels to reflect only the degree of dependence on imported middle product, A, as in eq. (20). The primary source of differential wage response is found in a difference in the flexibility of input substitution in both the input and output tiers of the economy.

3.3. Monetary disturbances

Before proceeding to some generalizations in the productive structure of this model, we mention that purely monetary disturbances have the expected results on a nation's wage level and exchange rate. For example, suppose the *world* prices of A and B are inflating at the same rate. If local monetary wealth is undisturbed, the exchange rate must adjust to keep Y constant. But with no change in the terms of trade (and no change in aggregate output since labor remains fully employed), $\hat{y} = 0$, so that the price level, p_O, is constant. This implies that:

$$\theta_{LO}\hat{w} + \theta_{AO}\hat{E} = -\theta_{AO}\hat{\bar{p}}_A.$$ (22)

That is, the $\overline{Y}$ schedule in fig. 2.3 would shift downwards as the world inflates.

But the OL ray rotates as well. In the input tier

$$\hat{L}_I = -\gamma_I(\hat{w} - \hat{E} - \hat{\bar{p}}_B),$$

while in the output tier

$$\hat{L}_O = -\theta_{AO}\sigma_O(\hat{w} - \hat{E} - \hat{\bar{p}}_A),$$

since real consumption, x_O, is undisturbed. By the full-employment condition, eq. (3), letting $\hat{\bar{p}} = \hat{\bar{p}}_B = \hat{\bar{p}}_A$, we have

$$\hat{w} = \hat{E} + \hat{\bar{p}},$$ (23)

so that in fig. 2.3 the OL ray shifts clockwise. Indeed, eqs. (22) and (23) jointly determine that the exchange rate falls by the same rate as the world price level rises, thus fully insulating the domestic wage rate, as at point K.

If, instead of a rise in world prices, the home country experiences a purely monetary expansion, the OL ray in fig. 2.3 would remain in position but the money value of produced income, Y, would be driven up. This is accommodated by an equi-proportionate increase in the wage rate and exchange rate as the negatively sloped curve in fig. 2.3 is shifted radially outwards from the origin.

4. Diversity in the input tier

The impact on real income of a rise in the price of an imported middle product is to some extent mitigated if local production takes place. In this section we allow each country to produce some middle product A (as well as B) in the input tier, but continue to assume that all x_B is exported in exchange for imports of A, which, in conjunction with local production (x_A), is used in the output tier to help produce the single non-traded consumption good, x_O. To be more specific, we assume that at initial prices the value of output in the input tier is unchanged, but now local x_A production replaces some x_B production. Furthermore, x_A is produced with labor and a factor specific to its production (V_A). Therefore comparisons of two potential initial equilibria, which differ in the extent of import-competing production (x_A) presuppose a different mix of specific factors (V_A, V_B).

The demand for labor in the input tier now depends on the wage rate relative both to p_A and p_B. If the world price of A, $\bar{p}_A$, rises with $\bar{p}_B$ constant, as we have been assuming, producers of A in the input tier find their demand for labor stimulated. With obvious notation,

$$\hat{L}_A = -\gamma_A(\hat{w} - \hat{E} - \hat{\bar{p}}_A)$$

and

$$\hat{L}_B = -\gamma_B(\hat{w} - \hat{E}),$$

so that if λ_{LA} denotes the fraction of the labor force in the input tier that is devoted to production of x_A,

$$\hat{L}_I = \lambda_{LA}\hat{L}_A + \lambda_{LB}\hat{L}_B$$

or,

$$\hat{L}_I = -\gamma_I\{\hat{w} - \hat{E} - \beta_A\hat{\bar{p}}_A\}, \tag{24}$$

where

$$\gamma_I \equiv \lambda_{LA}\gamma_A + \lambda_{LB}\gamma_B$$

and

$$\beta_A \equiv \frac{\lambda_{LA}\gamma_A}{\gamma_I}.$$

The fraction, β_A, answers the following question: if the domestic price of A should rise by one percent and the size of the labor force in the input tier is kept constant, by how much would the wage rate rise if p_B is kept constant? β_A is larger the greater the importance of the A-industry as an employer of labor in the input tier and the higher is the elasticity of labor demand in the A-sector, γ_A, relative to γ_B.

The existence of an import-competing sector in the input tier also affects the output tier's demand for labor since real consumption, x_O, is not as severely hit by a deterioration in the terms of trade. Let θ_M denote the fraction of income devoted to imports of A. Then θ_M falls short of θ_{AO}, the fraction of income represented by total demand for middle product, A. The expression for the real income (and consumption) loss in eq. (7) is replaced by:

$$\hat{x}_O = -\theta_M \hat{\bar{p}}_A. \tag{25}$$

As before,

$$\hat{a}_{LO} = -\theta_{AO}\sigma_O(\hat{w} - \hat{E} - \hat{\bar{p}}_A),$$

so that, by eq. (5),

$$\hat{L}_O = -\theta_{AO}\sigma_O(\hat{w} - \hat{E}) + \theta_{AO}\left(\sigma_O - \frac{\theta_M}{\theta_{AO}}\right)\hat{\bar{p}}_A. \tag{26}$$

Substituting eqs. (24) and (25) into the labor-market clearing eq. (3) reveals that:

$$\hat{w} = \hat{E} + \frac{\alpha_2}{\omega_1}\hat{\bar{p}}_A, \tag{27}$$

where

$$\alpha_2 \equiv \beta_A \cdot \lambda_{LI}\gamma_I + \lambda_{LO}\theta_O\left[\sigma_O - \frac{\theta_M}{\theta_{AO}}\right].$$

This solution should be compared to eq. (19). The existence of an import-competing sector, x_A, raises the chances that an increase in the world price of A will increase the wage rate (for any given exchange rate) for two reasons. First, a rise in p_A will directly stimulate demand for labor in the input tier (this is the $\beta_A \cdot \lambda_{LI}\gamma_I$ term in α_2). Secondly, the real consumption loss, $\hat{x}_O$ in eq. (25), is less than $\theta_{AO}\hat{\bar{p}}_A$. Thus in α_2 the second term is positive if the substitution term, σ_O, exceeds a fraction, θ_M/θ_{AO}. In terms of the diagram (fig. 2.4) showing the simultaneous solution for the wage rate and exchange rate, the more self-sufficient is the economy in producing A, the more likely the *OL* ray is to rotate in a clockwise direction when world $\bar{p}_A$ rises.

As before, we assume that the exchange rate adjusts to keep nominal income, *Y*,

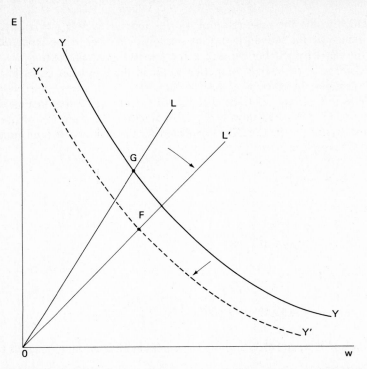

Figure 2.4. Wage and exchange rate determination with import-competing local production.

from changing. But eq. (16) is now replaced by (28),

$$\hat{p}_O = \theta_M \hat{\bar{p}}_A,$$ (28)

since the real income loss is proportional to imports, which is less than total (derived) demand for A. The price level is again shown to change as in eq. (17) so that subtraction reveals:

$$\theta_{LO}\hat{w} + \theta_{AO}\hat{E} = -(\theta_{AO} - \theta_M)\hat{\bar{p}}_A,$$ (29)

With θ_{AO} exceeding θ_M, this can be interpreted in fig. 2.4 as a downward shift in the YY schedule. The diagram reveals that with the OL ray more likely to shift clockwise, and the YY schedule shifting downwards as the economy approaches self-sufficiency, the home currency is more apt to appreciate, whereas the direction of the wage change seems in doubt. Pushing this to the extreme, suppose the input tier is completely dominated by production of A, which is still the only middle product assumed to be required in the output tier. The country becomes totally self-sufficient, the exchange rate falls by the same relative amount as the world price of A has risen, completely insulating the wage rate. This is identical to the case of world inflation discussed at the end of section 3.

If the economy is only partly dependent upon the rest of the world for imports of middle product A instead of totally dependent (as in section 3), is the wage rate more or less likely to rise when the world price of A rises? Ultimately this depends on the technological characteristics of the new x_A-industry in the input tier compared with the technology in the x_B-sector, which, by assumption, is being scaled down as import-competing production rises. Compared to x_B, if x_A is (1) labor-intensive, and (2) has a more elastic demand for labor (γ_A exceeds γ_B), the rise in $\bar{p}_A$ is more likely to raise the wage rate than in the case of total dependence on imports.[11]

If home and foreign countries are only partially dependent on imports of A, the rise in $\bar{p}_A$ affects their PPP rate as in eq. (30):

$$(\hat{p}_O - \hat{p}_O^*) = (\theta_M - \theta_M^*)\hat{\bar{p}}_A. \tag{30}$$

Thus ultimately the PPP rate depends upon real circumstances and, assuming the law of one price for middle product, A, these real circumstances refer only to the degree to which each country relies on imports of A. Any inter-country differences in the extent of import-competing local production affects relative wage rates and, through this route, the exchange rate between the home and foreign country. Thus

$$\hat{e} \equiv \hat{E} - \hat{E}^* = - \left\{ [(\theta_{AO} - \theta_M) - (\theta_{AO}^* - \theta_M^*)] + \left[\theta_{LO} \frac{\alpha_2}{\omega_1} - \theta_{LO}^* \frac{\alpha_2^*}{\omega_1^*} \right] \right\} \cdot \hat{\bar{p}}_A, \tag{31}$$

Local production of A has tended to insulate the price level in each country from the shock of a world price rise for imported A in each country [compare eq. (28) with

---

[11] Let θ_{AI} indicate the share of the x_A-sector in total output of the input tier. Then the expression for the wage rate change relative to $\hat{\bar{p}}_A$, obtained by solving eqs. (27) and (29), is

$$\frac{\hat{w}}{\hat{\bar{p}}_A} = \frac{\theta_{AO}}{\omega_1} \left\{ (\beta_A - \theta_{AI})\lambda_{LI}\gamma_I + (\sigma_O - 1)\lambda_{LO}\theta_{AO} \right\}.$$

If no A is produced in the input tier, the direction of change in the wage rate depends only on the comparison of σ_O with unity. If some A is produced, this comparison is modified by the term in $(\beta_A - \theta_{AI})$. But $(\beta_A - \theta_{AI})$ equals θ_{AI} times

$$\left\{ \frac{\lambda_{LA}}{\theta_{AI}} \cdot \frac{\gamma_A}{\gamma_I} - 1 \right\}.$$

The term $(\lambda_{LA}/\theta_{AI})$ exceeds unity if x_A is labor-intensive compared to x_B (in the sense of labor shares, $\theta_{LA} > \theta_{LB}$). The term (γ_A/γ_I) exceeds unity if and only if $\gamma_A > \gamma_B$.

(16)]. But the exchange rate between each country and the world currency (in which A is priced) picks up the difference. Comparing home and foreign countries, the total discrepancy, $\hat{\mu}$, between the actual exchange rate and the PPP rate, is much as in section 3's model with no import-competing production (save α_2 and α_2^* replace α_1 and α_1^*). But the share of this discrepancy borne by the PPP rate, on the one hand, and the actual (equilibrium) exchange rate, on the other, depends on the relative extent of import-competing productive activity.

5. Diversity in the output tier

In preceding sections no role was possible for differences in taste patterns between countries since only one final commodity was consumed. In order to discuss the role of tastes we revert to our earlier simplifications as to production in the input tier: each country produces only one middle product, B, which is traded on world markets. Some of its production of B is retained at home to be combined with labor to produce commodity x_2. The rest of its production of B is exported in exchange for A, which is used only to produce commodity x_1. As before, we concentrate on the relative impact at home and abroad of an increase in the world price of A.

A country importing A experiences a loss in real income when its terms of trade deteriorate. This real income loss is shown by eq. (15). Under flexible rates the price *index* of final consumables, p_O, must rise by the same amount [shown by eq. (16)] in order to keep nominal income, Y, unaltered. With two final consumption goods, the change in the price index, $\hat{p}_O$, is defined in eq. (32),

$$\hat{p}_O \equiv \theta_1 \hat{p}_1 + \theta_2 \hat{p}_2, \tag{32}$$

where θ_i denotes the share of national income devoted to consumption (and production) of commodity i. The term θ_{AO} refers to the fraction of national income paid for (imports of) middle product, A. By assumption, A is only used to produce the first commodity. Let θ_{A1} indicate its share of revenue produced by the first commodity so that

$$\theta_{AO} = \theta_{A1} \cdot \theta_1.$$

The change in the PPP rate between home and foreign country, each of whom experiences a rise in its national price level, is

$$(\hat{p}_O - \hat{p}_O^*) = (\theta_{A1}\theta_1 - \theta_{A1}^*\theta_1^*)\hat{p}_A. \tag{33}$$

The role of differences in national taste patterns is thus clearly revealed. Even if the technology of producing the first commodity is roughly comparable between countries, in the sense of θ_{A1} and θ_{A1}^* being approximately equal, the home price level inflates more than does the foreign to the extent that tastes at home are biased towards the commodity (x_1) which uses middle product A intensively (exclusively, by assumption). At the extreme, the foreign country might consume only the second commodity, in which case its price level is completely insulated from the rise in $\bar{p}_A$.

Changes in the PPP rate, however, need not accurately signal changes in the exchange rate between home and foreign currencies. Once again we must turn to two relationships that serve jointly to determine each country's wage rate and exchange rate with the rest of the world. Equation (32) defines the change in the price index. The competitive profit conditions in each sector of the output tier ensure that the $\hat{p}_i$ are linked to changes in costs. If world $\bar{p}_B$ is assumed constant,

$$\theta_{L1}\hat{w} + \theta_{A1}(\hat{E} + \hat{\bar{p}}_A) = \hat{p}_1, \tag{34}$$

$$\theta_{L2}\hat{w} + \theta_{B2}\hat{E} \quad\quad = \hat{p}_2. $$

Thus the change in the consumer price index can be expressed in terms of the change in the wage rate, the exchange rate, and the world price of middle product A:

$$\hat{p}_O = \theta_{LO}\hat{w} + \theta_{AO}\hat{\bar{p}}_A + (\theta_{AO} + \theta_{BO})\hat{E}. \tag{35}$$

The exchange rate changes so as to ensure p_O rises by the amount $\theta_{AO}\hat{\bar{p}}_A$ [see eq. (16)], so that subtraction reveals that:

$$\theta_{LO}\hat{w} + (1 - \theta_{LO})\hat{E} = 0. \tag{36}$$

By assuming away any import-competing production of middle product A, we have insured that in the absence of local monetary changes the wage rate and the exchange rate are inversely related as in the YY curve in fig. 2.3.

This schedule by itself, of course, does not determine the exchange rate and wage rate separately. Once again it is necessary to investigate the labor-market clearing conditions to obtain the second relationship among wage rate, exchange rate, and the world price of middle product A. With two commodities produced in the output tier, this relationship is more complex than in previous sections, so that here we only sketch the principal results.[12]

First, note that if consumer tastes are so rigid that x_1 and x_2 are always consumed in fixed proportions, the model is much like that described in section 3 with only one commodity consumed and produced in the output tier. In this case the determination of the wage rate is much as in eq. (19). Explicitly, we would have:

$$\hat{w} = \hat{E} + \frac{\alpha_3}{\omega_3}\hat{\bar{p}}_A, \tag{37}$$

---

[12] An explicit analysis of wage determination in a model with two activities in each tier of the economy is found in Sanyal and Jones (1982).

where

$$\alpha_3 \equiv \lambda_{LO} \theta_{A1} \lambda_{L1} \left[\sigma_1 - \frac{\theta_1}{\lambda_{L1}} \right],$$

$$\omega_3 \equiv \lambda_{LI} \gamma_I + \lambda_{LO} [\lambda_{L1} \theta_{A1} \sigma_1 + \lambda_{L2} \theta_{B2} \sigma_2].$$

With two commodities produced in the output tier, the expressions for α_3 and ω_3 are slightly different from the comparable expressions for α_1 and ω_1 in eq. (19). Most important, A is used only in the first industry so that the *OL* ray in fig. 2.3 would rotate clockwise as $\bar{p}_A$ rises only if σ_1 exceeds some critical value. This value now falls short of unity if the first industry (which uses A) is labor intensive. In any case the conflict between substitution and income effect is again apparent.

The case of such rigid taste patterns is extreme. At the opposite end of the spectrum we can imagine tastes captured by downward sloping *linear* indifference curves, which would insure that if both commodities are consumed, p_1/p_2 must remain constant. In such an event the competitive profit conditions in eq. (34) can be subtracted from each other to obtain:

$$\hat{w} - \hat{E} = - \frac{\theta_{A1}}{(\theta_{L1} - \theta_{L2})} \hat{\bar{p}}_A . \tag{38}$$

A rise in the world price of A squeezes the first industry which is the sole user of A. As in the theory of effective protection, if relative output prices cannot change, the real return to the factor used intensively in the first industry must fall. Suppose θ_{L1} exceeds θ_{L2}. This is a way of stating that the first industry is labor-intensive (relative to each industry's requirements of middle products). If so the wage rate (in world currency units) must fall.

The two extreme cases summarized by eqs. (37) and (38) are interesting because the more general link among $\hat{w}$, $\hat{E}$, and $\hat{\bar{p}}_A$ when tastes are captured by smoothly bowed-in indifference curves for the two final consumption goods is a convex combination of these two solutions. Without going into details,[13] let σ_D and σ_S denote, respectively, the elasticities of relative demand and supply for final consumption goods. With D_i indicating demand and x_i production,

$$\sigma_D \equiv - \frac{(\hat{D}_1 - \hat{D}_2)}{(\hat{p}_1 - \hat{p}_2)}$$

$$\sigma_S \equiv \frac{(\hat{x}_1 - \hat{x}_2)}{(\hat{p}_1 - \hat{p}_2)} . \tag{39}$$

---

[13]   These are spelled out in Sanyal and Jones (1982).

With reference to the extreme solutions shown by eq. (37) for the case in which $\sigma_D = 0$ and eq. (38) for the case in which $\sigma_D = \infty$, eq. (40) provides the general solution:

$$\hat{w} = \hat{E} + \left\{ \frac{\sigma_S}{\sigma_S + \sigma_D} \left(\frac{\alpha_3}{\omega_3} \right) + \frac{\sigma_D}{\sigma_S + \sigma_D} \left(-\frac{\theta_{A1}}{[\theta_{L1} - \theta_{L2}]} \right) \right\} \hat{\bar{p}}_A. \qquad (40)$$

The weights attached to each extreme case should be familiar from the theory of tax incidence and shifting; they involve the *relative* strength of the response of demanders and producers to changes in relative prices.

In the more simple case in which only one commodity is consumed, fig. 2.3 showed how a rise in world $\bar{p}_A$ caused the OL ray to rotate along a given YY curve to determine each nation's wage and exchange rate response. Precisely the same procedure is applicable here. Equation (36) reveals that the YY curve does not shift, while the coefficient of $\hat{\bar{p}}_A$ in (40), if positive, would imply a clockwise rotation of the OL ray.

The relevance of national differences in tastes and technologies in determining exchange rates can thus briefly be summarized:

(1) *Tastes.* The role of taste differences in affecting the PPP rate in eq. (33) has already been discussed and is traditional in the literature on purchasing power parity. Exchange rates are also affected. Suppose the home country has a taste bias (compared with the foreign country) towards consuming the commodity (x_1) which uses middle product A. This tends to make the absolute value of α_3 exceed that of α_3^*. The sign of α_3 depends on the elasticity of substitution. Suppose both σ_1 and σ_1^* are high so that α_3 and α_3^* are both positive; this tends to rotate OL clockwise as $\bar{p}_A$ rises. The taste bias is primarily captured in the λ_{L1} term in α_3; the fraction of home labor (in the output tier) devoted to producing the first commodity is higher than abroad $(\lambda_{L1} > \lambda_{L1}^*)$ if tastes are biased as we supposed. Other things being equal (and assuming high σ_1 and σ_1^*), such a taste bias would cause E to fall more at home than abroad, or for the home currency to appreciate relative to the foreign. By eqs. (2) and (33) such a taste bias causes a discrepancy between the PPP rate and the exchange rate *both* because the PPP rate is rising *and* because the exchange rate is falling. Should elasticities of substitution be small in both countries, the OL ray in fig. 2.3 would tend to rotate in a counter-clockwise direction, more so at home than abroad so that the home currency depreciates. In this case the PPP rate and the exchange rate move in the same direction.

(2) *Technology.* In the output tier two features of the technology are crucial. The size of the elasticity of substitution in the sector using the middle product that has risen in price helps determine the direction in which wages move. In addition, a factor intensity comparison between the commodities in the output tier is a key feature indicating the impact on wages of the squeeze implied by the rise in $\bar{p}_A$. If A is used in the labor-intensive sector at home and the non-labor intensive sector abroad, the rise in $\bar{p}_A$ will tend to lower w and raise w^*. This implies a rise in E, a fall in E^*, and therefore a strong depreciation of the home country's currency.

The degree of flexibility of technology in the input tier plays a more passive role. Of course large values for γ_I as well as for σ_1 and σ_2 will tend to increase the elasticity of supply, σ_S, and thus the weight attached to the α_3/ω_3 term in brackets in eq. (40). As well, large values for γ_I (which increases ω_3) tend to mitigate the extent of the required change in the wage rate, the direction of which depends largely on technology in the output tier (both the value of σ_1 and factor intensities).

(3) *Interaction of tastes and technology.*   In this paper we have focused on the case in which countries import A and, indeed, in this section there is no import-competing sector of the economy. In general, however, tastes, technology, and factor supplies interact to determine the pattern of trade and degree of dependence upon trade. The impact which a change in world prices has on any nation's price level is [by eq. (28)] directly dependent on the pattern and size of the trade flow. Thus the PPP rate depends upon this and essentially nothing else (in the presumed absence of local monetary changes). The exchange rate, however, depends on a different kind of interaction between tastes and technology, that reflected in the relative sizes of σ_D and σ_S. If, say, at home consumers are quite flexible in their taste patterns but inflexible in their ability to substitute inputs, with the opposite bias abroad, eq. (40) suggests that the movement of w and E depends largely on factor intensities in the output tier while that of w^* and E^* depends more heavily on the value of the elasticity of substitution in the industry using A. If σ_1^* is high and x_1 labor-intensive at home, a rise in world $\bar{p}_A$ could send wages rising abroad and dropping at home. With the OL ray in fig. 2.3 rotating clockwise for the foreign country and counter-clockwise at home, the home currency might suffer a severe depreciation even when the PPP rate might not change much.

5. Conclusions

This paper has put forward a view of the relationship between national price levels and exchange rates that is rather different from that traditionally found in the literature. The key organizing principle is that trade occurs only in middle products; final consumption goods contain some local valued-added, and the cost of this local value-added is reflected in the domestic price of final goods. International differences in technology and structure cause international differences in responses of local factor rewards in response to common disturbances, creating international differences in movements in exchange rate-adjusted national price levels, reflected in what we have called the PPP discrepancy, $\hat{\mu}$.

Under fixed exchange rates, these differences were of course reflected in movements in local currency price levels. Introducing flexible exchange rates, perhaps surprisingly, did not give rise to a different value for $\hat{\mu}$. And perhaps more surprisingly was the result that under flexible exchange rates national price levels became very "aggregative" variables movements in which reflected only changes in aggregate real income. Details of the technical structure of the economy held implications only for movements in the nominal exchange rates.

Elaborating the model to allow for local production of import-substitutes meant, of course, that the income effects from a deterioration in the terms of trade were mitigated, and the extent of profitable import-competing activity influenced the division of the PPP discrepancy between the price level and the exchange rate. Extension to two consumption goods allowed the introduction of price index problems. Again the response of the PPP rate depends only upon real income effects while the details of tastes and technology are reflected in movements in the nominal exchange rate.

An obvious extension would be to allow for short-run phenomena related to capital mobility and expectations. One approach is that suggested by Dornbusch (1976) who treats output prices as "sticky". In the current model real income effects are always negative; with p_O constant, monetary equilibrium would require that domestic interest rates fall. Hence E would have to rise relative to its long-run value in order for speculators to expect the domestic appreciation implied by the interest differential. If α is positive, the long-run equilibrium exchange rate rises; the short-run exchange rate would necessarily overshoot. If α is negative, the long-run exchange rate would fall and the short-run rate would then necessarily undershoot.

A more interesting possibility is to examine the implications of speculators being "confused, monetarist PPP advocates" who expect actual exchange rate movements in accordance with the PPP rate. Such implications, however, are beyond the scope of the present paper.

References

Balassa, Bela, 1964, The purchasing power parity doctrine: A reappraisal, Journal of Political Economy 72, 584–596.

Buiter, Willem and Douglas D. Purvis, 1980, Oil, disinflation, and export competitiveness: A model of the Dutch disease, NBER, Working Paper, no. 592.

Dornbusch, Rudiger, 1976, A model of exchange rate dynamics, Journal of Political Economy.

Frenkel, Jacob, 1980, The collapse of purchasing power parity, NBER, Working Paper, no. 569.

Noman, Kamran and Ronald W. Jones, 1980, A model of trade and unemployment, in: J. Green and J. Scheinkman (eds.), Essays in honour of Lionel McKenzie.

Samuelson, Paul A., 1956, Theoretical notes on trade problems, Review of Economics and Statistics.

Sanyal, Kalyan and Ronald W. Jones, 1982, The theory of trade in middle products, American Economic Review.

Usher, Dan, 1967, The price mechanism and the meaning of national income statistics (Greenwood Press).

Recent Issues in the Theory of Flexible Exchange Rates, edited by E. Claassen and P. Salin
© *North-Holland Publishing Company, 1983*

Chapter 3.1

THE NOMINAL AND REAL EXCHANGE RATE IN A QUANTITY-THEORETICAL TWO-COUNTRY MODEL

Emil CLAASSEN*

The nominal exchange rate is traditionally that of the purchasing power parity whereas the real exchange rate can be conceived either as the terms of trade to the extent that the traded goods are differentiated products or/and as the relationship of the relative prices between tradable and non-tradable goods in the domestic and foreign country.

For a rigorous determination of the real and nominal exchange rate, a two-country model is used representing the world economy being the only closed economy. We shall elaborate the model under the assumption of perfect capital mobility (in the sense that domestic and foreign financial assets are perfect substitutes). In the literature this assumption is normally set up in order to show that the regime of flexible exchange rates produces the highest transmission of disturbances between countries either on real national income in a Keynesian model [Mundell (1968)] or on the general price level in a quantity-theoretical framework [Dornbusch (1976b)]; the transmission mechanism is described for example in Claassen (1982). In this paper, the hypothesis of perfect capital mobility is used in order to analyse the effect of disturbances in terms of changes in the domestic quantity of money on the world interest rate and on other real variables like the real exchange rate within a quantity-theoretical framework. These real effects arise even in the long-run to the extent that monetary policy is conducted with open-market operations (inside money). The existing quantity-theoretical models operating under the assumption of perfect capital mobility are either one-country models [e.g. Dornbusch and Fischer (1980)] where the country is a small one exercising no influence on the world interest rate or two-country models [e.g. Dornbusch (1976b)] where the real exchange rate is absent.

Section 1 presents the model, which is essentially of the Metzler (1951) type, but transposed to the international economy. Furthermore, the Patinkin (1965) framework for a valid dichotomy of the pricing process is also applied to the international economy such that the real sector of the world economy determines the real variables, including

* This article has been supported by the Deutsche Forschungsgemeinschaft and elaborated within its special program "Inflation and Employment in Open Economies".

the real exchange rate, and the monetary sector determines the nominal variables: the price levels and the nominal exchange rate. Sections 2 and 3 investigate the long-run effects of an expansionary open-market policy on the nominal and real exchange rate. In section 2 it is shown that the rate of depreciation of the nominal exchange rate exceeds the rate of monetary growth (for a non-growing economy). However, there is also a depreciation of the real exchange rate which is necessary for equilibrating the national goods markets. Finally, section 3 restates the quasi neutrality of money with respect to the real exchange rate (but not with respect to other real variables) when one takes into account the readjustment of the economy towards the steady-state level of stocks with regard to financial and physical assets. A special assumption made in section 3 concerns the capital stock in both countries which is supposed to be variable in response to a change in the interest rate.

1. The model

The proposed classical or quantity-theoretical model has two characteristics.

(1) By following Patinkin's (1965) valid dichotomy of the pricing process, the world economy represented by the two-country model is divided into a real sector and into a monetary sector. Consequently, the markets for real cash balances belong to the real sector and real cash balances figure as an argument in the demand functions for goods to the extent that money is of the outside type.

(2) The real-balance effect in the goods markets, valid for the outside-money type, is introduced in form of the wealth effect according to the wealth-saving relationship of Metzler (1951). Wealth, for an open economy, is defined as:

$$w = \gamma a_1 + \lambda a_2^* + m, \tag{1}$$

$$w^* = \gamma^* a_1^* + \frac{1}{\lambda} a_2 + m^*, \tag{2}$$

where w represents the real value of non-human wealth which is supposed to be composed by equities (a) and money holdings m (where $m = M/P$, M being the quantity of money and P the price level). Residents in the home country hold domestic equities (a_1) and foreign equities (a_2^*); a similar relationship exists for the equities held in the foreign country (a^*) where $a^* = \gamma^* a_1^* + (1/\lambda) a_2$. The asterisk stands for the foreign country. γ is the proportion of common stock that is privately held; we assume for simplicity that open-market operations are conducted in terms of equities which are issued by the domestic economy. For an economy which has only outside money, $\gamma = 1$ while an exclusively inside money economy has $w = a_1 + \lambda a_2^*$ since $m = (1 - \gamma) a_1$. The real exchange rate is defined as the relation between the foreign price of imported goods (P^*) converted into the home currency by the exchange rate e and the domestic price of exported goods (P):

$$\lambda = \frac{e\,P^*}{P} \tag{3}$$

The *real sector* of the world economy is composed as follows:

goods markets

$$S(r, w) - I(r) = I^*\,(r) - S^*(r, w^*) = T\,(\lambda), \tag{4}$$

domestic market for real cash balances

$$L(r) = m, \tag{5}$$

foreign market for real cash balances

$$L^*\,(r) = m^*, \tag{6}$$

where S denotes saving, I investment, T the current account surplus and r the interest rate which is identical in both countries because of the assumption of perfect capital mobility. We have omitted wealth as a scale factor of the demand for money in order to simplify the analysis.

The real sector of the world economy represented by four equilibrium conditions determines simultaneously the four real variables: the world interest rate (r), the domestic and foreign stock of real cash balances $(m$ and $m^*)$ and the real exchange rate (λ). The equilibrium in the world market for goods can be accompanied by a disequilibrium in the national goods markets in the sense that

$$\underbrace{S(r, w) - I(r) = I^*(r) - S^*(r, w^*)}_{\substack{\text{world market} \\ \text{equilibrium}}} \underbrace{\neq T(\lambda).}_{\substack{\text{national market} \\ \text{disequilibria}}}$$

Take, for instance, the case of an excess supply of goods in the domestic country $(S - I > T)$ which must correspond exactly to an excess demand for goods in the foreign country $(I^* - S^* > T)$ because of the equilibrium in the world market for goods $(S - I = I^* - S^*)$. A depreciation of the home currency must take place which switches part of the foreign demand to the domestic country lowering the excess supply in the latter and the excess demand in the foreign country. Consequently, a disequilibrium in the national goods market is eliminated by an appropriate change in the real exchange rate.[1]

---

[1] The depreciation of the home currency (and, correspondingly, the appreciation of the foreign currency) exercises two effects in the national goods market: the relative price effect as men-

Having solved the equilibrium value for all real variables, *the monetary sector* can be added in the following way:

$$P = \frac{M}{m} , \qquad\qquad (7)$$

$$P^* = \frac{M^*}{m^*} , \qquad\qquad (8)$$

$$e = \lambda \frac{P}{P^*} . \qquad\qquad (9)$$

which determines the price levels for a given domestic and foreign nominal quantity of money (M and M^*) and, thus, the nominal exchange rate according to the ratio of the national price levels as in eq. (9).

2. Long-run effects of monetary policy

We are only interested in the long-run effects of an expansionary monetary policy.[2] Assume first that the domestic economy pursues the expansionary monetary policy in terms of outside money. In this case, the expansion of the domestic money supply increases proportionately the domestic price level and, by this, the nominal exchange rate while the foreign price level and the real variables (r, m, m^*, λ) remain unchanged.

Take now an expansionary monetary policy of the inside-money type: an open-

---

tioned above and the wealth effect via λa_2^* (via a_2/λ, respectively). The latter reinforces the elimination of the equilibrium in the national goods market such that in the absence of the wealth effect, the depreciation should be higher (see the Appendix). To the extent that the individuals would not hold equities issued by the foreign country, the determination of real variables can be conceived in two successive stages. During the first stage, the world market for goods and the national markets for real cash balances would determine r, m and m^*. A possible remaining disequilibrium in the national goods markets would be eliminated by a change in λ.

[2]   The impact effect can be derived from the interest-rate parity which allows for a short-run discrepancy between the domestic and foreign interest rate by the amount of the expected rate of change in the exchange rate. Following Dornbusch (1976a) who assumes that asset markets react more quickly to a disequilibrium than the goods market, the impact effect is identical to the effect in a one-country model: fall in the domestic interest rate, maintenance of the foreign interest rate and depreciation of the home currency overshooting the long-run exchange rate (by assuming that the expected long-run exchange rate determined by purchasing power parity has risen immediately) — a necessary condition in order to create the expectation of an appreciation. From the one-country model we know that a subsequent appreciation will take place accompanied by a rising domestic price level and a rising domestic interest rate. Taking into account a two-country model after the impact effect has taken place, the foreign interest rate begins to decline (in the case of open-market operations) which produces a lower interest-rate differential and, by this, a lower expected rate of appreciation of the home currency. This lower expected rate is induced by a subsequent bigger appreciation than the one which is normally derived in a one-country model.

market operation increases m and decreases privately held equities (γa_1) by the same amount such that total wealth remains unchanged. At the initial interest rate there is an excess supply in the world market for real cash balances which may correspond to an excess demand for financial assets driving down the world interest rate in both countries. The interest-rate effect creates an excess demand in the world market for goods. There is an excess supply in the domestic money market pushing up domestic prices. The excess supply of domestic money exceeds the excess demand in the foreign money market driving down the foreign price level; consequently, the *nominal* exchange rate will adjust in the sense that the domestic currency depreciates by the rise in the domestic price level and by the fall in the foreign price level.

As far as the precise rise of the nominal exchange rate is concerned, it should be emphasized that the issue of the relative size of each country within the world economy matters only for the absolute amount of the fall in the world interest rate. If, for instance, the home country is not a very small country and thus being able to influence the world interest rate *and* if the interest elasticity of the foreign demand for money is higher than the one of the home country, the rate of the depreciation of the ("nominal") exchange rate will exceed the rate of increase of the domestic money supply.[3]

What is happening to the *real* exchange rate? Assuming that the price level changes have fully taken place in both countries, they have pushed the effective wealth level in the home country below the initial (long-run desired) wealth level and in the foreign country above the initial one. The negative wealth effect in the home country produces an excess supply of goods in the domestic economy and the positive wealth effect in the foreign country creates an excess demand for goods in the foreign economy. Assume that there is an equilibrium in the world market for goods (which may be brought about by a temporary fluctuation in the interest rate with temporary repercussions on the national price levels) such that the excess supply of goods in the home country is matched by the excess demand for goods in the foreign country. In order to equilibrate the national goods markets, a further depreciation has to take place, now in terms of a rise in the real exchange rate which switches parts of the foreign demand towards domestic goods.

The depreciation of the real component (λ) of the exchange rate can be conceived within the traditional framework of differentiated tradable goods between the domestic and foreign economy or/and with respect to the price relation between homogeneous tradable goods and non-tradable goods in both countries. In the first case, λ refers to the terms of trade, i.e. to the relative price between domestic and foreign (tradable) goods.[4] In the second case, λ is defined as

---

[3] For a precise formulation see the Appendix. It should be noted that we have neglected the interest rate effect on wealth (a lower interest rate increases the value of equities) and, by this, on saving. See the Appendix.

[4] Dornbusch's (1976b) quantity-theoretical two-country model is similar to ours with respect to the saving function. Assuming investment in each country equal to zero, equilibrium in the world goods market and in the national goods markets is realized without any change in the real exchange rate λ:

$$\lambda \equiv \frac{e\,P^*}{P}$$

$$\equiv \frac{\theta^*}{\theta} \; . \tag{3a}$$

where θ contains the relation between the price of non-tradable goods (P_N) and the price of tradable goods (P_T).[5]

When λ is interpreted in terms of eq. (3a) where λ represents strictly two relative prices, the equilibrium mechanism of the national goods markets must be reformulated in the following way. The equilibrium condition in the world market for goods

$$S - I = I^* - S^*, \tag{10}$$

is equivalent to

$$(S_T - D_T) + (S_N - D_N) = (D_T^* - S_T^*) + (D_N^* - S_N^*), \tag{11}$$

where S_T and D_T stand for supply and demand of tradable goods, respectively and S_N and D_N for supply and demand of non-tradable goods. The equilibrium in the national goods markets is obtained when

$$\overbrace{S(r,w) - I(r) = I^*(r) - S^*(r,w^*)}^{\text{world market equilibrium}} \; \overbrace{= T(\lambda)}^{\text{national markets equilibria}}$$
$$= S_T(\theta) - D_T(\theta)$$
$$= D_T^*(\theta^*) - S_T^*(\theta^*).$$

$$S(r,w) = S^*(r,w^*) = T.$$

This is a possible case to the extent that one uses a one-commodity model for the world economy. In the quantity-theoretical one-country model Dornbusch and Fischer (1980) uses a differentiated good such that they introduce T as a function of λ where λ represents the terms of trade.

[5]   By defining the general price level (P) as the weighted average

$$P = \alpha P_T + (1 - \alpha) P_N,$$

and by denoting β the equilibrium relative price between tradable and non-tradable goods ($\beta = P_N/P_T$), the general price level can be written as

$$P = [\alpha + (1 - \alpha)\beta] P_T,$$

where the expression within the brackets represents θ.

It should be noted that an equilibrium in the national markets for tradable goods implies an equilibrium in the markets for non-tradable goods because of the equilibrium in the world market for goods [see eq. (11)].

Remember that a depreciation of the real exchange rate took place because there was an excess supply of goods in the home country which corresponded to an excess demand for goods in the foreign country. Two extreme cases can be conceived. Either the excess supply and the excess demand comprise only tradable goods; if we assume homogenous tradable goods, there is no need for a change in θ and θ^* and, consequently, in λ. Or the excess supply and the excess demand concern only non-tradable goods; the domestic market for non-tradable goods will clear through an appropriate decline of θ and the foreign market for non-tradable goods will be in equilibrium with a certain rise in θ^*. In this latter case, we have the highest conceivable depreciation of the real exchange rate. Consequently, all intermediate cases where the excess supply (demand) is related to tradable *and* non-tradable goods will be characterized by a lower depreciation of the real exchange rate. Finally, it should be noted that in the presence of differentiated tradable goods and of non-tradable goods the depreciation of the real exchange rate is caused by the simultaneous changes in the terms of trade and in the relative prices of tradable and non-tradable goods.

3. Steady-state effects of monetary policy

The explicit consideration of the wealth argument in the saving functions makes it possible to predict the amount of the current account surplus in the home country and the fluctuation of the real exchange rate during the long-run. Assume for a moment that we are in a stationary economy and that there was full-stock (i.e. steady-state) equilibrium in both countries before the implementation of expansionary monetary policy.

The increase of the price level in the domestic economy reduces wealth by the amount $m\,(dP/P)$. Consequently, there will be a cumulative positive saving of the same amount. This saving is allocated for the accumulation of foreign assets representing the (cumulative) current account surplus and for the accumulation of domestic assets because the capital stock is supposed to be variable in response to the interest rate.

We apply here a modified (and also a simplified) Metzler (1951) model to the international economy. The modification refers to a flexible capital stock whereas Metzler assumes a fixed one. Our saving and investment function can be specified in the following way:

$$\underbrace{S(r, w)}_{\delta\,(r)\,(\bar{w} - w)} - \underbrace{I(r)}_{\eta\,[\bar{K}\,(r) - K]} = T\,(\lambda), \qquad (12)$$

where $\bar{w}$ and $\bar{K}$ are the long-run desired targets of the stock of wealth and capital, respectively. δ and η reflect the speed of adjustment of the actual stock towards the desired one ($0 < \delta, \eta < 1$). For reasons of simplicity, we assume that $\bar{w}$ is not a function of the interest rate.[6]

In the steady state w is equal to $\bar{w}$ and K equal to $\bar{K}$. Differentiating the wealth definition, eq. (1), we obtain[7]

$$d\bar{w} = \gamma \, da_1 + a_1 \, d\gamma + \lambda \, da_2^* + a_2^* \, d\lambda + \frac{dM}{P} - m \, \frac{dP}{P} = 0. \tag{13}$$

Open-market operations imply that $dM/P + a_1 \, d\gamma = 0$. Furthermore, da_1 is equal to $d\bar{K}$ (in the expression $\gamma \, da_1$ the coefficient γ is equal to unity because there are no open-market operations with respect to the additional capital stock). Consequently, the change in the wealth composition is

$$d\bar{K} + \lambda \, da_2^* + a_2^* \, d\lambda - m \, \frac{dP}{P} = 0. \tag{14}$$

To the extent that the real exchange rate is unchanged after having again reached the steady state, the loss in wealth due to the rise in the price level $[- m/(dP/P)]$ will be compensated via the saving process by the aquisition of additional foreign assets ($\lambda \, da_2^*$) and by the increase in the domestic capital stock ($d\bar{K}$); the composition between the additional domestic and foreign assets depends on the sensitivity of the optimal capital stock with respect to the interest rate.

In the foreign country we have just the opposite interpretation of eq. (14); the latter should be written as

$$d\bar{K}^* + \frac{1}{\lambda} \, da_2 - \frac{a_2}{\lambda} \, \frac{d\lambda}{\lambda} - m^* \, \frac{dP^*}{P^*} = 0. \tag{15}$$

For the moment, it is assumed that the real exchange rate of the steady state has reached its initial level such that $(a_2/\lambda)(d\lambda/\lambda)$ equals zero. The foreign wealth has risen beyond the long-run desired level ($\bar{w}^*$) for two reasons: firstly, because of the fall in the foreign price level $[- m^*(dP^*/P^*)]$ and secondly, because of the increase in the foreign optimal capital stock ($d\bar{K}^*$). The increase in the two wealth items gives rise to a corresponding cumulative dissaving which is equal to the cumulative foreign current account deficit and, thus, to the (increase of) debt of the foreign country *vis-à-vis* the domestic country (da_2/λ) where da_2 is negative.

Remember from the end of section 2 that there was a depreciation of the real ex-

---

[6] Furthermore, η could be conceived as depending on the price of capital goods (or on Tobin's q) which complicates the adjustment process of the capital stock.

[7] Remember that in the long-run equilibrium there was a fall in the world interest rate which will be maintained in the new steady-state equilibrium. Again, we neglect the interest-rate effect on wealth which is taken into account in the Appendix with respect to the long-run effects of the expansionary monetary policy.

change rate in the home country. What is now the level of λ when the steady state has been reached? When the desired wealth level has been attained, saving falls to zero so that there is not any more an excess supply in the domestic goods market. Consequently, the real exchange rate has to fall to its original level, otherwise there would be an excess demand for goods arising from the foreign demand for domestic goods due to the relative price effect. The same situation, only with an opposite sign, exists in the foreign country where a depreciation has to take place to the original level of the exchange rate which equilibrates the foreign goods market and the current account turns from a deficit towards an equilibrium.[8]

However, the home country will experience a slight appreciation of the real exchange rate with respect to its initial level because it now receives more interest payments from abroad; we assume implicitly that at the beginning the home country is a net creditor and, thus, the foreign country a net debtor. Consequently, the trade-balance deficit of the domestic economy must be larger; which is brought about by the appreciation. Again, the opposite situation holds for the foreign country.

4. Concluding remarks

Money is (quasi-) neutral with respect to the real exchange rate, once the steady-state of stocks has been reached. At this moment, only the nominal exchange rate has moved according to the purchasing power parity. However, during the (long-run) adjustment process which is initiated by the expansionary open-market operations of the domestic economy, it is essential for the equilibrium of the national goods market that the real exchange rate depreciates in the home country and, consequently, appreciates in the foreign country. During this process a certain amount of savings in the home country corresponds to the foreign dissavings inducing capital movements between both countries. They have to be accompanied by a corresponding current account imbalance which is made possible by the temporary change in the real exchange rate. But strictly speaking, in the steady-state, money is only quasi-neutral with respect to the real exchange rate if one takes into account additionally the increase in interest payments from abroad which imply a larger trade-balance deficit brought about by a slight appreciation of the real exchange rate. As a matter of course, with respect to all other variables (real interest rate, real cash balances, capital stocks) open-market operations are not neutral — a conclusion which can equally be drawn from standard models of a closed economy.

---

[8] To the extent that the adjustment of the actual wealth towards the desired, steady-state level of wealth is different between the two countries, the adjustment process may be accompanied by a disequilibrium in the world markets implying temporary fluctuations in the interest rate and in the national price levels.

Appendix

The Appendix derives the long-run effect of the domestic expansionary monetary policy (section 2) on the nominal and real exchange rate for the quantity-theoretical two-country model described by the equation system (1)–(9).

According to purchasing power parity, the equilibrium exchange rate (e) of formula (9) consists of a real component (λ) and a nominal component (P/P^*) the latter being specified by the quantity-theory of money, i.e. by eqs. (7) and (8):

$$e = \lambda \, \frac{M}{M^*} \, \frac{m^*}{m} \, . \tag{A.1}$$

Strictly speaking, the real component of the exchange rate should refer to λ *and* to the expression m^*/m, both being determined by the real sector of the international economy.

Writing (A.1) in terms of rates of change by assuming $dM^* = 0$, we obtain:

$$\frac{de}{e} = \frac{dM}{M} + \left(\frac{dm^*}{m^*} - \frac{dm}{m} \right) + \frac{d\lambda}{\lambda} \, . \tag{A.2}$$

The value for dm^*, dm and $d\lambda$ can be derived by differentiating the equations of the real sector, i.e. the equations (1)–(2) and (4)–(6).

In order to take into account explicitly the interest-rate induced wealth effect, we shall reformulate the wealth definition (1) and (2) as:

$$w = \gamma \, \frac{A_1}{r} + \lambda \, \frac{A_2^*}{r} + m, \tag{A.3}$$

$$w^* = \gamma^* \, \frac{A_1^*}{r} + \frac{A_2}{\lambda r} + m^*. \tag{A.4}$$

The terms A and A^* represent the permanent income stream from equities. Differentiating (A.3) we obtain:

$$dw = \frac{A_1}{r} \, d\gamma$$

$$+ \frac{\gamma}{r} \, dA_1 + \frac{\lambda}{r} \, dA_2^*$$

$$- \left(\frac{A_1}{r^2} + \frac{\lambda A_2^*}{r^2} \right) dr$$

$$+ \frac{A_2^*}{r} \, d\lambda$$

$$+ \, dm.$$ (A.5)

The first line describes the expansionary open-market policy which implies a fall in γ such that $dM/P + (A_1/r) \, d\gamma = 0$. We shall continue to write A_1/r as a_1. The second line is relevant for the accumulation of the capital stock $(d\bar{K})$ and for the cumulative current-account surplus (ΣT), both taking place between the long-run and the steady-state. Determining the change of the real exchange rate only for the "beginning" of the long-run period, dA_1 and dA_2^* will still be zero. The third line stands for the interest-rate induced wealth effect which we shall denote $-J \, dr$ and the fourth line for the real-exchange rate induced wealth effect which we shall express as $E \, d\lambda$. Consequently eq. (A.5) is reduced to

$$dw = a_1 \, d\gamma - J \, dr + E \, d\lambda + dm.$$ (A.6)

Similarly, the differentiation of (A.4) has the reduced form of

$$dw^* = -J^* \, dr - E^* \, d\lambda + dm^*.$$ (A.7)

In the foreign country, there are no open-market operations. J^* and E^* are defined, respectively, as

$$J^* = \frac{\gamma^* A_1^*}{r^2} + \frac{A_2}{\lambda r^2} \quad \text{and} \quad E^* = \frac{A_2}{\lambda r^2}.$$

By taking into account (A.6) and (A.7), the differentiation of eqs. (4)–(6) can be written as:

$$(S_r - I_r - S_w J) \, dr - (T_\lambda - S_w E) \, d\lambda + S_w \, dm = -S_w a_1 \, d\gamma,$$ (A.8)

$$(S_r^* - I_r^* - S_w^* J^*) \, dr + (T_\lambda - S_w^* E^*) \, d\lambda + S_w^* \, dm^* = 0,$$ (A.9)

$$L_r \, dr - dm = 0,$$ (A.10)

$$L_r^* \, dr - dm^* = 0.$$ (A.11)

Writing the equation system in matrix form, the determinant Δ is:

$$\Delta = (S_r - I_r - S_w J + L_r S_w) \, (T_\lambda - S_w^* E^*)$$

$$+ (S_r^* - I_r^* - S_w^* J^* + L_r^* S_w^*) \, (T_\lambda - S_w E) > 0.$$ (A.12)

The interest-rate induced wealth effects and the real-exchange-rate induced wealth effects increase the positive value of Δ. Δ is positive provided that the Marshall–Lerner conditions hold ($T_\lambda > 0$).

The values for dm^*, dm and $d\lambda$ are, respectively:

$$dm^* = -\frac{1}{\Delta} L_r^* S_w (T_\lambda - S_w^* E^*) a_1 d\gamma > 0, \tag{A.13}$$

$$dm = -\frac{1}{\Delta} L_r S_w (T_\lambda - S_w^* E^*) a_1 d\gamma > 0, \tag{A.14}$$

$$d\lambda = \frac{1}{\Delta} S_w (S_r^* - I_r^* - S_w^* J^* + L_r^* S_w^*) a_1 d\gamma > 0. \tag{A.15}$$

Dividing eqs. (A.13), (A.14) and (A.15) by m^*, m and λ respectively, and expressing $-L_r^*/m^*$ as $r\epsilon_{L*/r}$ and $-L_r/m$ as $r\epsilon_{L/r}$ where $\epsilon_{L*/r}$ and $\epsilon_{L/r}$ stand for the absolute value of the elasticity of the demand for real cash balances with respect to the interest rate, we can formulate (A.2) as follows:

$$\frac{de}{e} = \frac{dM}{M}$$

$$+ \frac{1}{\Delta} rS_w (\epsilon_{L*/r} - \epsilon_{L/r}) (T_\lambda - S_w^* E^*) a_1 d\gamma$$

$$+ \frac{1}{\lambda\Delta} S_w (S_r^* - I_r^* - S_w^* J^* + L_r^* S_w^*) a_1 d\gamma.$$

The second right-hand expression stands for $dm^*/m^* - dm/m$ and the third one for $d\lambda/\lambda$.

The rate of depreciation of the home currency as a consequence of the expansionary open-market policy is equal to the rate of monetary expansion *plus* the differential rate of increase between the foreign and domestic demand for the real cash balances (provided that, in absolute terms, $\epsilon_{L*/r} > \epsilon_{L/r}$) *plus* the rate of increase in the real exchange rate.

References

Claassen, E., 1982, The Keynesian and classical determination of the exchange rate in a two-country model, Weltwirtschaftliches Archiv, forthcoming.

Dornbusch, R., 1976a, Expectations and exchange rate dynamics, Journal of Political Economy, December, 1161–1176.

Dornbusch, R., 1976b, Capital mobility, flexible exchange rates and macroeconomic equilibrium, in: E. Claassen and P. Salin (eds.), Recent issues in international monetary economics (North-Holland, Amsterdam), 261–278.

Dornbusch, R. and S. Fischer, 1980, Exchange rates and the current account, American Economic Review, December, 960–971.

Metzler, L.A., 1951, Wealth, saving and the rate of interest, Journal of Political Economy, April, 93–116.

Mundell, R.A., 1980, International economics, Appendix to chapter 18 (New York).

Patinkin, D., 1965, Money, interest, and prices, 2nd ed. (New York).

Recent Issues in the Theory of Flexible Exchange Rates, edited by E. Claassen and P. Salin
© *North-Holland Publishing Company, 1983*

Chapter 3.2

COMMENT ON CLAASSEN

Giorgio BASEVI

The contemporary literature on exchange rates — nominal and real — is essentially devoted to the analysis of their paths of adjustment from the short to the long run, and of the respective roles played by asset markets and the balance of payments in driving nominal and real exchange rates along these paths toward equilibrium. In his contribution to this conference Professor Claassen takes a more detached view of exchange rates, by concentrating on the comparative static relationships between long-run and steady-state equilibria, and thus disregarding the dynamic processes of adjustment that lead to them. The object of Professor Claassen's analysis is the classical question whether money is neutral or not with respect to real variables; a question which he casts in the framework of a simplified Metzler–Patinkin model. The real variables upon which the analysis is initially concentrated are the world interest rate, the domestic and foreign stocks of real cash balances, and the real exchange rate. In the last section, when the horizon is extended to the steady state, real capital stocks are also allowed to change through physical investment.

However, the mathematical appendix to the paper, which is more illuminating than the main text, is not similarly extended to deal with the steady state, but only limited to the analysis of the long-run effects of open-market policy on the nominal and real exchange rates. This is unfortunate because by extending the formalized analysis to the steady state the author could have refined and extended his own results. In particular, since in the steady state the real capital stock is higher in both countries, the world rate of interest must be lower. Moreover, in the long-run position, that precedes the full steady state, the rate of interest cannot be equal in the two countries. In fact such equality is not allowed by the reverse change in the real exchange rate that — as Claassen shows — must take place between the long run and the steady state. If this final real exchange rate change is brought about by a change in the nominal exchange rate which is perfectly anticipated during the long-run position, the nominal interest rate in the domestic economy must be different from that abroad during that same long-run intermediate position. If, on the other hand, the real exchange rate change takes place through price adjustment with fixed nominal exchange rate, then the real rate of interest must be different in the two countries during the same long-run intermediate position.

Thus, notwithstanding the author's care to concentrate on and to compare equilibrium positions, the interest rate cannot be collapsed into a unique real variable during the long-run position, since further nominal and real adjustment has to take place between the long run and the steady state, and presumably this is fully anticipated by rational economic agents.

My final comment concerns a point of no real consequence to Professor Claassen's analysis, which however seems in need of more precision. In discussing the relationship between saving and investment in the two countries and their balance of current account, the author allows for inequality between the latter and the former but not between the two countries' differences between saving and investment. He labels this as a possible case of national goods market disequilibrium but world goods market equilibrium. This may be confusing since if investment minus saving is said to be different from a country's balance on current account the terms investment and saving are used in the sense of planned investment and planned saving. And if this is so, then there is no continuous constraint to make them always equal at the world level. On the other hand, if the terms investment and saving are used in the realized *ex post* meaning so as to be always equal at the world level, it must also be true that their difference at the national level always equals the balance on current account.

PART II

MACROECONOMICS OF FLEXIBLE EXCHANGE RATES

Recent Issues in the Theory of Flexible Exchange Rates, edited by E. Claassen and P. Salin
© North-Holland Publishing Company, 1983

CHAPTER 4.1

MACROECONOMIC ADJUSTMENT TO INTEREST RATE DISTURBANCES: REAL AND MONETARY ASPECTS

Pentti J.K. KOURI*

1. Introduction

With the rapid growth of international money and capital markets, and increasing financial openness of national economies, adjustment to changes in international interest rates has become an important policy concern. Flexibility of exchange rates does not insulate national economies from changes in the *real interest rate* in the international capital market, but leaves policymakers with difficult adjustment alternatives. Should the domestic interest rate increase, or decrease, *pari passu* with the world interest rate? Or should the domestic currency instead be allowed to depreciate (appreciate) to a point at which an expectation of future appreciation (depreciation) would just match the difference between domestic and foreign interest rates? Or, should the central bank simply follow monetarist advice and keep the money supply unchanged, leaving the exchange rate and the interest rate to market forces? Or, as yet another policy option, is there an economic case for interfering with free international movements of capital?

These questions have not been systematically discussed and analysed in the literature, despite their obvious importance for macroeconomic policy. The purpose of this paper is to present such an analysis, and in the process to discuss some theoretical issues concerning the modelling of capital movements and capital market integration.

Rather than developing one model, I start the paper by discussing the implications of interest rate disturbances in familiar models of the open economy.

Discussion of the Mundell—Fleming model brings out the result that under flexible exchange rates and with *nominal* wage rigidity, an increase (decrease) in the "world interest rate" is expansionary (contractionary), provided that the Marshall—Lerner condition holds. Expansion in output and unemployment occurs because improvement in the trade balance, caused by real depreciation, more than outweighs the deflationary effect of the interest rate increase on investment and consumption. If the Marshall—

* This research has been supported in part by a grant from the Ford Foundation.

Lerner condition does not hold, there is a problem of stability in the Mundell—Fleming model. One way out of this problem is to assume regressive exchange rate expectations, but in that case, an increase in the foreign interest rate must be accompanied by a decline in the domestic interest rate.

The results of the Mundell—Fleming model carry over to full employment equilibrium with price flexibility: an increase in the world interest rate leads to a deterioration in the domestic terms of trade, and an increase in the domestic price level. The Dornbusch model, discussed in the third section of the paper, bridges the gap between full employment equilibrium and the short run unemployment equilibrium *à la* Mundell—Fleming.

The Mundell—Fleming—Dornbusch model completely ignores the intertemporal balance of payments constraint, and, as is shown in the fourth section, leads to incorrect conclusions. In particular, the deterioration in the terms of trade that occurs in the short run, has to be reversed over time because of the increase in net foreign asset holdings and net interest income. In long run stationary (or steady state) equilibrium, an increase in the foreign interest rate leads to a improvement in the domestic terms of trade, or "real appreciation" of the domestic currency. The domestic price level will, however, be higher because of higher velocity while the nominal exchange rate may either depreciate or appreciate depending on the relative strengths of the price level effect on the one hand, and terms of trade improvement on the other.

A further implication of portfolio balance models noted in the discussion is that with rational expectations the domestic real rate of interest measured in terms of domestic output does not increase by the full amount of the increase in the foreign interest rate except in long run stationary (or steady state) equilibrium. The less open the economy in *goods markets*, the less is the short run effect of an increase in the foreign interest rate on the domestic interest rate, and the greater is the effect on the terms of trade.

The Mundell—Fleming model does not justify the concern recently expressed by many European governments that the increase in U.S. real interest rates prolongs stagnation in their economies. It is argued in this paper that the explanation is the assumption of nominal wage rigidity, and the neglect of imported raw materials in the Mundell—Fleming model. With wages responding to prices, and currency depreciation having a direct effect on production costs, capital outflow caused by an increase in the world interest rate adds to domestic inflation at each level of unemployment. If policymakers attempt to fight "imported inflation" by tight monetary policy, there will indeed be an increase in unemployment following an increase in the world interest rate. It is argued further that with complete real wage rigidity capital outflow reduces domestic output and increases 'classical" unemployment without monetary policy being able to do anything about it except in the very short run.

The paper also discusses the implications of models that are derived from individual optimizing behaviour: Ramsey—Sidrauski type models with infinitely lived families that maximize an additively separable utility function; Uzawa-type models in which the rate of time preference is an increasing function of the level of consumption; and life-cycle-overlapping generations models in which distribution effects across cohorts of different age play a key role. This discussion has less immediate relevance for policy but it brings up a number of important issues in the rigorous modelling of the open economy with capital movements.

The effects of interest rate changes on the cost of fixed capital, as well as working capital is then discussed and compared to the cost effects of oil price increases. It is argued that although capital costs are typically ignored in macroeconomic models, they are important and pervasive. In the small open economy changes in relative capital costs are a potentially important source of external disturbances.

The paper concludes with a discussion of restrictions of capital movements and argues that the economic case for free capital movements is basically the same as the case for free trade in goods and services. In the same way that terms of trade disturbances do not justify interference with the structure of free trade, "interest rate disturbances" do not justify interference with free movement of capital. In particular, a small open economy cannot insulate itself from the effects of an "adverse" change in the world interest rate by imposing capital controls *ex post*. On the contrary, such controls add to the cost imposed by the external disturbance. With price rigidities, capital controls can, however, increase domestic output and welfare. However, if that justification is accepted, the same logic also applies to using tariffs in place of devaluation to maintain full employment following a disturbance in the trade balance.

The paper concludes with some remarks on how individuals and firms can hedge against terms of trade and interest rate disturbances through futures markets and the use of other available methods of hedging. It is argued that policy can best support adjustment to interest rate changes by adhering to a steady course as far as the expansion of nominal income is concerned, without interfering with the adjustment of the exchange rate and domestic interest rates. Such policy does not imply constant money supply but requires that the money supply be reduced (increased) so as to offset the increase (decrease) in the velocity of circulation.

2. The Mundell–Fleming model

The standard Mundell–Fleming model[1] deals only with the short term aggregate demand effects of international capital movements. The basic result of the model is that an increase in "the world interest rate" is expansionary, and a decrease contractionary under flexible exchange rates.[2] The reason for this is that an increase (decrease) in the world interest rate causes a shift away from domestic to foreign assets and thus leads to currency depreciation (appreciation), and an improvement in the trade

---

[1] Mundell (1968) and Fleming (1962).
[2] For the most part we shall be discussing adjustment to an increase in the rate of interest. The effects of a decline in the rate of interest can be readily inferred. Mathematical derivations are left out because they are staightforward, or readily available in the literature.

balance provided that the Marshall—Lerner condition holds. If the Marshall—Lerner condition does not hold, an increase in the foreign interest rate is, however, deflationary because of the deflationary impact of the trade balance deterioration.

With perfect capital mobility, and static exchange rate expectations, as is assumed in the standard Mundell—Fleming model, the domestic nominal interest rate must increase (or decrease) by the same amount as the foreign interest rate. Since prices are stable, and expected to remain stable, in the Mundell—Fleming model, the interest rate increase represents an increase in the real interest rate. Therefore, there will be a decline in domestic consumption and investment. Yet the model implies that total domestic output must increase if the central bank holds the supply of money unchanged. The formal explanation of this surprising implication is that the increase in the domestic interest rate increases the velocity of circulation of money: since prices are assumed to remain stable, domestic output must increase to restore equilibrium between the demand for and the supply of money. The economic mechanism that leads to the increase in output is the depreciation of the domestic currency, induced by initial excess demand in the foreign exchange market. The stimulative effect of the devaluation is more than sufficient to offset the contractionary effect of the higher interest rate on consumption and investment. Obviously, the Marshall—Lerner condition must hold for this analysis to be correct.

An increase in the foreign interest rate is expansionary in the Mundell—Fleming model even with regressive exchange rate expectations as long as there is some increase in the domestic interest rate.[3] The result does not depend on the assumption of perfect capital mobility either. With zero capital mobility there is obviously no effect on the domestic economy; with some responsiveness of capital movements to interest rate differentials, the expansionary effects goes through. Inclusion of wealth in the demand for money function as in most portfolio balance models is unlikely to change the conclusion and may well strengthen it. The latter is true if the net wealth effect of interest rate and exchange rate changes is negative: in that case domestic output has to increase by even more to make up for the "slack" in money demand.

If the Marshall—Lerner condition does not hold, as is reasonable to assume in short run analysis, the issue becomes more problematic. Currency depreciation will then depress domestic output. But how can output fall if the supply of money is fixed, and most importantly, prices remain stable? Only if the domestic interest rate declines in response to the increase in the foreign interest rate! This would enable excess money supply to be absorbed by a decline in the velocity of circulation. For this paradoxical situation to be consistent with equilibrium in the foreign exchange market, domestic currency would have to depreciate so much that from its low point the market would then expect it to appreciate at a rate equal to the nominal interest rate differential. It would not be difficult to construct a dynamic model which would allow for this sort of perverse short term response, with the perhaps equally para-

---

[3] Argy and Porter (1972) were the first to develop the implications of the Mundell—Fleming model with regressive exchange rate expectations.

doxical expansionary Mundell—Fleming effect taking over as the J-curve unwinds. But the implication that the domestic interest rate would have to decline when the foreign interest rate increases does not square well with economic intuition, nor does there appear to be any empirical evidence of such response.

As far as policy is concerned, the Mundell—Fleming model has different implications depending on whether one assumes that the Marshall—Lerner condition holds, or that it does not. If it is assumed to hold, then the supply of money should be *reduced* in response to an interest rate increase in order to offset the net expansionary effect of depreciation. Some currency depreciation would, however, be necessary to offset the contractionary effect of the higher interest rate level. If policy attempted to maintain both the exchange rate and the level of output unchanged, it would be necessary to introduce a fiscal stimulus and at the same time to reduce the supply of money.

When the Marshall—Lerner condition does not hold, the only policy option to offset an interest rate disturbance is a mix of expansionary fiscal policy and restrictive monetary policy.

Yet another policy option that suggests itself in the Mundell—Fleming model is a tax on foreign investment. It would appear to be possible in the Mundell—Fleming model to offset interest rate disturbances completely by means of an "interest equalization tax", but as we shall see this result does not hold true in a correctly specified model.

3. The Dornbusch model

Dornbusch's celebrated 1976 paper on exchange rate dynamics bridges the gap between long run full employment equilibrium and short run Keynesian unemployment equilibrium by assuming a Phillips curve relationship between domestic inflation and the rate of unemployment.[4] A key result of the model is the demonstration of the possibility of overshooting the exchange rate to monetary disturbances with rational exchange rate expectations.

The Dornbusch model implies that an increase in the world real interest rate causes a permanent deterioration in the domestic terms of trade in full employment equilibrium: this is necessary to offset the contractionary effect of the higher real interest rate on aggregate demand. Furthermore, there is a permanent increase in the domestic price level, with a constant money supply, because of the increase in velocity caused by the rise in the interest rate. For both of these reasons, there is a permanent depreciation of the domestic currency in full employment equilibrium.

In the short run the Dornbusch model behaves like the Mundell—Fleming model with regressive exchange rate expectations around the long run equilibrium value of the exchange rate. Depending on the values of the parameters, the domestic interest

---

[4] Dornbusch (1976).

rate may increase by less than the foreign interest rate in the short run. In that case, the exchange rate would have to overshoot its long run equilibrium value.

Qualitatively, the response of the domestic economy to an interest rate disturbance is the same in the Dornbusch model as in the Mundel–Fleming model: domestic currency depreciates, interest rate increases and output expands. Over time domestic prices and wages increase to a new and higher equilibrium level. To offset the inflationary impact, the central bank should reduce the supply of money in response to an increase in the world interest rate. The only way to keep both the exchange rate and domestic output and price level unchanged, would again be a mix of tight monetary and expansionary fiscal policy. An "interest equalization tax" would appear to be another policy option to completely offset the domestic effects of a change in the world interest rate. We shall see later on, however, that such policy will not provide insulation in a properly specified model.

4. Effects of changes in the world interest rate in portfolio balance models

The Mundell–Fleming model, and Dornbusch's extension of it, are both *ad hoc* models designed to capture some macroeconomic relationships that are perceived as particularly relevant and important. The simplifications that are made in these models do not matter in the analysis of some problems but they do matter in the analysis of capital movements.

Consider Dornbusch's full employment version of the Mundell–Fleming model. The model implies that in response to an increase in the world interest rate the current account will be *permanently* in surplus. Clearly, this cannot be a sustainable equilibrium, but rather reflects a misspecification of the model. The misspecification that is responsible for this conclusion is the neglect of the intertemporal budget constraint, or, what comes to the same, of the effects of interest earnings (payments) on domestic absorption.

In portfolio balance models the intertemporal budget constraint is recognized by the inclusion of interest earnings on foreign assets as part of disposable income, and by the direct effect of foreign asset holdings, as part of total private wealth, on consumption. With this change of specification, an automatic mechanism of current account adjustment is introduced.[5] As long as the current account is in surplus (deficit), domestic wealth increases (decreases) and thus domestic consumption also increases (decreases). Provided that the marginal propensity to spend out of interest income exceeds one, and that the Marshall–Lerner condition holds, the stock of foreign assets will eventually reach a stationary equilibrium value (assuming no secular growth).

---

[5] The automatic current account adjustment mechanism is formalized in Dornbusch and Fischer (1980), Kouri (1975, 1976, 1980) and Kouri and de Macedo (1978), and C.A. Rodriguez (1977).

In the stationary equilibrium the current account is equal to zero, and the trade account surplus (deficit) is equal to net foreign interest income.

Consider now the effect of an increase in the foreign interest rate once the requirement of long run portfolio balance is recognized. Assume initially that full employment prevails both in the short run and in the long run. In the short run an increase in the foreign interest rate causes an outflow of capital, a deterioration of the terms of trade and an increase of the domestic price level. Over time, the stock of foreign assets increases and causes an improvement in the terms of trade. In the new long run equilibrium, the stock of foreign assets is higher, and the interest account surplus is greater than in the initial equilibrium. Therefore, the long run effect of an increase in the foreign interest rate on the domestic terms of trade is *favourable*. The effect on the exchange rate is ambiguous: *real* appreciation may, or may not, be offset by an increase in the domestic price level caused by an increase in the velocity of circulation. Furthermore, there may not be any decrease in the demand for money in the long run, if the demand for money depends on total disposable income, or total expenditure, rather than on domestic income only, or if there is a wealth effect on money demand.

The implications of the Mundell—Fleming model with the inclusion of the requirement of long run portfolio balance are very sensitive to the specification of the demand for money function. Obviously, if one assumes that the demand for money depends only on the level of domestic output, the price of domestic output and the nominal interest rate, and that the domestic price level is fixed, an increase in the foreign interest rate is expansionary both in the short run and in the long run. The long run effect on the exchange rate is, however, ambiguous: on the one hand, there is an improvement in the interest service account but on the other hand, there is an increase in import demand because of higher levels of domestic income, foreign interest earnings and wealth.

If the demand for money is assumed to depend on total income, or total expenditure, and wealth, the long run effect of an increase in the foreign interest rate on domestic output is ambiguous.

If one does not assume perfect substitutability between domestic assets and claims issued by domestic residents on the one hand, and foreign assets on the other, there is another adjustment mechanism at work restoring equilibrium in the current account. A surplus (deficit) in the current account increases (decreases) the supply of foreign assets relative to domestic assets and thus causes the domestic interest rate to decline and the price of foreign currency to decrease so as to maintain equilibrium in financial markets. Both of these effects are independent of the wealth effect on expenditure and on their own tend to restore equilibrium in the current account.

In the portfolio balance models with imperfect substitutability, an increase in the foreign interest rate has two conflicting effects on the domestic interest rate in the long run. On the one hand, there is a substitution effect, a shift away from domestic to foreign assets at a given level of wealth, and on the other, there is a wealth effect, which causes the stock of wealth and therefore, the demand for domestic assets to *increase*. It is possible that the wealth effect dominates in the long run, in which case an increase in the foreign interest rate would paradoxically lead to a decline in the domestic interest rate.[6]

Descriptive portfolio balance models suffer from all the shortcomings of *ad hoc* models in that they do not really enable one to narrow down the range of outcomes, nor to condition the outcomes on parameters or considerations that have a clear interpretation in terms of the behaviour of individuals, or in terms of distribution effects across individuals. Below, we shall therefore discuss the implications of models that are explicitly derived from optimizing behaviour by individuals.

In summary of the brief review of the literature, we note that once the requirement of long term portfolio balance is taken into consideration, an increase in the foreign interest rate (in real terms) leads to an immediate depreciation of the domestic currency followed by a period of appreciation. Therefore, with rational expectations the domestic interest rate does not increase by the full amount of the increase in the foreign interest rate.

In the long run there will be real appreciation of the domestic currency because of the increase (decrease) in foreign interest earnings (payments). The long run effect on the nominal exchange rate, as well as on the domestic price level is, however, ambiguous.

The reversal of the initial effect does not occur in the Mundell—Fleming model, or in Dornbusch's extension of it, because there is no requirement of long run current account equilibrium in these models.

Finally, we note that except for the problems caused by the "J-curve", an increase in the foreign interest rate is expansionary in the short run in the standard macroeconomic models.

5. Real wage rigidity, raw material imports and the inflation—unemployment trade-off

The nature of the short run effects of disturbances under flexible exchange rates depends critically on whether one assumes that wages are rigid in nominal or real terms. This is also true as far as the effects of interest rate disturbances are concerned.

If wages are indexed *de factor* or *de jure* in such a way that the real wage rate in terms of domestic and imported goods is rigid, an increase in the world interest rate leads to an increase in unemployment, a decrease in domestic output and an increase in the domestic price level.[7] The domestic price level increases for two reasons: because of the increase in velocity and because of the reduction in domestic output.

Even with real wage rigidity, however, the current account moves into a surplus if

---

[6]   See Kouri (1980).
[7]   The importance of "real wage rigidity" has been emphasized by Bruno and Sachs (1981), Branson and Rotemberg (1980), Modigliani and Padoi—Schioppa (1978) and Sachs (1979), who have also developed the Mundell—Fleming model from the assumption of real rather than nominal wage rigidity.

the Marshall–Lerner condition holds. Therefore, the initial deterioration of the terms of trade will be offset by subsequent real appreciation. In the long run, the improvement in the terms of trade permits an increase in the real wage rate and/or in the level of employment.

If the wage rate is 100 percent indexed and adjusts with virtually no time delay to price changes, monetary policy has no real effects and, in particular, has no effect on employment. In that case monetary policy might as well aim directly at price stability. To the extent that fiscal policy could be used to shift demand from foreign to domestic products, and thus to improve the terms of trade, it could be assigned to domestic employment and output targets.

With some delay in wage adjustment there would still be some room at least in the short run to buy more output and employment by tolerating more inflation.[8] In this case, an increase in the foreign interest rate could be interpreted as causing an adverse shift in the short run Phillips curve: the outcome would be stagflationary or inflationary depending on the policy choice.

The stagflationary effect of depreciation is reinforced once we incorporate imports of intermediate inputs such as oil into our model.[9] Even without any wage response, there will be an increase in the domestic price level. Without monetary accommodation, domestic output will decrease or increase depending on the relative magnitudes of the price level increase on the one hand, and the increase in velocity on the other.

From another perspective, an increase in the price of raw materials causes an adverse shift in the short run Phillips curve, and is stagflationary if the central bank chooses to fight "imported inflation" by means of a more restrictive monetary policy.

Figure 4.1 illustrates the effect of an increase in the foreign interest rate on the domestic inflation–unemployment trade-off. Because of the increase in import prices caused by the depreciation of the domestic currency, and the response of wages to higher prices, the short run Phillips curve shifts from PP to $P'P'$. With no change in the supply of money, the economy may end up at a point such as B with more inflation and less unemployment because of the expansionary effects discussed above. If, on the other hand, policy attempts to keep the rate of inflation unchanged, then there has to be an increase in unemployment to a point such as B' in fig. 4.1.

If the real wage rate is completely rigid, there is an increase in the "noninflationary rate of unemployment", from U to U' in fig. 4.1, because of the deterioration in the terms of trade. Over time, however, the accumulation of foreign assets leads to an improvement in the terms of trade, and thus, to a decrease in the noninflationary rate of unemployment below the initial unemployment rate.

---

[8] Delay in the adjustment of nominal wages to past price increases gives rise to a downward sloping Phillips curve in Modigliani and Padoi–Schioppa (1978).

[9] Raw material imports were introduced into the Mundell–Fleming model by Findlay and Rodriguez (1977). Schmid (1976) is another early reference.

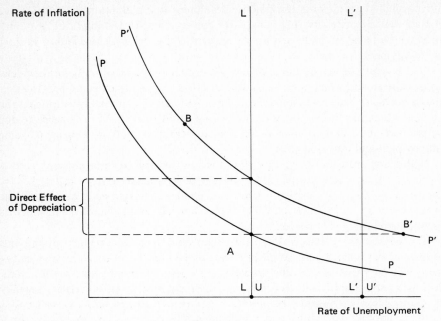

Figure 4.1

6. Implications of models derived from optimizing behaviour

Optimizing models of the open economy are still at their infancy. There are three different classes of models, each with quite different implications: a Ramsey–Sidrauski type model with an intertemporally additive utility function, an Uzawa-type model with endogenous time preference and life-cycle model.[10]

A Ramsey–Sidrauski type model has the unfortunate implication for the open economy that unless the foreign interest rate happens to equal the rate at which domestic residents discount future utility, there is no stationary equilibrium. An increase in the foreign interest rate, for example, would lead to a permanent surplus in the current account and to a steady increase in the stock of foreign assets and consumption, with the rate of decrease of the marginal utility of consumption equal to the difference between the world interest rate and the domestic rate of time preference. With inelastic foreign demand for domestic exports, or with non-traded goods,

[10] Sidrauski (1967) is the basic reference on the "Ramsey–Sidrauski approach"; Uzawa (1968) on the variable time preference model; and, in the trade context, Gale (1971) on the life-cycle-overlapping generations model. Frenkel (1971) develops an illuminating diagrammatic analysis of growth and the balance of payments. Onitsuka (1974) is another basic reference. Obstfeld (1981) develops a Sidrauski–Uzawa model to study exchange rate dynamics.

an increase in the foreign interest rate would lead to continuous real *appreciation* after an initial real depreciation.

A further implication of the Ramsey model is an indeterminacy of equilibrium in the sense that there is no tendency for the economy to converge to a long run equilibrium which is independent of initial conditions. If, for example, the foreign rate of interest was equal to the domestic rate of time preference, a windfall increase in domestic wealth would increase domestic wealth permanently, and thus it would have a permanent effect on equilibrium prices.

In a model with two or more countries, the Ramsey model has the disturbing implication that if the rates of time preference happen to be unequal between the residents of the two countries, the country with the lower rate of time preference will end up consuming total world output, and earning total world income, with the income and consumption of the "impatient" country converging asymptotically to zero.

If, on the other hand, one assumes that for some reason the rates of time preference happen to be equal between the two countries, the distribution of wealth, and therefore, the entire relative price structure have no equilibrium values which are independent of initial conditions.

The Uzawa model assumes that the rate of time preference is an increasing function of the rate of consumption, and thus implies a long run target level of consumption which is an increasing function of the rate of interest. In this model savings behaviour can be interpreted in the Metzlerian way as an adjustment of the stock of wealth to its long run desired level.

In an Uzawa-type model an increase of the foreign interest rate increases consumption in the long run, and therefore increases the demand for domestic output in the long run. In a model in which the domestic economy produces one good which is consumed at home and exported, and faces inelastic demand, the long run effect of an interest rate increase is an improvement in the terms of trade, or real appreciation. In a model with non-traded goods, the relative price of non-traded goods must increase in the long run. Figure 4.2 illustrates this result.

The economy is initially in equilibrium at E_0 with utility $U_0 U_0$. An increase in the world interest rate increases the long run target rate of consumption — measured in terms of utility — to $U_L U_L$. The consumption target is outside the initial production and consumption possibilities frontier of the economy, so that it can be achieved only through saving. Since we are ruling out domestic capital accumulation (and, in any case, domestic capital stock would decrease in response to a higher foreign interest rate), the only way that wealth can increase is through accumulation of assets. Eventually, long run equilibrium is obtained with consumption at C_L and production at P_L, and the real exchange rate equal to the slope of the production possibilities frontier at P_L and of the indifference curve at C_L. In comparison with initial equilibrium at E_0, the relative price of home goods at (P_L, C_L) is higher reflecting the increase in the relative scarcity of home goods whose supply is constrained to be on the production possibilities frontier, while the supply of traded goods can be increased through

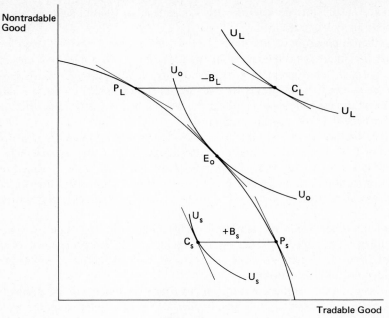

Figure 4.2

saving. In the long run equilibrium, the trade account is in deficit by B_L.

In order for the increase in the stock of foreign assets to be possible, the current account must be in surplus in the process of adjustment. In fig. 4.2 consumption (measured in terms of utility) initially declines to $U_s U_s$. Short run equilibrium obtains with production at P_s, consumption at C_s and the trade account in surplus by B_s. At (C_s, P_s) the price of traded goods is higher than in the equilibriun at E_0, implying "real depreciation" of the domestic currency. In the process of adjustment from (C_s, P_s) to (C_L, P_L) the domestic currency continuously appreciates in real terms as long as the current account is surplus. Therefore, the domestic interest rate must be below the foreign interest rate until long run equilibrium is reached at (P_L, C_L).

The behaviour of the nominal exchange rate cannot be inferred without specifying the demand for and the supply of money. In the short term there has to be depreciation also in nominal terms, but whether there is nominal depreciation in the long run is ambiguous. On the one hand, there is an increase in the velocity of circulation because of the higher interest rate, but on the other, there is also an increase in the demand for money because of the increase in consumption and wealth. Therefore, the direction of change of the price level is ambiguous in the long run. And even if the price level increases, the increase may be offset by real appreciation, implying the possibility that the domestic currency appreciates also in nominal terms in the long run.

A third framework of analysis which starts from a specification of individual optimizing behaviour is a model with finitely lived overlapping generations. As is well known such model gives rise to a long run "wealth demand function" which resembles the type of function typically assumed in portfolio balance models. The behaviour of an economy with selfish overlapping generations also resembles the behaviour of an Uzawa-type economy of infinitely lived families. There is, however, one important difference. In the life-cycle-overlapping generations model, capital and human wealth are complementary, whereas in the Uzawa model they are sub- stitutable. Thus, in the overlapping generations model an exogenous increase in wage income would lead to an increase in the supply of capital, whereas in the Uzawa model there would be a *decrease* in the supply of capital. The intuitive reason for the complementarity between wage income and capital income in the overlapping generations model is that to enjoy part of their increased wage income in retirement years, individuals need to accumulate a larger stock of assets for consumption in those years. In the Ramsey model the supply for capital is infinitely elastic in the long run, so that the question of complementarity versus substitutability is not even well defined.

Figure 4.3 illustrates the effects of an interest rate increase in a life-cycle model. It portrays the lifetime consumption-savings plan of an individual at the beginning of his active life. For simplicity it is assumed that the individual earns a constant wage income in his active years (assumed to be of duration L), and earns no wage income in his retirement years. Assuming that the individual chooses his consumption-cum- savings plan so as to maximize an additively separable utility function and plans to leave no bequests, his consumption profile might look like the *CC* schedule in fig. 4.3. It is assumed that the rate of interest is greater than the individual's rate of time

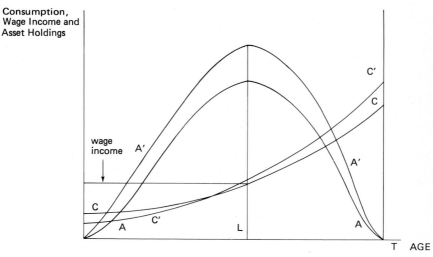

Figure 4.3

preference, so that the marginal utility of consumption decreases — and therefore consumption increases — along the planned consumption path. The AA schedule illustrates the planned time path of asset holdings.

An increase in the rate of interest tilts the consumption path up and reduces consumptions in the early years. Thus, for young people saving is unambiguously an increasing function of the rate of interest. This is because the substitution effect and the income effect go in the same direction: an increase in the rate of interest reduces the present value of wage income. For older people with substantial non-human wealth (or young people with inherited wealth) the wealth effect of an interest rate increase is positive and thus consumption may be an increasing rather than a decreasing function of the rate of interest.

The effect of an interest rate increase on total saving is the net outcome of substitution and income effects at the individual level, and distribution effects across individuals in different age groups. The distribution effects work against the substitution effects because an increase in the rate of interest reduces the human wealth of young people with relatively high savings propensity.

The long run effects of an interest rate increase on the demand for wealth — or the supply of capital — can be inferred from the life-cycle plan of the individual if we assume a stationary population with a rectangular demographic profile. In fig. 4.3 the effect of an interest rate increase on the supply of capital is measured by the difference between the area under the $A'A'$ curve on the one hand, and the AA curve on the other. As the curves are drawn the supply of capital ubambiguously increases, but that need not be the case.

Total long run consumption can also be inferred from fig. 4.3: it is the area under the CC ($C'C'$) schedule. Whether total long run consumption is an increasing or decreasing function of the rate of interest is also ambiguous, but in general the presumption is that it is an increasing function. Obviously, the requirement that long run consumption be an increasing function of the rate of interest is less stringent than the requirement that the supply of capital be an increasing function of the rate of interest.

Although the life-cycle model implies a long run consumption function, there is an important difference with the Uzawa model. Unlike in the Uzawa model, long run consumption is not independent of wage income in the life-cycle model but is instead an increasing function of wage income. In the Uzawa model wage income (or other non-capital income such as transfers) and capital income are perfect substitutes; in the life-cycle model they are complements. This difference has an important bearing on a number of issues, such as the long run effects of transfer payments, or of a terms of trade deterioration on the balance of payments. For example, the Uzawa model implies that following a permanent deterioration in the terms of trade with no change in the real rate of interest, the current account moves into a *surplus* and remains in surplus until the economy is able to support the same level of consumption as before from a higher level of interest earnings abroad. In contrast, the life-cycle model implies the intuitively more plausible response, that a deterioration in the terms of trade will be followed by a period of current account deficits and will lead to a permanent reduction in non-human wealth and long run consumption.

In the Uzawa model the real rate of return on capital investments, or saving, is the sole determinant of long run consumption and it is therefore the most crucial relative price that a small open economy faces in the world market. In the life cycle model the real wage rate is an equally important determinant of long run consumption and welfare.

Population growth, demographic profile, productivity increase, social provision of retirement benefits and so forth are all important considerations in the life cycle framework in analyzing the savings behaviour of different economies and the flow of capital between them.

In international economics, the full implications of the life-cycle model are yet to be worked out. With a great diversity of demographic profiles, productivity growth rates and social security systems between countries, one can expect rich rewards from that line of research.

7. Effects on the cost of capital, the demand for capital and investment

So far we have abstracted from the effects of interest rate changes on the supply side of the economy. For permanent interest rate changes such effects are profound, while short term changes mainly affect consumption and the timing of investment projects.

From the long run point of view capital cost in the open economy is exactly like the cost of imported raw materials or other intermediate inputs. Therefore, long run adjustment to an increase in the real rate of interest presents the same adjustment problems as the much analyzed increase in the relative price of energy. In particular, other factors being given, and abstracting from ambiguities that might arise because of reswitching, an increase in the cost of capital requires a reduction in the real wage rate. Indeed, in the standard neoclassical model with labour and capital as the only inputs in a production process that exhibits constant returns to scale, the real wage is uniquely determined by the cost of capital. At the real wage rate so determined, the long run demand for labour is infinitely elastic! Allowing for non-reproducible specific factors of production, such as land and human talent, the long run demand for labour function becomes downward sloping, but still an increase in the cost of capital reduces the marginal product of labour, and therefore its demand.

In the long run, the distinction between traded and non-traded goods is further blurred by the fact that the non-tradable sector uses capital services, which are tradable inputs. An increase in the rate of interest increases the cost of housing, or of hospital services, much in the same way that an increase in the cost of oil does in the short run.

An increase in the cost of capital changes the structure of relative prices in the long run with the relative price of capital intensive products likely to increase. There is no reason to expect that the relative price of "non-traded goods" should change in any particular way. Although some sheltered sectors, such as restaurants and government bureaucracies, are very labour intensive, others, such as housing services, electric utilities, public roads and other transportation infrastructures are very capital intensive.

Finally, we should note that the cost of capital measured in terms of domestic output, depends not only on the rate of interest but also on the relative price of capital goods in terms of domestic output. If capital goods are mostly imported, an improvement in the terms of trade can have a substantial effect on the cost of capital. This introduces a potential link between domestic saving and the domestic cost of capital. An increase in saving leads, in the short run, to a deterioration in the terms of trade because of capital outflow, and therefore to an increase in the relative price of capital goods. Over the long run, however, there will be an improvement in the terms of trade because of the higher level of interest earnings, and therefore a reduction in the cost of capital. Whether the cost of capital, as opposed to the relative price of capital goods, increases or decreases in the short run depends on whether the anticipated improvement in the domestic terms of trade offsets the effect of the temporarily higher price of capital goods.

Increase in the cost of capital reduces the demand for capital in the long run both because of substitution from capital to labour intensive methods of production, and also because of the shift of demand from capital to labour intensive products. Therefore, there is a decline in gross investment in the short run and a permanent decline in replacement investment in the long run. Accordingly, there will be a reallocation of resources from industries producing capital goods to sectors that produce consumer goods and services.

8. Effects on the cost of working capital, inventories and money balances

For reasons that are not altogether clear, the cost of working capital, inventories and money balances is typically totally ignored in macroeconomic models although such costs are far from being trivial. Furthermore, such costs provide an immediate link between the cost of output and the rate of interest, unlike in the case of fixed capital that earns quasi-rent in the short run.

The cost of inventories of finished products and raw materials is the sum of storage costs and the opportunity cost of the capital that is tied up in inventories. These costs are considerable and they must be covered by the price of the product even in the short run. Therefore, an increase in the rate of interest increases the supply price of output. With inventories equal to 30—40 percent of annual output, the capital cost of inventories cannot be ignored.

Because investment projects take time to be completed, the interest cost of resources that are tied up during the construction phase must be included in the cost of capital goods. Thus, if it takes two years to build a steel plant, the price of the plant in two years is not equal to the sum of wages, raw materials, machines and so forth that were paid during the two years, but rather the relevant price is the *augmented cost*, with each month's expenditure multiplied by an interest rate factor.

Yet another cost that is almost always ignored in macroeconomic models, is the capital cost of time that elapses in the shipment of goods from producers to users. In the input-output model, for example, each entry in the cost matrix contains a capital cost element of this nature.

The opportunity cost of holding money balances that yield nominal interest below the market rate of interest is recognized in monetary theory but again, macroeconomic models never include the cost of money balances as part of the total cost of output. In a correctly specified model such costs should obviously be included as a part of total variable costs. This addition to the standard macroeconomic model would introduce the *nominal rate of interest* (minus the nominal rate of return on money balances) as one of the determinants of the supply price of output.

Finally, we should also note here that in most countries the cost of housing is incorrectly measured in the consumer price index. In a well-functioning market for housing services, the short term rental cost of housing does not depend on the rate of interest, given the fixed supply of space for housing services. In practice, however, given rent controls, rents are often adjusted on the basis of the cost of interest service; and in any case, the imputed cost of owner-occupied housing is measured on the basis of the cost of interest service.

This bias in the construction of the CPI index exaggerates the extent of inflation, or of the decline of real wages when the nominal interest rate increases because of higher inflation.

9. Effects on the cost of public debt service and seignorage

A potentially important effect of interest rate changes is the effect on the interest burden of public debt. The governments of many small countries have borrowed extensively in the international capital market, and typically with variable interest rates, so that they are immediately affected even if the domestic capital market was not integrated to the international capital market. With capital market integration, the cost of domestic debt service increases *pari passu* with the cost of external debt service. Because the government, too, faces an intertemporal budget constraint, an increase in the rate of interest must either lead to a reduction in government expenditure or to an increase in taxes, or some combination of the two. Both alternatives are politically unattractive, and the second, in addition, magnifies the costs of distortions caused by taxes.

The central bank will benefit from higher interest rates: its interest earnings on domestic and foreign assets increase; or from the other side of the balance sheet the seignorage on reserve money increases. This will partly offset the higher cost of public debt service.

Private banks too may benefit, if their deposit rates do not adjust while loan rates go up with other interest rates.

10. International capital movements and domestic welfare

The analysis of the effects of interest rate changes has established that they are pervasive both in the short run and in the long run, and often pose difficult macroeconomic adjustment problems. In part for this reason, freedom of capital movements has never been advocated with the same conviction as freedom of trade in goods and services. The current international trade and payments system requires neither convertibility nor absence of restrictions on capital account transactions.

Yet the economic case for freedom of capital movements is as clearcut as the case for free trade. And free trade, too, contributes to macroeconomic adjustment problems, as recent years clearly demonstrate. It is taken for granted however, that "macroeconomic reasons" do not justify interference with the basic long term structure of free trade.

With capital movements countries do, however, have such freedom. Should an individual country then use it when faced, for example, by an increase in "the world interest rate".

To discuss this question let us consider a prototype Fisherian two-period model of a small open economy which produces a single internationally traded good. Let us assume further that this good can be either consumed or invested to augment future consumption.

The *PP* schedule in fig. 4.4 illustrates the consumption possibilities of such an economy under autarchy. Indifference curves, such as *UU* and *U'U'*, represent consumers' preferences between current and future consumption. In the absence of international capital movements equilibrium obtains at the point of tangency of indifference curve *UU* and the consumption possibilities frontier at *A*. The common slope of the *UU* and *PP* schedules at *A* is equal to the relative price between next period's and current period's consumption, or $1 + r$ where r is the rate of interest.

If the world interest rate is different from the domestic interest rate that obtains under autarchy, "capital market integration" increases domestic welfare. Figure 4.4 illustrates a case when the world interest rate is less than the domestic interest rate. New consumption equilibrium obtains now at point *C* and new production equilibrium at *B*. Social welfare increases from *UU* to *U'U'*. This increase can be divided in the usual way into a consumption gain — move from *A* to *C'* in the figure — and a production gain — move from *C'* to *C*.

Trade balance surpluses and deficits measure the extent of intertemporal trade, in the same way that the levels of imports and exports measure the extent of contemporaneous trade. In fig. 4.4 the trade balance is in surplus in the second period by *BD* and in deficit in the first period by *DC*. It follows from the budget constraints that the present value of trade surpluses or deficits, or $DC + [1/(1 + r^*)]BD$ in the figure, is equal to zero.

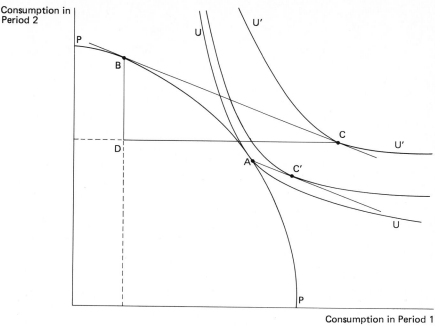

Figure 4.4

Although the trade account is in deficit in period 1 in our example, the deficit does not represent a policy problem, nor does it imply that the society is sacrificing future consumption to maintain current consumption. A large enough tariff on foreign borrowing could eliminate the deficit and restore autarchic equilibrium at A in fig. 4.4 but only at the cost of a decline in social welfare from $U'U'$ to UU. In the example illustrated in fig. 4.4 elimination of the trade deficit means less consumption in the future as well as in the present.

After these preliminaries consider the effects of interest rate changes. Let us assume an "overlapping generations" model, with each generation living for two models. Let us also assume for simplicity that both the consumption possibilities frontier and the indifference map are the same for each generation. Suppose, with reference to fig. 4.5, that the old generation faced interest rate r_0^* and was in equilibrium at points B_0 and C_0 with utility level $U_0 U_0$. In the current period, the world interest rate is r_1^*, which is assumed to be higher than the previous period's interest rate. The old generation is unaffected by this "disturbance" but the young generation's real income is now lower than what it would be had the world interest rate stayed at r_0^*. In the absence of policy intervention new equilibrium obtains at points B_1 and C_1. The young generation's consumption plan is on indifference curve $U_1 U_1$; at the old interest rate it would be on indifference curve $U_0 U_0$. There is, however, nothing that the government can do to reduce this welfare loss.

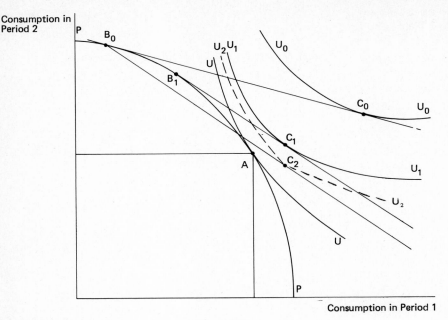

Figure 4.5

The government might decide to keep the domestic interest rate unchanged despite the increase in the world interest rate. It could do so by means of a tax on foreign investment equal to the change in the world interest rate. Producer's equilibrium would remain at B_0, but, as consumers, domestic residents would be made worse off with consumption plan C_2 on indifference curve $U_2 U_2$.

The marginal change in real income measured in terms of current consumption is given by:

$$du = -\frac{r-r^*}{1+r} dB - (X_2 - C_2) \frac{dr^*}{1+r^*} , \qquad (1)$$

where r = domestic interest rate, r^* = world interest rate, B = trade surplus and X = domestic output. The second term measures the unavoidable primary loss (gain) from an exogenous change in the world interest rate. If r is initially equal to r^*, there is no secondary loss on the margin. But once the domestic interest rate is below the world interest rate, an improvement in the trade balance entails a *reduction* in utility.

Change in real income (utility) can be further expressed in terms of an interest rate change as follows:

$$du = -\frac{(r-r^*) \, \mu_c C_1 + \mu_I I}{1+r - \pi_1 \, (r-r^*)} \left(\frac{dr}{1+r}\right) - \frac{(1+r)(X_2 - C_2)}{1+r - \pi_1 \, (r-r^*)} \left(\frac{dr^*}{1+r^*}\right) , (2)$$

where μ_c = absolute value of the interest elasticity of current consumption, μ_I = absolute value of the interest elasticity of investment (I), and π_1 = marginal propensity to consume.

We note that if the domestic interest rate is below the world interest rate, a further reduction of it reduces domestic welfare, the more so the greater are the interest elasticities of consumption and investment. Once autarchy is reached, $X_2 = C_2$, and domestic welfare is no longer affected by changes in the world interest rate. This insulation is achieved, however, at the cost of a permanently lower real income.

The relationship between interest rate changes and the trade balance is also of some interest. It is given by:

$$\mathrm{d}B = \frac{\mu_c C_1 + \mu_1 I}{1 + r - \pi_1 (r - r^*)} \; \mathrm{d}r \; - \; \frac{(1 + r)^2 \; \pi_1 (X_2 - C_2)}{(1 + r^*) \left[1 + r - \pi_1 (r - r^*)\right]} \; \mathrm{d}r^*. \quad (3)$$

An increase in the domestic interest rate unambiguously improves the trade balance (for all "reasonable" values of r), and thus causes an outflow of capital. The effect of a change in the foreign interest rate depends on whether the domestic economy is a net debtor or a net creditor. In the first case the effect is negative (trade balance deteriorates) whilst in the second case the effect is positive (trade balance improves).

In summary, taxes on international capital movements work like tariffs on trade in goods and services. They distort intertemporal production and consumption plans in a way that entails a deadweight welfare and efficiency loss.

There are two economic arguments for restricting capital movements despite the *prima facie* case for free trade. One is the familiar argument that the rate of interest that domestic residents earn on their foreign investments, or the rate of interest that they have to pay on foreign loans, depends on total domestic foreign investment or borrowing. In that case the usual optimal tariff argument applies. Also, if the domestic economy has some monopoly power in commodity trade but cannot impose tariffs on trade, some restriction, or subsidization, of capital movements may be optimal from the viewpoint of national interest.[11]

The second argument for controls on capital movements is the macroeconomic argument. Figure 4.6 illustrates the argument by means of an example. The domestic economy is initially in equilibrium at E_0 with output of traded goods equal to X_0^T and output of nontraded goods X_0^{NT}. The consumption vector is (C_0^T, C_0^{NT}) and it puts domestic residents on indifference curve $U_0 U_0$. For simplicity, it is assumed that trade is initially in balance. It is assumed further that in the second period the production possibilities frontier is the same and equilibrium obtains at the same point E_0.

Suppose now that there is an increase in the world interest rate. At the given relative price between traded and non-traded goods, and with production still at E_0 in both periods, the consumption plan would be (A_0, A_1). This plan is clearly not consistent with equilibrium in either period. To effect the intertemporal adjustment, there has to be real depreciation in the first period and real appreciation in the second. If domestic prices are rigid, price adjustment is not possible and therefore, there will be adjustment in quantities.

There will clearly be excess supply of non-traded goods in the first period and a surplus in the trade account. Therefore, the output of non-traded goods has to decline: thus, there will be Keynesian unemployment in the first period. Consumption equilibrium might obtain at a point like B_0 and production equilibrium at D_0, implying a trade surplus of $B_0 D_0$. In the second period domestic production of traded goods remains unchanged because relative prices remained unchanged. The supply of traded goods is, however, then greater because of the accumulation of foreign assets, and interest earnings on them, in the first period. Therefore, there will be excess demand for non-traded goods in the second period.

Thus, an increase in the world interest rate causes a problem of Keynesian unemployment in the first period and one of excess demand, or "repressed inflation", in the second. If prices are completely rigid in *real terms*, it is possible that an increase in the world interest rate leads to a quantity equilibrium that is worse than equilibrium that would prevail under autarchy. In that case capital controls might be justifiable as a second best device to support domestic output and employment.

However, this same justification applies also to tariffs on trade in goods and ser-

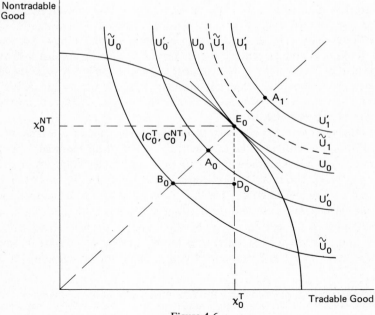

Figure 4.6

vices and it is not accepted as a valid justification. A better alternative from the long run point of view is to improve the workings of the domestic labour market in such a way that required relative price adjustments can be achieved by means of devaluations and revaluations of the domestic currency.

11. Appropriate policy

Capital market integration improves efficiency of intertemporal resource allocation and increases domestic welfare, but is also exposes the domestic economy to fluctuations of equilibrium interest rates in the international capital market. There is, however, no reason to think that the level of interest rates would necessarily be less stable if the domestic economy is integrated into the international capital market, than if it is not.

Nevertheless, with capital market integration the domestic economy has to adjust to changes in international interest rates in the same way that it has to adjust to changes in the terms of trade or in the relative prices of raw materials. Various aspects of such adjustments have been examined in this paper.

An increase in international interest rates requires some increase in the level of domestic interest rates and some deterioration in the terms of trade, and some increase in the relative price of traded *versus* non-traded goods, in order that domestic resources be efficiently reallocated. A reduction in international interest rates requires adjustments in the opposite direction.

Under flexible exchange rates, domestic interest rates and the exchange rate move automatically in the right direction to effect the required adjustment. However, a policy of constant money supply (or steadily growing money supply) is not appropriate in an economy that is integrated into the international capital market, because the velocity of circulation of money then changes with the level of international interest rates. Instead, monetary policy should aim to stabilize the level of *nominal GNP*.[12]

Such policy would not completely stabilize the domestic price level: a terms of trade deterioration, or an increase in the relative price of imported raw materials, would still increase the domestic price of *final output*. Achievement of complete price stability would, however, require more flexibility of nominal wages than one is likely to have in any country in order for employment to be maintained in the face of changes in the terms of trade, or in the relative price of raw materials.

From a different point of view, absolute price level stability is not desirable in any case when the economy is subject to unavoidable real disturbances, such as terms of trade or real interest rate changes. In most economies individuals cannot completely hedge against real disturbances of that nature by means of contingent contracts or equity claims. That being the case it is desirable to have the price level affected by

---

[12] This argument is developed in Kouri (1981).

real disturbances: nominal bonds and other nominal contracts become then vehicles of risk sharing between borrowers and lenders. To improve the efficiency of such risk sharing, macroeconomic policy should aim to eliminate the "noise" of purely nominal disturbances.

This point applies to exchange rate fluctuations also. It is desirable to eliminate nominal exchange rate fluctuations, and have the exchange rate correlate closely with "the real exchange rate". In that case, forward and futures currency markets enable individuals and firms to hedge against unpredictable changes in the terms of trade.

The same point holds true for hedging in the bond market as well. If the price level is negatively correlated with real income in each period, borrowers can hedge their real income risk by matching the term structure of their nominal bond holdings by the term structure of their expected income stream. If real income in some future period turns out to be lower than expected, the real burden of a nominal discount loan of the same maturity will then also be less.

References

Argy, V. and M. Porter, 1972, The forward exchange market and the effects of domestic and external disturbances under alternative exchange rate systems, IMF Staff Papers, Nov.

Branson, W.H. and J. Rotemberg, 1980, International adjustment with wage rigidities, European Economic Review.

Bruno, M. and J. Sachs, 1981, Supply versus demand approaches to the problem of stagflation, in: P. Kouri and F. Modigliani (eds.), Macroeconomic policies for growth and price stability: The European perspective (Mohr, Tübingen).

Dornbusch, R., 1976, Expectations and exchange rate dynamics, Journal of Political Economy 81, Dec.

Dornbusch, R. and S. Fischer, 1980, Exchange rates and the current account, American Economic Review, Dec.

Findlay, R. and C.R. Rodriguez, 1977, Intermediate imports and macroeconomic policies under flexible exchange rates, Canadian Journal of Economics.

Fleming, J.M., 1962, Domestic financial policies under fixed and under floating exchange rates, IMF Staff Papers 9, Nov.

Frenkel, J.A., 1971, A theory of money, trade and the balance of payments in a model of accumulation, Journal of International Economics 1, May.

Gale, D., 1971, General equilibrium with imbalance of trade, Journal of International Economics 1, May.

Karekan, J. and N. Wallace, 1977, Portfolio autarchy: A welfare analysis, Journal of International Economics 7, Feb.

Kemp, M., 1966, The gain from international trade and investment: A neo-Heckscher–Ohlin approach, American Economic Review 56, Sep.

Kouri, P., 1975, Essays on the theory of flexible exchange rates, Ph.D. dissertation, M.I.T., Cambridge, Mass.

Kouri, P., 1981, The effect of risk on interest rates: A synthesis of the macroeconomic and financial views, in: Hawkins, Levich and Wihlborg (eds.), The internationalization of financial markets and national economic policy (JAI Press).

Kouri, P. and J. de Macedo, 1978, Exchange rate and the international adjustment process, Brooking Papers on Economic Activity.

MacDougal, G.D.A., 1960, The benefits and costs of private investment from abroad: A theoretical approach, Economic Record 36, March.

Modigliani, F. and T. Padoi-Schioppa, 1978, The management of an open economy with "100% plus" wage indexation, Essays in International Finance, no. 130 (Princeton University).

Mundell, R.A., 1968, International economics (Macmillan, New York).

Obstfeld, M., 1981, Macroeconomic policy, exchange-rate dynamics, and optimal asset accumulation, Journal of Political Economy 89, Dec.

Onitsuka, Y., 1974, International capital movements and the patterns of economic growth, American Economic Review 65, March.

Rodriguez, C.A., 1977, Flexible exchange rates and imported inputs: A dynamic analysis of the interactions between the monetary and real sectors of a small open economy. Discussion Paper 76-7708, Department of Economics, Columbia University, March.

Sachs, J., 1979, Wage indexation, flexible rates and macroeconomic policy, International Finance Discussion Paper, no. 137, Federal Reserve Board, April.

Schmid, M., 1976, A model of trade in money, goods and factors, Journal of International Economics 6, Nov.

Sidrauski, M., 1967, Rational choice and patterns of growth in a monetary economy, American Economic Review, May.

Uzawa, H., 1968, Time preference, the consumption function, and optimum asset holdings, in: J.N. Wolfe (ed.), Value, capital, and growth: Essays in honor of Sir John Hicks (Aldine, Chicago).

Recent Issues in the Theory of Flexible Exchange Rates, edited by E. Claassen and P. Salin
© *North-Holland Publishing Company, 1983*

Chapter 4.2

COMMENT ON KOURI

Florin AFTALION

Under the title "Macroeconomic Adjustment to Interest Rate Disturbances: Real and Monetary Aspects", Professor Kouri has written a very ambitious paper. He should be commended for his effort which is not only academically significant but also relevant from a policy making point of view. When interest rates reach historic heights in the United States, European governments among others seem to be groping for the proper course of action. This paper should shed some light on this problem.

More precisely the author's purpose is to present an analysis of policy adjustment alternatives for a small country when there are changes in the real interest rates in the international capital market. His method does not consist in developing one model, but in discussing "implications of interest rate disturbances in various familiar models of the open economy". Such models are numerous and it would be quite useless to criticize the choice that has been made: the most important "classes" of models are adequately represented.

Since implications derived in the different instances studied appear to be correct, my comments will only deal with the organization of the paper.

The first section of the paper deals with well known monetary models under flexible exchange rates. First are discussed the Mundell—Fleming and the Dornbusch (vintage 1976) models, and policy responses to a change in the foreign interest rate are derived. It is recognized that such models suffer from presenting no long run equilibrium adjustment mechanism to balance of trade deficits. More theoretically adequate portfolio balance models are then presented. Unfortunately, as a class they produce different policy responses due to different possible specifications of the demand for money functions.

A possible alternative to the author's presentation could have been to select one specific portfolio balance model and analyze its implications more in depth. This could have been done at the expense of the discussion in terms of shifts in the short run Phillips curve which follows that of the monetary models. Indeed this discussion implies an *ad hoc* model, the assumption of which are far from being clear.

In the next section, which is not recognised as such, the author discusses "models derived from optimizing behavior". Three types of models are presented. Their microfoundations are of course sound, but they contribute very little to the author's purpose of presenting policy adjustment alternatives. This is due on the one hand to the fact that they have divergent properties and on the other hand that they all deal only with real quantities. The lack of a monetary sector makes it very difficult to derive policy prescriptions.

In what could be the next section of the paper the author studies the effect of a change in the foreign interest rates on the cost of capital and the demand for capital and investment, the cost of working capital, inventories and money balances and the cost of public debt service and seignoriage. Many interesting points are made here which fit the author's secondary objective of discussing "some theoretical issues concerning the modelling of capital movements". However, the problems discussed here involve long run effects and imply policy responses of a totally different nature from those recommended in the first section.

The last section of the paper deals with the effects of changes of interest rate on welfare. More precisely the author presents the case for freedom of capital movements. This is done in relationship with some of the conclusions in the first part which seemed to call for some restrictions.

The author's strategy is just to present a Fisherian model analogous to the one used to defend free trade. A more complex model is analyzed next, where a policy reaction to a foreign increase in interest rates is accounted for. This is the only place in the paper where a quantitative analysis is given. This seems also to be an original model (as opposed to the previous standard ones) and for this reason should have been presented at greater length. The same thing holds for the third model of this section which is used to defend an argument in favor of controls.

Finally in his conclusion Professor Kouri analyses "appropriate policy" responses. He very briefly sums up the numerous points made in the course of the paper and states that "monetary policy should aim to stabilize the level of nominal GNP". Unfortunately this conclusion is drawn from two of his papers which are not discussed here. It is therefore somewhat disappointing to read a long, rich, stimulating paper such as this one only to be told that answers to the initial policy question should be found elsewhere.

Recent Issues in the Theory of Flexible Exchange Rates, edited by E. Claassen and P. Salin
© *North-Holland Publishing Company, 1983*

Chapter 5.1

ASPECTS OF THE CURRENT ACCOUNT BEHAVIOR OF OECD ECONOMIES

Jeffrey SACHS*

1. Introduction

Many aspects of international capital mobility among developed economies are not well understood. There are puzzles about the size and distribution of current account imbalances and their counterpart, international capital flows, within the OECD. There are competing theories about the links of exchange rate movements to the current account that have not yet been sorted out empirically. Most fundamentally, there is doubt about the basic degree of capital mobility, with some [like Feldstein and Harioka (1981)], arguing that national capital markets are highly segmented, and others [like Harberger (1980)] arguing that high international capital mobility effectively equalizes rates of return in disparate financial centers. Harberger (1980) recently bemoaned this professional "schizophrenia" in thinking about capital flows, indicating that it points to "a genuine ignorance on our collective part of how the world capital market works."[1]

This essay examines some aspects of capital flows within the OECD, and outlines a framework for analyzing current account movements. In both the theoretical and empirical sections, I argue for the importance of including investment and growth in analyses of the current account, in contrast to much recent work which emphasizes savings (but not investment) decisions in current account determination. I present empirical evidence confirming that shifts in investment rate explain a large part of recent OECD current account behavior.

In addition, the links in theory and practice between exchange rates and the current account are scrutinized. There has been amazingly little evidence brought to bear on the basic assertion that exchange rate depreciation is correlated with current account deficits, and appreciation with surpluses. The assertion is made, but

* I wish to thank Barry Eichengreen and Charles Wyplosz for discussions, and Joy Mundy for secretarial assistance.

[1] Harberger (1980, p. 331).

not tested, in Kouri and Macedo (1980), for example. The hypothesized link holds
up well for the larger OECD economies and not for a number of smaller European
economies characterized by large deficits and exchange rate appreciation in the 1970s.
But on closer scrutiny, the exchange rate behavior in the smaller countries can be
explained by their specific exchange rate policies. For these countries, a link is found
between deficits and rising nominal interest rates rather than depreciating currencies.

2. An overview of current account behavior: 1960–1979

The broad outlines of current account behavior for fourteen OECD countries may be
gleaned from table 5.1. From the final line of the table, we see the well known fact
that the OECD as a whole went into deficit upon the 1973 oil price hike, after a
decade-and-one-half of aggregate surpluses. Even at the point of deepest deficits,
though, the ratio of the current account to gross national product, CA/GNP, for the
fourteen countries in the aggregate never fell below −0.005 during 1974 to 1979. Note

Table 5.1
Current accounts as a proportion of GNP, 1960–79.

	1960–65	(CA/GNP) 1966–73	1974–79	$(-CA/I)$ 1974–79	Proportion of surplus years
Large countries					
Canada	−0.019	−0.003	−0.020	0.011	0.15
France	NA	NA	−0.006	0.024	0.42
Germany	0.002	0.010	0.010	−0.007	0.85
Italy	0.010	0.018	−0.002	0.002	0.75
Japan	−0.005[a]	0.011	0.003	−0.011	0.53
Netherlands	0.010	0.005	0.010	−0.050	0.65
U.K.	−0.002	0.003	−0.012	0.058	0.45
U.S.	0.007	0.001	0.000	−0.004	0.75
Average, large eight	0.004[a]	0.004	0.004	−0.003	0.58
Small countries					
Australia	−0.029	−0.021	−0.023	0.094	0.10
Austria	−0.001	−0.008	−0.029	0.105	0.20
Denmark	−0.015	−0.021	−0.033	0.138	0.05
Finland	−0.016[a]	−0.014	−0.027	0.080	0.16
Norway	−0.025	−0.015	−0.080	0.226	0.10
Sweden	0.000	0.001	−0.016	0.076	0.35
Average, small six	−0.012[a]	−0.012	−0.030	0.118	0.16
Average, all	0.003[a]	0.004	−0.002	0.009	0.39

Source: Current account balance is from the OECD Main Economic Indicators, Historical Statistics. GNP and *I* are from the International Financial Statistics, International Monetary Fund.
   [a] 1961–65.

that the smaller countries have consistently run deficits since 1960, and that *CA/GNP* worsened after 1973 considerably more for this group than for the larger countries, a fact which we will take up soon.

The position of a country as a capital importer (i.e. with a current account deficit) or exporter is remarkably steady over time, and is also tied closely with economic size. The largest economies (by total *GNP*), Germany, Japan and the United States, have been fairly consistent capital exporters, at least until the large U.S. deficits of 1977 and 1978. The small countries have all been capital importers for twenty years, with remarkable consistency. For the six small countries during 1961–79, there are only 19 observations of surplus of a total of 119 annual observations. The proportion of surplus years between 1960 and 1979 is shown in the last column of table 5.1. Of the large countries, only Canada is consistently in deficit; of the small, none is typically in surplus.

An indicator of the persistence of surpluses and deficits across years is given by the correlation of *CA/GNP* for the list of countries across subperiods. Between 1960–65 and 1966–73, the correlation for thirteen countries (excluding France) is 0.81. For the periods 1966–73 and 1974–79, the correlation is $r = 0.72$.

Also, the absolute magnitude and variability of *CA/GNP* is negatively related to economic size. For the group of large countries as a whole, the 1960–79 range of *CA/GNP* is 0.004 to −0.004, while for the small countries, the range is 0.003 to −0.044. The standard deviation of *CA/GNP* for the large eight economies is 0.003, much less than 0.011 for the smaller countries. This same point was made by Harberger (1980), using the ratio of *CA* to gross investment I rather than to *GNP*. The result probably reflects the fact that small countries are truly "small" in international capital markets, and can borrow and lend international at a fairly fixed interest rate, while larger economies face an upward sloping schedule of international funds. We return to this point later in the paper.

Note that the deficits are a substantial fraction of gross domestic investment in many of the countries. For the smaller countries as a group, international capital inflows accounted for more than 11 percent of the funds for gross domestic investment during 1974–79. This ratio is an astonishing 22.6 percent for Norway; Norway's deficits, we shall note later, reflect international borrowing to finance Norway's North Sea oil development.

My regression analysis to date has focused more on the sources of *shifts* in the current account, than on the reasons for persistent imbalances, though the theoretical discussion below clearly points to factors which can explain long periods of international borrowing. Current account flows over decades can be expected between countries with similar tastes but unequal marginal productivities of capital, either because of different technologies, a different industrial mix, or different initial endowments of capital. Alternatively, *CA* imbalances can occur between countries with similar technologies, but differing intertemporal consumption preferences (i.e. savings behavior). If differing technologies or capital endowments are the main source of capital flows, we would expect to see persistent deficits in economies with high investment rates. This is indeed the case for the large *versus* small OECD economies.

The *I/GNP* ratio for the smaller six countires is consistently three to four percentage points above the same ratio among the large eight economies. For our three subperiods, these rates are given by:

	1960–65	1966–73	1974–79
(*I/GNP*), large 8	0.21[a]	0.22	0.22
(*I/GNP*), small 6	0.26	0.26	0.25

[a] 1961–65
Source: International Financial Statistics.

On a country-by-country basis, Japan is the significant exception to the negative link of *CA/GNP* and *I/GNP*. The Japanese *CA/GNP* ratio is usually positive although the investment share *I/GNP* is the highest among the fifteen countries studied. My guess is that Japanese capital controls until the late 1970s explain the low *CA/GNP* ratio.[2] In the absence of controls, Japan's extraordinary savings rates would probably have led to large CA surpluses, and smaller investment rates. Since the capital controls effectively bottled up the savings domestically, in spite of Japanese home interest rates much below international levels, *CA/GNP* was reduced and *I/GNP* was raised.

As a further check on the investment relation, I ran a cross-section of *CA/GNP* and *I/GNP* for a number of subperiods, with and without Japan included. These are shown as regressions (1) to (3) in table 5.2. The correlation between investment rates and *CA/GNP* is particularly strong after 1970.

If differing endowments of capital, rather than differences in technologies or product mix are behind the persistent differences in investment rates, the international flow of capital would be from high per capita income countries to lower per capita income countries. Surprisingly, the simple relationship between *CA/GNP* and real per capita income is negative, not positive, and extremely weak, as shown in regression (4). Other writers have found a weak or negative relationship between per capita income and the current account balance in examining flows between developed and developing countries.[3] Apparently low per capita incomes are as much evidence of low total factor productivity as of low endowments of capital per head.

It is often thought that the recent pattern of current account deficits and surpluses reflects in part the distribution of oil import dependence among nations. I have argued at length in Sachs (1981) that the links between oil dependence and deficits were rather weak in the 1970s, for good theoretical reasons. As an illustration of this proposition, regression (5) and (6) show *CA/GNP* as a function of *I/GNP* and M^{oil}/GNP, where M^{oil} is the value of net petroleum imports into the country. All variables are

[2] For background on the extensive role of Japanese Capital Controls until the mid-1970s, see Seki (1980).
[3] Halevi (1971).

averaged over 1970–79. There is no overall negative relationship between oil dependence and *CA/GNP* and the oil variable is weak and statistically insignificant. The basic explanation here is that while countries with higher oil dependence, *ceteris paribus*, suffered greater real income losses after the oil price increases in the 1970s, real income losses *per se* do not lead to international borrowing. In principle, it is crucial whether the income losses are perceived as permanent or temporary; only in the latter case will deficits be greatest in countries with the largest income losses. A second part of the explanation is that oil-rich countries, such as Canada, Norway and the U.K., experienced a sharp rise in investment expenditures on energy resource development, and these expenditures contributed to current account deficits.

The links between investment and the current account are even stronger when we

Table 5.2
Regression analysis of CA/GNP[a].

	Country		R^2
(1)	Excluding Japan	$\left(\dfrac{CA}{GNP}\right)_{1961-70} = \underset{(1.57)}{0.037} - \underset{(1.82)}{0.172} \left(\dfrac{I}{GNP}\right)$	0.23
(2)	Excluding Japan	$\left(\dfrac{CA}{GNP}\right)_{1971-79} = \underset{(3.58)}{0.084} - \underset{(4.10)}{0.39} \left(\dfrac{I}{GNP}\right)$	0.60
(3)	All	$\left(\dfrac{CA}{GNP}\right)_{1971-79} = \underset{(1.49)}{0.039} - \underset{(1.89)}{0.20} \left(\dfrac{I}{GNP}\right)$	0.21
(4)	All	$\left(\dfrac{CA}{GNP}\right)_{1961-70} = \underset{(0.03)}{-0.0004} - \underset{(0.47)}{-0.002} (\$\, GNP/population)_{1961-70}$	0.02
(5)	All	$\left(\dfrac{CA}{GNP}\right)_{1971-79} = \underset{(1.27)}{0.03} - \underset{(1.9)}{0.20}\,(I/GNP) + \underset{(1.0)}{0.28}\,(M^{oil}/GNP)$	0.28
(6)	Excluding Japan	$\left(\dfrac{CA}{GNP}\right)_{1971-79} = \underset{(3.2)}{0.08} - \underset{(4.0)}{0.39}\,(I/GNP) + \underset{(0.43)}{0.09}\,(M^{oil}/GNP)$	0.61
(7)	Excluding Japan	$\Delta\left(\dfrac{CA}{GNP}\right)_{\substack{(1971-79) \\ -(1961-70)}} = \underset{(4.2)}{-0.01} - \underset{(4.6)}{0.65}\,\Delta(I/GNP)$	0.65
(8)	Excluding France[b]	$\Delta\left(\dfrac{CA}{GNP}\right)_{\substack{(1971-79) \\ -(1961-70)}} = \underset{(1.1)}{-0.01} - \underset{(0.34)}{0.15}\,\Delta(S/GNP)$	0.01

Sources: CA from OECD Main Economic Indicators; *GNP* from International Financial Statistics. *I* is total gross investment, including inventory accumulation, from IFS. Savings, *S*, are defined as $I + CA$. The notation $(\quad)_{1961-70}$ or $(\quad)_{1971-79}$ indicates a simple arithmetic average over the years indicated. $\Delta(\quad)_{\substack{(1971-79) \\ -(1961-70)}}$ indicates $[(\quad)_{71-79} - (\quad)_{61-70}]$. The full country list is as in table 5.1.

[a] Numbers in parentheses are *t*-statistics.
[b] Missing observations for France prevented inclusion.

consider *shifts* in international borrowing. With great consistency, the countries that had the largest increase in CA deficits in the 1970s were those with the sharpest rise in gross investment. As seen in regression (7) $[(I/GNP)_{71-79} - (I/GNP)_{61-70}]$ accounts for 65 percent of the variance in $[(CA/GNP)_{71-79} - (CA/GNP)_{61-70}]$. Since the coefficient on investment is -0.65, a 1 percent rise in the investment rate was financed on average 0.65 percent by foreign capital inflows, and only 0.35 percent by gross national savings.

In principle, exogenous increases in domestic savings rates, in addition to shifts in investment, might explain the recent current account behavior. Indeed the theoretical section stresses that a great variety of shocks can potentially account for *CA* movements. Our empirical task is to sort out which of the possible shocks is the likely candidate for having moved the current account in any particular period, and here the evidence strongly points to investment shifts as opposed to savings shifts as the major influence. As seen in regression (8) in table 5.2, shifts in national savings rates are virtually uncorrelated with CA shifts between the decades of the 1960s and 1970s. The R^2 is only 0.01, and $\Delta(S/GNP)$ is statistically insignificant.

On a country-by-country time series basis, we again find a large role for shifts in investment rates in *CA* swings and apparently smaller role for shifts in savings rates. The simple correlation (not shown) during 1961–1979 between (detrended) *CA/GNP* and (detrended) *I/GNP* is negative in thirteen of the fourteen countries, with $r < -0.50$ in six cases. The (detrended) savings rates, as expected, are positively correlated to (detrended) *CA/GNP*, for twelve of the fourteen countries, though the correlation is generally weaker; $r > 0.50$ in three countries.

3. An overview of exchange rate–current account linkages: 1973–80

With the great extent of theorizing about current account effects on the exchange rate, there has been remarkably little attempt to verify competing hypotheses. Before we explore what theory says the links *should* be, let us examine what the links have been. While there are many potential hypotheses to test, I will focus on the view that deficit countries will have depreciating nominal and real exchange rates, and surplus countries the opposite. With respect to the current account influences on the nominal exchange rate, Kouri has dubbed this view the "accelerationist" hypothesis.

Proponents of this view, of course, recognize that domestic financial policies can upset any simple link between deficits and depreciation, but argue that the hypothesis is supported empirically in spite of potential complications. As Kouri and Macedo (1981) write:

> "Allowing for the effects of intervention, changes in interest rates and so on there is still a clear tendency of currencies of surplus countries to appreciate continuously and those of deficit countries to depreciate continuously.
>
> ... [referring to evidence on the large 7 countries] cumulative autonomous capital flows have been insufficient to finance the substantial imbalances that

have existed since 1973. Year after year, furthermore, they have often accentuated the pressure on the exchange rate of deficit countries ...".

Table 5.3 offers the basic data to test this proposition. The exchange rate for each country is a geometric weighted average of the country's bilateral exchange rates with the other countries, where the weights are country shares in total international trade during 1968–73. The real exchange rate EP^*/P is similarly calculated, using the wholesale price index as the price variable. Among the large countries, there is a clear pattern of nominal and real exchange rate appreciation among surplus countries (Germany, Japan, the Netherlands) and depreciation among the rest (Canada, France, Italy, U.K., and U.S.). The correlation of both nominal and real exchange rate changes with (CA/GNP) are negative for all of the large countries except Canada. Regression equa-

Table 5.3
The current account and exchange rate movements.

| Country | (CA/GNP) 74–79 | End 1973–End 1979 | | Correlation[a] of CA/GNP, $\%(E)$ | Correlation[b] of CA/GNP, $\%(EP^*/P)$ |
		$\%(E)$ (annual rate)	$\%(EP^*/P)$ (annual rate)		
Large eight					
Canada	−0.020	5.0	3.8	0.09	0.28
France	−0.006	−1.2	−0.2	−0.38	−0.59
Germany	0.010	−7.5	−2.1	−0.28	−0.29
Italy	−0.002	7.5	−0.7	−0.31	−0.26
Japan	0.003	−1.0	0.3	−0.58	−0.71
Netherlands	0.011	−5.4	−1.1	−0.10	−0.50
U.K.	−0.012	3.5	−2.6	−0.14	−0.06
U.S.	0.000	3.0	2.6	−0.40	−0.58
Small six					
Australia	−0.023	4.5	2.5	−0.11	−0.54
Austria	−0.029	−6.6	−1.6	0.27	0.29
Denmark	−0.033	−1.1	−1.3	0.04	−0.05
Finland	−0.027	0.7	−1.4	0.01	0.49
Norway	−0.080	−1.9	−1.0	0.04	−0.19
Sweden	−0.016	0.5	−1.1	−0.29	0.05

Source: CA and *GNP* as in table 5.1. The exchange rate for country i is calculated as $\log(E_i) = [\Sigma_{j \neq i} w_j \log(E_{ij})]/(1 - w_i)$, where w_j is the share of country j in total exports plus imports, on average, during 1968–73. That is, $w_j = (X_j + M_j)/[\Sigma_k (X_k + M_k)]_{1968-73}$, with X_j, M_j equal to the dollar values of total exports and imports for country j. E_{ij} is an index of the end-of-period bilateral exchange rate between countries i, j, in units of currency i per unit of currency j ($E_{ij} \equiv$ 1 in 1975). The series E_{ij} is calculated from the International Financial Statistics, IMF, using the series Lae for each country. EP^*/P is analogously calculated as $\log(E_i P^*/P_i) = [\Sigma_{j \neq i} w_j \log(E_{ij}P_j^*/P_i)]$, with P_j the wholesale price index of country j (also from IFS data).
 [a] Quarterly, 1974:1–1979:4.
 [b] Annual, 1973–1979.

tions of %$\Delta(E)$ on lagged %$\Delta(E)$ and (CA/GNP), shown in table 5.4, tell a similar story.

Interestingly, the pattern seems to break down for many of the smaller countries, where we observe large deficits together with nominal and real exchange rate appreciations. Norway, for example, had deficits of over 10 percent of *GNP* in 1976, accompanied by real and nominal exchange rate appreciation of over 6 percent throughout the year. Austria, similarly, experienced real appreciation in the midst of seven consecutive years of deficit. Nor is there a negative correlation between exchange rate movements and the current account on an annual or quarterly basis. In almost all cases the correlations are positive or weakly negative, and the regression coefficients are statistically insignificant.

Table 5.5 packages the data in a slightly different format, by simply counting for each country the number of observations in which surpluses and deficits are associated with nominal and real appreciations and depreciations. An χ^2 statistic is used to test for independence of the current account position and the direction of exchange rate movement. Again, there is a clear pattern of nominal and real depreciation *cum* deficits in the large countries, *versus* nominal and real appreciation *cum* deficits in many of the smaller countries. There are as many observations of deficits with appreciation as with depreciation for the smaller countries.

What explains this difference in behavior? Clearly, a major step towards explanation is a difference in exchange regimes in the small and large countries. Of the large countries, the U.S., U.K., Canada and Japan have been floating throughout the entire period 1973–80, and France and Italy floated for most of the period.[4] Germany has been at the center of a series of cooperative exchange arrangements, first the "Snake" and since March 30, 1979, the European Monetary System (EMS). The Dutch guilder has remained fairly closely linked to the Deutschmark, first in the Snake and now in the EMS.

The smaller countries, with the exception of Australia, have all maintained some linkage to a group of currencies, either formally as members of the Snake and EMS (Belgium, Denmark, Norway for a period), or informally by pegging to a basket of currencies (Austria, Finland, Norway, Sweden).[5] Since the theory of nominal exchange rate movements and the current account is predicated on a floating regime, it is perhaps not surprising that the smaller countries fail to support the "accelerationist" view. With respect to real exchange rates, the difference in exchange regime provides little answer to the differences in behavior of large and small countries. Most of the links between CA/GNP and P/EP^* that have been described in the literature apply to both fixed and flexible rate regimes, as we shall see.

---

[4]   Until joining the European Monetary System in 1979.
[5]   Finland began pegging to a basket of currencies on November 1, 1977. Norway was in the Snake until December 12, 1978, at which point it began pegging to a basket of currencies. Austria was in the Snake off and on throughout the 1970s, alternating between the joint European float and a closer connection with the Deutschmark. Denmark was a member of the Snake, and now the EMS. Sweden has pegged to a basket of currencies since the mid-1970s.

Table 5.4
Regressions of $\%\Delta E$ on CA/GNP, quarterly 1974:1−1980:4.

Country	Interval	Independent variables				R^2	D.W.
		C	$\dfrac{CA}{GNP}$	$(\%\Delta E)_{-1}$	$(\%\Delta E)_{-2}$		
Large eight							
Canada	74:1−	0.01	0.08			0.00	1.69
		(0.89)	(0.14)				
	80:4	0.01	0.16	0.16	−0.027	0.02	1.98
		(0.89)	(0.27)	(0.81)	(0.14)		
France	74:1−	−0.007	−0.79			0.15	1.6
		(1.2)	(1.9)				
	79:4	−0.007	−0.72	0.06	0.0005	0.15	1.77
		(1.1)	(1.2)	(0.28)	(0.002)		
Germany	74:1−	−0.006	−0.81			0.16	2.21
		(0.91)	(2.2)				
	79:4	−0.012	−0.82	−0.30	−0.27	0.29	1.68
		(1.7)	(2.4)	(1.7)	(1.5)		
Italy	74:1−	0.016	−0.45			0.09	2.6
		(1.8)	(1.5)				
	79:4	0.020	−0.64	−0.32	0.07	0.19	1.9
		(2.0)	(2.0)	(1.4)	(0.37)		
Japan	74:1−	−0.008	−1.13			0.11	1.12
		(0.98)	(1.8)				
	80:4	−0.006	−0.12	0.55	−0.03	0.28	1.92
		(0.72)	(0.14)	(2.3)	(0.12)		
Netherlands	74:1−	−0.008	−0.19			0.03	2.24
		(1.6)	(0.85)				
	80:3	−0.014	−0.20	−0.24	−0.33	0.19	1.78
		(2.4)	(0.95)	(1.4)	(1.9)		
United Kingdom	74:1	−0.012	−0.41			0.04	1.46
		(0.15)	(1.0)				
	80:3	−0.001	−0.34	0.26	0.09	0.13	2.10
		(0.22)	(0.84)	(1.3)	(0.5)		
United States	74:1−	0.003	−1.6			0.09	2.40
		(0.49)	(1.6)				
	80:4	0.005	−2.3	−0.28	−0.36	0.27	2.03
		(0.76)	(2.3)	(1.6)	(2.1)		
Small six							
Australia	74:1−	0.005	−0.252			0.008	2.04
		(0.36)	(0.46)				
	80:4	0.005	−0.279	−0.07	−0.006	0.013	1.91
		(0.35)	(0.48)	(0.35)	(0.03)		
Austria	74:1−	−0.004	0.179			0.02	2.08
		(0.54)	(0.84)				
	80:4	−0.012	0.180	−0.290	−0.35	0.18	1.61
		(1.31)	(0.88)	(1.5)	(1.8)		

(Table 5.4 continued)

Denmark	74:1–	–0.000 (0.02)	0.057 (0.19)			0.001	1.77
	79:4	–0.006 (0.48)	–0.12 (0.32)	–0.03 (0.13)	–0.24 (0.91)	0.04	1.78
Finland	74:1–	0.003 (0.47)	0.008 (0.05)			0.000	1.93
	79:4	0.001 (0.09)	–0.05 (0.30)	0.06	0.20	0.039	2.04
Norway	74:1–	–0.0003 (0.03)	0.019 (0.17)			0.0	1.82
	79:4	0.0 (0.0)	0.02 (0.19)	0.09 (0.46)	–0.22 (1.03)	0.06	1.95
Sweden	74:1	–0.01 (1.16)	–0.60 (1.41)			0.08	1.30
	79:4	–0.02 (1.36)	–0.70 (1.61)	0.33 (1.62)	–0.03 (0.147)	0.19	1.92

Table 5.5
The "accelerationist" hypothesis: *CA* and exchange rate changes, annual observations, 1973–1980.

Country	Number of years in which:				Percent of observations in support of hypothesis
	Surplus appreciation	Deficit depreciation	Surplus depreciation	Deficit appreciation	
Large eight					
Canada					
Nominal	0	3	1	4	37.5
Real	0	4	1	3	50
France					
Nominal	2	2	0	4	50
Real	2	5	0	1	87.5
Germany					
Nominal	5	1	1	1	75
Real	5	2	1	0	87.5
Italy					
Nominal	1	3	2	0	67
Real	2	2	1	2	57
Japan					
Nominal	3	2	0	3	62.5
Real	3	3	0	2	67
Netherlands					
Nominal	4	0	1	2	57
Real	4	1	1	1	71

(Table 5.5 continued)

U.K.

Nominal	1	4	1	2	62.5
Real	2	2	0	4	50

U.S.

Nominal	3	3	2	0	75
Real	2	2	3	1	50

Subtotal, large eight

Nominal	19	18	8	16	60.5
Real	20	21	7	14	77.5

Small six

Australia

Nominal	1	5	0	2	75
Real	1	4	0	3	67.5

Austria

Nominal	0	2	0	6	25
Real	0	4	0	4	50

Denmark

Nominal	0	4	0	4	50
Real	0	4	0	4	50

Finland

Nominal	0	2	1	5	25
Real	0	1	1	5	12.5

Norway

Nominal	0	3	1	4	37.5
Real	1	4	0	3	62.5

Sweden

Nominal	0	3	1	4	37.5
Real	0	3	1	4	37.5

Subtotal, small six

Nominal	1	19	3	25	41.5
Real	2	20	2	24	46.0

Total (15) countries

Nominal	20	37	11	41	52.0
Real	22	41	9	38	57.0

$\chi_1^2 = 3.3^a$, Large eight, nominal $\qquad p < 0.10$

$\chi_1^2 = 7.1$, Large eight, real $\qquad p < 0.01$

$\chi_1^2 = 1.5$, Small six, nominal $\qquad p > 0.10$

$\chi_1^2 = 0.0$, Small six, real $\qquad p > 0.10$

$\chi_1^2 = 1.3$, Total, nominal $\qquad p > 0.10$

$\chi_1^2 = 4.7$, Total, real $\qquad p < 0.05$

[a] Pearson statistic.

There is still a quandry, though, with the smaller countries. If we maintain the assumption of the imperfect substitutability of home and foreign assets which underlies the accelerationist view, we know that a deficit country can peg its exchange rate only at the expense of continued official reserve outflows, or increasingly contractionary monetary policies with rising domestic interest rates. There is no evidence of significant use of official reserves to finance the post-73 deficits, and indeed for these countries official reserves increased in almost all of the years between 1973 and 1979. With respect to interest rates, we can check the imperfect capital mobility assumption by examining whether interest rate differentials with Deutschmark assets tended to increase during deficit years for the currencies pegged to the DM (Austria, Denmark, the Netherlands, and Norway until December 12, 1978). As seen in table 5.6, there is a clear pattern of rising differentials during the deficit years for all of the countries. Correlations of annual changes in interest rate differentials with CA/Y show a negative link for each of the countries except Denmark (see table 5.6).

With this brief overview, we turn to the theoretical section. The goal is to embed international capital flows in a model that can explain: (1) the persistence of current account deficits and surpluses; (2) the large role of investment shifts in current account movements; (3) the co-occurrence of deficits and exchange depreciation in floating exchange rate economies; and (4) the ambiguous links between the real exchange rate and the current account.

4. A theoretical model of the current account

In a series of recent papers, I have developed an infinite-horizon, two-country model of the current account under assumptions of economic growth with far-sighted households, value-maximizing competitive firms, and efficient asset markets. Since an analytical solution to the model is apparently beyond reach, I have examined the model with computer simulations. In this section I sketch a two-period, one country analog to the model, that preserves the basic structure and results of the more complete analysis. The strength of the approach is that it illustrates how specific exogenous shocks induce particular correlations between key variables, such as CA with P/EP^* and I.

Most recent models analyzing the links of the current account to the exchange rate and to other variables, have failed to model current account behavior properly. Typically, the current account balance is written as a simple function of the exchange rate and current financial wealth [as in Kouri (1981), Dornbusch and Fischer (1980), and Rodriguez (1981)]. There is almost never any treatment of physical capital accumulation, and its relationship to wealth holdings. Moreover, these current account equations give inadequate results for many types of questions, since the savings behavior that is implied by the equations is not credible. Thus, in Dornbusch and Fischer (1980) for example, consumption is not a function of human wealth, or the discounted value of domestic output. We will see the many disturbances affect the

Table 5.6
Interest rate differential in pegged exchange rate economies. (Government bond yield minus German bond yield, end of year)

Country	1973	1974	1975	1976	1977	1978	1979	1980	Correlation of $\Delta(i-i^*)$, CA/GNP (1973−79)
Austria									
$(i-i^*)$	−0.62	0.38	1.11	1.25	3.3	1.61	0.30	0.72	−0.34
(CA/GNP)	−0.013	−0.014	−0.009	−0.037	− 0.063	−0.025	−0.026	NA	
Belgium									
$(i-i^*)$	−1.8	−0.8	0.23	2.00	2.72	2.39	3.10	3.71	−0.18
(CA/GNP)	0.027	0.012	0.004	−0.001	− 0.009	−0.010	−0.031	NA	
Denmark									
$(i-i^*)$	2.57	3.93	4.78	2.35	6.36	8.17	8.10	8.67	0.03
(CA/GNP)	−0.016	−0.029	−0.014	−0.046	− 0.037	−0.027	−0.045	NA	
Norway									
$(i-i^*)$	−3.4	−2.5	−1.0	−0.06	2.67	1.89	2.14	1.38	−0.81
(CA/GNP)	−0.018	−0.048	−0.086	−0.121	− 0.143	−0.055	−0.023	NA	

Sources: The interest rate data for each year are the December observations of government bond yields from the IFS (LGI at the Country Code).
For year t, $\Delta(i-i^*)$ is $(i-i^*)_t - (i-i^*)_{t-1}$.

current account precisely by altering the discounted value of domestic output, and such channels are necessarily ignored in the Dornbusch–Fischer model. In Rodriguez (1980), all anticipated disturbances to the economy have an impact on the current account *only* through real balance effects, probably the least important of all the relevant channels.

Failure to treat investment and capital accumulation is not an innocent simplification, if we are to draw real-world conclusions from our models of exchange rate behavior. By excluding all wealth accumulation except in the form of foreign assets, these models set up a one-to-one link between the change in wealth and the current account balance. With domestic investment, however, real wealth may be increasing or decreasing along with *CA* surpluses and deficits. Again, in Dornbusch–Fischer, the exchange-rate links to the current account are mediated entirely by changes in wealth. A deficit signals declining wealth and thus declining money demand *cum* depreciation. With investment explicitly treated, a CA deficit may easily be matched with *rising* wealth and appreciation, particularly if the deficit reflects an investment boom.

It is not enough to add investment as a component of expenditure to arrive at a general theory of the current account. In addition, we must include the returns to investment as part of the wealth of firms' shareholders and allow that wealth to affect current consumption decisions. This general equilibrium structure is readily built into the simple model now presented.

We consider an economy which produces a single final output, with price P. The economy is small in the world capital market, so that domestic agents can borrow and lend in foreign denominated bonds at a fixed interest rate r^*. The domestic output is an imperfect substitute in consumption for a foreign final good that has world price P^* and domestic price EP^*, where E is the exchange rate. The home country is assumed to be small in its import market, so that P^* is exogenous, and may be considered fixed.

All international capital flows take place in one-period foreign denominated bonds; I denote the end-of-period domestic net holdings of these bonds as Z_t. Domestic equity is internationally tradable, and is a perfect substitute for Z, so that the required return on equity in foreign currency units is r^*. The only outside asset denominated in domestic currency is non-interest bearing money, M. Inside domestic bonds have interest rate i, which may differ from the return on foreign assets because of the portfolio preferences of domestic agents. Neither domestic money nor the domestic bond is held by foreigners.

In assuming perfect substitutability of home equity and foreign bonds (or foreign equity), but imperfect substitutability of domestic and foreign bonds, I am deviating from a typical assumption that home assets are better substitutes for each other than each is for foreign assets. Of course, there is no theoretical assumption that is "right" in this regard: relative asset substitutability depends on the nature of underlying stochastic shocks in the economy, and on the structure of trade. Kouri (1981) has pursued the hard work of linking an array of exogenous disturbances to optimal asset demand functions in a general equilibrium model. We are still far off from concrete results in this area for open-economy macroeconomic models, and I do not pursue the ambitious task of solving endogenously for the structure of portfolio choices.

Households make their consumption decisions to maximize a two-period, additively separable utility function, subject to the constraint that the discounted value of consumption must equal initial wealth

$$\max_{C_1^D, C_1^F, C_2^D, C_2^F} U(C_1^D, C_1^F) + \frac{1}{1+\delta} U(C_2^D, C_2^F), \tag{1}$$

$$\text{s.t. } (\pi_1 C_1^D + C_1^F) + \frac{1}{1+r^*} (\pi_2 C_2^D + C_2^F) = W_1.$$

In this equation, π_t is the period t relative price of home goods to foreign goods $(\pi = P_t/EP^*)$, and W_1 is the initial wealth, in units of the foreign final good. C_t^D is consumption of the home good, and C_t^F is consumption of the foreign good. By additive separability, the household first determines total spending each period $\pi_t C_t^D + C_t^F$, and then determines the composition of spending between C_t^D and C_t^F.

To stay as simple as possible, I choose $U(\cdot, \cdot)$ to be $\log (C_t^{D\alpha} C_t^{F(1-\alpha)})$. Then the optimal expenditures are given by:

$$C_1^D = \frac{\alpha(1+\delta)}{(2+\delta)\pi_1} W_1, \qquad C_1^F = \frac{(1-\alpha)(1+\delta)}{(2+\delta)} W_1,$$

$$C_2^D = \frac{\alpha(1+r^*)}{(2+\delta)\pi_2} W_1, \qquad C_2^F = \frac{(1-\alpha)(1+r^*)}{(2+\delta)} W_1. \tag{2}$$

The discounted value of expenditure on each of the goods C_1^D, C_1^F, C_2^D, C_2^F is a constant share of wealth by the assumption on utility.

Managers are assumed to maximize the market value of firms. By the assumption that the cost of capital r^* is set in the world equity market, firm valuation is simply the present discounted value of total earnings, net of investment expenditure (I_1):

$$V = (\pi_1 Q_1 - \pi_1 w_1 L - I_1) + \frac{(\pi_2 Q_2 - \pi_2 w_2 L)}{1+r^*}, \tag{3}$$

where w_t is the nominal wage deflated by domestic output price.

Output is produced according to the production function $Q_t = F(K_t, L_t)$ and $K_2 = K_1 + I_1$. (I assume that all capital goods are imported, so that investment expenditure in terms of the foreign good I_1 also equals the quantity of new capital.) We will assume continuous full employment $L_i = \bar{L}$. Obviously, first-order conditions for value maximization are given by:

$$\frac{\partial Q_t}{\partial L_t} = w_t; \qquad \pi_2 \frac{\partial Q_2}{\partial K_2} = (1+r^*). \tag{4}$$

In the spirit of simplicity, I will assume that the production function is Cobb–Douglas, with $Q_t = \bar{L}^\beta K_t^{1-\beta}$.

Domestic wealth is given by the sum of human wealth (H), domestic ownership of equities, and net foreign investment. I will assume that households own the entire domestic capital stock, and that all international capital flows are changes in Z. There are no initial holdings of Z. In this model, the issue of portfolio composition between equity and Z is unimportant since equities and Z earn the same rate of return. All that matters is that at the beginning of the first period, domestic households own the claims to the domestic firms. Human wealth is the present value of total labor earnings $\pi_1 w_1 L_1 + (\pi_2 w_2 L_2)/(1 + r^*)$. Adding up the components of wealth, $H + V$, we have

$$W = \pi_1 Q_1 + \frac{\pi_2 Q_2}{1 + r^*} - I_1. \tag{5}$$

Domestic money demand is set, without formal justification, according to a transaction demand specification

$$\frac{M_t}{P_t} = Q_t^\phi (1 + i)_t^{-\theta}. \tag{6}$$

Here, real balances are an increasing function of domestic output and a declining function of the domestic interest rate i. Because this is a two-period model, second period money demand is inherently problematic as there are presumably no alternative assets to money in the last period (and thus no second-period interest rate i) and no explicit reason to hold money. I will arbitrarily fix i_2 to the exogenous world interest rate i^* (any constant would do); a better solution only emerges in an infinite horizon model, or in a finite-horizon model with a very explicit transactions technology.

The domestic interest rate is determined according to portfolio preferences for home *versus* foreign assets. As I have noted, in more sophisticated models the portfolio problem is solved with explicit attention to the types of shocks in the economic environment. Here I fall back to a reduced form specification, as in a model of Kouri (1981), in which the nominal interest rate differential between the home and foreign asset, net of expected exchange rate changes, is a declining function of the stock of foreign assets held domestically:

$$[1 + i_t] \bigg/ \left[\frac{E_{t+1}}{E_t} (1 + i^*) \right] = f(Z_t) \quad f'(Z_t) < 0, f(0) = 1, f > 0. \tag{7}$$

In our two period case, $Z_1 = CA_1$. In a multiperiod model, $Z_t = \sum_{i=1}^t CA_i$.

The model is completed by adding an export demand equation and market clearing conditions:

$$X_t = \frac{Y^*}{\pi_t}, \tag{8}$$

and

$$Q_t = C_t^D + X_t. \tag{9}$$

Y^* is a world export demand shift variable, presumably reflecting foreign income or wealth.

Our goal is to solve for CA_1, the first period current account, and to relate CA_1 to the parameters of the model, and to E_2/E_1 and π_2/π_1, the rates of nominal and real exchange rate change. The first-period current account at world prices is simply given by

$$CA_1 = \pi_1(Q_1 - C_1^D) - C_1^F - I_1, \tag{10}$$

and $CA_2 = -CA_1$ by the household budget constraint. From (2), we have consumption as a function of W, and in (5), we have the definition of W. Thus, substituting in (10), we can write CA_1 as

$$CA_1 = \frac{\pi_1 Q_1 (r^* - \delta)}{(2+\delta)(1+r^*)} - \frac{(\pi_2 Q_2 - \pi_1 Q_1)(1+\delta)}{(2+\delta)(1+r^*)} - \frac{I_1}{2+\delta}. \tag{11}$$

Of course this expression is not yet in final form, since π_1, π_2, Q_2 and I_1 are endogenous, and indeed Q_2 is a function of I_1. Still, (11) points up the three fundamental determinants of current account balance. The first term on the right hand side shows that CA_1 is an increasing function of the difference between the world interest rate and the rate of time preference $(r^* - \delta)$. This difference determines the desire to save income for later consumption. In the continuous time version of the present model, $\dot{W} = (r^* - \delta)W$, so that $r^* - \delta$ in fact determines the path of overall wealth accumulation.

The second term might be described as capturing the role of transitory fluctuations in current account determination. When export demand falls temporarily in a given year, pulling down real income, households dissave not because they are poor but because their *transitory* income is less than permanent income. In the attempt to smooth the income stream, households borrow in early periods if the real income stream is rising, and lend initially if the real income stream is falling. Thus, CA_1 decreases with $(\pi_2 Q_2 - \pi_1 Q_1)$.

The third term highlights the special role of investment in current account determination. Since $CA_1 = \pi_1 Q_1 - (C_1^F + \pi_1 C_1^D + I_1)$, the effects on CA_1 of an exogenous shock that causes I_1 to rise depend on the effects of the shock on $C_1^F + \pi_1 C_1^D$. To the extent that the shock has no effect on household wealth, consumption will not change; $(\pi_1 C_1^D + C_1^F + I_1)$ and thus the deficit $(= I_1 + \pi_1 C_1^D + C_1^F - \pi_1 Q_1)$ will rise *one-for-one* with the investment boom. This is precisely the case for a rise in investment projects that just earn the market rate of return, r^*. If domestically owned firms retain earnings to invest in projects with return r^*, households dissave by the same amount, keeping C_1 constant. Though the first-period dividend flow to households is reduced by the rise in I_1, households "pierce the corporate veil," and dissave. They effectively substitute the firms' investment for their household savings, so that total absorption is increased one-for-one with I_1.

Sometimes a rise in I_1 also signals "good news" that raises household wealth. For instance an anticipated rise in future world demand for domestic output raises both I_1 and W. In this case, both $\pi_1 C_1^D + C_1^F$ and I_1 rise, and the deficit worsens more than one-for-one with the increase in I_1.

To solve for the reduced form for CA_1, and π_1 and π_2, we must first determine wealth W in terms of the underlying parameters: $Y_1^*, Y_2^*, r^*, K_1, \delta$. A couple of facts are helpful here. First, by the assumption of Cobb–Douglas technology, $(1 + r^*)K_2 = (1 - \beta)\pi_2 Q_2$, so that investment I_1 $(= K_2 - K_1)$ is given by

$$I_1 = \frac{(1 - \beta)\pi_2 Q_2}{1 + r^*} - K_1. \tag{12}$$

Second, $\pi_1 Q_1$ and $\pi_2 Q_2$ are linear in W, Y_1^*, and Y_2^*. When the consumption and investment equations are plugged into (5) and (9), we find W and CA_1:

$$W = \Delta^{-1} (2 + \delta) \left(Y_1^* + \frac{\beta Y_2^*}{1 + r^*} + K_1 \right), \tag{13}$$

$$\Delta = (2 + \delta) - \alpha(1 + \delta) - \alpha\beta > 0,$$

$$CA_1 = \Delta^{-1} \{ [1 - \alpha]Y_1^* - [(2 + \delta) - \alpha(1 + \delta) - \beta]/[1 + r^*]Y_2^* +$$
$$+ [1 - \alpha]K_1 \}. \tag{14}$$

We will interpret this expression shortly. To find the terms of trade π_1, note that $\pi_1 Q_1 = [\alpha(1 + \delta)/(2 + \delta)W + Y_1^*]$ from (2), (8) and (9). Thus

$$\pi_1 = \frac{1}{Q_1} \left[\frac{\alpha(1 + \delta)}{2 + \delta} W + Y_1^* \right].$$

[Remember that Q_1 is fixed, since K_1 is predetermined, $L_1 = \bar{L}$, and $Q_1 = F(K_1, L_1)$.] π_2 is found similarly, though now Q_2 is endogenous. To find Q_2, we use the investment eq. (12), $K_2 = K_1 + I$, and $Q_2 = L^\beta K_2^{1-\beta}$. The solution for π_2 is

$$\pi_2 = \left[\frac{1 + r^*}{1 - \beta} \right]^{1 - \beta} \left[\frac{1}{\bar{L}} \right]^\beta \left[\frac{\alpha(1 + r^*)}{2 + \delta} W + Y_2^* \right]^\beta. \tag{15}$$

Finally, the ratio π_2/π_1 is given, after a bit of algebra, by:

$$\frac{\pi_2}{\pi_1} = \frac{\alpha(1+r^*)Y_1^* + [(2+\delta) - \alpha(1+\delta)]Y_2^* + \alpha(1+r^*)K_1}{[(2+\delta) - \beta\alpha]Y_1^* + [\alpha(1+\delta)/(1+r^*)]\beta Y_2^* + \alpha(1+\delta)K_1}$$

$$\times \left[\left(1 + \frac{I_1}{K_1}\right)^{-(1-\beta)} \right]. \tag{16}$$

These bulky equations are in fact easy to interpret. To start with CA_1, a rise in Y_1^* *ceteris paribus* necessarily improves the current account and an anticipated rise in Y_2^* necessarily worsens the current account. In both cases, the rise in world demand causes an increase in wealth, and in π_1, π_2, and I_1. But when Y_1^* rises, households save some of the first period income gain (i.e. run a surplus) to spread the consumption windfall across time; when Y_2^* rises, households borrow against the anticipated future windfall to enjoy higher consumption in the initial period. Since an increase in Y^* in *either* period leads to a demand increase in *both* periods, π_1 and π_2 both rise. Also, I_1 rises, since $\pi_2 Q_2$ is increased, and I_1 is linear in second-period real income [see (12)].

An equal rise in Y_1^* and Y_2^* has an ambiguous effect on CA_1. But in the benchmark case $r^* = \delta$, a "permanent" rise in Y^* (i.e. $dY_1^* = dY_2^*$) leads to a *deficit* on CA_1! This is sharply counter to the conventional view that the current account improves when demand shifts permanently towards a country. But the reason in clear enough. Higher Y^* increases investment demand, throwing $\pi_1(Q_1 - C_1) - C_1F - I_1$ negative. In a model without investment (e.g. $\beta = 1$, $K_1 = 0$ in the present case), and with $Y_1^* = Y_2^*$, $r = \delta$, a rise in Y^* has *no* effect on the current account. Rather, π_1 and π_2 rise in equal proportion, and the value of exports and imports rise by the same amount.

Finally, note that CA_1 is an increasing function of the initial endowment of capital. Higher K_1 *ceteris paribus*, reduces I_1/K_1, which in turn induces an improvement in the current account. All other things equal, capital flows should lead from highly capital-endowed economies to poorly capital-endowed economies.

What can we say about the links of CA_1 and real depreciation? It is possible to find every combinations of $CA_1 \gtrless 0$ together with $\pi_2/\pi_1 \gtrless 1$. What is crucial is the *source* of the current account imbalance. Consider two countries that are identical except for δ. We can easily verify from (16) that $\partial(\pi_2/\pi_1)/\partial\delta < 0$, and from (14) that $\partial CA_1/\partial\delta < 0$. Thus, when current account differences reflect *taste* differences, high deficit countries will experience real depreciation. On the other hand, for two countries that are identical except for future demand Y_2^*, the opposite conclusion is reached. Higher Y_2^* unambiguously leads to higher π_2/π_1, and to a fall in CA_1. Similarly, a temporary decline in world demand ($dY_1^* < 0$; $dY_2^* = 0$) causes π_2/π_1 to rise and CA_1 to fall. First-period deficits are again associated with real exchange rate appreciation. If the countries differ only in K_1 the effects on the relative π_2/π_1 are ambiguous. In general, with $Y_1^* \doteq Y_2^*$ and $\delta \doteq r^*$, faster growing countries will see a larger decline in π_2/π_1. Since growth in Q_2/Q_1 is inversely related to K_1, we should expect, *ceteris paribus*, countries with initially poor endowments of capital to experience relative large real exchange rate depreciation over time. As noted above, such countries will also, *ceteris paribus*, have larger CA deficits.

At this point, we can bring in the monetary side to find the links between CA_1 and *nominal* exchange rates. The monetary subsystem was given in (6) and (7). Noting that $P_1 = (E_1 P^*)\pi_1$ and $P_2 = (E_2 P^*)\pi_2$ and substituting into the money demand equations, we can write:

$$\frac{E_2}{E_1} = \left(\frac{M_2}{M_1}\right)\left(\frac{\pi_1}{\pi_2}\right)\left(\frac{Q_1}{Q_2}\right)^\phi \cdot \left[\frac{(1 + i^*)}{(1 + i)}\right]^\theta. \tag{17}$$

From the portfolio eq. (7), $(1 + i^*)/(1 + i) = (E_1/E_2)f(CA_1)$. Remember that f measures the substitutability of home and foreign denominated nominal bonds, with $f \equiv 1$ for the case of perfect substitutability. Thus, plugging into (17), we have

$$\frac{E_2}{E_1} = \left[\left(\frac{M_2}{M_1}\right)\left(\frac{\pi_1}{\pi_2}\right)\right]^{1/(1 + \theta)}\left(\frac{Q_1}{Q_2}\right)^{\phi/(1 + \theta)}[f(CA_1)]^{-\theta/(1+\theta)}. \tag{18}$$

For the individual periods we have:

$$E_1 = M_1^{1/(1 + \theta)} M_2^{\theta/(1 + \theta)} Q_1^{-\phi/(1 + \theta)} Q_2^{-\theta\phi/(1+\theta)} \pi_2^{-\theta/(1 + \theta)}$$
$$\pi_1^{-1/(1 + \theta)}[f(CA_1)]^{-\theta/(1+\theta)}, \tag{19a}$$

$$E_2 = M_2 Q_2^{-\phi}(1 + i^*)^\theta/(\pi_2 P^*). \tag{19b}$$

Not surprisingly, both real and purely monetary factors affect the exchange rates. Changes in M_1 and M_2 can move E_1 and E_2 with no effects on CA_1, π_1, π_2, etc. under the assumptions of the model. For given M_1, M_2, *real* exchange rate appreciations and depreciations tend to cause nominal exchange rate appreciations and depreciations. Thus, as Stockman (1980) has indicated, much of the observed correlation between changes in E and EP^*/P may be due to common responses to underlying shocks. This is in contrast to the more typical assumption that changes in E cause EP^*/P to move because of nominal price rigidity.

We also see a direct effect of CA imbalance on the nominal exchange rate, working through the Kouri–Branson portfolio demand channel. Thus, even if a deficit economy is on a path of real appreciation, rising output, and stable money supply, it may experience nominal depreciation as its net indebtedness grows over time. Of course only in the case of perfect capital mobility, $f' = 0$, does this effect go away.

Thus, to sum up, a deficit country will surely experience nominal and real depreciation if the deficit is caused by high δ. If, on the contrary, the deficits arise from a path of increasing Y^*, then π_2/π_1 will be large, and the nominal exchange rate will tend to appreciate unless $-f'$ is also large.

5. Extensions and conclusions

There are at least three important directions for extending the theoretical framework described above. These are: a multiperiod or infinite-horizon analysis with more general functional forms; the introduction of capital control restrictions as a policy instrument; and an explicit treatment of portfolio considerations in a setting with uncertainty and risk averse agents.

The first is, in a sense, easy and already accomplished [cf. Sachs (1982), Lipton and Sachs (1980)]. An infinite horizon, two-country version of the model here has been developed and analyzed through simulation. There is no reason to stick with particular functional forms as in the model in this paper once recourse is made to computer simulation. Thus, in work now underway with Michael Bruno, a three-sector infinite-horizon model of the U.K. is being developed, that incorporates a complete input–output structure in the production technology.

The second extension, explicitly to treat restrictions on capital mobility, would allow a more accurate depiction of the degree of capital mobility among the OECD economies. Most of the major economies have or continue to resort to restrictions on international capital flows to help achieve current account and other objectives. Foreign access to the U.S. bond market was effectively closed until 1974, and until much more recently in Japan. Our understanding of theoretical aspects of capital controls is still rather limited, and controls are rarely brought in explicitly into theoretical work.

The third direction is by far the hardest. To this point we have very little feel for the relevant sources of risk that lead to the imperfect substitutability of assets across national borders. Our models will have radically different conclusions if imperfect substitutability is based on inflation risk, default risk, political risk, or hedging behavior against still other types of real disturbances. It seems that the most fruitful way to proceed here is to build theoretical models, with attention to a limited number of key stochastic elements, so that portfolio behavior may be derived endogenously.

References

Dornbusch, Rudiger and Stanley Fischer, 1980, Exchange rates and the current account, American Economic Review, Dec.

Feldstein, Martin and Charles Harioka, 1981, Domestic savings and international capital flows, Economic Journal.

Halevi, N., 1971, An empirical test of the "balance of payments stages" hypothesis, Journal of International Economics, Feb.

Harberger, Arnold C., 1980, Vignettes on the world capital market, American Economic Review, Papers and Proceedings, 331–337.

Kouri, Pentii J.K., 1981, Balance of payments and the foreign exchange market: A dynamic partial equilibrium model, NBER, Working Paper, no. 644, March.

Kouri, Pentii J.K., 1981, The effect of risk on interest rates: A synthesis of the macroeconomic and financial views, NBER, Working Paper, no. 643, March.

Kouri, Pentii J.K. and Jorge Braga de Macedo, 1980, Perspectives on the stagflation of the 1970s, Woodrow Wilson School of Public and International Affairs, Princeton, Discussion Paper no. 91, Dec.

Lipton, David and Jeffrey Sachs, 1981, Accumulation and growth in a two-country model, NBER, Working Paper, no. 570, forthcoming on the Journal of International Economics.

Obstfeld, Maurice, 1980, Imperfect asset substitutability and monetary policy under fixed exchange rate, Journal of International Economics, May.

Rodriguez, C., 1980, The role of trade flows in exchange rate determination: A rational expectations approach, Journal of Political Economy 88, Dec.

Sachs, Jeffrey, 1981, The current account and macroeconomic adjustment in the 1970s, Brookings Papers on Economic Activity.

Sachs, Jeffrey, 1982, Energy and growth under flexible rates, in: J. Bhandari and B. Putman (eds.), The international transmission of economic disturbances under flexible exchange rates (M.I.T. Press, Cambridge, Mass.).

Stockman, Alan, 1980, A theory of exchange rate determination, Journal of Political Economy 88, Aug.

Recent Issues in the Theory of Flexible Exchange Rates, edited by E. Claassen and P. Salin
© *North-Holland Publishing Company, 1983*

Chapter 5.2

COMMENT ON SACHS

Charles WYPLOSZ

In his stimulating paper, Jeffrey Sachs shakes a number of conventional explanations of the effects of the oil shock on OECD countries' current accounts and exchange rates. The central intuition of the paper follows from his use of the accounting identity in an intertemporal optimizing framework instead of the standard Keynesian income flow version. The result is a theoretically innovative model and a fresh look at the data: Sachs discounts very much the importance of the dependence on oil and stresses the empirical role of investment in shaping the current account.

Recent macroeconomic models dealing with perfect foresight have directed attention to intertemporal choices: if economic agents correctly anticipate future events, it is presumably to include these expectations in their own intertemporal optimising problems. As a result, we now have investment behaviour as a function of Tobin's q or future returns and the consumption function is of the life-cycle or permanent income type.

When applied to the open economy, this line of research has been emphasizing the role of wealth, present and future, in driving the current account and the exchange rate. The dynamic properties are very much tied around the wealth effects of current account imbalances, i.e. through the accumulation or decumulation of tradable assets. Sachs' contribution is a healthy reminder that tradable assets, although important, are probably a small component of total domestic wealth so that changes in human wealth and the value of fixed capital are likely to play a major role which had been overlooked recently. In a way, Sachs brings the absorption approach back, with its heavy emphasis on savings and investment, but with the notable difference that their behaviours now derive from intertemporal optimisation.

In this theoretical model, a simplified pedagogic version of the larger models that he has built, Sachs actually eliminates the wealth effects of current imbalances, allowing him to get results in sharp contrast with recent theorizing. This is obtained by resorting to a two-period framework, so that current accounts balance in present value terms, because of the household budget constraint, thus having no impact on either period's wealth. In a multi-period framework this property would carry through if the domestic interest rate used to discount future revenues is always equal to the foreign one, an assumption that does not square well with the imperfect asset substitutability of eq. (7).

The interpretation to be given to the two periods is not specified by Sachs. With the assumption of flexible prices and full employment, one would be tempted to think in terms of two "steady states", where goods and labour markets have settled to an equilibrium, while the current account imbalances translate the growth process of the economy in between these two states. If so, the model does not say anything about the shorter run processes during which unemployment and inflation interfere with long run trends and may lead to policy measures. As a matter of fact, no policy experiments are envisaged in this paper. Monetary policy cannot have any real effect in this perfectly dichotomised model. As for fiscal policy, with perfect foresight, budget deficits or surpluses are likely to be doomed as long as they are financed by Barro (1979) bonds, which would seem to be a natural assumption in this framework. There is some scope, however, for taxes or subsidies directed at investments as long as the rate of return (r^*) differs from the rate of time preference (δ).

Sachs uses this model to validate his interpretation of the data. His views differ from more traditional ones which stress the income flow effects on the current account. For example, a standard Keynesian model would predict that a greater dependence on oil implies larger income losses and larger current account deficits following an oil shock. This does not seem to fit the data well. An alternative explanation, offered by Sachs, stresses that permanent income reductions should be matched by an equal cut in absorption, with no impact on the current account. With temporary income losses, on the contrary, absorption should not fall significantly, which might explain initial deficits while the lasting effects of higher oil prices were being recognised. I think that this explanation carries a lot of weight but I would be reluctant to accept it as the only one, because when the second oil shock came about in 1979, the lesson of 1973 should have been learned, the lag in reaction should have disappeared, and the current accounts should not have changed considerably. The data on table 5.7 show that oil-rich countries as the U.K. and Canada improved their current account, while Germany, Japan, Italy and France went from surpluses in 1978 to large deficits in 1980. One other explanation would follow Bruno and Sachs (1979) in treating the oil shock as a technical regress proportional to the degree of oil dependence which vanishes in the longer run as the elasticity increases. In this story, the drop of income in the short run greatly overshoots the long run effects and justifies a moderate reduction in absorption, making the current account deficit proportional in the short run to oil imports. Furthermore, there is evidence that cyclical factors, as measured in the last line of table 5.7 also played a major role, for example, in the strong 1980 U.S. surplus.

In an intertemporal framework, one would expect the opposite result: a cyclical, therefore temporary, drop in income should not be accompanied by a reduction in absorption and should lead to a current account deficit. This last remark directly concerns Sachs' main empirical point, namely the assertion that in the identity $CA = S - I$, investment is empirically the main driving force behind current account fluctuations, with savings shifts largely irrelevant. I have just argued that savings fluctuations

means by which *real wages* can be lowered, thereby leading to greater employment when there exists an excess supply of labor and idle resources at going wages [Alexander (1952), Purvis (1976) and Salop (1974)].

Mundell has countered, however, that this

> "... argument is based on money illusion. The community is unwilling to accept variations in real income through changes in money prices, but it will accept the same changes in real income through adjustments in the rate of exchange." [Mundell (1960 p. 152)]

Purvis and Salop have argued that lower wages following devaluation might reduce the supply of labor rather than increase the demand for it, thereby *contracting* rather than expanding output.

In addition, a somewhat neglected possibility is the *resource allocation* effect. In Machlup's terms:

> "... The 'resource allocation effect' of devaluation may be especially significant when the 'idle resource effect' is negligible or zero; total employment may remain practically unchanged while the output produced may increase through a more efficient use of the resources employed." [Machlup (1955, p. 266)]

This effect is potentially important insofar as countries frequently use exchange depreciation as a vehicle for dismantling exchange controls and restrictions on imported inputs [Cooper (1971) and Connolly and Taylor (1976)]. Finally, the higher domestic price of *imported inputs*, such as oil and machinery, may lead to a contraction of aggregate supply [Findlay and Rodriguez (1977)], tending to offset favorable effects.

In what follows, simple tests are devised to examine the relationship between exchange rate changes and changes in growth rates from a sample of 22 exchange rate changes taken independently for the most part by small, open economies in the 1960s.

1.2. Empirical results

This section reports the results of simple tests of the hypothesis that devaluation is expansionary. The first test examines the change in growth rates after devaluation by country, the second performs a simple t-test on the mean change in growth rates, and the third regresses changes in growth rates upon the percentage rate of devaluation and the magnitude of the slump prior to devaluation. In matrix form, the model to be estimated for the five years before and after devaluation is:

$$
\begin{bmatrix} y_1 \\ y_2 \\ y_3 \\ y_4 \\ y_5 \\ y_6 \\ y_7 \\ y_8 \\ y_9 \\ y_{10} \end{bmatrix} = \begin{bmatrix} 1 & 1 & 0 \\ 1 & 2 & 0 \\ 1 & 3 & 0 \\ 1 & 4 & 0 \\ 1 & 5 & 0 \\ 1 & 5 & 1 \\ 1 & 5 & 2 \\ 1 & 5 & 3 \\ 1 & 5 & 4 \\ 1 & 5 & 5 \end{bmatrix} \begin{bmatrix} \alpha \\ \gamma_1 \\ \gamma_2 \end{bmatrix} + \begin{bmatrix} \mu_1 \\ \mu_2 \\ \mu_3 \\ \mu_4 \\ \mu_5 \\ \mu_6 \\ \mu_7 \\ \mu_8 \\ \mu_9 \\ \mu_{10} \end{bmatrix} \tag{1}
$$

where y_i is the logarithm of gross domestic product in constant prices for year i, $\gamma_2 - \gamma_1$ the estimated change in growth rate in the five years after devaluation, and μ_i error terms.

The standard errors of the change in growth rates are computed by:

$$
\mathrm{SE}(\gamma_2 - \gamma_1) = \left([0, -1, 1]\, [X' \cdot X]^{-1} \begin{bmatrix} 0 \\ -1 \\ 1 \end{bmatrix} \mathrm{MSE} \right)^{\frac{1}{2}} \tag{2}
$$

where X is the design matrix in (1), X' its transpose, and MSE the mean square error of the regression [Johnston (1972), pp. 125–6)].

This formulation constrains growth after devaluation to begin from predicted year 5 income rather than actual income. The reason for this is that the year before devaluation is frequently one of a recession in economic activity, so that constraining growth afterward to start from gross domestic product the year before would unduly bias the test in favor of the expansionary hypothesis.[3]

Table 6.1 reports the estimated change in growth rates, along with the corresponding standard errors in parentheses, as well as the magnitude of the recession in the year prior to devaluation. Of the 20 devaluing countries, 7 experienced increases in growth rates that were significant at the 5% level. The average change in the growth rate is 0.9 percent, which in light of the corresponding variance, gives a t-value of the *mean* change in growth equal to 1.97, significant at 5%. Regressing the change in the growth rate $\Delta G = \gamma_2 - \gamma_1$ upon the change in the exchange rate ΔE gives

$$
\begin{aligned}
\Delta G = -0.001 + 0.027\,\Delta E \quad R^2 &= 0.13 \\
(0.007)\ (0.016) \qquad\qquad& \\
\text{(standard errors in parentheses)}&
\end{aligned} \tag{3}
$$

[3] Of the 20 devaluations, 13 countries had income less than 10 year trend income in the year before devaluation, and in the 2 revaluations, both had income higher than trend the year before. On the average, income was 1.2 percent lower than trend income the year before.

The rate of devaluation is significant at the 10% but not at the 5% level, and the fit is rather poor.[4]

Regressing the change in the growth rate upon the change in the exchange rate and the magnitude of the previous slump on economic activity gives a much better fit, suggesting that the acceleration in growth following devaluation may reflect primarily recovery from the previous recession.

Table 6.1
Expirical results.

Country	Date	Exchange rate change (ΔE in %)	Change in growth rate (ΔG in %)	Magnitude of previous slump[a] (+ if boom, − if slump) (ΔY in %)
1. Argentina	January 1959	58	0.60 (1.65)	2.32
2. Ecuador	July 1961	20	0.91 (0.57)	−1.21
3. Ecuador	August 1970	39	6.31[b] (1.67)	−7.02
4. Finland	September 1957	39	2.02 (1.59)	−1.61
5. Finland	October 1967	30	2.25[b] (0.92)	−2.85
6. France	December 1958	17	0.84 (0.55)	−0.69
7. France	August 1969	12	−0.07 (0.34)	0.34
8. Germany	March 1961	−5	−0.87 (0.61)	2.26
9. Iceland	February 1960	56	3.63[b] (1.47)	−1.67
10. India	June 1966	58	2.73[b] (1.20)	−4.18
11. Israel	February 1962	67	−1.16 (1.29)	−0.36
12. Korea	May 1964	96	4.62[b] (0.77)	−7.06
13. Netherlands	March 1961	−5	1.73 (1.04)	1.23
14. New Zealand	November 1967	24	−0.44 (0.90)	−0.91
15. Peru	October 1967	44	−0.06 (1.18)	2.00
16. Philippines	January 1962	94	1.20 (0.76)	0.15
17. Philippines	February 1970	65	1.29[b] (0.39)	−0.79
18. Spain	November 1967	16	−0.31 (0.43)	−0.12
19. Tunisia	September 1964	24	−2.67 (1.10)	2.64
20. Turkey	August 1970	65	1.42[b] (0.47)	−2.67
21. United Kingdom	November 1967	16	−0.63 (0.38)	0.20
22. Venezuela	January 1964	42	−1.80 (1.03)	0.74
Averages[c]		41	0.90	−1.19

Standard errors in parentheses; t-statistic of average: 1.97[b] for growth rate column, −2.22[b] for magnitude of "previous slump" column.

  [a] The measure of the previous slump results from estimating the 10 year trend line of gross domestic product, then calculating the slump in the year before devaluation (year 5) as the logarithm of actual income minus the logarithm of predicted income. A negative number thus indicates the percentage "slump", while a positive one indicates a "boom".
  [b] Significant at 5% level (one-tail test).
  [c] For all averages, Germany and Netherlands data were averaged in with sign reversed since they were revaluations.

---

  [4] Measurement error in the rate of devaluation may, however, bias the coefficient in eq. (3) toward zero [Connolly and Taylor (1976a, p. 854)].

$$\Delta G = 0.004 + 0.001 \, \Delta E - 0.658 \, \Delta Y \qquad R^2 = 0.70. \tag{4}$$
$$(0.005) \ (0.011) \qquad (0.111)$$

(standard errors in parentheses)

The magnitude of the devaluation is not significant at all when the depth of the previous slump is taken into account.[5]

In short, while the evidence is mixed, expansion frequently occurred after devaluation in the 1960s. In a third of the cases, growth rates increased significantly, and on the average, growth was higher. However, the relationship between changes in growth rates and the magnitude of devaluation is a weak one. Of perhaps more importance, changes in growth appear to be closely related to the magnitude of the previous slump so that any stimulus recorded may reflect primarily recovery from a recession rather than the expansionary effects of a devaluation *per se*.

To conclude this section, our results can be compared to those of Cooper (1973) who finds that for a sample of 23 developing countries:

> "In fact, some depression in economic activity is frequently found following devaluation in developing countries, sometimes lasting only a few months, not infrequently lasting more than a year. While it is impossible to disentangle the deflationary effects of devaluation from those of autonomous policy measures designed to facilitate success of the devaluation, there is much circumstantial evidence to suggest that the extent of depression is a surprise to the authorities in the devaluing countires, that they have not adequately taken into account the depressing effects of the devaluation itself, or that they have exaggerated its expansionary impetus." [Cooper (1973, pp. 189–90)]

Cooper is quite right that there is frequently a slump in the year after devaluation. In our sample (which was based on his), there was a depression in 13 of 20 devaluing countries the year after devaluation, and on the average for the 20 the slump was 1.9 percent below 10 year trend income. However, of these 13 cases of slumps, 11 were already in a recession the year before devaluation so that it would be difficult to fully attribute the pause in economic activity to devaluation.[6] Further, as Cooper suggests, contractionary policies to ensure the success of devaluation were indeed undertaken the year after devaluation since 16 of the 20 devaluing countries decelerated the rate of growth in the rate of domestic credit creation.[7] Thus, one could not expect a devaluation to turn around a recession rapidly, that is, within a year or so.

---

[5] Larger slumps caused larger devaluations which may explain the positive coefficient in regression eq. (3). The estimated relationship is

$$\Delta E = 0.358 - 4.46 \, \Delta Y, \quad R^2 = 0.18$$
$$(0.058) \quad (2.13)$$

[6] Nine of the thirteen did, however, have larger slumps the year after than the year before devaluation.

[7] See Connolly and Taylor (1976a, 1979a).

2. Devaluation, credit restraint and the balance of payments

There is clear evidence that the success or failure of exchange rate depreciation as a policy measure to improve the balance of payments hinges almost totally upon the accompanying domestic credit policy pursued by the central bank. Indeed, the extent of improvement in the balance of payments is, for a number of reasons, nearly unrelated to the percentage rate of devaluation, but rather, is rigidly linked to the domestic credit policy carried out in the year or two following the change in the peg. This is not a matter of conjecture, nor does it result from a monetary identity. It is a question of evidence.

In fig. 6.1, the increase in growth of domestic credit as a percentage of the monetary stock is plotted along the horizontal axis, while the improvement in the balance of payments as a percentage of the money stock is plotted along the vertical exis.[8]

A cursory glance at fig. 6.1 illustrates that nearly every unsuccessful devaluation was associated with an acceleration in the rate of growth of domestic credit. In those cases, the previous exchange rate peg possibly played the disciplinary role of an anchor on domestic monetary expansion which was lifted by the change in the peg. In other instances, the banking authorities apparently took measures to decelerate the rate of growth of domestic credit, possibly to insure improvement in the balance of payments. This deceleration in domestic credit growth bore the desired fruits.

Paradoxically, the improvement in the balance of payments appears unrelated to the magnitude of the change in the peg. Theoretically, the observed point should lie above the 45° line through the origin by an amount equal to the percentage rate of devaluation. However, the actual points typically do not. This is so for a number of reasons, the principal one being that exchange devaluation was a means by which exchange controls and multiple exchange rates could be abolished. The change in the official parity was to some extent to ratify *de facto* disguised devaluation in the form of export subsidies, import surcharges, multiple exchange rates, restrictions on purchases of foreign exchange and the like. Consequently, with the abolition of the paraphernalia of exchange control, the *effective* rate of devaluation was much less than the nominal rate.[9] Furthermore, the exchange rate change has the effect, at least in the short run of primarily raising the *relative* price of traded goods rather than accelerating *absolute* prices. This is so because prior to the devaluation, home prices get out of line, and a decision to change the peg is made in order to bring domestic prices in line with world prices. Thus, devaluation is, once again, a response to a domestic disequilibrium that plays a further role in realigning domestic prices. For this reason,

---

[8] Both are measured as the change in the two years after devaluation relative to the two years before.

[9] It is not at all the case that exchange controls flourish only in the warm climes of the tropics. Almost without exception, the developed countries in the sample also took advantage of devaluation to dismantle exchange and import controls. See Connolly and Taylor (1979, p. 292) for actions taken by each country.

the exchange rate depreciation will not have the full impact predicted by a simple monetary model.

The evidence on the *relative* price effect of devaluation is illustrated in fig. 6.2.

The average movement of export and import prices as a ratio of the consumer price for each country is plotted to highlight the change in relative prices. The decline in the relative price of traded goods typically reflects rises in consumer prices, possibly of

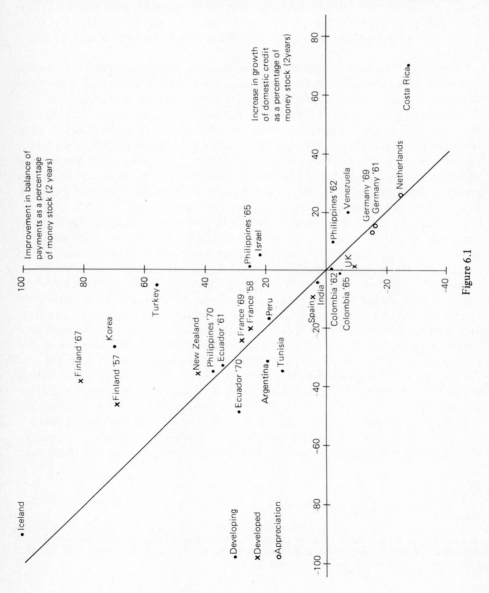

Figure 6.1

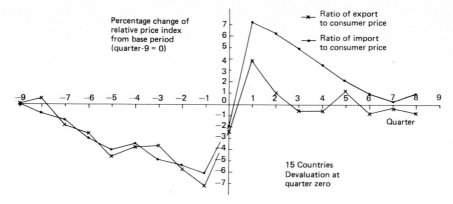

Figure 6.2

monetary origin, but sometimes declines in export prices, possibly of real origin. Price adjustment appears complete after two years. As for absolute prices, a rough calculation indicates that about $2\frac{1}{2}$ percent per annum were added on the average to the rise in the consumer price index in the two years after devaluation, which is negligable relative to the magnitudes of the devaluations. [10]

In any event, a simple regression of the improvement of the balance of payments as a proportion of the money stock on the rate of devaluation and the rate of growth of domestic credit as a proportion of the money stock over a two year period before and after devaluation gives: [11]

$$\left[\frac{B_t}{M_t} - \frac{B_{t-1}}{M_{t-1}}\right] = \underset{(0.08)}{0.28} \frac{\Delta r_t}{r_t} - \underset{(0.12)}{0.87} \left[\frac{\Delta D_t}{M_t} - \frac{\Delta D_{t-1}}{M_{t-1}}\right], \tag{5}$$

$R^2 = 0.73$ (standard errors in parentheses).

The coefficient for the rate of devaluation, while significant, falls well short of its theoretical value of approximately +1, but the coefficient for the rate of acceleration of domestic credit is consistent with the monetary prediction of -1. This regression captures what is evident from fig. 6.1: the success or failure of a devaluation in improving the balance of payments depends critically, indeed, almost uniquely, upon decelerating the rate of growth of domestic credit. Incidentally, credit restraint is typically an important component of IMF stabilization programs, a point to which we shall return later.

[10]   See Connolly and Taylor (1979) for further evidence.
[11]   *Source:* Connolly and Taylor (1979, p. 283). This regression is on data for 25 countries listed in the Appendix and is available upon request from the author. France, 1958 was excluded since there was a devaluation in August of the previous year, and Germany, 1969 also, since the mark began to float in May, 1971 making a two year comparison difficult.

3. The international monetary fund in the tropics

There has been some criticism in the past few years of the role played by the International Monetary Fund in its stabilization programs applied to developing countries. One critic appears to be Lance Taylor (1981) who states:

> "There is growing consensus that orthodox IMF-style stabilization policies do not work well when administered to semi-industrialized countries, the usual victims of inflationary balance-or-payments disease ... The conclusion is that the stabilization tools normally applied – monetary restraint, fiscal control, and devaluation – all have stagflationary impacts to a greater or lesser extent. Moreover, their efficacy in improving the balance of payments may also be small." [pp. 465 and 486]

These conclusions follow not from the examination of any evidence in particular, but rather from a peculiar exercise applying static IS–LM analysis to the tropics, which leads, as Peter B. Clark correctly points out in his comment, to absurd conclusions: "Taylor's study can have the absurd policy implications that in the face of inflation and balance of payments deficit, the country should expand the money supply and revalue." (p. 506). This is so because Taylor's IS–LM analysis informs us that monetary expansion is deflationary (pp. 485–6), devaluation reduces output (p. 486), and its effect on the balance of payments is unclear (p. 490).

The evidence reported here suggests firstly that devaluation does not have adverse real effects on output in developing countries, and secondly this is so despite the tendency toward monetary restraint. Further, credit restraint plays an important role in the success or failure of devaluation in improving the balance of payments. IMF

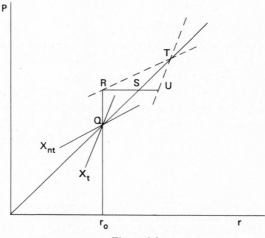

Figure 6.3

orthodoxy or not, the vast majority of devaluing countries contracted the rate of growth of domestic credit, and with one exception, all those that did experienced an improved balance of payments.

It is easy to agree with Taylor on one institutional point. In many developing countries, there is hardly any market for governmental or private bonds, particularly long term ones, because of a long history of high and unstable money growth bringing about high and unstable inflation that has crippled bond markets. For this problem, however, the solution is monetary stability, not the remedy prescribed by Taylor.

Apart from these remarks, a strong economic case can be made for an IMF-like stabilization program involving the abolition of exchange controls, exchange rate depreciation when necessary, and domestic credit restraint. The customary litany of the ills of exchange controls involving inefficiencies in production, consumption, and resource allocation can be skipped here. Rather, the evidence reported here suggests that (1) exchange depreciation does not restrain growth and (2) a slowdown in the rate of growth in domestic credit is particularly helpful in improving the balance of payments.

To illustrate the arguments, consider the Mundellian traded, non-traded goods model in fig. 6.3, where p measures the price of non-traded goods along the vertical axis and r the exchange rate or price of traded goods along the horizontal axis.

Suppose the small country in question initially has a pegged exchange rate at r_0, but for one reason or another, does not put up with monetary discipline and expands the money stock, thereby shifting the excess demand schedules of traded goods (X_t) and non-traded goods (X_{nt}) to point T. The rules of a fixed currency peg would normally require the monetary authorities to sell off foreign reserves, thereby reversing the monetary expansion. [12] The authorities may not obey these rules because they are not willing to deflate the price of home goods which has risen to R. Exchange controls may be applied to maintain the currency peg at r_0, thereby suppressing the excess demand for foreign exchange (measured by RU), but this is not a necessary assumption of the analysis. In either case, the relative price of non-traded goods is out of line (which shows up in the evidence reported in section 2). To restore equilibrium, a reform package could be administered involving the elimination of exchange controls, devaluing the currency to S, and restraining domestic credit moderately which shifts the excess demand schedules downward along the ray from the origin from T to S. The theory suggests this policy will work, and further, the evidence reported here unambiguously supports, I believe, the theory.

[12] This is an old point, but is worth repeating. See Connolly (1981) for a formal analysis applied to Latin America and Connolly (1982b) for a theoretical framework.

4. Concluding remarks

The evidence reported here suggests:

(1) Countries frequently devalue their currency in a situation involving a slump in real economic activity, a rise in the price of home goods compared to traded ones, and the presence of various exchange controls.

(2) A primary purpose of the abandonment of a particular peg appears to be the relaxation of exchange and trade controls which seems to accompany most devaluations.

(3) The devaluation realigns the relative price of traded goods but does not appear to play a role in the subsequent mild acceleration in real economic activity.

(4) The success or failure of the stabilization package in improving the balance of payments depends almost entirely upon the domestic credit policy pursued after devaluation, rather than upon the size of the devaluation. In particular, a moderate domestic credit slowdown *à la* IMF stabilization programs appears sufficient to guarantee an improved balance of payments.

Finally, it should be noted that the analysis and results presented here apply mainly to the 94 countries belonging to the IMF that still maintain a fixed currency peg of one sort or another.

Appendix

1. Definitions and sources

As a rule of thumb for the tests on real economic activity, the year of devaluation is treated as "the year before" if the exchange rate change came in the last half of the year and as the "year after" if it came in the first half as in Cooper (1971). Data on Gross Domestic Product in constant prices are from the May, 1977 issue (line 99b.p.) of *International Financial Statistics* except for Ecuador 1961, The Netherlands and the Philippines, 1962 where various issues of the United Nations' *Yearbook of National Accounts Statistics* were used.

Nearly all exchange rate changes were taken from the 1973 Supplement to the *International Financial Statistics*, line a. However, in two cases, Argentina and Iceland, the existence of prior multiple exchange rates was taken into account. For Argentina the rate reported is the increase in the free rate of the third quarter of 1958 to the IMF rate of the second quarter of 1959, and for Iceland it is the increase from the mid-point of the selling rate in the quarter of devaluation to the new IMF rate at the end of the quarter. The 1964–66 and 1966–67 Supplements were consulted for these two rates. For France, 1958 and Finland, 1957, the 1961–62 Supplements were used. In all other cases, the exchange rate is from the 1973 Supplement.

Data: Gross domestic product at constant prices.

Year	Argentina 1959	Ecuador 1961	Ecuador 1970	Finland 1957	Finland 1967	France 1958	France 1969	New Zealand 1967	Peru 1967
1	47.09	12347	29.81	18.30	30.24	349.0	614.5	4350	173.0
2	50.15	12609	31.64	19.96	32.22	365.4	648.8	4620	185.0
3	51.38	13261	33.44	21.47	33.88	387.2	680.5	4899	193.9
4	53.82	14140	35.07	21.89	34.68	410.1	711.8	5085	207.5
5	57.49	14357	34.64	22.23	35.60	421.8	763.9	5040	214.6
6	54.43	15008	36.19	22.21	36.46	434.7	808.4	5149	214.4
7	61.77	15597	39.22	23.82	40.27	464.9	851.1	5408	219.4
8	67.28	16809	45.50	26.18	43.59	490.9	899.2	5609	240.7
9	64.83	17366	51.68	28.29	44.64	524.0	951.5	5752	253.0
10	70.50	18430	54.42	29.50	47.78	552.5	987.5	6001	267.8

Year	Germany 1961	Iceland 1960	India 1966	Israel 1962	Korea 1964	Netherlands 1961	Venezuela 1964
1	334.9	23.92	294.9	na	1099	3459	28.12
2	353.8	24.20	307.0	na	1121	3576	29.23
3	365.2	24.34	309.6	7727	1178	3544	30.68
4	390.7	26.52	333.1	8217	1213	3719	33.47
5	425.3	26.94	317.4	9134	1320	4080	35.81
6	448.3	27.94	323.3	10037	1434	4203	39.26
7	466.3	28.10	348.8	11072	1521	4389	41.63
8	482.4	30.55	358.6	12183	1704	4530	42.67
9	514.5	33.58	382.1	13290	1828	4928	44.30
10	543.3	36.87	403.7	13441	2061	5208	46.46

Year	Philippines 1962	Philippines 1970	Spain 1967	Tunisia 1964	Turkey 1970	United Kingdom 1967
1	na	32.11	1658	440.4	118.6	41.99
2	10818	33.67	1761	498.0	123.6	44.45
3	11507	35.53	1888	501.3	131.8	45.38
4	11843	37.42	2044	554.7	138.9	46.29
5	12415	39.59	2132	576.4	146.9	47.53
6	12469	41.75	2254	605.2	161.9	49.18
7	13708	44.48	2430	624.0	173.9	49.85
8	14162	46.67	2575	623.1	183.3	51.02
9	14902	51.17	2698	676.2	196.8	52.31
10	15838	54.22	2928	705.3	212.6	53.70

Countries and rates of devaluation.

(1)	Developing	%
1.	Argentina, January, 1959	58
2.	Colombia[a], November, 1962	34
3.	Colombia[a], September, 1965	50
4.	Costa Rica, September, 1961	18
5.	Ecuador, July, 1961	20
6.	Ecuador, August, 1970	39
7.	Iceland, February, 1960	56
8.	India[a], June, 1966	58
9.	Israel, February, 1962	67
10.	Korea, May, 1964	96
11.	Peru, October, 1967	44
12.	Philippines[a], January, 1962	94
13.	Philippines[a], November, 1965	11
14.	Philippines[a], February, 1970	65
15.	Tunisia, September, 1964	24
16.	Turkey[a], August, 1970	65
17.	Venezuela, January, 1964	42

(2)	Developed	%
1.	Finland[a], September, 1957	39
2.	Finland[a], October, 1967	30
3.	France, December, 1958	17
4.	France[a], August, 1969	12
5.	Germany[a], March, 1961	−5
6.	Germany, October, 1969	−7
7.	New Zealand[a], November, 1967	24
8.	Netherlands[a], March, 1961	−5
9.	Spain[a], November, 1967	16
10.	United Kingdom, November, 1967	16

For a detailed description of the date sources and uses, see Connolly and Taylor (1979a, p. 291). These data are also available upon request from the authors.

[a] Price data are available.

References

Aizenman, Joshua and Jacob Frenkel, 1981, Real and monetary disturbances and the economics of a managed float, Paper presented at the Carolina Currency Conference on the Choice of an Exchange Rate System, May (University of South Carolina, Columbia, S.C.).

Alexander, Sidney, 1952, Effects of a devaluation on a trade balance, IMF Staff Papers 2, April.

Cardoso, Eliana and Rudiger Dornbusch, 1980, Equilibro externo do Brasil: uma avaliação da perspectiva monetarista, Pesquisa e Planejamento Econômico, August, 481–54.

Connolly, Michael and Dean Taylor, 1976a, Testing the monetary approach to developing countries, Journal of Political Economy 84, August, 849–59.

Connolly, Michael and Dean Taylor, 1976b, Adjustment to devaluation with money and non-traded goods, Journal of International Economics 6, August, 289–99.

Connolly, Michael and Dean Taylor, 1979, Exchange rate changes and neutralization: A test of the monetary approach applied to developed and developing countries, Economica 46, August, 281–94.

Connolly, Michael and José Dantas da Silvéira, 1979, Exchange market pressure in postwar Brazil: An application of the Girton–Roper monetary model, American Economic Review 69, June, 448–54.

Connolly, Michael, 1981, Optimum currency pegs for Latin America, Paper presented at the second International Conference on Financial Development and Capital Markets in Latin America and the Caribbean, Caraballeda, Venezuela, April. To be published in the Journal of Money, Credit, and Banking.

Connolly, Michael, 1982a, Currency questions in the Caribbean, Department of Economics, University of South Carolina (Columbia, S.C.).

Connolly, Michael, 1982b, The choice of an optimum currency peg for a small country in a monetary model with rational expectations, Journal of International Money and Finance, forthcoming.

Cooper, Richard, 1971, Currency devaluation in developing countries, Princeton Essays in International Finance, no. 86, June (Princeton University Press, Princeton).

Cooper, Richard, 1973, An analysis of currency devaluation in developing countries, in: Michael Connolly and Alexander Swoboda (eds.), International Trade and Money (Allen & Unwin, London), 167–96.

Findlay, Ronald and Carlos Rodriguez, 1977, Intermediate imports and macroeconomic policy under flexible exchange rates, Canadian Journal of Economics 10, May, 208–17.

Harberger, Arnold, 1950, Currency depreciation, income, and the balance of trade, Journal of Political Economy 58, February, 47–60.

International Monetary Fund, International financial statistics, May 1977 issue, 1973 supplement, and other issues cited (Washington, D.C.).

Johnston, J., 1972, Econometric methods (McGraw-Hill, New York), 125–6.

Machlup, Fritz, 1955, Relative prices and aggregate spending in the analysis of devaluation, American Economic Review 45, June, 255–78.

Mundell, Robert, 1960, The monetary dynamics of international adjustment under fixed and flexible exchange rates, Quarterly Journal of Economics 74, May, 227–57.

Mundell, Robert, 1971, Devaluation, in: R.A. Mundell, Monetary theory (The Goodyear Company, Pacific Palisades).

Mundell, Robert, 1982, The case for a managed international gold standard, in: Michael Connolly (ed.), The international monetary system: Choices for the future (Praeger, New York), forthcoming.

Mussa, Michael, 1976, The exchange rate, the balance of payments, and monetary and fiscal policy under a regime of controlled floating, Scandinavian Journal of Economics 78, May, 227–48.

Purvis, Douglas, 1976, Wages, the terms of trade, and the exchange rate regime, Cowles Foundation, Discussion Paper, no. 438, November.

Robinson, Joan, 1974, Beggar-my-neighbour remedies for unemployment, Essays in the theory of employment, 2nd edition (Basil Black, Oxford).

Salop, Joanne, 1974, Devaluation and the balance of trade under flexible wages, in: G. Horwich and P. Samuelson (eds.), Trade, stability and macroeconomics: Essays in honor of Lloyd A. Metzler (Academic, New York).

Taylor, Lance, 1981, IS–LM in the tropics: Diagrammatics of the new structuralist macro-critique, in: William Cline and Sidney Weintraub (eds.), Economic stabilization in developing countries (Brookings Institution, Washington), 465–507.

United Nations, Yearbook of national accounts statistics, various issues (New York).

Recent Issues in the Theory of Flexible Exchange Rates, edited by E. Claassen and P. Salin
© *North-Holland Publishing Company, 1983*

Chapter 6.2

COMMENT ON CONNOLLY

Jürgen Schröder

Much theoretical and empirical work has been done on the effects of devaluation on the balance of trade. This question was and is of interest because the main reasons for a devaluation in a system of fixed exchange rates is the removal of an existing deficit in the current account. However, countries have attempted in the past, and especially in the 1930s, to use devaluation in order to expand economic activity and employment. Connolly's paper addresses these two interesting questions. With respect to the first he gives a clear answer: the chances that a devaluation improves the balance of payments increase when deceleration of domestic credit expansion accompanies the devaluation. Here Connolly found empirically what economic theory tells us. Concerning the second question there is unfortunately not such a clear-cut answer. I will concentrate in my comment on this second question, that is: How does a devaluation affect economic activity at home?

Connolly's empirical results for twenty countries in the 1960s show that the relationship between changes in growth rates and magnitude of devaluation is rather weak. In fact, his empirical findings demonstrate that changes in growth appear to be closely related to the magnitude of previous slumps so that any positive effect on economic activity may be due to the recovery from a recession rather than to the stimulative effect of a devaluation. If it is doubtful whether a devaluation increases economic activity at home, one has to search for the possible reasons. Obviously production and employment at home will decrease if as a consequence of a devaluation either aggregate demand — that means home and foreign demand — for home produced goods decreases at given prices and a given positively sloped aggregate supply curve, or the aggregate supply of domestically produced goods decreases at given prices and a given negatively sloped aggregate demand curve. Or lastly, a positive effect on production and employment caused by a devaluation via aggregate demand will be overcompensated by a negative devaluation effect via aggregate supply or *vice versa*. What do we know about the effects of a devaluation on aggregate demand and on aggregate supply in different economic situations? Let me first deal with the demand side.

Neglecting a possible terms of trade or Laursen—Metzler effect and a possible wealth effect associated with the devaluation, the demand for home produced goods increases only if the devaluation improves the current account. We know that at least for two reasons one should not be too optimistic in this respect. First, it is not excluded that in the short run there exists a *J*-curve effect; and second, the effective devaluation is usually substantially smaller than the nominal devaluation when countries take advantage of devaluation to dismantle exchange rate and import controls as well as export subsidies.

What do we know about the impact of a devaluation on the demand for domestically produced goods via the money market? A devaluation implies a decrease in the real money supply so that we have a negative effect on home produced goods if there exists no liquidity trap and if the demand for home produced goods is interest-rate elastic. This negative effect will be mitigated if we take into consideration the impact of a terms-of-trade change on the demand for real money and assume that the devaluation worsens the terms of trade and thereby reduces real income.[1] If the elasticity of real money demand for transactions purposes is unity, then the negative devaluation effect of the money supply side will be exactly compensated by the effect of the money demand side. If the elasticity is smaller than one then there remains still a net negative effect. But if we take the terms of trade effect on the money market into consideration then we must also consider this effect in the goods market. Here a terms of trade deterioration leads via a decrease in real income to a negative effect on aggregate demand. Hence, a devaluation-induced terms-of-trade effect has opposite influences on aggregate demand via the money and the goods markets. The negative effect via the money supply side can be mitigated or even overcompensated if the devaluation is accompanied by an increase in the nominal money stock. Even with no improvement in the current account, the overall balance of payments can improve and the net foreign reserves of the central bank can increase if a huge short term capital reflux takes place after devaluation. According to international portfolio theory there will be a capital import after a devaluation; the likelihood and magnitude of this reflux increases as people expect the devaluation to be successful. The increase in the central banks' net foreign position leads to an increase in the nominal money supply unless the central bank sterilizes this effect by reducing domestic credit. Connolly's empirical results show that in most of the countries the balance of payments improved after devaluation and furthermore in most of the countries there was a deceleration in domestic credit expansion after devaluation. But this deceleration in domestic credit only partly offset the expansionary monetary effect of the balance of payments improvement. So there was a net positive effect on the nominal money supply.

Here I think we arrive at an important point concerning the impact of a devaluation

---

[1] Though it is well known from international trade theory that a country which is small compared to the rest of the world can hardly change its terms of trade by a devaluation of its currency, empirical evidence tells us that at least in the short run even in small countries the terms of trade are not unaffected by a devaluation. The main reason for this is the existence of various market imperfections.

on economic activity at home. When the economy is not in a deep depression, the chance that a devaluation will improve the current account at least in the medium or in the long run increases if the devaluation is accompanied by a tight monetary and fiscal policy. Tot the extent such policy measures reduce home demand for domestically produced goods, the devaluation-induced foreign demand can be satisfied. It is, on the other hand, clear that such a demand-switching policy does not increase economic activity at home via the demand side, although the devaluation is successful in improving the current account. The picture is of course different when the economy faces a deep depression so that there are idle resources on the labor market, the capital market and on the money market (the umemployed of the money market are the free liquidity reserves of the private banks). In such a situation a devaluation can be successful without being accompanied by a contractionary policy at home. In this case there will probably be more of an increase in economic activity at home. But this was not the picture in the 1960s, at least not in the developed countries.

Nevertheless this could perhaps help a little to explain Connolly's empirical results. His finding that the increase in growth — or in economic activity — is closely related to the magnitude of the previous slump could also be interpreted that the impact of a devaluation on domestic economic activity increases with the magnitude of the previous slump. I calculated the rank correlation between the previous slump, that is the last column in table 6.1, and the exchange rate change, the first column in table 6.1. The rank correlation is about 0.4 which does at least slightly support the point made here.

If all these points concerning the demand side are correct, then there is not too much room for optimism that a devaluation increases economic activity via aggregate demand in a country which does not suffer from a recession or a depression.

Now let me come to the supply side which I think is, in this context at least, as important as the demand side. How does a devaluation affect aggregate supply? I think there are three points which have to be mentioned here. First, how does a devaluation affect aggregate supply via the labor market? Second, how does a devaluation affect aggregate supply via the import of inputs or primary products and third, can there be an efficiency effect of a devaluation on aggregate supply?

To point one: let us assume first for simplicity that only consumption goods are imported. Then a devaluation increases the consumer price index according to the proportion of imports in the consumption bundle. If it is the trade unions' goal to keep real wages constant this leads to an increase in nominal wages. At given prices for home produced goods this nominal wage increase raises real labor costs. As a consequence employment and production will decrease, unless entrepreneurs are satisfied with less profit. This negative effect on the aggregate supply curve is larger the more the devaluation worsens the terms of trade. There will be no negative effect when there is either money or exchange rate illusion on the worker's side or workers refrain from wage increaes because they want to avoid a possible negative effect on employment and production. I think that a least nowadays the time of money illusion or exchange rate illusion is over, though it might have been different in the 1960s.

A voluntary sacrifice of nominal wage increases after a devaluation-induced consumer price increase is probably more likely as the slump preceding the devaluation increases. Thus, when Connolly found that the positive impact on the growth rate seems to be more related to the magnitude of the previous slump than to devaluation, then one possible explanation for this result can be that because of the previous slump the devaluation-induced increase in nominal wages may have been very moderate so that there was no or little negative effect on domestic economic activity via aggregate supply. I think it might be interesting to examine how nominal wages developed in the 1960s in the various countries, especially in the two years before and after devaluation.

Now let me briefly mention the second point. If there are not only consumption goods but also primary products or inputs imported, then a devaluation increases the price of these products so that we have in addition to the labor market effect another, negative effect on the aggregate supply curve for home produced goods. At least since the first oil price shock economists and also politicians of those countries which are very dependent on imported inputs pay particular attention to these two points. The main reason for this is that at least in the short run the import demand elasticities for these imports are rather low, while the export supply elasticities probably increase with the size of the slump. Such elasticity combinations suggest a deterioration in terms of trade after a foreign price increase for inputs or a devaluation, so that these two negative effects on the aggregate supply curve play an important role.

Now let me come to the third point, the efficiency argument of a devaluation which was first mentioned by Machlup in his famous AER article in 1955. There are many reasons for a persistent balance of payments deficit which leads finally to a devaluation. There can be changes in demand preferences on the international level or differences in the growth rates in the various countries which make a devaluation necessary. There can also be different Phillips curves or with identical Phillips curves governments can have different preferences concerning unemployment and inflation, so that an exchange rate change becomes inevitable. Whatever the reason for a balance of payments deficit, a proper devaluation leads away from a disequilibrium to an equilibrium exchange rate. This increases efficiency for several reasons so that it has a positive impact on aggregate supply. The main reason is probably that due to the devaluation the foreign exchange supply out of exports will sooner or later increase so that it is no longer necessary to ration the demand for imports. An increase in the volume of exports and imports will take place and with it the international division of labor and competition at home increases. It is clear that because of this positive efficiency effect even a more or less full employed economy can have an increase in economic activity at home after a devaluation. But a *conditio sine qua non* is that the country must conduct its internal economic policy so as to keep the exchange rate in equilibrium. If it was a loose economic policy which made the devaluation necessary — and this is the case in most devaluations — then the devaluation has to be accompanied by tight internal measures; otherwise this positive efficiency effect can hardly be called forth.

What is the resumé of my comment? First, considering all the possible effects on the aggregate demand and the aggregate supply it is rather doubtful that a devaluation *per se* will increase domestic economic activity. Connolly's empirical findings seem to support this point of view. In fact, this could be one reason why governments are so reluctant to devalue despite huge balance of payments problems.

Second, a very cautious interpretation of the empirical findings, although different from Connolly's interpretation, could at least to some extent support the hypothesis that the likelihood of a positive impact of devaluation on economic activity increases with the size of the slump before devaluation.

Third, if this interpretation is correct, then it follows that the observed negative influence of a devaluation on domestic economic activity in countries which had no slump before devaluation can be attributed to the fact that the efficiency effect did not work because the devaluation was either not large enough and/or was not accompanied by the necessary tight economic policy at home so that the currency was overvalued again soon after devaluation. From this point of view it might be interesting to see empirically whether and to what extent contractionary internal measures and exchange control liberalizations accompanied the devaluation in the various countries and to compare these findings with the change in economic activity after devaluation. Using Connolly's empirical findings I took a first little step in this direction. I calculated the rank correlation between the change in the growth rate, column 2 in table 6.1, and the decrease in the growth of domestic credit as a percentage of the money stock, which I took from fig. 6.1. So, for instance Iceland was No. 1 in deceleration of domestic credit and No. 3 in the increase in the growth rate. The calculated rank correlation is about 0.4, which I think is of some interest and supports at least to some extent the hypothesis that the positive impact of a devaluation on domestic economic activity seems to increase when it is accompanied by contractionary internal monetary measures.

Recent Issues in the Theory of Flexible Exchange Rates, edited by E. Claassen and P. Salin
© North-Holland Publishing Company, 1983

Chapter 7.1

A SMALL MACROECONOMIC MODEL OF AN OPEN ECONOMY: THE CASE OF CANADA

David LAIDLER, Brian BENTLEY, David JOHNSON and
Susan THOMPSON JOHNSON*

1. Introduction

It is a commonplace that, when it comes to the interpretation of economic history or the discussion of practical economic policy, the data do not speak for themselves. They must be organised in terms of some sort of theoretical structure. All too often that structure is an informal one, rather than being an explicit model, but there is nevertheless much to be said for discussing practical matters in terms of a fully articulated model. If policy debates are cast in such terms, it becomes much easier to recognise the extent to which differences of opinion arise from ideological considerations on the one hand, and from disagreements about the logic of economic theory or about simple matters of fact on the other.

There already exist many formal econometric models that can be used in such discussions, but these models are typically large and cumbersome. Their mechanics are extremely difficult to understand, even for those who are actively engaged in building and maintaining them, let alone for anyone else. There is frequently a "small model" underlying such large models. We often hear one block of equations being referred to as "The IS block", and another as "The LM block", when attempts are made to describe such large scale systems, but we seldom come across attempts to formulate and test explicitly the small model whose existence is implicit in such a description. However, over the last seven or eight years, one of us has been involved in a number of attempts to construct macroeconomic models that are both small scale enough to be readily comprehensible, and sufficiently relevant empirically to withstand econometric testing [see e.g. Laidler (1973), Laidler and O'Shea (1980), Laidler and Bentley (1981)].

It goes without saying that a small scale model can deal only with a few phenomena.

* We are grateful to Greg Turnidge and Susan Lawler for help with constructing some of the data used in this study, and to the Social Science and Humanities Research Council of Canada for financial support.

The models under discussion here have focussed on what one might reasonably refer to as the central issues of short run macroeconomics. They have dealt with the inter-action of inflation and output (and therefore, indirectly, unemployment), as well as with the influence of the quantity of money and various fiscal variables on these policy targets. Some of the work in question has dealt only with these factors, and hence data drawn from the relatively "closed" United States economy have been used in empirical tests [Laidler (1973), Laidler and Bentley (1981)].

It is by now well established that closed economy macroeconomics, no matter how relevant it might be (or perhaps might have been before the end of the Bretton—Woods System) to the United States, must be applied with the greatest care to more open economies. At the very least the exchange rate and the balance of payments are vari-ables of key importance in any open economy. The model developed by Laidler and O'Shea (1980), dealing as it does with the United Kingdom, recognises this fact and pays particular attention to these variables while still dealing with interactions among output, prices, and monetary and fiscal policy variables. Spinelli (1980) has shown that the very same structure seems to fit Italian data rather well, with only minimal modification, and in this paper we deal with yet a third attempt to confront the frame-work in question with empirical evidence. In the pages that follow we shall give an account of our attempts to test it against data from Canada.

This application to Canadian data is interesting for a number of reasons. First, it represents an attempt of a type not too often encountered in applied economics at replicating an empirical experiment. A model that purports to show how monetary and fiscal policy influence real income and prices in an open economy, originally developed using United Kingdom data, is confronted with evidence that did not influence its initial construction. Thus, as with Spinelli's work applying the model to Italy, so here we have something akin to a true test of the model in question. Second, and perhaps more important, the U.K. and Italian data against which the model has earlier been tested are drawn from fixed exchange rate periods. In both of these cases, it turned out to be impossible to use the model to deal with data drawn from the 1970s, when the world economy was operating a system of flexible exchange rates and when the international monetary system was in much turmoil. Canada operated a flexible exchange rate during the period 1954—1962, at a time when the world econ-omy was relatively tranquil. Thus Canadian data present us with the opportunity to discover the extent to which it was the existence of exchange rate flexibility *per se* that undermined the model in the cases of the U.K. and Italy in the 1970s and how much it was the general state of upheaval in the world economy that accounted for the difficulties in question.

As we shall see, it does turn out to be necessary to modify the model to get it to perform well in the face of Canadian data, even for the 1950s and 1960s, thus con-firming that the nature of the exchange rate regime is an important matter in deter-mining the way in which monetary and fiscal policy interact with prices and output in an open economy. We shall also see that further problems arise when attempts are made to model the early 1970s in the case of Canada, even after the model has ap-parently been adapted successfully to deal with exchange rate flexibility *per se* although these extra problems are relatively minor. Thus our results suggest that the simple adoption of exchange rate flexibility is the main source of our difficulty (and every-one else's) in dealing with data generated by the United Kingdom and Italy in the 1970s. Further comments on this conclusion will be more readily comprehensible when the model and the results of testing it have been presented, and it is to this task that we now turn.

2. The basic model

Detailed descriptions of the basic framework that generated the results to be present-ed below, and of its analytic properties, are already available in Laidler and O'Shea (1980) and Spinelli (1980) and there is no need to repeat all the relevant analysis here. Nevertheless it will be convenient if we first of all set out the model as it was used in those two papers. The reader may then make up his own mind about how basic are the modifications which we have made to it in order to deal with data generated under a flexible exchange rate regime.

The basic model is in the tradition of open economy monetarism and was designed to cope with data generated under fixed exchange rates. Thus the interaction of the balance of payments with the supply and demand for money, and the interaction of actual and expected inflation rates with fluctuations in real income, are its key ingre-dients. The model is log linear in form, and may be set out as follows:

$$y = \alpha_1 (m_s - m_d)_{-1} + \alpha_2 (\pi + e + a - p)_{-1} + \alpha_3 t_{-1} + \alpha_4 g, \tag{1}$$

$$\Delta r = \gamma_1 (m_s - m_d)_{-1} + \gamma_2 (\pi + e + a - p)_{-1}, \tag{2}$$

$$m_d = \delta_0 + \delta_1 y^* + p, \tag{3}$$

$$\Delta p = \beta y_{-1} + (p^e - p)_{-1}, \tag{4}$$

$$(p^e - p) = \epsilon_1 \Delta \pi + \epsilon_2 (\pi + e + a - p), \tag{5}$$

$$\Delta m_s = (1 - \mu) \Delta c + \mu \Delta r, \tag{6}$$

$$y^* = \theta_0 + \theta_1 \tau. \tag{7}$$

The variables used above are all, with the exception of τ (time) logarithms, and are defined as follows: y the transitory component of the log of real income; m_s the log of the nominal money supply; m_d the log of the long-run quantity of nominal money demanded; π the log of the price level ruling in the world economy; e the log of ex-change rate or price of foreign currency; p the log of the domestic price level; p^e the value that the log of the domestic price level is expected to take next period; t the deviation of the log of the economy's average tax rate from trend; g the deviation of the log of government expenditure from trend; r the log of the stock of foreign exchange reserves; y^* the permanent component of the log of income; c the log of domestic credit extended by the consolidated banking system; and a a constant to be described below.

Equation (1) may be regarded as a reduced form of an income expenditure system that tells us that deviations of output from its "permanent" level (or "natural" level, the concepts are interchangeable in this model) depend upon the size of any difference between the supply of money on the one hand and the long run demand for money on the other, the deviation of domestic prices from some equilibrium value relative to world prices and the exchange rate (with units of measurement chosen so that the equilibrium value of that relative price term is zero) and the deviation of the tax rate and government expenditure from trend. In fact, eq. (1) is a log linear approximation to the following, more conventionally expressed, relationship, where capital letters are used to indicate the natural values of the relevant variables, with C being real consumption, I investment, and X net exports. The approximation in question is obtained by linearising the logarithmic form of the relationship about the steady state values of the logarithms of the variables following a procedure set out in Wymer (1976).

$$Y = (C + I + X) + G = k \left[\frac{M_s^{\alpha_1^1}}{M_d} \cdot \frac{\Pi}{P} E^{\alpha_2^1} \cdot T^{\alpha_3^1} \right]_{-1} Y^* + G. \tag{8}$$

The parameters of eq. (1) bear the following relationships to those of eq. (8):

$$\alpha_1 = k\alpha_1^1, \quad \alpha_2 = k\alpha_2^1, \quad \alpha_3 = k\alpha_3^1, \quad \alpha_4 = 1 - k.$$

It is worth noting two points explicitly here. First, to enter fiscal policy variables as deviations from trend, as we have done here, while making permanent, or steady state, income solely a function of time *imposes* long-run crowding out of fiscal policy on the behaviour of the model, while leaving short-run crowding out open as an empirical matter. Second, the relative price level term includes a constant a: in our empirical work, prices and the exchange rate are measured as index numbers with a base of $1970 = 1$ so their logs are zero in that year, and the constant a is thus a measure of the proportion by which the home currency, in this case the Canadian dollar, was undervalued in 1970.

Equation (2) is an equation that determines the balance of official settlements concept of the balance of payments and makes it depend upon the excess supply of money, as well as upon relative price levels and the exchange rate. Equation (3) tells us that the long run demand for real money balances depends upon permanent income, and omits an opportunity cost argument. This last omission might disturb some readers, but the following points should be noted. First, and most important, because this is a model in which the economy is allowed to be "off" its long run demand for money function, to leave an interest rate out of this relationship does not, as it would in a conventional IS–LM framework, ensure that only money matters as far as the determination of real income and prices is concerned. Second, some preliminary work carried out using ordinary least squares on eq. (1) suggests that to add an interest rate to the demand for money function makes no important difference to the results obtained for other parameters of the system, a conclusion that receives further support from the work of Laidler and Bentley (1981) on United States data. Third, and of considerable importance, the omission of interest rates from the model enables us to keep the structure simple. Were such a variable included, the model would have to be extended in order to cope with its determination, and that would be no easy matter. Finally, in omitting the interest rate from our model, we do not imply that that variable is unimportant in the transmission mechanism of monetary policy. The model may be interpreted as ignoring interest rate variations, not because they do not matter, but because they are an intermediate step in that mechanism. Equation (4) is a conventional expectations augmented Phillips curve while eq. (5) tells us that inflation expectations depend both upon the rate of inflation ruling in the world economy, and on the deviation of the domestic price level from its long-run equilibrium level. Equation (6) is a standard log linear approximation to the money supply identity while eq. (7) defines the permanent, or natural, component of the logarithm of income as being given by a simple time trend.

The only differences between the model set out above and that fitted already by Laidler and O'Shea, and Spinelli to U.K. and Italian data lie in some minor adjustments to eqs. (2) and (6) that were made to adapt the textbook money supply identity to the accounting conventions actually used in generating U.K. and Italian balance of payments data. The model was further modified in both studies in the following ways in the light of empirical results. In the case of the U.K. the parameter α_1 turned out to be zero, indicating that the only measurable effects of monetary policy in that country over the period studied were on the balance of payments, while the parameter ϵ_1 was estimated so close to unity that it was constrained to take that value; in the case of Italy the role of relative price levels in the output equation turned out to be better determined if the term was entered unlagged, while the "catch up" parameter ϵ_2 in the inflation expectations equation turned out to be zero and ϵ_1 took a unit value as in the British case, indicating that the Italian price level had never deviated far enough from equilibrium *vis-à-vis* the rest of the world for a catch up effect to be measurable. This result contrasted with the U.K. case where the 1967 devaluation caused a major shock to this relationship whose subsequent influence on inflation was, statistically speaking, well determined.

Unlike the U.K. and Italy, Canada operated a flexible exchange rate regime for much of the period 1954–1970, and so the question must arise as to whether the framework set out here needs any modification in the light of this fact. This is, of course, an empirical question. The exchange rate appears on the right-hand side of three of our equations and there is nothing in the pure logic of our model to stop us treating it "as if" an exogenous variable for estimation purposes. Even so, it is one thing to say that it is logically possible to formulate the model in this way, but quite another to say that the procedure will yield sensible results, and as we shall see in a moment, it emphatically did not in this case. Before turning to this, and other, aspects of our empirical work, however, we must first of all say something about the data we have used.

3. The data

The data from which our empirical results are derived are straight-forward enough and are listed in the Appendix. The output variable upon which y and y^* are based is real gross domestic product. The price variable is the consumer price index, chosen because it is the index most readily comparable with the data upon which our world price level variable is based. The latter variable is a GNP weighted geometric average of the consumer or retail price indices of sixteen other countries, while the exchange rate, defined as the domestic currency price of foreign currency, is a similarly weighted index of the individual exchange rates on the same sixteen countries. A considerable amount of effort was devoted at an early stage of our work to investigating whether or not the use of trade weights would make any difference to the outcome of experiments involving these "world economy" variables. In the case of Canada the choice between GNP and trade weights makes virtually no difference to the series, since with either set of weights United States' data dominate the index.

The government expenditure and tax variables which we use appertain to federal, provincial and local government activities. As with the output series, they represent deviations of the logs of the variables in question from trends fitted by ordinary least squares to the original data. Care was taken to ensure that time patterns of these series were not heavily dependent on the choice of years over which the original trends were fitted. They do not seem to be, and in every case the variables used in our study are deviations from a log linear trend fitted to the period 1952–1975.

Our money supply series is for a "broad" M3 definition of money, and this choice was made for three reasons. First, and least important, broad money variables were used by Laidler and O'Shea in dealing with Britain and Spinelli in dealing with Italy, and there seemed to be some point in maintaining this practice to facilitate comparisons among the modelling exercises in question. Second, and crucially, as we have already noted, our model's demand for money function contains no opportunity cost variable. We believe that the demand for a broad definition of money, encompassing as it does many interest-bearing assets, is relatively insensitive to this omission, and preliminary experiments with ordinary least squares confirmed that the addition of an interest rate variable to the demand for money equation used in this model made an, at best, marginal improvement to its explanatory power. Laidler and Bentley (1981) have investigated this same question in the course of their work on the U.S. economy with a closed economy version of this type of model, and their results further confirm this conclusion. Third, ours is an open economy model that seeks to exploit the basic balance sheet identities of the banking system. It is easier to do this when a broad definition of money is utilized, given the way in which published data are put together.

As it is, it is precisely when we come to deal with these balance sheet identities that our data are less than straightforward. In the simple textbook open economy monetary model, an equation such as (2) determines the balance on official settlements concept of the balance of payments, and this in turn is usually treated as identical with the change in the banking system's holdings of foreign exchange reserves. In the real world, a number of problems intrude to make matters more complex. First, official borrowing and lending overseas is an alternative to reserve movements as a means of financing payments inbalances, and second, the domestic currency value of foreign exchange reserves varies as a result of exchange rate changes.

Our solution to the accounting difficulties posed by these facts is essentially the same as that adopted by Jonson (1976) and followed by Laidler and O'Shea. Our "reserve" series is constructed by starting in a benchmark year and then adding to the value of reserves observed in that year the current Canadian dollar value of the balance of official settlements concept of the balance of payments observed in the next and each successive year. This practice ensures that the proportional change in reserves variable on the left-hand side of eq. (2) is appropriately measured. The money supply identity, to which eq. (6) is a log linear approximation, is then preserved by subtracting our reserves variable from the money supply to generate a series for domestic credit. The latter variable is treated as exogenous in our model, and all changes in foreign exchange reserves arising from exchange rate changes that were at any time permitted to influence the money supply rather than the net worth of the banking system are hence included in it. They are thus treated as exogenous, as we believe they should be. The money stock, domestic credit, and reserves figures are end period statistics, as they should be, given the timing of the flow data in our model.

The only other variable used in our empirical work is the deviation of the logarithm of U.S. real GNP from trend. This variable was introduced into our work at a rather late stage, and its role is best discussed in the context of the relevant empirical results. Suffice it to say for the moment that this variable was generated in exactly the same way as the Canadian output and fiscal variables by fitting a log linear trend to real GNP data for the period 1952–1975, and taking deviations from that trend.

4. A test of the basic model

We now turn to a discussion of the results generated by our attempts to fit the model described in section 2 above, to annual data on the Canadian economy for the period 1954–1970. Implicit in the model's structure are a number of constraints on parameter values both within and across equations. Therefore, as in virtually all our empirical work, we used full information maximum likelihood techniques to fit the model as a whole, employing programs originally developed by Dr. Clifford Wymer.

The model as actually estimated is obtained by substituting eqs. (3) and (5) in the relevant places, and, because eq. (7) determining "permanent" income as a time trend was estimated first and the relevant variable entered as exogenously measured, consists of four equations.

These are:

$$y = (\alpha_1 \delta_0 + \alpha_2 a) + \alpha_1 (m_s - p - \delta_1 y^*)_{-1} +$$
$$+ \alpha_2 (\pi + e - p)_{-1} + \alpha_3 t + \alpha_4 g, \tag{9}$$

$$\Delta r = (\gamma_1 \delta_0 + \gamma_2 a) + \gamma_1 (m_s - p - \delta_1 y^*)_{-1} + \gamma_2 (\pi + e - p)_{-1}, \tag{10}$$

$$\Delta p = \beta y_{-1} + \epsilon_1 \Delta \pi + \epsilon_2 (\pi + e - p) + \epsilon_2 a, \tag{11}$$

$$\Delta m_s = (1 - \mu) \Delta c + \mu \Delta r. \tag{12}$$

Table 7.1 presents the results of estimating this model (using annual Canadian data for the period 1954–1970). It presents a set of parameter estimates for the model with the figures in brackets underneath the parameters being asymptotic standard errors. These are the results obtained when the same form of the model as fitted by Laidler and O'Shea to U.K. data was used. That model, set out above, clearly does not perform in a satisfactory way, thus suggesting strongly that simply to treat Canada "as if" it were a fixed exchange rate economy that had a large number of "exogenous" exchange rate changes over the period in question will not do. Note in particular that the parameters of the demand for money function are nonsense, and that only the parameters α_2 and α_4 are of the correct sign at convention levels of statistical significance as far as eq. (1) is concerned. As to the Phillips curve, the parameter ϵ_1, which ought not to be different from unity, clearly is, while the balance of payments equation fails completely. All in all, the attempt to replicate the results obtained by Laidler and O'Shea and Spinelli using Canadian data fails miserably.

Table 7.1
Parameter estimates based on the original model: 1954–1970.

δ_0	14.445 (72.330)	β	0.162 (0.061)
δ_1	−3.450 (20.946)	ϵ_1	0.492 (0.120)
α_1	−0.023 (0.115)	ϵ_2	0.152 (0.044)
α_2	0.556 (0.141)	γ_1	0.022 (0.108)
α_3	−0.118 (0.075)	γ_2	−0.173 (0.559)
α_4	0.462 (0.129)	a	0.146 (0.026)
		μ	0.122 (0.009)

5. Modifying the model

This failure of our first attempt to replicate U.K. and Italian results using Canadian data is perhaps not all that surprising, because in estimating our model we have treated years of flexible and fixed exchange rates identically. That is to say the results presented in table 7.1 are, among other things, based upon the hypothesis that the exchange rate regime makes no difference to the behavior of the economy, and this is a dubious hypothesis to say the least. As we shall now show, some rather simple modifications to the model, designed to account for the differences between fixed and flexible exchange rate regimes, lead to a remarkable improvement in its empirical performance.

We made two changes to the structure of the model in order to deal with the flexible exchange rate years.

(1) The first of these involved the hypothesis that, under a fixed exchange rate, inflation expectations are given by eq. (5) but that under a flexible rate, they could usefully be modelled as depending solely on domestic factors. We took the lagged value of the domestic inflation rate as an appropriate variable to use here. According to the monetarist style analysis from which our model is derived, inflation in an open economy is determined abroad if the economy operates a fixed exchange rate, and at home if it operates a flexible rate. This is a plausible, and indeed obvious, modification to make to our basic model. Thus eq. (5) was modified to take the form

$$p^e - p = \epsilon_1((1 - D)\Delta\pi + D\Delta p) + (1 - D)\epsilon_2(\pi + e + a - p). \qquad (5)$$

where D is a dummy variable taking the value 1 when a flexible exchange rate regime was in place and zero when the exchange rate was fixed. We investigated this equation's properties by substituting it into eq. (4), the Phillips curve, and estimating the resulting expression with ordinary least squares. This investigation confirmed (i) that the formulation was not obviously inappropriate, (ii) that the parameter ϵ_1 was roughly equal to unity, (iii) that the Phillips curve equation's performance was indeed improved by switching between expectations proxies as the exchange rate regime changed. As we shall note below, the first two of these three conclusions hold up well when the question is estimated as part of the complete system, while the third finds a certain amount of marginal support as well.

(2) If the level of the exchange rate cannot be treated as an exogenous variable when rates are flexible, then at such times one's first inclination would be to treat it as the appropriate dependent variable for an equation such as (2). Unfortunately, though textbook models can and do take it that reserve changes are equal to zero when the exchange rate is flexible, the real world does not behave in that way. Here therefore we followed Girton and Roper (1977), in arguing that pressure on the foreign exchange market can manifest itself both in reserve losses and exchange depreciation. They further argue that it is appropriate to define a variable called "exchange market

pressure" (EMP) as the sum of the change in log of reserves and the change in the log of the exchange rate, and we used such a variable as the dependent variable of eq. (2) for both fixed and flexible exchange rate periods, thus:

$$\text{EMP} \equiv \Delta r - \Delta e = \gamma_1 (m_s - m_d)_{-1} + \gamma_2 (\pi + e + a - p) \tag{2'}$$

Girton and Roper treat exchange market pressure as the simple sum of the percentage change in the exchange rate and the percentage change in reserves, but, because we could think of no compelling *a priori* reason why this should be the case in the context of our model, we experimented extensively with versions of our model which allowed exchange market pressure to be a weighted sum of the two variables, with the weights in question being estimated as part of the model. It turned out that the data seldom rejected the hypothesis of equal weights, and that the results for other parameters in the system were not affected in any important, or statistically significant, way by what we did here. Thus the results we actually present are in fact based upon this simplifying, and as it turned out, innocuous assumption.

When eq. (2) is modified in the way just described, it becomes a moot point as to whether the model is still "complete". As far as the fixed exchange rate regime is concerned, it certainly is, because exchange rate changes were to all intents and purposes zero during the 1963–1969 period – the one exception being provided by the influence of the British devaluation of 1967, but that was clearly exogenous. For flexible rate years the question is more open. Certainly the float of the 1954–1962 period was not a clean one, and it is arguable that, with exchange market pressure in any year being determined by an equation such as (2'), the authorities decided in each instance how much of that pressure to absorb by reserve changes and how much by an exchange rate change. This in effect is to argue that this division is the result of a decision exogenous to the model. However, it is natural to ask whether or not there might not exist some systematic principles underlying such a decision that could be captured in a well determined policy reaction function.

We did expend a considerable amount of energy investigating this matter, but to no avail. Thus, the empirical results that we present below are to be interpreted, depending on the taste of the reader, either as resting on the hypothesis that during the floating rate period, the division of exchange market pressure between reserves and exchange rate changes was at the exogenous discretion of the authorities, or that it was determined by an as yet undiscovered policy reaction function. Those who choose the latter alternative will, of course, be more skeptical about the results that we present than those willing to accept the former. They will also note that our treatment of domestic credit expansion as an exogenous variable, independent of the fiscal variables, is a further symptom of our inability to find a simple way of rendering monetary policy endogenous in this model.

The two modifications we have just described proved sufficient to enable the model to generate sensible estimates for most parameters, with the bulk of the improvement arising from the introduction of exchange market pressure as the dependent variable in eq. (5). Nevertheless, the parameter ϵ_2, representing what we have termed the "catch up" factor in inflation expectations under fixed exchange rates, remained essentially equal to zero in all these experiments, seldom becoming larger than 0.1, and always being considerably smaller than its standard error once exchange market pressure became the dependent variable of eq. (2). Thus, at this stage the parameter in question was dropped from the model although it was from time to time reintroduced in subsequent work in order to ensure that its absence was not affecting the outcome of the experiments in question. These spot checks confirmed our earlier decision to exclude it. The reader might note that in having expectations solely determined by past domestic inflation under flexible rates, our model rules out the exchange rate from playing a role in the transmission mechanism of domestic monetary policy to inflation under flexible rates. We will return to this matter below in section 6.

As did Laidler and O'Shea in dealing with U.K. data, so we too attempted to add a number of other variables to various equations of our model in order to check the robustness of our results. In particular we added lagged domestic transitory income to the output equation (to pick up potential multiplier effects) and to the exchange market pressure equation (to pick up propensity to import effects). We also added U.S. transitory income to these two equations to pick up any direct links between U.S. income fluctuations and Canadian output and exchange market pressure. By and large, the addition and subtraction of various permutations and combinations of these variables did not disturb the estimates we obtained for the other parameters of the model, the exception here being the fiscal policy parameters α_3 and α_4 whose statistical significance is higher when the various lagged income variables are omitted from eq. (1), the problem here obviously being one of multicollinearity.

Be that as it may, lagged domestic income turned out to be potentially important in the output equations, but not in the balance of payments, while lagged U.S. income turned out to influence significantly only the balance of payments. The parameters of these variables are α_5 and γ_4 respectively and estimates of them appear in table 7.2. The two variables in question are highly correlated with one another, of course, and the reader might note that, because the programmes used to estimate the model do not tell us anything about the serial correlation properties of the residuals generated by the model, the presence of lagged transitory income in eq. (1) might simply be picking up first order serial correlation in the residuals from that equation. It is worth repeating, therefore, that nothing of any importance as far as the rest of the model is concerned hinges upon the presence of these variables, so that the reader who is suspicious of the role that they are playing should not discount the rest of our results for this reason.

The results presented in table 7.2 largely speak for themselves. The demand for money function is well determined with *a priori* reasonable estimate of the income elasticity of demand for money. The parameter α_1 satisfies tests based on conventional levels of statistical significance and this result suggests that monetary disequilibrium has exerted a systematic influence on domestic output, while an important role for fiscal policy in influencing output is confirmed by the statistical significance of the

Table 7.2
Parameter estimates based on the modified model: 1954–1970.

δ_0	−1.657 (0.628)	β	0.122 (0.055)
δ_1	1.212 (0.170)	ϵ_1	1.016 (0.079)
α_1	0.276 (0.135)	ϵ_2	− −
α_2	0.522 (0.141)	γ_1	−0.529 (0.299)
α_3	−0.216 (0.087)	γ_2	−0.149 (0.388)
α_4	0.275 (0.131)	γ_4	0.983 (0.540)
α_5	0.417 (0.142)	a	0.088 (0.026)
		μ	0.157 (0.007)

parameters α_3 and α_4. The level of prices in Canada relative to that in the rest of the world also displays a well determined influence on output. Excess demand systematically influences inflation, while the expected rate of inflation influences current inflation with the theoretically predicted unit coefficient.

The weakest equation of the model is that dealing with exchange market pressure, for although domestic monetary disequilibrium does produce a correctly signed though not too well determined effect here, the relative price level term takes a negative sign, albeit not significantly so. Although this result does not contradict anything in economic theory, it does differ from the well determined positive influence that Laidler and O'Shea found for the U.K. This absence of a relative price level effect in the balance of payments is not a characteristic only of the results presented here but turned up in all our experiments with various forms of the model and presents an as yet unresolved puzzle that merits further investigation. Spinelli encountered similar problems, though not so acutely, in the case of Italy.

Of the variables added to our basic model, the only one whose presence creates something of a problem of interpretation is United States' transitory income. This variable is on the margin of significance in the exchange market pressure equation but was never significant to the output equation. If this variable was capturing a simple Keynesian marginal propensity of the U.S. to import Canadian goods, one would have expected it to appear in both equations. Our tentative suggestion is that it is standing, instead, as a proxy for the influence of U.S. monetary disequilibrium on the capital account of the balance of payments, but we have not as yet carried out any work to check this conjecture. It should be noted that the coefficient μ which measures the share of "reserves" in the assets that match the money supply is of an appropriate order of magnitude. Moreover the estimate of a suggests that the Canadian dollar was undervalued by a little under 9 per cent in 1970. Given that Canada had not by then imported much of the Vietnam War inflation from the United States, but was in that year forced by balance of payments pressures to float the dollar (upwards) this estimate is not obviously wrong, though one might argue that, if anything, it somewhat exaggerates the degree of overvaluation ruling at the time.

Perhaps the most striking thing about the results presented in table 7.2 is the way in which relatively small modifications to the original model, introduced in order to cope with exchange rate flexibility, cause the results to fall into line. Indeed, given the well determined effects of the quantity of money on domestic output, and the sensible estimate of the income elasticity of demand for money, it is possible to make the case that the framework under test here actually fits the Canadian data rather better than it does the United Kingdom data in terms of which it was first developed by Laidler and O'Shea. They could find no well determined effect of money on domestic output, and their estimate of the permanent income elasticity of demand for money was implausibly low.

However, the question must naturally arise as to whether this relatively good performance is merely accidental or rather will hold up in the face of further modifications to the model. We shall now turn to discussing some further experiments which we carried out with our model, and as the reader will see, our basic results do hold up quite well in the face of such further testing.

6. Further tests

It is often remarked that the nature of the inflation—unemployment trade off in an open economy is crucially different given the nature of the exchange rate regime, and our model provides a vehicle, even though a crude one, for investigating this question. As we have already noted, one characteristic of the model which generated the results presented in table 7.2 is that the expected inflation rate is proxied by lagged world inflation under a fixed exchange rate, and lagged domestic inflation under a flexible exchange rate. To see how important this modification actually was to the outcome of our empirical work, we tried the experiment of using each proxy in turn for the entire sample period. Here the results were indecisive, and therefore disappointing. Neither of these two variants of the model gave results that were *quite* as well determined as those presented in table 7.2 but the deterioration in the model's overall performance was on the whole trivial. In particular the coefficient ϵ_1 remained equal to unity and well determined in either case, and although the statistical significance of the parameter β linking excess demand to inflation did fall off notably, the rest of the model remained essentially unchanged. Indeed the deterioration of β was the only characteristic of the results that could be used to defend the proposition that it is important to model inflation expectations separately for fixed and flexible exchange rate periods. We must conclude therefore that both the world and Canadian economies were too

Table 7.3
Further modifications to the model.

δ_0	−1.679 (0.553)	β	0.204 (0.043)
δ_1	1.216 (0.149)	ϵ_1	1.306 (0.081)
α_1	0.306 (0.129)	ϵ_3	0.622 (0.084)
α_2	0.604 (0.137)	γ_1	−0.656 (0.324)
α_3	−0.217 (0.083)	γ_2	0.359 (0.440)
α_4	0.265 (0.127)	γ_4	0.937 (0.572)
α_5	0.427 (0.142)	μ	0.156 (0.007)
		a	0.081 (0.025)

tranquil in the 1954–1970 period to generate data that would enable us to get a sharp test of the importance of this matter.

In order to check into these issues further, another experiment was carried out. Instead of forcing the parameter on world inflation under fixed rates and domestic inflation under flexible rates to be the same, they were estimated separately. The relevant results are given in table 7.3, where the parameter ϵ_1 is attached to lagged world inflation under fixed rates and ϵ_3 to lagged domestic inflation under flexible rates. The reader will see that the unit coefficient on expected inflation that appears in table 7.2 is the result of averaging two components, the new ϵ_1 which is slightly greater than unity, and ϵ_3 which is markedly below unity. He will also see that the rest of the model is insensitive to this modification. A further probe involved modelling the expected inflation rate under flexible rates not just by lagged domestic inflation, but rather by the outcome of applying the error-learning hypothesis to past domestic inflation rates. The results of doing this were not impressive. The error-learning parameter took a point estimate of 0.350, but its standard error was so large that it could not be concluded that it differed either from zero or one. All in all, the most striking feature of this test and of that reported in table 7.3 is not the evidence it generated about "new" parameters, but rather the way in which it showed that the estimates of the other parameters of the model were robust in the face of the changes made to the model's price determination equations.

In addition to those described in tables 7.1, 7.2 and 7.3, a large number of other permutations and combinations of experiments were performed with the various specifications of the model using data for 1954–1970. In particular much fruitless time and effort was put into testing various policy reaction functions designed to make exchange rate changes endogenous to the model. None of this work added anything startling, either for or against the model, to the results already presented. The reader may take it that, as far as the period 1954–1970 is concerned the results set out in tables 7.2 and 7.3 are representative of those obtained and robust in the face of many small modifications to the model.

As we noted in the introduction to this paper, one of the objects of our work was to see whether the 1970s differed from earlier times in being a flexible exchange rate period, or whether the general instability of the world economy over that period was also a factor underlying the difficulties encountered by Laidler and O'Shea and Spinelli in extending their work on the U.K. and Italy beyond 1970. Hence we also put some effort into extending our Canadian model's period of application to encompass the flexible exchange rate years 1971–1975. We found this quite a difficult task, and were never able to do so entirely satisfactorily.

Tables 7.4 and 7.5 present results for the forms of the model earlier presented in tables 7.2 and 7.3 respectively, but with these extra five years of data added. These results are typical of those we obtained. Although certain aspects of our earlier results proved quite robust, particularly as far as the output equation and the demand for money are concerned, other aspects did not. The intercept of the demand for money function, and the "undervaluation" parameter a are essentially undetermined. Since these parameters turn up in the intercepts of equations (9) and (10), this indicates that at least one of these equations is incapable of dealing with data drawn from the 1970s. In this respect our model as specified is obviously inadequate. It might be noted that our estimate of ϵ_3 is not different from 1.0 when the new data are added and to this

Table 7.4
Model as presented in table 7.2, estimated for 1954–1975.

δ_0	7.116 (656.581)	β	0.090 (0.061)
δ_1	1.197 (0.109)	ϵ_1	1.113 (0.061)
α_1	0.249 (0.094)	ϵ_3	–
α_2	0.416 (0.105)	γ_1	−0.574 (0.304)
α_3	−0.137 (0.064)	γ_2	−0.950 (0.495)
α_4	0.212 (0.107)	γ_4	1.942 (0.709)
α_5	0.264 (0.107)	μ	0.114 (0.007)
		a	5.329 (394.519)

Table 7.5
Model as presented in table 7.3 estimated for 1954–1975.

δ_0	3.507 (195.841)	β	0.083 (0.070)
δ_1	1.201 (0.112)	ϵ_1	1.093 (0.145)
α_1	0.248 (0.094)	ϵ_3	1.118 (0.073)
α_2	0.419 (0.106)	γ_1	−0.561 (0.304)
α_3	−0.138 (0.064)	γ_2	−0.935 (0.495)
α_4	0.215 (0.108)	γ_4	1.984 (0.715)
α_5	0.261 (0.107)	μ	0.114 (0.007)
		a	3.110 (116.500)

extent the model's performance is improved by their addition. Also, the improvement in the model's performance, brought about by splitting the expectations variable between fixed and flexible rate periods, which was only marginal for the 1954–1970 period, was more marked for the longer period as results not reported in detail here showed. However, against this improvement must be offset the poor performance of the parameter β as displayed in tables 7.4 and 7.5, not to mention the fact that the parameter γ_2 becomes almost significantly negative in sign.

As we noted above, one characteristic of the flexible exchange rate version of our model is troublesome. It makes inflation expectations depend solely upon the past behaviour of the domestic price level, and therefore eliminates any possibility of a line of transmission running between domestic monetary policy and prices by way of the exchange rate. As the reader will easily see, if we were to use eq. (5) as an expectations formula for flexible exchange rate periods this particular problem would not arise. Then, monetary disequilibrium would influence exchange market pressure, and to the extent that this pressure manifested itself in an exchange rate change, it would also influence domestic prices by way of the "catch-up" term in the expression determining inflation expectations. The results presented in table 7.1 suggest that this form of the model might be worth trying.

Table 7.6 presents the results of estimating our model, modified to use eq. (5) for both fixed and flexible rate periods for the years 1954–1970 and 1954–1975. These results are in some respects more satisfactory than those already described and in some ways less so. To begin with, note that certain characteristics of the model's performance are robust in the face of this change. The output equation continues to perform well —

Table 7.6
Version of the model with inflation expectations modelled according to eq. (5).

	1954–1970	1954–1975
δ_0	−3.305 (1.772)	−2.463 (0.889)
δ_1	1.718 (0.552)	1.480 (0.269)
α_1	0.168 (0.105)	0.149 (0.073)
α_2	0.824 (0.132)	0.539 (0.103)
α_3	−0.295 (0.070)	−0.171 (0.055)
α_4	0.369 (0.106)	0.312 (0.087)
α_5	0.372 (0.140)	0.273 (0.100)
β	0.132 (0.041)	0.194 (0.065)
ϵ_1	0.580 (0.118)	0.509 (0.121)
ϵ_2	0.113 (0.029)	0.168 (0.048)
γ_1	−0.295 (0.210)	−0.445 (0.253)
γ_2	−0.892 (0.517)	−1.272 (0.613)
γ_4	1.461 (0.613)	1.780 (0.697)
a	0.125 (0.023)	0.130 (0.023)
μ	0.155 (0.007)	0.119 (0.007)

with the exception of a fall off in the statistical significance of the parameter α_1 for the shorter time period. On the other hand, the parameter β, which links the inflation rate to excess demand retains its significance in this experiment even when the years 1971–1975 are added to the sample. Moreover, although γ_2 remains negative in this formulation of the model, there is no longer any difficulty in estimating the parameters δ_0 and a for the longer period. The inclusion of the latter parameter in a third equation apparently enables it to be estimated with a fair degree of precision.

The key problem with the results set out in table 6 lies with the parameter ϵ_1

which is systematically estimated at less than unity, as it was in table 7.1. A number of comments may be made about this result. To begin which, on the basis of results presented earlier, one might have thought that this estimate was produced solely by data generated during flexible exchange rate periods. However we did try a number of experiments in which ϵ_1 was estimated as a separate parameter for fixed and flexible exchange rate periods, and this turned out not to be the case. To use eq. (5) to model expectations during the flexible exchange rate years makes sufficient difference to the quantitative estimates of the other parameters of the model as to yield an estimate of significantly below unity for ϵ_1 for the fixed rate period too. It should also be pointed out that we attempted to apply the error-learning hypothesis to the world inflation rate, to see if the low parameter estimate of ϵ_1 reported in table 7.6 was the result of inflation expectations responding with a distributed lag to changes in the world inflation rate. This experiment was to no avail, because the error-learning coefficient was found to be not different from unity in this case while ϵ_1 remained well below that value.

The time periods 1954–1970 and 1954–1975 are both characterised by rising inflation in the world economy. It is, therefore, by no means impossible to take the position that our estimate of the parameter ϵ_1 might indeed give a true measure of the link between actual world inflation and expected world inflation during those periods. Perhaps agents did indeed systematically expect the world inflation rate to fall below recently experienced values over the years in question. However to accept this interpretation of our results is to argue that the estimate of ϵ_1 does not represent a structural parameter describing an aspect of the Canadian economy so much as it represents an *ex post* statistical description of the relationship between the actual and expected value of the world inflation rate over a particular time period. It is thus to argue that the formulation of the model upon which the results presented in table 7.6 are based is only partly satisfactory. All in all then, the particular modification to our model whose results we have just described cannot be regarded as any more satisfactory than earlier formulations.

7. Conclusions

By no means all of the empirical results that we have presented, or referred to, in this paper have been successful and clearcut, but it is important to maintain a certain sense of proportion here. The broad aim of the study reported in this paper was to replicate, if possible, an experiment first carried out using United Kingdom data (Laidler and O'Shea) and later Italian data (Spinelli) with information gathered from a third economy, Canada, and covering the same time period as those originally used. In this not unimportant respect our study has been in good measure successful. Once certain simple modifications were made to the basic model, which amounted to little more than recognising that, under a flexible exchange rate regime, the exchange rate cannot be treated as an exogenous variable, results at least qualitatively like those obtained elsewhere were found to hold for Canada.

A model that attributes output fluctuations mainly to variations in the quantity of money and fiscal policy does seem to account rather well for Canadian experience and indeed in this respect the model performs better for Canada than the U.K. Moreover, output fluctuations in their turn do appear to have a systematic effect on the domestic inflation rate, once due allowance is made for "expectations". Monetary factors also turn out to have an, albeit not too well determined, effect on the behaviour of the foreign exchange market. Though perhaps none of these conclusions is startling, it is nevertheless notable that so simple a model as the one we have used here can account for data on such variables drawn from three separate economies (or four if one counts the closed economy Laidler—Bentley version of the model that been used on United States data).

By no means all of our results have been positive, but even negative or indecisive results can be instructive. We expended a good deal of effort on investigating the way in which the foreign exchange rate regime has impinged upon the interaction of output and prices in Canada, but the results we have obtained here cannot be regarded as being more than suggestive. Our initial hypothesis was that to allow foreign inflation to influence domestic inflation under fixed rates but not under flexible rates would permit a more satisfactory explanations of the relevant data. The results we obtained here were, unfortunately, disappointing. They were consistent with this hypothesis, but, particularly for the 1954—1970 period the improvement in our model's performance which arose from the modification in question was trivial. Moreover we have seen that to use the original "world inflation plus a catch-up" hypothesis, as used by Laidler and O'Shea, to capture inflation expectations throughout the sample period enables us to produce results that in some respects are satisfactory and in some respects are not.

In the light of these indecisive results it is hard to resist the conclusion that our, admittedly rudimentary, efforts at modelling the formation of inflation expectations in an open economy under alternative exchange rate regimes have been inadequate. Of course the whole of the literature on the "rational expectations" hypothesis tells us that the next step in such an investigation ought to involve incorporation of information about the conduct of policy into the formation of expectations. Our inability, noted above, to find any simple policy reaction function which could be incorporated in our model, however, has precluded us from making even a preliminary investigation along these lines.

One reason for using Canadian data in order to test the model underlying this paper was that this might permit us to isolate the effects of exchange rate flexibility *per se* on the model's performance from those of the instability in the international economy that so dominates the data drawn from the early 1970s. In this respect our results are of some interest, because although the addition of the years 1971—75 to our sample did increase the difficulties we encountered in our empirical work, this addition stopped far short of destroying the model's viability as it had done in the case of Laidler and O'Shea's work on the United Kingdom. In some formulations of the model the difficulties we encountered were confined to estimating a couple of intercept terms, and in one formulation — whose results are set out in table 7.6 — extending the sample period created no difficulties that were not already present in the short period results. All this suggests that the structure of the model we have been testing is rather robust both with respect to changes in the exchange rate regime, and with respect to changes in the stability of the world economy. Certainly our model proved more robust in this respect than we initially expected. Nevertheless, we did, as we have already pointed out, run into difficulties, particularly as far as modelling inflation expectations are concerned. In this respect our exercise has been relatively unsuccessful. However, it is easy enough to suggest further lines of enquiry that would be worth pursuing and which might solve these problems.

First, we have already noted that the modelling of the policy formation process needs to be carried out successfully if further progress is to be made in dealing with expectations. Perhaps just as important is the matter of dealing with the influence of the rest of the world on the home economy. In the exercises we have described in this paper, that "rest of the world" has been described by a price level variable and a United States real income variable, both of which have been treated as exogenous. Obviously, these variables are themselves generated by economic processes in the rest of the world which could themselves be modelled along the lines which we have followed in dealing with the home country Canada. It would be an interesting endeavour, though by no means an easy one, to build a "rest of the world" model that could be linked through the exchange market pressure equation, and perhaps the expectations equation as well, to a home country model such as we have described here.

To sum up, some of the key characteristics of the model under test in this paper have survived confrontation with data from yet another country and with data generated under a flexible exchange rate, and this is not an unimportant result. In some respects, however, notably in the treatment of inflation expectations, our model has proved fragile and clearly needs further, perhaps quite extensive work. Thus, though we hope that the results we have described in this paper are interesting, they should be regarded as the outcome of work still in progress rather than of work which purports to provide a definitive account of the interaction of prices, output, the exchange rate and the balance of payments in the post-Korean-war Canadian economy.

Appendix
Data 1952–1975.

	Real GDP ($ billion)	Consumer prices (1970 = 100)	World prices (1970 = 100)	Exchange rate ($/FCU 1975 = 100)	Money supply ($ Canadian billion)	Reserves ($ Canadian billion)	Domestic credit ($ Canadian billion)	Real government expenditure ($ Canadian billion)	Taxes as a proportion of GDP
1952	31.84	69.5	64.5	96.8	9.26			5.21	0.176
1953	33.46	68.9	65.0	97.1	9.32	1.75	7.57	5.55	0.174
1954	33.57	69.3	65.5	96.2	10.14	1.88	8.26	5.52	0.161
1955	36.93	69.4	65.7	97.3	10.88	1.38	9.50	5.82	0.164
1956	40.65	70.5	67.0	97.1	11.19	1.88	9.31	6.28	0.172
1957	41.38	72.7	68.7	94.3	11.50	1.77	9.73	6.29	0.166
1958	41.63	74.7	71.0	94.7	12.93	1.89	11.04	6.50	0.137
1959	43.48	75.5	71.9	92.5	12.79	1.87	10.92	6.59	0.149
1960	44.75	76.4	73.2	93.4	13.40	1.47	11.57	6.91	0.146
1961	45.84	77.2	74.2	97.9	14.58	2.13	12.45	7.24	0.164
1962	49.14	78.1	76.0	103.5	15.12	2.28	12.84	7.59	0.168
1963	51.83	79.4	77.9	104.6	16.15	2.42	13.73	7.81	0.166
1964	55.25	80.9	79.6	104.6	17.35	2.78	14.57	8.29	0.179
1965	59.05	82.8	81.8	104.6	19.34	2.94	16.40	8.88	0.187
1966	63.75	85.9	84.6	104.5	20.58	2.59	17.99	9.96	0.199
1967	66.06	89.0	87.0	103.3	23.68	2.60	21.08	10.96	0.202
1968	69.30	92.6	90.4	103.2	27.19	2.96	24.23	11.92	0.209
1969	73.12	96.8	94.7	100.0	27.91	3.02	24.89	12.75	0.224
1970	75.43	100.0	100.0	97.5	31.16	4.56	26.60	14.46	0.221
1971	80.53	102.8	104.9	99.7	36.35	5.33	31.02	15.49	0.214
1972	86.01	107.8	109.5	106.2	41.42	5.55	35.87	16.31	0.207
1973	94.76	115.9	117.7	102.3	49.03	5.08	43.95	17.22	0.205
1974	102.85	128.6	132.5	107.6	57.44	5.10	52.34	18.68	0.212
1975	105.87	142.5	145.8		67.38	4.70	62.68	20.16	0.172

Data sources

Real GDP.   *International Financial Statistics.* May 1977, line 99b deflated by consumer prices.

Consumer prices.   *International Financial Statistics.* May 1977, line 64, rebased on 1970 = 100.

World prices.   A GDP weighted average of the Consumer Price index of sixteen Industrial Countries: Australia; Austria; Belgium; Denmark; France; Ireland; Italy; Japan; Netherlands; New Zealand; Norway; South Africa; Sweden; Switzerland; United States; West Germany. Data from *International Financial Statistics.* May 1977.

Exchange rate.   A GDP weighted average of the Canadian dollar price of the currencies of sixteen industrial countries as listed above. Data from *International Financial Statistics*, May 1977.

Money supply.   Currency plus privately held Canadian dollar deposits at chartered banks. End of period. *Source*: Bank of Canada mimeo.

Reserves.   1953 Canadian dollar value of Official International Reserves. Thereafter the series is generated by adding Series for "Net Official Monetary Movements". (CANSIM No. B50212) net of any allocation of Special Drawing Rights (CANSIM No. D50210).

Domestic credit.   Money supply − reserves, as defined above.

Real government expenditures.   Outlays of Federal, Provincial, and Local Governments for currently produced goods and services. 1952−1970 *National Income and Expenditure Accts.* 1926−1974 (13−531). 1971−1975 *National Income and Expenditure Accts.* 1978 4th Quarter.

Taxes as a proportion of GDP.   Total Federal, Provincial and Local Government revenue minus current transfers divided by GDP. Data from *National Income Expenditure Accounts*, as above.

References

Girton, L. and D. Roper, 1977, A monetary model of exchange market pressure applied to the post-war Canadian experience, American Economic Review 67, 537−548.
Jonson, P.D., 1976, Money and economic activity in the open economy. The United Kingdom 1880−1970, Journal of Political Economy 84, 979−1012.
Laidler, D.E.W., 1973, The influence of money on real income and inflation − a simple model with some empirical evidence for the United States, 1963−1972, Manchester School 41.
Laidler, D.E.W. and P. O'Shea, 1980, An empirical macromodel of an open economy under fixed exchange rates: The United Kingdom, 1954−1970, Economica 47, 141−158.

Laidler, D.E.W. and B. Bentley, 1981, A small macro-model of the post-war United States, University of Western Ontario Research Report, no. 8101, mimeo.

Spinelli, F., 1979, Fixed exchange rates and monetarism — the Italian case, University of Western Ontario Research Report, no. 7915, mimeo.

Wymer, C.R., 1976, Linearisation of non-linear system — Supplement no. 15, Computer Programmes, London School of Economics, mimeo.

Recent Issues in the Theory of Flexible Exchange Rates, edited by E. Claassen and P. Salin
© *North-Holland Publishing Company, 1983*

Chapter 7.2

COMMENT ON LAIDLER, BENTLEY, JOHNSON AND JOHNSON

Herwig LANGOHR

Laidler, Bentley, David Johnson and Susan Thompson Johnson (LBJJ) estimate the small analogue economy model designed to replicate inflation and transitory income behaviour of the United Kingdom (Laidler and O'Shea, 1980) fixed exchange rate regime of 1954–1970 on Canadian data for the same period. That model, they find, "clearly does not perform in a satisfactory way, thus suggesting strongly that simply to treat Canada 'as if' it were a fixed exchange rate economy that had a large number of 'exogenous' exchange rate changes over the period in question will not do" (LBJJ, section 4). This finding is not surprising, as in fact Canada operated from 1954 to 1962, the first half of the total sample period, with a flexible exchange rate. To improve the replicating performance of the analogue economy, LBJJ make three successive specification changes in it and report each time the estimation results for different sample periods.

Before commenting on the empirical results, it will be useful to highlight the key characteristics of the LBJJ models. Designed to be "readily comprehensible" and standard in appearance, the LBJJ hypothesis is in fact complex and novel. These features are best pointed out in three stages. The system represented by eqs. (1) through (7) is first simplified to a closed economy case. Its open economy benchmarks are analyzed next. Lastly, the modified open economy model, in which eqs. (2') and (5') are substituted for (2) and (5) respectively, is discussed.

The closed economy model is obtained by setting, in eqs. (1) through (7),

$$\alpha_2 = \gamma_1 = \gamma_2 = \epsilon_1 = \epsilon_2 = \mu = 0.$$

The following three equations determine y, p, and m_d:

$$y = \alpha_1 (m_s - m_d)_{-1} + \alpha_3 t_{-1} + \alpha_4 g, \tag{1'}$$

$$\Delta p = \beta y_{-1} + (p^e - p)_{-1}, \tag{4'}$$

$$m_d = \delta_0 + \delta_1 y^* + p. \tag{3'}$$

In this domestic version, the money supply and the expected inflation rate are exogenous. The model has four innovations relative to Laidler's previous work [Laidler 1975a), Laidler (1975b), Laidler and O'Shea (1980), Laidler (1981)]: the disequilibrium real balance effect term $(m_s - m_d)$ in eq. $(1')$, the error in inflation expectations term $(p^e - p)$ in eq. $(4')$, the demand for money determined by the permanent income y^* rather than current income in eq. $(3')$, and, lastly, the aggregate supply relationship interpretation of the expectations augmented Phillips curve. Besides its aggregate supply interpretation in view of aggregate demand in $(1')$, eq. $(4')$ is somewhat novel in formulation. It does not tell that, ignoring transitory income, prices will increase at the same rate as the price level is expected to increase, but rather, that they will increase at the same rate as previous period inflation forecasting error. It implies that, ignoring transitory income, it would be sufficient for market participants to anticipate correctly the inflation rate in order that inflation is eliminated.

The steady state of eqs. $(1')$, $(3')$ and $(4')$ has to be characterized by zero inflation which agents expect to be maintained and by money supply growth proportional to long term output growth. If it were not for the inflation and output repercussions created by errors in inflation expectations, any rate of monetary expansion would in the long run be compatible with full employment and that rate would only affect the rate of inflation. Indeed, let $y = t = g = 0$, then $(1')$ and $(3')$ yield the quantity equation:

$$\Delta p = \Delta m_s - \delta_1 \Delta y^*, \tag{8}$$

and $(4')$ yields:

$$\Delta p = (p^e - p)_{-1}. \tag{4''}$$

Equation $(4'')$ indicates that the quantity equation would only be compatible with consistent overestimation of the inflation rate. Therefore, the model assumes implicitly zero inflation monetary policy which furthermore is credible enough that agents expect it to be maintained permanently.

Paradoxically, the lack of endogenisation of the expectation formation process combined with the impulse of expectational errors upon the inflation rate and, hence — through the real balance effect — on output, rigidifies the model to extreme rationality and policy discipline to reach the steady state. But nothing in the model forces the authorities or the agents to behave eventually in such a way. The model is essentially one of a fragile economy in which nothing guarantees a return to steady state equilibrium once it is pushed off balance. To converge to long run equilibrium the model needs either a process by which expectations are formed rationally in the sense that expectation errors are white noise or money supply growth in constant proportion to long term output growth. Neither of these requirements is fulfilled in the model. Therefore, if the hypothesis wants to be consistent it suffers from lack of generality. Alternatively, in the general terms in which it is stated, the model does not guarantee consistency.

The openness of the economy enriches the closed economy case in three ways. Errors in inflation expectations are made proportional to the contemporaneous world inflation rate $\Delta\pi$ and are endogenized through their dependency on the domestic price difference between foreign and domestic products. The money supply is endogenized through the balance of payments constraint reflected in international reserves; the quantity of these reserves responds inversely to domestic excess money supply and proportionally to the domestic price difference between foreign and domestic products. Lastly, this price difference positively affects transitory income. In the open economy model, the evolution of relative prices between domestic and foreign produced goods is quite central to the movement of the system. Increased foreign prices relative to domestic ones fuels inflation directly [eqs. (4) and (5)], and indirectly through excess money and demand growth [eqs. (2), (6) and (3), respectively, eqs. (1) and (4)]. The role played by these relative prices combined with exogenous inflation expectations and the demand for money provide for the classical specie flow characteristics of the model, namely that domestic inflation kills itself rather than feeding itself.

It is unfortunate that the authors do not discuss the properties of the open economy model. A glimpse of it is provided though in the original paper on the United Kingdom [Laidler and O'Shea, (1980)] when eqs. (8) and (9) in that paper are discussed. The unattractive feature reappears that the formation of inflation expectations implicitly needs a given policy rule to be maintained by the monetary authorities for the steady state to reach the natural level of income. Nothing in the model guarantees that these requirements are satisfied.

As discussed in Laidler and O'Shea (1980) the open economy model has also the property that an increase in the world inflation rate produces domestic unemployment unless the domestic authorities accelerate domestic credit expansion. What is the story behind this? The story is that domestic inflation converges to the foreign inflation rate through the formation of expectations and the aggregate supply function derived by the expectations augmented Phillips curve. This convergence holds, regardless of the rate of domestic credit expansion. To a certain extent, the transmission of inflation bypasses the monetary transmission mechanism, operating directly through expectations and producers' price setting behavior. Consequently, the open economy model is capable of generating domestic inflation without needing prior money growth expansion to make it happen. Thus, world inflation creates domestic unemployment because it creates domestic inflation without concomitant financing of inflation-induced increased demand for nominal balances. When the demand for nominal balances increases and the supply of it does not follow, aggregate demand is reduced and unemployment increases. That is, by and large, the story behind the LBJJ open economy hypothesis.

In our view, this story is unsatisfactory, because it produces the results (inflation) without providing for the means to achieve them (excess money growth). We would suggest that current and past money growth, rather than foreign inflation and price relations, enter the agents' inflation expectations formation process. This would not

is the hypothesis that the widespread adoption of floating exchange rates in the 1970s might have been the root of the international economic instability. However, the Canadian experience (where floating exchange rates seem not to have introduced more instability into the system) led the authors to suppose that "there seems to have been more at work than floating exchange rates in producing the puzzling results of the 1970s."

The "something else" (LBJJ) might lie in the absence of a supply block in the model. It is not at all difficult to argue that the "oil-shock" imposed by the Opec cartel upon the industrial countries introduced a deeper instability in the world economy than the adoption of flexible exchange rates. What the LBJJ model seems to render specifically obsolete for the 1970s is eq. (7), the assumption that the economy moves along a long term equilibrium growth path with the "natural" rate θ_1. Equation (7) should be replaced by a "supply block" consisting of a labor market (allowing for disequilibrium configurations) and a production function. The "oil shock", i.e. the increase in the relative price of energy must shift both the demand for labor function and the production function. This makes the model undoubtedly more complex, but it would still be simple enough to be handled by small research teams (one of the goals of LBJJ). Developing the model in this direction and distinguishing between regimes with nominal wage rigidity and regimes with real wage rigidity would permit a more satisfactory explanation of the stagflation experience in the 1970s in the three countries.

References

Friedman, M., 1970, A theoretical framework of monetary analysis, Journal of Political Economy 78, March/April, 2.

Johnson, H.G., 1972, The monetary approach to the balance of payments, in: J.A. Frenkel, and H.G. Johnson, (eds.), The monetary approach to the balance of payments, pp. 147–167.

Tobin, J., 1981, The monetarist counter-revolution today – An appraisal, Economic Journal 91, March, 361.

Recent Issues in the Theory of Flexible Exchange Rates, edited by E. Claassen and P. Sa.
© *North-Holland Publishing Company, 1983*

Chapter 8.1

EXCHANGE RATE OSCILLATIONS AND CATASTROPHE THEORY

Paul DE GRAUWE*

1. Introduction

An important feature of a floating exchange rate system is the oscillatory nature of exchange-rate movements in the short-run. This is illustrated in fig. 8.1. A substantial amount of theoretical research has now emerged explaining this phenomenon. The most widely accepted explanation (at least in the academic literature) is based on the role of new information ("news") which reaches the market in an unpredictable way.[1] These random information shocks lead to changes in expectations, which in efficient markets, are immediately reflected in the exchange rates. As a result, the latter will

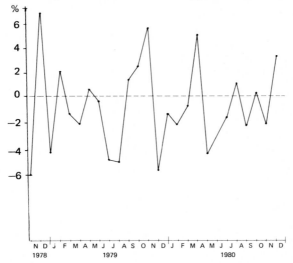

Figure 8.1(a). Sterling/dollar rate, monthly change (in percent). Sources: IMF, IFS.

* This paper benefited from the many comments made at the Seminar of International Economics of the University of Michigan.
[1] See Frenkel (1981) and Mussa (1979).

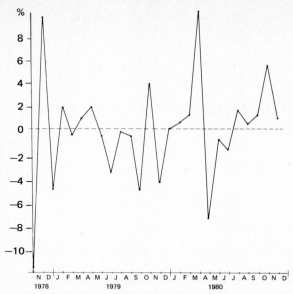

Figure 8.1(b).   Deutschmark/dollar rate, monthly change (in percent). Sources: IMF, IFS.

show sharp movements. Thus, the ultimate cause of the short-term oscillation of ex-change rates is to be found in the rapid successions of exogenous shocks.

The purpose of this paper is to suggest an alternative explanation. More specifically, an attempt will be made to endogenize the short-term exchange rate oscillations. In order to do so, we rely on the Dornbusch–Frankel model of exchange rate determination and the dynamic theory known as "catastrophe theory" is applied to this model.

In section 2 the essentials of the catastrophe theory are explained. In section 3 the Dornbusch–Frankel (1976) model is briefly explained and in section 4 catastrophe theory is applied. In the further sections some additional complications are added to the model.

2. Catastrophe theory[2]

Catastrophe theory is a mathematical theory of dynamic systems. In its simplest form it can be described as follows. Start from a simple differential equation,

$$\dot{x} = f(x, y). \tag{1}$$

where $\dot{x}$ is the time derivative of the state variable x. We refer to x as the "fast" variable and y as the "slow" variable, i.e. x adjusts immediately to a short-term equili-

---

[2]   We shall use the presentation of catastrophe theory in Varian (1979).

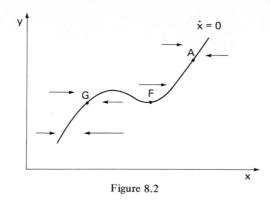

Figure 8.2

brium whereas y changes over time to a long-run equilibrium. It will be immediately evident that this distinction between slow and fast variables is directly applicable to the theory of exchange rate determination where exchange rates are the fast variables and goods prices and output are the slow variables moving the system to a long-run equilibrium.

Catastrophe theory analyzes how the short-run equilibrium behaves when the system moves the slow variable towards long-run equilibrium. During this movement "catastrophes" can occur, i.e. the short-run equilibrium jumps from one region of the state space to another. An example of a simple catastrophe is provided in fig. 8.2, where the locus $\dot{x} = 0$ is non-linear. x is the fast variable and it adjusts immediately so that a (stable) equilibrium point on $\dot{x} = 0$ is reached. Suppose that the initial conditions are such that the point A is reached. We now assume that y slowly decreases. As a result, the short-run equilibrium point moves continuously downwards along the $\dot{x} = 0$ line. When it reaches the critical point F (the fold point) any further decline in y will lead to a jump of the short-run equilibrium point towards G.

3. The model with exogenous oscillations

We start from the simple Dornbusch (1976) model as extended by Frankel (1979)[3]. *Asset market equilibrium* is described by the interest parity condition, the money demand equation and an equation describing expectations formation. The interest parity condition can be written as

$$r = r^* + \mu, \tag{2}$$

where r is the log of one plus the domestic interest rate, r^* is the log of one plus the foreign interest rate and μ is the expected rate of depreciation of the domestic currency.

---

[3] See Dornbusch (1976) and Frankel (1979).

Domestic monetary equilibrium is obtained when the demand for domestic money equals its supply. Thus

$$h - p = -\lambda r + \phi y, \tag{3}$$

where variables are expressed in logarithms, h is the log of the nominal money stock, p is the log of the domestic price level and y is the log of real income.

The expectations formation assumption is the following:

$$\mu = \theta(\overline{e} - e) + \pi - \pi^*, \tag{4}$$

where e is the log of exchange rate (the price of the foreign currency) and $\overline{e}$ is its long-run equilibrium value; π is the expected rate of domestic inflation and π^* is the expected rate of foreign inflation.

Equation (4) states that the expected rate of depreciation of the domestic currency is proportional to the gap between the current exchange rate and its long-run equilibrium value and is a function of the difference between the domestic and foreign expected inflation rate. When in long-run equilibrium $e = \overline{e}$, the domestic currency is expected to change at the rate of $\pi - \pi^*$.

Substituting eq. (4) into (2), and (2) into (3) yields the asset market equilibrium equation

$$h - p = -\lambda r^* - \lambda\theta\overline{e} + \lambda\theta e + \phi y - \lambda(\pi - \pi^*). \tag{5}$$

Equation (5) defines the short-run equilibrium condition of the system, i.e. given the real money stock, $h - p$, it determines the exchange rate needed to instantaneously clear the asset markets (for any given level of expectations and the variables r^* and y). In the jargon of catastrophe theory the exchange rate is the "fast" variable and the price and output levels are the "slow" variables.

A distinctive feature of the short-run equilibrium condition represented by eq. (5) is that an increase in the current exchange rate (a depreciation of the domestic currency) increases the demand for the domestic money ($\lambda\theta > 0$), necessitating an increase in the real money stock ($h - p$). The latter can be brought about either by an increase in the nominal money stock or by a decline in the price level. This negative relationship between the price level and the exchange rate needed to maintain instantaneous asset market equilibrium is essentially due to the regressive nature of the expectation formation assumption.

The modelling of the goods market is left general enough to encompass various dynamic scenarios. First we impose a long-run equilibrium condition that purchasing power parity be satisfied, i.e.

$$\overline{e} = \overline{p} - p^*, \tag{6}$$

and

$$e = \overline{e},$$

where p^* is the log of the foreign price level and $\bar{p}$ is the long-run equilibrium of the domestic price level.

Second, we postulate that when the current exchange rate exceeds its long-run value $(e > \bar{e})$ an expansionary process is set in motion in the goods market. Output will be above its long run-value $\bar{y}$ and the rate of price increases accelerates. The opposite occurs when $e < \bar{e}$.

The long-run equilibrium value of output, $\bar{y}$, is exogenously determined and assumed to be stationary. The equilibrium value of the price level, $\bar{p}$, can be found by setting $e = \bar{e}$ and $y = \bar{y}$ in eq. (5) and solving for p.[4]

Equation (5) together with the long-run equilibrium condition $e = \bar{e}$ can also be used to determine the long-run equilibrium level of the real money stock, $h - p$,

$$h - p = -\lambda r^* + \phi\bar{y} - \lambda(\pi - \pi^*). \tag{7}$$

It can now easily be established that in the long-run equilibrium h and p must grow at the same rate, π, i.e.

$$\dot{h} = \dot{p} = \pi. \tag{8}$$

Note also that from eq. (4) it follows that the long-run equilibrium rate of change of the exchange rate is equal to the differential in the expected domestic and foreign rates of inflation. The latter is equal to the interest differential. We have:

$$\dot{e} = \mu = \pi - \pi^* = r - r^*. \tag{9}$$

This model has a simple graphical interpretation (see fig. 8.3). On the vertical axis we set out the real money stock per unit of output $(m = h - p - \phi y)$ and on the horizontal axis the "real" exchange rate $(e - \bar{e})$.

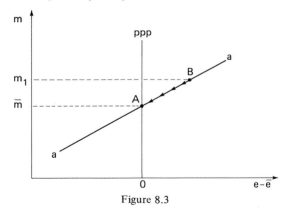

Figure 8.3

[4]   The dynamics of this model are developed in greater detail in Dornbusch (1980).

The *aa*-line defines the relationship between the real money stock per unit of output (for short, the effective real money stock) m and the real exchange rate $e - \overline{e}$ which maintains asset market equilibrium. It is derived from eq. (5). The slope of the *aa*-line is given by $\mathrm{d}m/\mathrm{d}(e - \overline{e}) = \lambda\theta > 0$. The *aa*-line can be interpreted as the locus of short-run equilibrium points: an increase in the effective real money stock (produced for example by an increase in the nominal money stock) must lead to an increase of the real exchange rate (e increases above its long-run value $\overline{e}$), in order to maintain asset market equilibrium. The nominal exchange rate here is the "fast" variable, which maintains instantaneous asset market equilibrium.

The long-run equilibrium condition is given by the vertical line PPP. This is the collection of points for which $e = \overline{e}$, i.e. purchasing power parity holds. The full equilibrium of the system is determined by the intersection of the *aa*-line and the PPP line. The intersection point A determines the long-run equilibrium level of effective real cash balances, $\overline{m}$.

The dynamics of the system can be described as follows. Since e is the fast variable, it adjusts instantaneously to keep the short-run equilibrium point on the *aa*-line. If this short-run equilibrium point is to the right of the PPP line, say at B, the exchange rate, e, is above its long run value $\overline{e}$ (the domestic currency is too cheap). This produces excess demand in the domestic goods market, pushing the price and output levels (the "slow" variables) upwards, and the real money stock downwards. Over time the short-run equilibrium point moves downwards along the *aa*-line. The opposite occurs if the short-run equilibrium point is to the left of the PPP-line.

As is well-known this model produces the "over-shooting" phenomenon when the equilibrium is disturbed. For example, an increase of the nominal money stock h increases the real money stock above its long-run value $\overline{m}$, because the price level cannot adjust immediately. In fig. 8.3 it increases to m_1. As a result, the short-run equilibrium point moves to B and the exchange rate must immediately increase above its long-run value. This increase of the exchange rate above its long-run value leads economic agents to expect a lower future rate of depreciation of the currency than the long-run rate of depreciation given by $\pi - \pi^*$, and induces them to hold the increased money stock. Over time the price level increases and the real money stock declines. The economy moves down along the *aa*-line until it reaches the initial point A.

Note that in this scenario we assumed a once and for all increase in the level of the money stock and an unchanged rate of growth of the money stock thereafter, so that the expected rate of inflation is unchanged. Other types of shocks can be analyzed leading to similar overshooting phenomena.

Finally it should be stressed that in order to explain rapid oscillations in the model, random disturbances in the exogenous variables have to be introduced. In addition, the dynamics of the model is crucially dependent on the assumption about expectations formation. The regressive expectations assumption ensures that the *aa*-line is positively sloped. As pointed out earlier, this implies that when the domestic currency depreciates below its long-run value (e is above $\overline{e}$), excess demand is created in the domestic money market, necessitating a decline in the price level or in the output level to keep the money market in equilibrium. In the following, we will be mainly interested in the conditions under which the *aa*-line is not positively sloped over a particular domain.

4. The model with endogenous oscillations

We now introduce a different set of assumptions about the way expectations are formed. Instead of assuming a regressive expectations behavior, as in eq. (4), it will be assumed here that expectations reflect both a regressive and an extrapolative part.

The *regressive* expectations behavior will be assumed to be non-linear, i.e.

$$\mu = \theta \, (\overline{e} \, - e) + \pi - \pi^*, \tag{10}$$

where θ is an increasing function of the gap between the observed and the equilibrium exchange rate. The graphical representation of eq. (10) is given in fig. 8.4.

The rationalization of this non-linear regressive expectations assumption is the following. In a world of uncertainty about the true equilibrium exchange rate, movements away from the equilibrium exchange rate do not lead to the same proportional expectational change. The closer e is to the equilibrium value $\overline{e}$, the greater the uncertainty whether or not the observed exchange rate deviates from the equilibrium value. As a result, a movement of e, when e is close to the equilibrium, induces only small changes in expectations. On the other hand, the farther away the observed exchange rate is from the equilibrium level the greater the likelihood that e deviates from the true equilibrium exchange rate. As a result, any further movement away from equilibrium leads to stronger expectations that this movement will have to be reversed in the future.

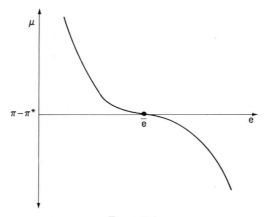

Figure 8.4

An example may clarify this expectational assumption. Suppose the equilibrium DM/dollar rate is 0.5, but it is not known with certainty by economic agents. If the current DM/dollar rate increases to 0.51 economic agents will be highly uncertain whether this constitutes a departure from the equilibrium rate. As a result, the increase of the exchange rate will have a low impact on the expected future rate of depreciation of the dollar (θ is low). If, however, the current exchange rate is, say, 0.6 and now increases to 0.61 this upward movement of the observed exchange rate will be associated with less uncertainty with a departure from the equilibrium exchange rate and induce a stronger response in expectations (θ will be larger).

The existence of an *extrapolative* expectations behavior is a matter of considerable controversy. In the non-academic literature this kind of behavior is often assumed as a matter of course, and is usually based either on an assumed irrationality of speculators, or on the existence of speculators without access to relevant information. This expectations behavior leads to bandwagon effects and destabilizing speculation.

Another, and in our view more attractive way to rationalize an extrapolative expectations formation, is to recognize the existence of ratchet effects in the goods market and the possibility of policy accommodations which then may lead to "vicious" or "virtuous" circles.

The scenario runs as follows. An overshooting exchange rate leads to an acceleration of import prices and nominal wages. These cost push effects of a depreciating currency tend to offset the demand pull effects of a depreciation of the currency. To the extent that the monetary authorities react by expansionary policies to accommodate the deflationary consequences of the cost push, the expected rate of inflation will be adjusted upwards. We can formalize this as follows:

$$\pi = \epsilon(e - \overline{e}) + \overline{\pi}, \tag{11}$$

where $\epsilon > 0$. The expected rate of inflation is adjusted upwards when the current exchange rate overshoots its long-run value $\overline{e}$.

Whether this expectational assumption is reasonable is an empirical issue. In general, it is more likely to occur the more widespread wage indexing is, and the greater the propensity of the monetary authorities to accommodate the cost push influences of exchange rate changes.

Combining (11) with (10) leads to

$$\mu = \theta(\overline{e} - e) + \epsilon(e - \overline{e}) + \overline{\pi} - \pi^*. \tag{12}$$

Imposing global stability on the model requires that for large enough deviations of e from $\overline{e}$ the regressive expectations behavior will dominate. Given the non-linear nature of θ, for small enough deviations of e from its equilibrium value the extrapolative part will dominate. We then have the following graphical representation of eq. (12) (fig. 8.5). For values of e below e_L and above e_U the regressive part of expectations formation dominates ($\theta > \epsilon$). For values of e between e_L and e_U the extrapolative part of the expectations formation dominates so that an increase in the exchange rate leads to a further expected depreciation of the domestic currency.

We can now incorporate this non-linear expectation formation function into the asset market model of the previous section.[5] One then obtains

$$h - p = -\lambda r^* + \phi y + \lambda(\theta - \epsilon)(e - \overline{e}) - \lambda(\overline{\pi} - \pi^*), \qquad (13)$$

where $(\theta - \epsilon)$ is a function of $e - \overline{e}$ as described in fig. 8.5. Graphically we obtain a non-linear asset market equilibrium line which is represented in fig. 8.6 by the line *aa*. It has the following interpretation. Suppose, the short-term equilibrium point is in *A*

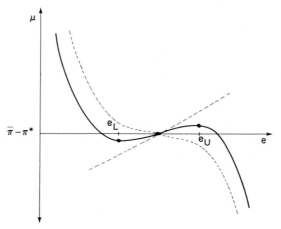

Figure 8.5

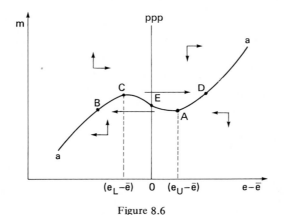

Figure 8.6

[5] We continue to assume here that the risk premium is zero. In a later section a non-zero risk premium is added.

and assume that the real money stock per unit of output, m, declines. (This decline in m can be due to a decrease in the nominal money stock or to an increase in the price level or the output level.) As a result, the domestic interest rate must increase. In order to maintain interest parity (i.e. equality of yield of domestic and foreign assets), the domestic currency must be expected to depreciate. Such an expected depreciation, however, can only come about by a jump of the exchange rate (a "catastrophe"). The new short-term equilibrium point will be in B.

Another way to interpret the non-linear asset market equilibrium line is the following. A movement of the current exchange rate between e_L and e_U generates expectational changes of the extrapolative type. As a result, by increasing the expected rate of depreciation a current depreciation of the domestic currency raises the domestic interest rate and leads to a decline in the demand for money. Thus, within the range set by e_L and e_U, an increase in the exchange above its long-run value must be compensated by a lower real money stock to maintain asset market equilibrium. Only when the real exchange rate is below or above the critical value $e_L - \overline{e}$ and $e_U - \overline{e}$ is an increase in the exchange rate associated with an expected appreciation of the domestic currency, leading to the "normal" positive relationship between the short-run equilibrium levels of real money stock and real exchange rate.

The dynamics of the system can now be analyzed as follows. We know that when the short-term equilibrium point is to the left of the PPP-line (i.e. when the real exchange rate is too low) the currency is overvalued. As a result, a deflationary process is set in motion in the domestic goods market, tending to reduce the rate of growth of the domestic price and output level. The real money stock per unit of output then tends to increase. The opposite occurs if the short-term equilibrium point is to the right of the PPP-line. The dynamics of the adjustment are illustrated by the arrows in fig. 8.6. Note that the assumption of instantaneous market clearing in asset markets ensures that the short-run equilibrium point is always located on the aa-line.

The long-run equilibrium point is obtained at E. However, it is unstable, and will never be reached. This can be shown as follows. Suppose we start from the short-run equilibrium point B in fig. 8.6. The currency is overvalued and a deflationary process is set in motion in the goods market. Over time the real money stock per unit of output, m, increases because the price level and/or the output level tend to increase at a lower pace. The short-run equilibrium point moves up. When it reaches the critical point C, the upward movement of the real money stock tends to move the short-term equilibrium point off the aa-line. In order to maintain asset market equilibrium, the short-term equilibrium jumps to point D. In D the dynamics of the adjustment in the goods market are reversed, pushing the short-term equilibrium point down until we have a new jump in A. Thus, the exchange rate will oscillate around its long-run equilibrium value $\overline{e}$.

Note that the amplitude of the oscillations critically depends on the range within which the extrapolative part of expectations is operative (given by the points $e_L - \overline{e}$ and $e_U - \overline{e}$ in fig. 8.6). As pointed out earlier this depends on several factors. First, with an increasing uncertainty about the true equilibrium rate $\overline{e}$ the range between

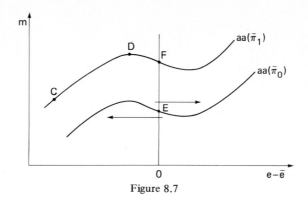

Figure 8.7

$e_L - \bar{e}$ and $e_U - \bar{e}$ will be large leading to larger oscillations around the equilibrium exchange rate. Second, the more the monetary authorities are believed to accommodate exchange-rate changes the stronger will be the extrapolative part of exchange rate expectations, thereby increasing the range between $e_L - \bar{e}$ and $e_U - \bar{e}$. This will also lead to a greater amplitude of exchange rate oscillations.

The effect of exogenous shocks can now be analyzed as follows. Suppose the monetary authorities announce a reduction in the rate of growth of the money stock, and economic agents are confident that the monetary authorities will stick to their intentions. As a result, the expected rate of inflation compatible with the rate of growth of the money stock declines. This shock increases the long-run equilibrium level of the real money stock, because it reduces the nominal interest rate thereby increasing the willingness to hold domestic money. This can be seen from eq. (13). Graphically we have an upward shift of the *aa*-line (see fig. 8.7). The effect is to shift the short-run equilibrium point to C^6 so that the real exchange rate declines. Over time the deflationary effect of this shock will tend to reduce the rate of growth of the price level thereby increasing the real money stock. The exchange rate starts oscillating again once the critical point D is reached. Note that the oscillations are around a lower long-term rate of change of the exchange rate given by $\dot{e} = \mu = \bar{\pi}_1 - \pi^*$.

It is also worth noting here that when an exogenous shock occurs, the uncertainty about the equilibrium exchange rate is likely to increase, at least "until the dust settles". This then may increase the upper and lower limits $e_L - \bar{e}$ and $e_U - \bar{e}$, and lead to strong short-term oscillations.

6. Risk premium

In the model of the previous sections it was assumed that interest parity holds perfectly, i.e. that there is no risk involved in holding foreign assets. This may seem im-

---

[6] Note that the exact location of C on the new *aa*-line depends on where the oscillatory exchange rate was when the shock was instituted.

plausible in a model where uncertainty exists about the equilibirum exchange rate. Therefore, in this section a risk premium is introduced explicitly.

The risk premium on the domestic asset can be defined as

$$\rho = r - (r^* + \mu) \gtrless 0. \tag{14}$$

It can be positive or negative, depending on the net foreign asset position of the country.[7] In general the higher the risk premium, ρ, the more attractive it is for domestic and foreign residents to invest in domestic assets. With a decreasing risk premium it becomes more attractive to invest in foreign assets. Thus, there is a relation:

$$A = A(\rho), \tag{15}$$

where A = the net foreign asset position of domestic residents, and $\partial A/\partial \rho < 0$.

In a flexible exchange rate system, changes of the net foreign asset position of the country can only occur through current account surpluses or deficits. If the country has a current account surplus (deficit) it will increase (decrease) its net foreign asset position. At any point in time, however, the net foreign asset position is fixed. This also means that at any given point in time the risk premium is given, and determined by the past current account surpluses and deficits. It can now easily be seen that the (linear) asset market equilibrium condition becomes

$$h - p = -\lambda r^* - \lambda \theta \overline{e} + \lambda \theta e + \phi y - \lambda \rho, \tag{16}$$

where an increase in the risk premium, ρ, reduces the demand for the domestic money. At any given point in time, however, ρ is exogenously given. Thus, the short-run equilibrium relation between p and e is described by the same *aa*-line as in the previous sections. It is also clear that the non-linear *aa*-line derived in the previous sections can be derived in a straightforward manner. The difference here is that the *aa*-line shifts over time as the risk premium changes. For example, if a current account deficit exists, the risk premium increases so that excess supply of money results (for any given real money stock). Thus, the *aa*-line shifts downwards, so that the exchange rate must increase for any given price level. These shifts of the *aa*-line alter the dynamics of the adjustment of the system, however, without changing the oscillatory pattern of short-term exchange rate movements.

---

[7]   The relation between risk premium and net foreign asset position is analyzed in detail by Fukao (1981); see also Isard (1980). The empirical evidence about the existence of risk premiums in foreign exchange markets is inconclusive. Frankel does not find evidence of a time-varying risk premium [see Frankel (1980); Meese and Singleton (1980) find a time-varying risk premium].

7. Conclusion

The limitations of the present paper are obvious, but need to be emphasized. One is that the expectations assumption used in this paper is based more on intuition than on theory. In particular, it should be shown that the non-linear expectation assumption is consistent with rational expectations. This has not been done here. In order to do so one would have to show that the assumed non-linearity in the expectations behavior follows from the structure of the model. Such a model would, most likely, have to exhibit J-curve effects and policy induced "vicious circles" in the exchange rate adjustments.

References

Dornbusch, R., 1976, Expectations and exchange rate dynamics, Journal of Political Economy, Dec.

Dornbusch, R., 1980, Open economy macroeconomics (Basic Books).

Frankel, J., 1979, On the mark: A theory of floating exchange rates based on real interest differentials, American Economic Review, September.

Frankel, J., 1980, A test of the existence of the risk premium in foreign exchange markets, International Finance Discussion Papers, Federal Reserve Board.

Frenkel, J., 1981, Flexible exchange rates, prices and the role of "news": Lessons from the 1970's, Journal of Political Economy, August.

Fukao, M., 1981, The risk premium in the foreign exchange market (University of Michigan) mimeo.

Isard, P., 1980, Expected and unexpected changes in exchange rates, International Finance Discussion Papers, Federal Reserve Board, no. 156, April.

Meese and Singleton, 1980, Rational expectations, risk premia and the market for spot and forward exchange, International Finance Discussion Papers, Federal Reserve Board.

Mussa, M., 1979, Empirical regularities in the behavior of exchange rates and theories of the foreign exchange market, Journal of Monetary Economics.

Varian, H., 1979, Catastrophe theory and the business cycle, Economic Enquiry.

Recent Issues in the Theory of Flexible Exchange Rates, edited by E. Claassen and P. Salin
© *North-Holland Publishing Company, 1983*

Chapter 8.2

COMMENT ON PAUL DE GRAUWE

Pascal SALIN

The paper by Paul De Grauwe offers an imaginative explanation of a usual — and still mostly unexplained — feature of floating exchange rates, namely their short-run oscillations. He starts from the now traditional Frenkel—Dornbusch model of over-shooting with regressive expectations and he adds two specific assumptions:

(1) the non-linearity of regressive expectations;
(2) the existence of extrapolative expectations in the neighbourhood of the equilibrium exchange rate $\bar{e}$.

The first assumption is quite acceptable. However, one may have the feeling that it is an *ad hoc* assumption: in fact, one has to utilize this assumption in order for extrapolative expectations to be dominant in the area around $\bar{e}$. Thus, when there is over-shooting, the process is amplified by extrapolative expectations until regressive expectations become dominant. There is then a turning point and, later, a "jump", i.e. an overshooting in the other direction, etc. ...

To explain this process of recurrent overshooting around an equilibrium point which is more or less unknown, De Grauwe makes use of catastrophe theory. In fact, his model bears some relation to the more traditional cobweb model, which is also a theory of imperfect information and different speeds of adjustment between variables.

We shall not discuss the basic structure of the model and we shall focus on two categories of problem: its empirical relevance and the justifications for extrapolative expectations.

1. Empirical relevance of the model

The graphs given by De Grauwe are somewhat misleading (see fig. 8.1 in his paper). It seems that there are oscillations around an equilibrium value, which is precisely the phenomenon that he aims to explain. In fact, the horizontal line is only a statistical trend. The model which implies short-run fluctuations around the equilibrium exchange rate seems to fit with these facts. But the equilibrium exchange rate is unknown and it may, for instance, be above or under the actual band of fluctuations.

Recent experience with floating exchange rates might suggest that an important and somewhat puzzling feature of such regimes is the existence of large swings with short-run oscillations at levels which may be considered as far from the equilibrium one, as is illustrated by the following figure:

As was confirmed by De Grauwe in the discussion, he is not interested in the large swings, but only in the short-run oscillations. However, if it can be considered that the actual exchange rate has often stayed far from its long-run equilibrium value for a long time, it would be interesting to know why such a situation can last, although everyone knows that the exchange rate is far from its equilibrium value. Does it mean that extrapolative expectations play a role when the actual exchange rate is far from $\bar{e}$ rather than when it is in its neighbourhood, contrary to De Grauwe's assumption?

As was mentioned in the discussion by Jacob Frenkel, it is true that, when one observes that the actual exchange rate has remained far from the equilibrium rate for a long time, such a judgment may depend on the personal prejudice of the observer about the value of the equilibrium exchange rate and one could as well assume that the so-called disequilibrium exchange rate was in fact an equilibrium exchange rate.

However, such a situation may also imply that the equilibrium exchange rate is volatile, which makes it difficult to test such a model as that of De Grauwe, for instance against a model which would explain the short-run oscillations of the exchange rate by a random process. Do we get a better explanation by analysing rigorously oscillations around a volatile equilibrium exchange rate or by assuming a random process around a more or less well known equilibrium exchange rate?

We cannot criticize De Grauwe for not giving empirical tests of his model, but we can fear that they would be difficult to do, since the lack of information he assumes in the neighbourhood of $\bar{e}$ about the precise value of $\bar{e}$ exists both for the speculator and the observer.

2. Justifications for extrapolative expectations

In the traditional overshooting model, individuals expect a return to $\overline{e}$. In De Grauwe's model, there is a move away from $\overline{e}$ until regressive expectations become dominant. As mentioned already, one could possibly assume rather a random process in the neighbourhood of $\overline{e}$, which would be consistent with studies on efficient markets. The assumption, made by De Grauwe, about the existence of extrapolative expectations around $\overline{e}$ could in fact correspond to two different situations.

(1) Extrapolative expectations are a normal way for speculators to behave in the neighbourhood of $\overline{e}$: information is scarce and costly and, by using extrapolative expectations, individuals get cheap information. They assume that the market knows better than they do.

Contrary to what is often accepted, such an assumption does not mean that individuals are irrational, since rationality does not mean perfect information, but optimum information, which is the result of a trade-off between the cost of information and its expected return.

However, as is well known, speculation is destabilizing in such a case and speculators lose as a whole. According to the traditional argument, speculators should no longer exist. Moreover, this assumption is not consistent with the fact that in the neighbourhood of $\overline{e}$ the change in the actual exchange rate seems — *ex post* — to follow a more or less random process, since there are frequent jumps, which are difficult to explain. Even if these jumps can be explained, as De Grauwe tries to do, they seem to occur at random from the point of view of an observer. From past experience, speculators ought to know that extrapolative expectations give cheap but bad information. They ought to know that, in the case where there is uncertainty on the expected direction of the change in the exchange rate, extrapolative expectations are a bad instrument, which may not be the case when the exchange rate is far from the equilibrium exchange rate.

(2) Another justification for extrapolative expectations is introduced by De Grauwe, so that he can avoid the inconsistency we have just underlined. He introduces an *ad hoc* assumption according to which there is an accommodating monetary policy. This, in turn, raises two series of problems:

(a) In the neighbourhood of $\overline{e}$, the changes in exchange rate are small and unpredictable. There is a contrast — not to say an inconsistency — between the uncertainties which then exist and the implicit assumption made by De Grauwe about monetary policy, its flexibility and its effects, which are all supposed to be perfectly known and predictable. Monetary policy adjusts very rapidly and precisely to the possible changes in income and in prices potentially brought about by changes in import prices and wages due to the change in the exchange rate!

Therefore, there is some paradox in the fact that extrapolative expectations, which — as we have seen — are a cheap way of getting information in a world of uncertainty, occur because there is certainty for all variables (except the exchange rate).

(b) As regards monetary policy, two outcomes are possible:

(i) in the first case one can assume that, starting from the usual point of over-shooting, monetary authorities are following an expansionary monetary policy. Individuals anticipate its effects and there is more inflation, therefore an expected depreciation, a new point of overshooting, etc. ... There may be an acceleration of inflation and depreciation in such a case of accommodating monetary policy.

In this situation, $\bar{e}$ is steadily increasing and speculation is not destabilizing. It correctly forecasts the steady change in $\bar{e}$. Extrapolative expectations could be said to be similar to rational expectations since individuals forecast correctly the reactions of the authorities.

(ii) The second possibility is that the expansionary monetary policy is transitory, which, in turn, raises two questions: First, what makes monetary policy reverse? We have to assume random turning points for monetary policy, which implies that the oscillations around $\bar{e}$ are of a random nature, contrary to De Grauwe's assumption of an endogenous explanation. Second, speculators lose in that case and — as we have said already — they ought to disappear or to learn from experience.

PART III

BEHAVIOUR OF MONETARY AUTHORITIES UNDER FLOATING EXCHANGE RATES

Recent Issues in the Theory of Flexible Exchange Rates, edited by E. Claassen and P. Salin
© North-Holland Publishing Company, 1983

Chapter 9.1

ASPECTS OF THE OPTIMAL MANAGEMENT OF EXCHANGE RATES

Jacob A. FRENKEL and Joshua AIZENMAN*

1. Introduction

This paper deals with the problem of the choice of an optimal exchange rate regime for a small open economy. Previous analyses of the choice between fixed and flexible exchange rate systems centered around questions of stabilization policies, the effect of capital mobility on the efficacy of monetary and fiscal policies, the role of speculation in the foreign exchange market, the nature and origin of exogenous disturbances, and the like. Subsequent discussions originating with contributions in the 1960s by Mundell (1961), McKinnon (1963) and Kenen (1969) have shifted the focus of analysis to the choice of the optimal currency area. The shift of emphasis reflected the recognition of the fact that the optimal exchange rate regime need not be the same for all countries. Rather, a country might find it useful to maintain a fixed rate with some currencies while having a flexible exchange rate with some other currencies.

The analysis in this paper recognizes that the spectrum of possibilities open for the various economies is much broader than the one implied by the framework of analysis of the optimal currency area. Rather than dividing the world into currencies among which exchange rates are flexible and those among which exchange rates are fixed, one might consider the optimal degree of fixity of exchange rates between each pair of currencies. In this framework the choice of an exchange rate regime between any pair of currencies need not be a fixed or a flexible rate but rather it might be some optimal mix of the two extremes. The optimal mix is referred to as the optimal managed (or dirty) float and the determinants of the optimal degree of exchange rate management is the subject of this paper.

The analytical framework that is outlined below builds upon, and extends the analysis of recent papers by Fischer (1976) and Gray (1976). Fischer analyzes the choice

* An earlier version was presented at a conference on the Choice of an Exchange Rate System, held at the University of South Carolina, May 1–2, 1981. J.A. Frenkel is indebted to the National Science Foundation, grant SES-7814480 AO1 for financial support. The research reported here is part of the NBER's Research Program in International Studies. Any opinions expressed are those of the authors and not necessarily those of the NBER.

between the two extreme exchange rate systems in terms of the source of exogenous disturbances. He demonstrates that when the exogenous shocks are real, the variance of steady-state consumption is lower under a fixed exchange rate system than under a flexible rate system. On the other hand, when the exogenous shocks are monetary, the opposite holds and the flexible rate system is preferred to the fixed rate system. Gray's paper deals with wage indexation in a closed economy and develops the concept of the optimal degree of wage indexation when the system is subject to real and monetary shocks which occur simultaneously. Lack of complete information precludes identifying the effect of each shock separately, and thus results in the optimal degree of wage indexation. In what follows we combine the two approaches of Fischer and Gray into a framework which yields an index measuring the optimal degree of fixity of exchange rates, i.e. the optimal managed float. Section 2 describes the analytical framework and analyzes the problem for an economy whose production consists only of commodities that are traded internationally. It is shown that the major determinants of the optimal managed float are the variances of and the covariances among the various shocks that affect the economy.[1] In section 3 we extend the analysis to an economy which produces tradable as well as non-tradable goods and examine the dependence of the optimal managed float on the composition of production. Section 4 contains some concluding remarks.

2. Optimal managed float with only tradable goods

In this section we analyze the determinants of the optimal degree of exchange rate management for an economy which produces only tradable goods. We start with a presentation of the analytical framework.

2.1. *The analytical framework*

The key characteristic of the analytical framework is the specification of the stochastic structure of the economy. Consider a small economy that is subject to three types of repetitive and serially uncorrelated shocks. These shocks which are specified below are referred to as real, monetary, and foreign shocks.

Denote the supply of output by Y_t, and assume that

$$Y_t = y\,\mathrm{e}^{\mu}; \quad \mu \sim N(-\sigma_\mu^2/2, \sigma_\mu^2), \tag{1}$$

[1] The analytical framework is adapted from Frenkel (1976, 1980). For an early analysis of the optimal exchange rate regime in terms of the structure of the economy see Stein (1963). Modigliani and Askari (1973) have emphasized that the optimal exchange rate regime depends on the nature of the shocks and that the optimum may be an intermediate system between fixed and flexible rates, e.g. sliding parities. A similar emphasis on the origin of shocks is found in Flood (1979), Buiter (1977) and Enders and Lapan (1979) who also emphasize the stochastic nature of the various shocks.

where μ is a stochastic disturbance with a constant variance σ_μ^2. The mean of the distribution of μ is chosen to be $-\sigma_\mu^2/2$ so as to assure that the expected value of output $E(Y_t)$ equals y. Thus, y is referred to as permanent income and μ is referred to as the real shock. It can be shown that σ_μ is approximately equal to the standard deviation of current income as a percentage of permanent income.[2]

The second source of disturbances arises from the monetary sector of the economy. Let the demand for nominal balances L_t be

$$L_t = kP_t Y_t e^\epsilon; \quad \epsilon \sim N(-\sigma_\epsilon^2/2, \sigma_\epsilon^2), \tag{2}$$

where k is the Cambridge k denoting the desired ratio of money to income, P denotes the domestic price level and ϵ denotes the stochastic disturbance to the demand for money, where again its time subscript has been omitted. Analogous to the distribution of the real shock, the standard deviation of the monetary shock σ_ϵ is approximately equal to the standard deviation of the income velocity as a percentage of permanent velocity.

The third source of disturbances stems from the foreign sector. Denote the foreign price level by P_t^* and let it be related to its permanent value p_t^* according to

$$P_t^* = p^* e^{\chi_1}; \quad \chi_1 \sim N(-\sigma_{\chi_1}^2/2, \sigma_{\chi_1}^2). \tag{3}$$

Thus, χ_1 denotes the shocks due to variability of foreign prices. Again, σ_{χ_1} is approximately equal to the standard deviation of foreign prices as a percentage of their mean.

The domestic price level is linked to the foreign price level through the purchasing power parity which is assumed to be satisfied except for random deviations. The stochastic deviations from purchasing power parity are denoted by χ_2 and thus

$$P_t = S_t P_t^* e^{\chi_2}; \quad \chi_2 \sim N(-\sigma_{\chi_2}^2/2, \sigma_{\chi_2}^2), \tag{4}$$

where S_t denotes the exchange rate which is defined as the price of foreign exchange in terms of domestic currency. For further use it is convenient to combine eqs. (3) and (4) and to express the domestic price level as

$$P_t = S_t p^* e^\chi, \tag{4'}$$

where χ denotes the effective foreign price shock that is defined by the sum $\chi_1 + \chi_2$.

Let the flow demand for money ΔM_t^d correspond to a stock adjustment process by

---

[2] $E(Y_t) = y$, $E(Y_t^2) = y^2 e^{\sigma_\mu^2}$ and $\mathrm{var}(Y_t) = y^2(e^{\sigma_\mu^2} - 1)$; thus $\sigma_\mu/E(Y) = y(e^{\sigma_\mu^2} - 1)^{1/2}/y = (e^{\sigma_\mu^2} - 1)1/2 \simeq \sigma_\mu$ for small σ_μ. It should be clear that the choice of $-\sigma_\mu^2/2$ as the mean of the distribution of μ is made solely for analytical convenience. None of the results is affected by rescaling the distribution so as to move its mean to zero. To simplify notations we have suppressed in eq. (1) the subscript t that is attached to the realization of the shock μ. We will follow the same convention in subsequent specifications of shocks.

which individuals wish to restore stock equilibrium by a constant multiple of the discrepancy between desired and actual money holdings:

$$\Delta M_t^d = \alpha(L_t - \overline{M}_t).$$
(5)

In (5), α denotes the speed of adjustment while $\overline{M}_t$ denotes money holdings at the beginning of the period. The determinants of $\overline{M}_t$ will be discussed later.

Using eqs. (1), (3) and (4') in (2) we may express the demand for money as

$$L = kp^*S_t y e^{(\mu + \epsilon + \chi)}.$$
(2')

When the exchange rate is flexible, any stock disequilibrium in the money market will disappear automatically since the exchange rate will change so as to guarantee that $L_t - \overline{M}_t = 0$. Using eq. (2'), it follows that when the exchange rate is flexible the money market clears and therefore

$$kp^*S_t y e^{(\mu + \epsilon + \chi)} - \overline{M}_t = 0.$$
(6)

Thus, the equilibrium exchange rate is

$$S_t = (\overline{M}_t / kp^*y)e^{-(\mu + \epsilon + \chi)},$$
(7)

and the percentage change thereof is

$$\log S_t - \log S_{t-1} = \log(\overline{M}_t / kS_{t-1}p^*y) - (\mu + \epsilon + \chi).$$
(8)

For the other extreme regime of the fixed exchange rate system, the exchange rate does not change and therefore

$$\log S_t - \log S_{t-1} = 0.$$
(9)

Using (8) and (9) we may define an index γ such that $0 \leqslant \gamma \leqslant 1$:

$$\gamma \equiv (\log S_t - \log S_{t-1})/[\log(\overline{M}_t / kS_{t-1}p^*y) - (\mu + \epsilon + \chi)].$$
(10)

In eq. (10) the parameter γ characterizes the whole spectrum of exchange rate regimes. In the two extreme systems of a fixed and freely flexible exchange rates, the value of the coefficient γ is zero and unity, respectively. Between these two extremes there is the wide range of possible mixtures of the two extremes. The coefficient γ may be viewed as indicating the fraction of money market disequilibrium that is allowed to be eliminated through changes in the exchange rate. In what follows we will refer to γ as the coefficient of managed float. Equation (10) also implies that the current exchange rate is

$$S_t = S_{t-1}^{1-\gamma} (\bar{M}_t/kp^*y)^\gamma e^{-\gamma(\mu+\epsilon+x)}. \tag{11}$$

2.2. The objective function

The optimal managed float strategy is necessary because it is assumed that the government (as well as the private sector) possesses information that is incomplete. If information were complete and during each period the various shocks could be observed and identified separately, an optimal policy would be to allow changes in the exchange rates to correct only for the monetary disturbances and not for the real disturbances. This is essentially the main insight from Fischer's paper (1976). In introducing incomplete information it is assumed that during a given period only the joint outcome of the various shocks is known but not their separate values. Because complete information is not available, policymakers face a signal extraction problem and some second-best policy is required.

It is assumed that the objective is to minimize the losses due to imperfect information, and that the policymaker seeks to minimize the quadratic loss function H:

$$\text{Minimize} \quad H \equiv E[(c_t - E(Y_t)]^2 = \text{var}(c_t) + [E(Y_t) - E(c_t)]^2, \tag{12}$$

where c_t denotes the rate of consumption which, from the budget constraint, equals the rate of income minus the real value of additions to cash balances

$$c_t = Y_t - \frac{\Delta M_t}{p_t}. \tag{13}$$

The previous relationships imply that

$$[c_t - E(Y_t)] = y(e^\mu - 1) - \alpha k y[e^{\mu+\epsilon}$$
$$- (\bar{M}_t/ks_{t-1}p^*y)^{1-\gamma} e^{\gamma(\mu+\epsilon)+x(\gamma-1)}] \tag{14}$$

and using eq. (14) in (12) yields the loss function which is to be minimized with respect to the intervention index γ.[3]

Inspection of (14) suggests that in addition to finding the optimal γ, the policymaker might want to pursue what Fischer terms "active" monetary policy by setting the beginning of period holdings of cash balances $\bar{M}_t$, at some desired level. It is assumed that at the beginning of each period the monetary authority changes the money supply so as to compensate for past disturbances. Thus, the money supply is set at that level for which

---

[3]   In a recent analysis of the optimal foreign exchange intervention, Boyer (1978) extends and applies Poole's framework (1970) to the problem at hand. Boyer assumes that real income is fixed and that the objective function is to minimize the variability of prices.

$$\bar{M}_t = kS_{t-1}p^*y\mathrm{e}^{\delta}; \quad \delta \sim N(-\sigma_{\delta}^2/2, \sigma_{\delta}^2). \tag{15}$$

The stochastic term δ in (15) denotes the stochastic shock to the money supply. It reflects the possibility that in setting the money supply the monetary authorities are unable to avoid stochastic deviations from their target.[4] Recalling that the shock to the demand for money is denoted by ϵ, the *net* monetary shock, i.e. the shock to the excess demand for money, is $\epsilon - \delta$.

2.3. The optimal intervention index

Having outlined the objective function we now turn to the solution of the optimal intervention index which will be denoted by γ^*. To simplify the computations we approximate the discrepancy between consumption and expected income by the first two terms of a Taylor expansion of eq. (14). Thus

$$[c_t - \mathrm{E}(Y_t)] \simeq [\mu - (1-\gamma)\alpha k\theta]y, \tag{14'}$$

where the expansion is carried out around a zero value of the shocks.[5] In eq. (14') θ denotes the sum of all shocks, that is,

$$\theta \equiv \mu + \chi + \epsilon - \delta,$$

and, under full flexibility of exchange rates (when $\gamma = 1$), money market equilibrium implies that the percentage fall in the exchange rate equals θ.

---

[4] It should be noted that the specification of the "active" monetary policy is somewhat arbitrary since, in principle, other rules are possible. For example, one could specify a rule by which the monetary authority sets $\bar{M}_t$ so as to ensure equality between the values of the mathematical expectations of the streams of consumption and income, i.e. $\mathrm{E}(c_t) = \mathrm{E}(Y_t)$. Further, eq. (14) suggests that the monetary authority possesses two instruments for the attainment of its policy goals: a γ policy – the optimal intervention index and an $\bar{M}_t$ policy – the optimal stock of money at the beginning of each period. The general optimization procedure would then solve simultaneously for the optimal *combination* of $\bar{M}_t$ and γ so as to minimize the loss function. In the following section we report and analyze the results of computer simulations that are based on determining $\bar{M}_t$ according to Fischer's specification of "active" monetary policy. We have experimented with the other two alternative monetary rules. It turns out that, at least for the range of parameters that have been assumed, the resulting optimal intervention index is almost invariant among the various monetary rules for the choice of $\bar{M}_t$ and thus, for ease of exposition, we report only simulations using Fischer's rule. It is also relevant to note that under rational expectations the precise specification of the $\bar{M}_t$ policy is completely irrelevant for the key results; for an explicit demonstration of this point see Aizenman (1980).

[5] The expansion is around zero in order to ensure that the approximation would be around the expected value of the function; thus we approximate e^{μ} by $(1 + \mu)$ and thereby we have that $\mathrm{E}(\mathrm{e}^{\mu}) = 1$. Likewise, as was shown in footnote 2, $\sigma_{\mathrm{e}^\mu}^2 \simeq \sigma_{1+\mu}^2$. It should be noted that in computing the loss function, the second moment of the distributions is much more relevant than the mean and thus the choice of the mean may be made on the basis of convenience.

Minimization of the loss function requires that the value of γ in (14′) is chosen so as to minimize the squared discrepancy between μ and $(1 - \gamma)\alpha k\theta$. This minimization amounts to computing the ordinary least squares estimate of a regression of μ on $\alpha k\theta$. It follows that the optimal intervention index γ^* is

$$\gamma^* = 1 - \frac{\text{cov}(\mu, \theta)}{\alpha k\sigma_\theta^2}, \tag{16}$$

and when all shocks are independent of each other, the optimal intervention index becomes:

$$\gamma^* = 1 - \frac{\sigma_\mu^2}{\alpha k \left[\sigma_\mu^2 + \sigma^2{}_{(x + \epsilon - \delta)} \right]}, \tag{16′}$$

where σ_θ^2 is expressed as the sum of the variance of the real shock σ_μ^2 and the variance of the effective monetary shock $\sigma^2{}_{(x + \epsilon - \delta)}$.[6] The intuition underlying eqs. (16) and (16′) can be provided in terms of the signal extraction problem which is faced by the policymaker given the assumed informational structure. From his knowledge of the intervention rule and from the observed change in the exchange rate, the policymaker can infer the magnitude of the global shock θ. It is assumed that only the value of θ is known but not the individual components of the global shock. The signal extraction problem amounts to an attempt to estimate the unobserved value of the real shock μ from the known value of θ (that is inferred from the change in the exchange rate).

Inspection of (16) and (16′) reveals that when $\sigma_\mu^2 = 0$ so that the disturbances are composed only of effective monetary shocks, $\gamma^* = 1$ and the optimal exchange rate regime is that of complete flexibility. On the other extreme for which $\sigma^2{}_{(x + \epsilon - \delta)} = 0$ so that the disturbances are entirely of a real origin, the optimal intervention index is set to equal zero and the optimal exchange rate regime is that of fixed rates.[7] In general, when both types of shocks are present, the optimal intervention index is within the range $(0,1)$ and the optimal exchange rate system corresponds to neither of

---

[6] Since the effective foreign price shock x (which is composed of the shock to foreign prices, x_1, and the shock to purchasing power parities, x_2) exerts similar effects as shocks to the excess demand for money, $\epsilon - \delta$, their sum $(x + \epsilon - \delta)$ is referred to as the effective monetary shock. Since ϵ represents a change in taste, we assume that the objective function remains invariant with respect to this shock. If the objective function were to depend on ϵ, we would have had to assume that there are no shocks to money demand. In that case the effective monetary shock should be read as $x - \delta$ instead of $x + \epsilon - \delta$.

[7] From (16) and (16′), when the effective monetary shock is zero, $\gamma^* = 1 - 1/\alpha k$ where αk denotes the marginal propensity to save (hoard) out of transitory income. When $\alpha k = 1$, the loss function is minimized when $\gamma^* = 0$. For $\alpha k < 1$, γ^* is set to equal zero since we rule out negative values.

the extremes of a completely fixed or of a completely flexible rate regime. In that case the optimal system is an intermediate system, i.e. a system of an optimal managed float.

The magnitude of the optimal intervention index depends on the characteristics of the shocks. As may be inferred from eq. (16), as long as the covariance between μ and $(\mu + \chi + \epsilon - \delta)$ is positive, the optimal intervention index depends negatively on the variance of the real shock. Thus,

$$\frac{\partial \gamma^*}{\partial \sigma_\mu^2} < 0. \tag{17}$$

High variance of real shocks, *ceteris paribus*, tends to raise the desirability of greater fixity of exchange rates. Small economies, and in particular developing countries, tend to have concentrated production patterns and thus are likely to have higher variance of real shocks than more diversified economies. *Ceteris paribus*, these economies will find it optimal to have greater fixity of exchange rates.

Similarly, eq. (16) implies that as long as the covariance between the effective monetary shock $(\chi + \epsilon - \delta)$ and the global shock $(\mu + \chi + \epsilon - \delta)$ is positive, the intervention index depends positively on the variance of the effective monetary shock. Thus,

$$\frac{\partial \gamma^*}{\partial \sigma_{(\chi + \epsilon - \delta)}^2} > 0. \tag{18}$$

High variance of the effective monetary shock tends to raise the desirability of greater flexibility of exchange rates.

Equation (16) also implies a definite relationship between αk — the propensity to save out of transitory income — and the optimal intervention index. As long as the covariance between μ and $(\mu + \chi + \epsilon - \delta)$ is positive, a higher value of αk is associated with a higher value of γ^*.

$$\frac{\partial \gamma^*}{\partial \alpha k} > 0. \tag{19}$$

Thus, high speed of adjustment to asset disequilibrium (high α) and low velocity of circulation (high k) tend to raise the desirability of greater flexibility of exchange rates. This result may be rationalized by noting that the effect of any given value of real shock on the excess flow demand for money depends positively on αk. Since the desirability of greater flexibility increases with the extent of monetary shocks, and since the monetary disequilibrium which corresponds to a given real shock is larger the higher is the saving propensity, it follows that the effect of αk on γ^* is similar to the effect of a rise in the variance of the effective monetary shock.

From eq. (16') it is clear that the results in (17), (18) and (19) must hold when the various shocks are independent of each other. Further, inspection of eqs. (16) and

(16′) suggests that what is relevant for the optimal intervention index is not the absolute magnitude of the variances of the various shocks but rather their relative magnitude. In general, when the ratio between the variances of the effective monetary shock and the real shock approaches infinity (either because the former approaches infinity or because the latter approaches zero) the optimal exchange rate system is that of freely flexible rates. Likewise, when the same ratio approaches zero (either because the variance of the effective monetary shock approaches zero or because the variance of the real shock approaches infinity) the optimal exchange rate system is that of fixed rates.

Since the optimal intervention index depends negatively on the variance of real shocks and positively on the variance of the effective monetary shock, it is clear that its dependence on the covariance between these two types of shocks is ambiguous since it depends on the relative magnitudes of the two variances. Using eq. (16) it can be shown that

$$\text{sign } \frac{\partial \gamma^*}{\partial \text{cov}(\mu, \chi + \epsilon - \delta)} = \text{sign}(\sigma_\mu^2 - \sigma_{(\chi + \epsilon - \delta)}^2). \tag{20}$$

Thus, if the variance of the real shock exceeds the variance of the effective monetary shock, a rise in the value of the covariance between these shocks results in a higher value of the optimal intervention index and raises the desirability of greater flexibility of exchange rates. This result may be interpreted by noting that when the co-variance between the two types of shocks is zero while the variance of the real shocks is large relative to that of the effective monetary shock, the optimal intervention index is low since the optimal exchange rate regime is close to that of a fixed exchange rate. Under these circumstances, a rise in the covariance between the shocks implies that any given real shock is now being accompanied by a monetary shock. The induced rise in the importance of the monetary shock results in a higher value of the optimal intervention index, and increases the desirability of greater flexibility of exchange rates. A similar result as in (20) also applies to the analysis of the dependence of the optimal intervention index on the correlation between the two types of shocks.

2.4. Illustrative computations

The analysis of the properties and the determinants of the optimal intervention index was based on a Taylor approximation of the loss function. As is obvious, the accuracy of this approximation depends negatively on the magnitudes of the shocks. While the qualitative conclusions do not depend on the accuracy of the approximation, the quantitative estimates might be somewhat affected. To gain insight into the precise quantitative magnitude of the optimal intervention index we report in table 9.1 il-lustrative computations for the case in which the shocks are independent of each

Table 9.1
Optimal managed float for alternative values of real and effective monetary disturbances and saving propensities.

$\sigma_{\chi + \epsilon - \delta}$ σ_μ	$\alpha k = 0.5$					$\alpha k = 1$				
	0.01	0.03	0.05	0.07	0.09	0.01	0.03	0.05	0.07	0.09
0.01	0	0.80	0.92	0.96	0.98	0.50	0.90	0.96	0.98	0.99
0.03	0	0.47	0.69	0.80	0.87	0.10	0.50	0.74	0.85	0.90
0.05	0	0	0	0.33	0.53	0.04	0.27	0.50	0.67	0.77
0.07	0	0	0	0	0.25	0.02	0.16	0.34	0.50	0.63
0.09	0	0	0	0	0	0.01	0.10	0.24	0.38	0.51

other.[8] These computations are performed for alternative values of the propensity to save out of transitory income as well as for alternative assumptions concerning the magnitudes of the various shocks as measured by the standard deviations σ_μ and $\sigma_{(\chi + \epsilon - \delta)}$. These results illustrate the negative dependence of γ^* on σ_μ — the standard error of the real shock as well as the positive dependence of γ^* on $\sigma_{(\chi + \epsilon - \delta)}$ — the standard error of the effective monetary shock, and on αk — the propensity to save out of transitory income.

In computing the optimal intervention index in table 9.1, it was assumed that the covariances among the various shocks were zero. In table 9.2 we allow for various covariances among some of the shocks and we report the resulting optimal intervention index. Consider first the comparison between panels A and B of table 9.2. In panel A all three shocks are assumed to be of the magnitude of 3 percent while in panel B all three shocks are assumed to be of the magnitude of 9 percent. As is apparent, tripling of the magnitudes of the shocks while maintaining their ratios constant, does not seem to have a significant effect on the optimal intervention index. This illustrates the proposition that the optimal intervention index depends on the ratios of the various shocks rather than on their actual magnitude.

Panels C, D and E of table 9.2 illustrate the effects of changing the ratio among the various disturbances. When the magnitudes of the foreign price disturbance or of the domestic monetary disturbance are high relative to the other shocks (panels C and E, respectively) the optimal intervention index is close to unity and thus, the optimal regime is closer to that of a freely flexible rate. On the other hand, when the magnitude of the real shock is high relative to the other shocks (panel D), the optimal intervention index is low and the optimal exchange rate regime is closer to that of fixed exchange rates.

The various panels of table 9.2 also illustrate the effects of the covariances among foreign and domestic disturbances. Generally speaking, a positive covariance between

---

[8]   In these computations the optimal intervention index was obtained by using eq. (14) in the loss function (12) and minimizing with respect to γ. We are indebted to Michael Bazdarich for helpful assistance in the computations.

Table 9.2
Optimal managed float for alternative values of disturbances and their covariances.

A

$\sigma_\mu = 0.03$; $\sigma_\epsilon - \delta = 0.03$; $\sigma_\chi = 0.03$; $\alpha k = 1$

cov (χ, μ) / cov $(\chi, \epsilon - \delta)$	-0.6	-0.3	0	0.3	0.6
-0.6	0.33	0.66	0.78	0.83	0.87
-0.3	0.42	0.61	0.71	0.77	0.81
0	0.44	0.58	0.67	0.72	0.76
0.3	0.46	0.57	0.64	0.69	0.73
0.6	0.47	0.56	0.62	0.67	0.70

B

$\sigma_\mu = 0.09$; $\sigma_\epsilon - \delta = 0.09$; $\sigma_\chi = 0.09$; $\alpha k = 1$

cov (χ, μ) / cov $(\chi, \epsilon - \delta)$	-0.6	-0.3	0	0.3	0.6
-0.6	0.35	0.67	0.78	0.84	0.87
-0.3	0.42	0.62	0.71	0.77	0.81
0	0.45	0.59	0.67	0.73	0.76
0.3	0.46	0.57	0.64	0.69	0.73
0.6	0.47	0.56	0.62	0.67	0.71

C

$\sigma_\mu = 0.03$; $\sigma_\epsilon - \delta = 0.03$; $\sigma_\chi = 0.09$; $\alpha k = 1$

cov (χ, μ) / cov $(\chi, \epsilon - \delta)$	-0.6	-0.3	0	0.3	0.6
-0.6	1.0	1.0	1.0	1.0	1.0
-0.3	0.98	0.99	0.99	0.99	0.99
0	0.87	0.89	0.91	0.92	0.93
0.3	0.79	0.83	0.85	0.87	0.88
0.6	0.75	0.78	0.81	0.83	0.85

D

$\sigma_\mu = 0.09$; $\sigma_\epsilon - \delta = 0.03$; $\sigma_\chi = 0.03$; $\alpha k = 1$

cov (χ, μ) / cov $(\chi, \epsilon - \delta)$	-0.6	-0.3	0	0.3	0.6
-0.6	0	0	0.03	0.10	0.16
-0.3	0	0.06	0.12	0.17	0.22
0	0.08	0.14	0.18	0.22	0.26
0.3	0.15	0.19	0.23	0.26	0.29
0.6	0.19	0.23	0.26	0.29	0.32

E

$\sigma_\mu = 0.03$; $\sigma_\epsilon - \delta = 0.09$; $\sigma_\chi = 0.03$; $\alpha k = 1$

cov (χ, μ) / cov $(\chi, \epsilon - \delta)$	-0.6	-0.3	0	0.3	0.6
-0.6	0.94	0.95	0.96	0.97	0.97
-0.3	0.90	0.92	0.93	0.94	0.95
0	0.87	0.89	0.91	0.92	0.93
0.3	0.84	0.87	0.88	0.90	0.92
0.6	0.82	0.85	0.87	0.89	0.90

foreign price shocks and domestic monetary shocks tends to raise the optimal intervention index and thereby lower the desirability of fixed rates. Consistent with the results in eq. (19), the effect of a positive covariance between foreign price shocks and domestic real shocks is ambiguous and depends on the sign of the difference between the variance of the real shock and the variance of the effective monetary shock. When this difference is negative, as in panels C and E, a rise in $\text{cov}(\chi, \mu)$ is associated with a decline in γ^*. Likewise, when this difference is positive, as in panel D, a rise in $\text{cov}(\chi, \mu)$ results in a higher value of the optimal intervention index.

2.5. *Balance of payments variability*

The logic underlying the optimal degree of exchange rate management is that the optimal response to monetary shocks differs from the optimal response to a real shock. Monetary shocks are best dealt with through exchange rate changes while real shocks are best dealt with through trade flows. Using the terminology of Mundell (1973) and Laffer (1973), under the fixed exchange rates the current account (which equals the balance of payments in the absence of capital flows) cushions the effects of real shocks. As a result, large variability of real shocks yields large variability of the balance of payments. In what follows we examine the variability of the balance of payments under the optimal degree of managed float.

We first note that the discrepancy between consumption and expected income which is the key element in the objective function (12), can be written as

$$[c_t - \text{E}(Y_t)] = (c_t - Y_t) + [Y_t - \text{E}(Y_t)]. \tag{21}$$

The first term on the right-hand side denotes the deficit in the trade balance (which equals the balance of payments in the absence of capital flows) and the second term denotes transitory income. Minimization of the loss function amounts to choosing the optimal intervention index so as to minimize the average squared deviation of transitory income from the balance of payments deficit. Transitory income is μy and the balance of payments deficit is $(1 - \gamma)\alpha k\theta y$ which measures the fraction of money market disequilibrium that is not allowed to be cleared through exchange rate changes. It follows that the variance of the balance of payments, σ_B^2, can be expressed as the variance of $(1 - \gamma)\alpha k\theta y$. Substituting eq. (16') for the optimal value of γ (under the assumption that the shocks are independent of each other) yields eq. (22) as the expression for the variance of the optimal balance of payments σ_{B*}^2:

$$\sigma_{B*}^2 = \frac{(\sigma_\mu^2)^2}{\sigma_\theta^2} \, y^2, \tag{22}$$

or, expressed in terms of the standard deviation,

$$\sigma_{B*} = \frac{\sigma_\mu^2}{\sigma_\theta^2}\, y\sigma_\theta. \tag{22'}$$

Thus, given the variability of the global shock θ, a rise in the weight of real variability in total variability increases the variability of the optimal balance of payments. This relationship suggests that, *ceteris paribus*, countries for which real variability comprises a relatively large share of total variability should hold larger stock of international reserves in order to be able to facilitate the relatively high variance in the optimal balance of payments.

2.6. The capital account

An important limitation of the analysis in the previous sections has been the assumed absence of an integrated world capital market which reflects itself in the capital account of the balance of payments. As a result, the previous analysis identified the trade balance with the balance of payments. While such a simplification might be appropriate for economies with severe limitations on access to world capital markets, it may not represent the conditions faced by developed countries. In what follows we introduce some elements of the capital account.

It is assumed that the economy faces a perfect world capital market in which it can borrow and lend at a fixed rate of interest. Suppose that the desired ratio of money to securities depends on the rate of interest and, due to the assumed fixity of the world rate of interest, this ratio is also fixed. Since the economy may be a net debtor or a net creditor in the world capital market, the value of its permanent output need not equal the value of its permanent income. The analysis simplifies considerably by assuming that the world rate of interest is deterministic since in that case the stochastic characteristics of output are similar to those of income.[9] As a result, the previous analysis which minimized the squared deviation of consumption from permanent output remains relevant even though the concepts of income and output need not coincide. The only difference that has to be kept in mind is that when the economy has an access to world capital markets the previous analysis applies to the current account rather than to the overall balance of payments.

The signal extraction problem is similar to that in section 2.3. Individuals are assumed to observe the global shock $\theta \equiv \mu + \chi + \epsilon - \delta$, from which they attempt to estimate the real shock component μ and, thereby, the value of transitory income $\hat{\mu}y$ (where $\hat{\mu}$ denotes the estimated real shock given the realization of θ). The least squares estimate of the real shock is:

---

[9] Flood (1979) analyzes the implications of stochastic interest rates on the choice of the exchange rate system.

$$E(\mu|\theta) = \frac{\text{cov}(\mu,\theta)}{\sigma_\theta^2}\,\theta, \tag{23}$$

which, when multiplied by y, provides the estimated value of transitory income. In the previous analysis we argued that the optimal policy should aim at minimizing the squared discrepancy between transitory income and the current account (which was equal to the balance of payments). Suppose now that, given the rate of interest, portfolio holders wish to add to their holdings of securities a fraction β of their estimated transitory income. Under these circumstances, only a fraction $(1 - \beta)$ of the current account should be offset by monetary flows, and the analogous equation to (14') becomes

$$[c_t - E(Y_t)] \simeq [\mu - (1 - \gamma)\alpha k\theta - \beta\,\frac{\text{cov}(\mu,\theta)}{\sigma_\theta^2}\,\theta]y + \text{constant}, \tag{24}$$

where the constant in (24) is independent of the current values of the shocks and of γ, and where the term $[\beta\,\text{cov}(\mu,\theta)/\sigma_\theta^2]y\theta$ represents the desired change in security holdings given the (conditional) estimate of transitory income. Minimizing the squared value of (24) with respect to γ yields the optimal intervention index:

$$\gamma^* = 1 - (1 - \beta)\,\frac{\text{cov}(\mu,\theta)}{\alpha k\sigma_\theta^2}\,. \tag{25}$$

As is evident, when $\beta = 0$, the optimal intervention index in eq. (25) is identical to that in eq. (16). Further, as long as the covariance between μ and $(\mu + \chi + \epsilon - \delta)$ is positive, a rise in the fraction β raises the optimal intervention index. Thus

$$\frac{\partial\gamma^*}{\partial\beta} > 0. \tag{26}$$

The higher is the share of transitory income that is absorbed by changes in the holdings of securities, the larger becomes the desirability of greater flexibility of exchange rates. The rationale for that result is quite clear since a high value of β (which may be viewed as reflecting a high degree of capital mobility) implies that a larger fraction of the real shocks can be cushioned through the international capital market and, thereby, reducing the need for international reserves flows.

Finally, when some of the cushioning is provided by the capital account, the standard deviation of the optimal balance of payments becomes

$$\sigma_{B^*} = (1 - \beta)\,\frac{\sigma_\mu^2}{\sigma_\theta^2}\,y\sigma_\theta, \tag{27}$$

which is smaller than the magnitude corresponding to the case of no capital mobility. Again, in the special case for which $\beta = 0$, eq. (27) becomes identical to eq. (22').

2. The supply of output

Up to this point we have assumed that variations in the supply of output are determined exclusively by the characteristics of the stochastic shock μ. In what follows we modify the specification of eq. (1) and we assume a supply function of the Lucas and Rapping (1969) variety. Accordingly, output is assumed to depend on the ratio of realized to expected prices. Thus,

$$Y_t = y \left(\frac{P_t}{E_{t-1}P_t} \right)^h e^\mu, \tag{28}$$

where $E_{t-1}P_t$ denotes the expected price level for period t based on the information available at period $t - 1$, h denotes the elasticity of the supply of output with respect to the ratio of realized to expected prices and, as before, μ denotes a stochastic disturbance. The specification in eq. (28) may be rationalized in terms of models which allow for a confusion between relative and absolute price changes like in Lucas (1973) as well as in terms of models which postulate short-term fixity of nominal wages, e.g. Fischer (1977). Using the first two terms of a Taylor expansion, the supply of output in eq. (28) can be approximated as

$$Y_t \simeq y [1 + \mu + h(\chi + \hat{S}_t)], \tag{29}$$

where $\hat{S}_t$ denotes the percentage change in the exchange rate, i.e. $\hat{S}_t \equiv \ln S_t - \ln S_{t-1}$.

Under full flexibility of exchange rates, changes in the rate ensure that the money market clears. Thus, analogously to eq. (6),

$$kY_t e^\epsilon = \frac{\bar{M}_t}{S_t p^* e^\chi}, \tag{30}$$

where, from eq. (4'), $S_t p^* e^\chi$ designates the price level. Differentiating eq. (30) logarithmically and using eq. (15) and (29) for $\bar{M}_t$ and Y_t, the change in the exchange rate may be expressed as

$$\theta \equiv \frac{\mu + h\chi + \chi + \epsilon - \delta}{1 + h} = -\hat{S}_t. \tag{31}$$

The equality in eq. (31) between the change in the exchange rate and the sum of the shocks θ, is confined to the case in which the exchange rate is fully flexible. Under managed float $-\hat{S}_t = \gamma \theta$, and the supply of output becomes

$$Y_t \simeq y[1 + \mu + h(\chi - \gamma\theta)]. \tag{29'}$$

Using the previous expressions for the values of consumption and output, the discrepancy between consumption and expected income may be approximated by

$$[c_t - \mathrm{E}(Y_t)] \simeq [\mu + h\chi - \{(1 - \gamma)\alpha k + \gamma h\}\theta]y. \tag{32}$$

In this formulation, $\mu + h\chi$ may be referred to as a real shock. It is composed of two terms: the first is the genuine output supply shock μ, while the second is induced by the effective foreign price shock χ that is translated into changes in output through the supply elasticity h. Thus, in addition to its direct monetary effect on the price level, χ contributes to output variations. It is noteworthy that in the special case for which $h = 0$, the value of θ reduces to the one obtained in the previous analysis, and the real shock reduces to μ.

The optimal intervention index, γ^*, is computed so as to minimize the discrepancy between $\mu + h\chi$ and $[(1 - \gamma)\alpha k + \gamma h]\theta$. It follows that

$$\gamma^* = 1 - \frac{b - h}{\alpha k - h}, \tag{33}$$

where b denotes the regression coefficient of the real shock $\mu + h\chi$ on θ, i.e.

$$b = \frac{\mathrm{cov}(\mu + h\chi, \theta)}{\sigma_\theta^2}.$$

As is evident, in the special case for which the value of the output elasticity h is zero, eq. (33) coincides with (16).

As is revealed by eq. (33), the magnitude of γ^* depends on the stochastic structure of the economy and on whether αk – the propensity to save out of transitory income exceeds or falls short of h – the elasticity of output with respect to the ratio of realized to expected prices. As long as $\alpha k > h$, the relation between γ^* and the variances of μ and $(\epsilon - \delta)$ is similar to the one analyzed before: a rise in σ_μ^2 lowers γ^* while a rise in $\sigma_{(\epsilon - \delta)}^2$ raises it. On the other hand, when $\alpha k < h$, these relations are reversed and a rise in the variance of $(\epsilon - \delta)$ lowers it. The rationale for this reversal is that when the value of h is high (relative to αk), changes in the price level which result from monetary shocks induce relatively large changes in output. Thus, when $\alpha k < h$, monetary shocks act more like real shocks. Finally, since the foreign price shock exerts both real and monetary effects, the dependence of γ^* on σ_χ^2 depends on the variances of the real and the monetary shocks as well as on the sign of $\alpha k - h$:

$$\frac{\partial \gamma^*}{\partial \sigma_\chi^2} = (\alpha k - h)[(1 + h)\sigma_\mu^2 - h(1 + h)\sigma_{\epsilon - \delta}^2]. \tag{34}$$

3. Optimal managed float with tradable and non-tradable goods

The preceding analysis was confined to an economy whose production consists only of commodities that are traded internationally. This assumption implied that, except for random deviations from purchasing power parities, the domestic price level was tied to the foreign price. In this section we extend the analysis to an economy which produces both traded and non-traded goods. This production structure relaxes the constraint that was imposed by the small country assumption. Due to its relative size the economy is a price taker in the world traded goods market but it is obviously large in the market for its own non-traded goods. Thus, the relative price of non-traded goods may not be viewed as given to the small economy but rather it is determined endogenously by the market-clearing conditions. In extending the analysis we first specify the stochastic characteristics of the production structure and then proceed to determine the optimal intervention index.

3.1 Equilibrium in the market for non-traded goods

Production of traded and non-traded goods is assumed to be carried along a production possibility frontier which is assumed to be concave to the origin. Denoting the nominal prices of traded and non-traded goods by P^T and P^N, respectively, we define the relative price of non-traded goods by $q \equiv P^N/P^T$. Production of traded goods X^T is assumed to depend negatively on the relative price according to

$$X^T = X^T(q)e^{\mu}, \tag{35}$$

where μ, which denotes the real shock, is defined in eq. (1). Production of non-traded goods X^N is assumed to depend positively on the relative price according to

$$X^N = X^N(q)e^{\omega + \mu}; \quad \omega \sim N(-\sigma_{\omega}^2/2, \sigma_{\omega}^2), \tag{36}$$

where ω denotes a stochastic shock that is *specific* to the production of non-traded goods. Thus, μ may be viewed as an aggregative real shock which moves the transformation schedule in a uniform way while ω may be viewed as a sector specific real shock.

On the demand side it is assumed that the demand for the two goods is homothetic and that the share of spending on non-traded goods depends negatively on the relative price. Measuring income as the value of production in terms of traded goods and denoting the share of spending on non-traded goods by ψ, we can describe the equilibrium in that market (when income equals spending as under flexible exchange rates) by eq. (37):

$$\psi(q)[qX^N(q)e^{\omega} + X^T(q)]e^{\mu} = qX^N(q)e^{\omega + \mu}. \tag{37}$$

In eq. (37), the left-hand side denotes the demand for non-traded goods while the right-hand side describes the supply. Equation (37) implies that the equilibrium relationship between the relative price and the specific real shock may be expressed as

$$q = q_0 e^{-m\omega},$$

where q_0 denotes the equilibrium relative price in the absence of shocks and where m denotes the elasticity of the relative price with respect to the relative price shock, i.e.

$$m = \frac{1}{\eta/(1 - \psi) + 1 + \xi^N + \xi^T},$$

where η denotes the elasticity of the share of spending on non-traded goods (defined to be positive) and where ξ^N and ξ^T denote, respectively, the elasticities of supply of non-traded and traded goods with respect to their relative price.

3.2 The optimal intervention index

When the exchange rate is freely flexible, the demand for real balances equals the supply at each moment of time. Assuming, as before, that the demand is proportional to income and is subject to a stochastic shock ϵ, money market equilibrium obtains when

$$k[qX^N(q)e^{\omega} + X^T(q)]e^{\mu+\epsilon} = \frac{\bar{M}_t}{S_{t-1}p^*e^{\chi}e^{-\theta}}, \qquad (39)$$

where $\bar{M}_t$ is defined in eq. (15)[10] and where the denominator on the right-hand side denotes the price level P_t^T. The parameter θ denotes the percentage change in the exchange rate that is necessary to ensure stock equilibrium in the money market. By differentiating eq. (39) and using (38) for the equilibrium relative price we note that θ, the percentage change in the exchange rate that is required to clear the money market under a freely flexible exchange rate regime, is[11]

$$\theta = \mu + \chi + \epsilon - \delta + \omega\psi(1 - m). \qquad (40)$$

As before, θ denotes the global shock. In this case, however, it also contains terms that reflect the effects of changes in the relative price which result from the various shocks.

---

[10] Since the economy produces both goods, permanent income in this case is defined as the value of production in terms of traded goods when the relative price is q_0.

[11] In deriving eq. (40) we have used the envelope theorem for movements along the transformation curve according to which $\psi\xi^N - (1 - \psi)\xi^T = 0$.

It is relevant to note that when the specific real shock (ω) is zero, the required change in the exchange rate is, as before, $\mu + \chi + \epsilon - \delta$.

The above analysis characterized the equilibrium under a freely flexible exchange rate regime. When the exchange rate is managed, only a fraction γ of the stock disequilibrium in the money market is allowed to be eliminated through changes in the exchange rate. In terms of eq. (39), when the exchange rate is managed the domestic currency price of traded goods becomes $P_t^T = S_{t-1} p^* e^\chi e^{-\gamma\theta}$, and the money market remains in stock disequilibrium. Under such circumstances, the value of income diverges from the value of spending by the resultant flow demand for real balances [as indicated by eq. (13)]. Consequently, the demand for non-traded goods is not described any more by the left-hand side of eq. (37) — which was only appropriate for a freely flexible exchange rate regime. Rather, the demand for non-traded goods is equal to

$$\psi(q)\left[\bar{Y}_t - \frac{\alpha(L_t - \bar{M}_t)}{P_t^T} \right],$$

where $\bar{Y}_t$ denotes the value of output in terms of traded goods. By substituting the previous expressions for $\bar{Y}_t, L_t, \bar{M}_t$ and P_t^T and equating the demand for non-traded goods to the supply, we obtain the equilibrium relative price of non-traded goods:

$$q = q_0 e^{-m\omega - (1-\gamma)\theta z}, \tag{41}$$

where

$$z = \frac{m\alpha k}{\psi m\alpha k + (1 - \psi)} < 1.$$

Equation (41) reveals that the equilibrium relative price is influenced by both the specific shock ω and the global shock θ. The sensitivity of the equilibrium price to the specific shock depends on the elasticities of demand and supply which determine the value of the parameter m. This sensitivity is independent of the exchange rate regime. On the other hand, the dependence of the equilibrium price on the global shock depends on the intervention index γ. The higher the value of γ the smaller is the effect of the global shock. In the extreme case for which $\gamma = 1$, the exchange rate is freely flexible and the equilibrium relative price depends only on the specific real shock ω. In that case eq. (41) coincides with (38).

In order to find the optimal intervention index we turn to the specification of the objective function. We first note that the objective function (12) needs to be specified in greater care once there are traded and non-traded goods. In order to avoid an index number problem we express the value of consumption and production in terms of the general price index which is assumed to be a Cobb–Douglas function of the prices of the two goods. Thus, if we denote the values of spending and income (measured in terms of traded goods) by $\bar{c}_t$ and $\bar{Y}_t$, respectively, their corresponding values in terms of the general price index are $\bar{c}_t/q^\psi$ and $\bar{Y}_t/q^\psi$, and the loss function becomes

$$E\left[\frac{\bar{c}_t}{q^\psi} - E\left(\frac{\bar{Y}_t}{q^\psi}\right)\right]^2 .$$

Substituting the previous expressions for the real values of consumption and income and expanding in Taylor series we approximate the discrepancy between real consumption and expected real income by

$$\left[\frac{\bar{c}_t}{q^\psi} - E\left(\frac{\bar{Y}_t}{q^\psi}\right)\right] \simeq [(\mu + \omega\psi) - \alpha k\{(\mu + \omega\psi)$$

$$+ (\chi + \epsilon - \delta - \theta\gamma + \hat{q}\,\psi)\}] \frac{\bar{y}}{q_0^\psi} , \qquad (42)$$

where $\bar{y}$ denotes the permanent value of income in terms of traded goods and where $\hat{q}$ denotes the percentage change in the equilibrium relative price of non-traded goods. In eq. (42), $\mu + \omega\psi$ and $(\chi + \epsilon - \delta - \theta\gamma + \hat{q}\psi)$ may be referred to, respectively, as the real shock and the monetary shock.[12] Using eq. (40) as the definition of the global shock θ and substituting from eq. (41) for the relative price change, the discrepancy between consumption and permanent income can be expressed as

$$\left[\frac{\bar{c}_t}{q^\psi} - E\,\frac{\bar{Y}_t}{q^\psi}\right] \simeq [\mu + \omega\psi - (1 - \gamma)(1 - \psi z)\alpha k\theta] \frac{\bar{y}}{q_0^\psi} . \qquad (42')$$

Minimizing the loss function amounts to choosing γ so as to minimize the squared discrepancy between $\mu + \omega\psi$ and $(1 - \gamma)(1 - \psi z)\alpha k\theta$. Following the same logic of the signal extraction problem of the previous analysis, individuals who observe the global shock θ (through its effect on the exchange rate) attempt to estimate the real shock component which in this case is composed of the ordinary real shock μ plus $\omega\psi$ which represents the effect of the specific real shock on the real value of aggregate output in terms of the general price level. Computing the least squares estimate of the relevant regression coefficient yields the optimal intervention index:

$$\gamma^* = 1 - \left(1 + \frac{\psi}{1 - \psi}\,\alpha km\right) \frac{\text{cov}(\mu + \omega\psi, \theta)}{\alpha k\sigma_\theta^2} . \qquad (43)$$

As in the earlier sections, the magnitude of the optimal intervention index depends on the structure of the economy. In general, the optimal value of γ^* declines when the

---

[12]   As may be seen, the real shock does not include the effect of the relative price change, $\hat{q}$, since, due to the envelope theorem, the change in price does not affect the value of production. The effect of $\hat{q}$ is classified as a monetary shock since it induces a change in the price level (equal to $\hat{q}\psi$).

variance of the real shock rises. In this context both σ_μ^2 and σ_ω^2 are viewed as real shocks. Also, consistent with the previous results a higher value of αk is associated with a higher value of γ^*.

The new results of this section concern the relation between the optimal intervention index and the share of the non-traded goods sector (which may characterize the degree to which the economy is open), as well as between the optimal intervention index and the elasticities of demand and supplies of traded and non-traded goods. It can be shown that as long as the covariance between the real shock and the global shock is positive, a higher value of ψ is associated with a *lower* value of γ^*:

$$\frac{\partial \gamma^*}{\partial \psi} < 0. \tag{44}$$

Thus, a high share of spending on (and production of) non-traded goods, tends to reduce the desirability of a greater flexibility of exchange rates. This result seems to conflict with some of the well-known arguments on the relationship between the openness of the economy and the optimal exchange rate regime [e.g. McKinnon (1963)]. Likewise, by noting that m — the elasticity of the relative price of non-traded goods — depends negatively on η, ξ^N and ξ^T, it follows that

$$\frac{\partial \gamma^*}{\partial \eta} > 0, \quad \frac{\partial \gamma^*}{\partial \xi^N} > 0, \quad \frac{\partial \gamma^*}{\partial \xi^T} > 0. \tag{45}$$

Thus, the higher is the degree of flexibility in the structure of an economy the larger becomes the need for increased flexibility of exchange rates.

These results can be rationalized by noting from eq. (41) that, *ceteris paribus*, a given monetary shock induces a larger change in the relative price of non-traded goods the higher is the relative share of that sector and the lower are the elasticities of demand and supply. For a given exchange rate the change in the relative price is reflected in a change in the nominal price of non-traded goods which in turns affects the aggregate price level in proportion to the relative share ψ. The induced change in the price level mitigates the initial disequilibrium and thereby reduces the need for exchange rate flexibility. When all goods are internationally traded so that the internal relative price structure cannot be adjusted, the necessary changes in the price level can only be obtained through changes in the exchange rate. In contrast, the presence of non-traded goods provides for a flexible internal price structure which is capable of inducing some of the necessary adjustments in the price level. It follows that the need for exchange rate flexibility is reduced the higher is the degree of price level flexibility which, in turn, depends negatively on the elasticities of demand and supply, and positively on the relative share of non-traded goods.[13]

[13]   The conventional result that γ^* depends positively on γ reflects the assumption that both the foreign currency price of traded goods *and* the domestic currency price of non-traded goods are given. In that case changes in the exchange rate are the only source for changes in the price level

This discussion of the relationship between internal price flexibility and the optimal exchange rate regime has implications for the choice between tariffs and quotas as alternative forms of commercial policy. In some respects the imposition of an import quota (in contrast with the imposition of an import tariff) may be viewed as transforming a traded commodity whose relative price is determined in world markets into a non-traded commodity whose price is determined in the domestic market. It follows that the desirability of exchange rate flexibility is lower for economies with import quotas than for economies with equivalent import tariffs since the former enjoy a greater degree of internal price flexibility than the latter. Put differently, *ceteris paribus*, a rise in the degree of exchange rate flexibility provides an incentive to convert quota protection into tariff protection.

Inspection of eq. (43) and its comparison with (16) reveals that even when the specific shocks are zero, the optimal intervention index for an economy with non-traded goods is smaller than the corresponding coefficient for an economy that produces only traded goods. Therefore, the mere existence of non-traded goods raises the desirability of greater fixity of exchange rates. The explanation is that even in the absence of specific supply shocks changes in demand will be absorbed in part by changes in the price of non-traded goods. The induced change in the price level will mitigate the initial disequilibrium and thereby reduce the need for exchange rate flexibility. Finally, it can be seen that in the special case for which $\psi = 0$, eq. (43) coincides with (16).

4. Concluding remarks

In this paper we have analyzed aspects of the economics of managed float. We have shown that the choice of the optimal exchange rate regime depends on the nature and the origin of the stochastic shocks that affect the economy. Generally, the higher is the variance of real shocks which affect the supply of goods, the larger becomes the desirability of fixity of exchange rates. The rationale for that implication is that the balance of payments serves as a shock absorber which mitigates the effect of real shocks on consumption. The importance of this factor diminishes the larger is the economy's access to world capital markets. On the other hand, the desirability of exchange rate flexibility increases the larger are the variances of the shocks to the demand for money, to the supply of money, to foreign prices and to purchasing power parities. All of these shocks exert a similar effect and their sum was referred to as the effective monetary shock. We have also shown that the desirability of exchange rate flexibility increases the larger is the propensity to save out of transitory income. When we extended the analysis to an economy which produces traded and non-traded goods it was shown that the desirability of exchange rate flexibility diminishes the higher is the share of

---

and, as a result, the required change in the exchange rate is larger the smaller is the share of traded goods (i.e. the higher is γ). Our analysis shows that this dependence is reversed when the price of non-traded goods is flexible.

non-traded goods relative to traded goods and the lower are the elasticities of demand and supply of the two goods.

As a general comment it should be noted that in this paper monetary policy and foreign exchange intervention were treated as being close substitutes. In fact, as a first approximation, in our framework, these two policies are non-distinguishable. It is believed that this feature of the model is much closer to reality than would be the other extreme in which monetary policy and foreign exchange policies are viewed as two independent policy instruments.

The special role of the exchange rate should also be noted. In our framework the exchange rate (and thereby the price level) is determined to a large extent by considerations of asset market equilibrium. This characteristic is in accord with the recent developments of the theory of exchange rate determination.

An important characteristic of the approach is that the choice of an exchange rate regime is an integral part of a general optimization process. It calls, therefore, for an explicit specification of the objective function as a prerequisite to the analysis. This feature is emphasized since such a specification of the objective function has been neglected by much of the writings in the area.

A limitation of the analysis is that, except for the discussion in section 2.6, the model did not incorporate explicitly the implications of an integrated world capital market which reflects itself in the capital account of the balance of payments and which prevents insulation from stochastic shocks to world interest rates. It should be emphasized, however, that the mere access to world capital markets and the ability to borrow are unlikely to alter the essentials of our analysis since they are unlikely to eliminate the occasional need for using international reserves. Most countries cannot expect to be able to borrow any amount at a given rate of interest. Rather, the borrowing rate is likely to rise when the country's net debtor position rises. This rise reflects the deterioration of the quality of the loans which is due to the deterioration of the economy's credit worthiness. As a result, countries will find it useful to hold and use international reserves in order to reduce the likelihood of facing a steeply rising cost of borrowing. In that sense, the holdings of international reserves may be viewed as a form of forward borrowing that is likely to continue even when capital markets are highly integrated.

It should be noted that the present specification of the nature of the shocks is somewhat biased in favor of government intervention since to some extent the shocks have been presumed to originate from the instability of the private sector rather than from the actions of government policies. Furthermore, the concept of the optimal intervention index that is implied by the optimal managed float was developed as a policy prescription for the monetary authorities. This was motivated by realism and could be rationalized in terms of the presumption that, compared with the private sector, the monetary authorities possess superior information concerning their own actions. In principle, however, much of the optimal mix could also be performed by the private sector.

Finally, it is relevant to note that as a practical matter it is unlikely that a policymaker will be capable of implementing policies with sufficient precision so as to distinguish between cases in which, for example, $\gamma^* = 0.2$ and those for which $\gamma^* = 0.3$. Thus, when the optimal intervention index turns out to be about 0.3 or less, it is likely that the practical policy would be that of a fixed exchange rate; likewise, when the optimal intervention index turns out to be about 0.7 or more, it is likely that the practical policy would be that of flexible exchange rates. In that sense the choice of an exchange rate regime may be viewed as the outcome of the search for a second-best solution and the analysis in this paper should be interpreted as providing a qualitative guide for such a choice.

References

Aizenman, Joshua, 1980, Optimal managed flexibility of exchange rate, unpublished manuscript, University of Chicago.

Boyer, Russel S., 1978, Optimal foreign exchange market intervention, Journal of Political Economy 86, Dec. 1045–55.

Buiter, Willem, 1977, Optimal foreign exchange market intervention with rational expectations, unpublished manuscript, London School of Economics.

Enders, Walter and Harvey E. Lapan, 1979, Stability, random disturbances and the exchange rate regime, Southern Economic Journal 45, July, 49–70.

Fischer, Stanley, 1976, Stability and exchange rate system in a monetarist model of the balance of payments, in: R.Z. Aliber (ed.), The political economy of monetary reform (Allanheld, Osmun and Co., Monclair N.J.), 59–73.

Fischer, Stanley, 1977, Long-term contracts, rational expectations and the optimal policy rule, Journal of Political Economy 85, February, 191–206.

Flood, Robert P., 1979, Capital mobility and the choice of exchange rate system, International Economic Review 20, June, 405–16.

Frenkel, Jacob A., 1976, An analysis of the conditions necessary for a return to greater fixity of exchange rates, Report for the Department of State, U.S. Government, contract no. 1722–520100.

Frenkel, Jacob A., 1980, The demand for international reserves under pegged and flexible exchange rate regimes and aspects of the economics of managed float, in: H. Frisch and G. Schwödiauer (eds.), The economics of flexible exchange rates, supplement to Kredit und Kapital, Heft 6 (Duncker and Humblot, Berlin). Also reprinted in: D. Bigman and T. Taya (eds.), The functioning of flexible exchange rates: theory, evidence and policy implications (Ballinger, Cambridge).

Gray, Jo Anna, 1976, Wage indexation: A macroeconomic approach, Journal of Monetary Economics 2, April, 231–46.

Kenen, Peter B., 1969, The theory of optimum currency areas: an eclectic view, in: R.A. Mundell and A.K. Swoboda (eds.), Monetary problems of the international economy (University of Chicago Press, Chicago), 41–60.

Laffer, Arthur B., 1973, Two arguments for fixed rates, in: H.G. Johnson and A.K. Swoboda (eds.), The economics of common currencies (Allen & Unwin, London).

Lucas, Robert E., Jr., 1973, Some international evidence on output–inflation trade-offs, American Economic Review 63, June, 326–34.

Lucas, Robert E., Jr., and Leonard A. Rapping, 1969, Real wages, employment and the price level, Journal of Political Economy 77, September–October, 721–54.

McKinnon, Ronald I., 1963, Optimal currency areas, American Economic Review 52, September, 717–24.

Modigliani, Franco and Hossein Askari, 1973, The international transfer of capital and the propagation of domestic disturbances under alternative payment systems. Banca Nationale del Lavoro Quarterly Review 26, Dec. 295–310.

Mundell, Robert A., 1961, A theory of optimum currency areas, American Economic Review, Vol. 51, Nov. 509–17. Reprinted as chapter 12 in his International economics, 1968.

Mundell, Robert A., 1973, Uncommon arguments for common currencies, in: H.G. Johnson and A.K. Swoboda (eds.), The economics of common currencies (Allen & Unwin, London).

Poole, William, 1970, Optimal choice of monetary instruments in a simple stochastic macro-model, Quarterly Journal of Economics 83, May, 197–216.

Stein, Jerome L., 1963, The optimum foreign exchange market, American Economic Review 53, 384–402.

Recent Issues in the Theory of Flexible Exchange Rates, edited by E. Claassen and P. Salin
© *North-Holland Publishing Company, 1983*

Chapter 9.2

COMMENT ON FRENKEL AND AIZENMAN

Emil CLAASSEN

The "optimal management of exchange rates" concerns the optimum mix between two extremes, a fixed and a pure flexible exchange rate, for a given currency. It provides a rationale for the dirty float even though one result of an optimal management of exchange rates could be either of the two extremes: a fixed or a pure flexible exchange rate. According to a previous analysis by Stanley Fisher, the choice between the two extreme exchange rate regimes depended on the source of the underlying exogenous shocks to which the economy is exposed when the criterion for the choice of the exchange rate regime is that of minimizing the fluctuations around the steady-state consumption. A fixed exchange rate system is preferred to a flexible one when the exogenous shocks are of the real type and the opposite holds when the disturbances are of the monetary type. This view is not put into question by Jacob Frenkel and Joshua Aizenman, but it is embedded into a larger framework with, *inter alia*, two interesting results. If one takes into account explicitly capital movements, the desirability of the fixity of exchange rates diminishes even with the dominance of real shocks over monetary shocks. Secondly, the desirability of exchange rate fixity diminishes still more, the lower the share of non-traded goods relative to traded goods. Consequently, even in the presence of a predominance of real shocks, a high degree of flexibility of the exchange rate would be optimal when there is a high degree of capital mobility and when the sector of non-traded goods is relatively small, the first factor serving as a shock absorber and the second one dampening the relative price effect of traded and non-traded goods on the demand and supply of the two goods.

Any model has its restrictive assumptions. They do not invalidate it, but they may limit its explanatory power of real phenomena.

One restrictive assumption concerns the origin of shocks and, in particular, of real shocks which are supposed to come mainly from the instability of the private sector. However, if the real shocks are induced by the government sector, e.g. via monetary policy and interventions in the foreign exchange market, a monetary rule would be preferable to an exchange rate rule.

The other restrictive assumption relates to the objective the monetary authorities pursue which consists of stabilizing (of minimizing the variance of) steady-state income and, by this, steady-state consumption. In reality, there is often a mixture of targets — of an income-level target *and* of a price level target. When a currency tends to depreciate more than its PPP-value, monetary authorities intervene, often for reasons of price-level stability (in particular, in small open economies) so that monetary shocks (here the random deviation of the exchange rate from PPP) would lead to a lower degree of flexibility in the exchange rate whereas the Frenkel—Aizenman model would opt for a higher degree of flexibility. In the opposite case when a currency tends to appreciate more than its PPP-value, the Frenkel—Aizenman approach may become relevant to the extent that monetary authorities now look at the income-level target in such a way that they will allow a higher flexibility in the exchange rate. Consequently, there is some asymmetry in the behaviour of monetary authorities towards a (potential) depreciation and towards a (potential) appreciation which can be explained by the dominance of one policy objective over another.

I have two more remarks on the Frenkel—Aizenman paper. The first concerns the relation between the optimum degree of flexibility of the exchange rate and the optimum volume of international reserves. The second one relates to the issue of optimum flexibility under perfect capital mobility.

(1) In the Frenkel—Aizenman paper, the determination of the optimal degree of flexibility of the exchange rate (γ^*) implies implicitly the simultaneous determination of the optimal level of international reserves (R^*)

$$R^* = (1 - \gamma^*)\bar{R},$$

where $\bar{R}$ is that optimal level of international reserves which should be held in a system of fixed exchange rates. γ^* can also be designated as the degree to which the money supply is exogenous and $(1 - \gamma^*)$ as the degree to which the quantity of money is endogenous. Figure 9.1 illustrates a possible trade-off relationship between the two pol-

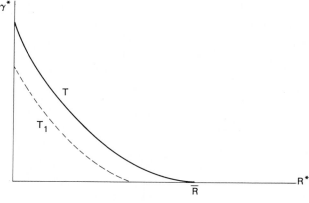

Figure 9.1.

icies. The line T implies that each policy operates under the principle of "decreasing returns" either to eliminate a balance-of-payments disequilibrium (γ^*) or to finance it (R^*), otherwise T would be a straight line.

But these two policies are not the only policies central banks dispose of and use effectively. If one looks at the literature on the demand for international reserves to which Frenkel has also made important contributions in the past, there is a whole range of balance-of-payments adjustment policies among which the degree of flexibility of the exchange rate constitutes only one among many others. There are expenditure-changing policies (e.g. fiscal policy) and expenditure-switching policies (e.g. parity changes) which influence the trade balance and there are other policies like monetary policy in terms of an interest-rate policy or exchange controls which are utilized to influence the capital balance. Thus, the question of the "optimal management of exchange rates" implies the determination of an optimal mix of several policies.

The most frequent mix which has been used over past years is that of exchange-rate flexibility, international reserves and interest-rate policy combined — always in the very short-run — with a sterilization policy of the monetary base. The interest-rate policy would shift the trade-off line T in fig. 9.1, e.g. towards T_1, such that for an unchanged reserves policy, the optimal degree of exchange-rate flexibility would be lower. Such an analysis must also answer the question of whether an extended policy mix is a desirable one and therefore to be recommended.

(2) My second remark concerns Frenkel—Aizenman's derivation of the optimum degree of exchange-rate flexibility under the assumption of capital movements. When there is no capital mobility and when real shocks are predominant, a low degree of flexibility is recommended, in particular for small open economies; then international reserves serve as a shock absorber which reduces the effect of real shocks on income and consumption. In the presence of capital mobility and neglecting the existence of non-traded goods, capital flows fulfill the same function such that perfect capital mobility could imply full flexibility. In the following, I would like to examine this special case.

Suppose for the moment that the individuals do not expect any change in the exchange rate. In this case, the domestic interest rate is always equal to the foreign interest rate and any interest-rate policy is excluded. I shall simplify the question of the optimal degree of exchange-rate flexibility in the traditional terms of either fixed or fully flexible exchange rates. Consequently, the money supply will be endogenous in the first case and exogenous in the second. Now I shall take into account the approach proposed by Poole (1970) who operates also with real and monetary shocks and I extend it to an open economy under perfect capital mobility as it is done in the paper by Melitz for this conference and, in particular, in one of his other publications (1979).

Jacques Melitz proposes figs. 9.2 and 9.3 — again our traditional IS-LM workhorses — in which the LM-curve is downward sloping because, for instance, wealth is an argument in the demand-for-money function and because wealth consists also of the holding of foreign assets. As a matter of course, the price level is absent in this simple Keynesian framework. The target income is $\bar{y}$ and income diverges from the target level by random shocks.

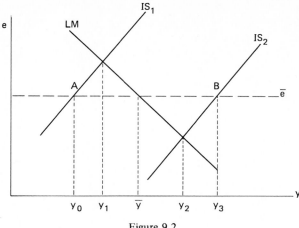

Figure 9.2.

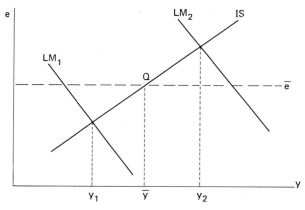

Figure 9.3.

From fig. 9.2 we can see that, if shocks are of the real type, the IS-curve shifts up-wards and downwards and income fluctuates between y_1 and y_2 under flexible ex-change rates. The income fluctuation is lower than under a fixed exchange rate $\bar{e}$ (y_0 and y_3) where the quantity of money is endogenous such that the LM-curve shifts to point A and to point B according to the monetary approach to the balance of pay-ments. Consequently, under perfect capital mobility, the flexibility of exchange rates would reduce fluctuations of real income as a consequence of real shocks.

Figure 9.3 tells us that fixed exchange rates are better when there is a dominance of nominal shocks shifting the LM-curve between LM_1 and LM_2. A flexible exchange rate would involve income fluctuations between y_1 and y_2. A fixed exchange rate ($\bar{e}$) together with an endogenous money supply would imply a LM-curve going through point Q and, by this, a tendency towards the maintenance of the target level of real income $\bar{y}$.[14]

The results of figs. 9.2 and 9.3 are in apparent opposition to Frenkel–Aizenman's observations. The difference may arise from the type of the underlying model. Frenkel and Aizenman use a classical model, whereas figs. 9.2 and 9.3 are pure Keynesian models.

References

Melitz, Jacques, 1979, Usage optimal des instruments monétaires en régime de changes flexibles, Revue Economique, September, 780–807.

Poole, William, 1970, Optimal choice of monetary policy instruments in a simple stochastic macro-model, Quarterly Journal of Economics, May, 197–216.

[14] In the case of expectations of a change in the exchange rate, the interest rate parity (in the case of flexible exchange rates) would imply that the LM-curve shifts also in fig. 9.2 giving rise to an even lower fluctuation in income and in fig. 9.3 provoking a greater fluctuation in income.

Recent Issues in the Theory of Flexible Exchange Rates, edited by E. Claassen and P. Salin
© *North-Holland Publishing Company, 1983*

Chapter 10.1

OPTIMAL STABILIZATION AND THE PROPER EXERCISE OF THE MONETARY-POLICY INSTRUMENTS UNDER FLEXIBLE EXCHANGE RATES

Jacques MELITZ*

By common experience, the advent of flexible exchange rates has brought monetary authorities new options. Recent theoretical efforts to frame their decision problems under this new regime draw their inspiration from Poole (1970). Poole considered a closed economy. But his model can be easily transposed to deal with a small open economy under flexible exchange rates [see Fortin (1980), Henderson (1979), Melitz (1979) and Sparks (1980)]. The current trend is to proceed very far in this direction [for example Boyer (1978), and Roper and Turnovsky (1980)], and to exploit an extreme form of Poole's analysis, which he himself was loath to follow. This involves his so-called "combination policy", which seems to do away with the problem of a choice of monetary-policy instruments. I shall argue, to the contrary, that there is no way to do away with the issue of this choice under any policy. Further, the choice is the only part of the problem of optimal stabilization that we are properly equipped to deal with at the moment, especially under flexible exchange rates. The rest of the problem of optimal stabilization is essentially a programme for research in the future.

The paper will also try to provide the simplest possible model that is capable of handling the question of this choice of instruments under flexible exchange rates. The proposed model goes beyond the mere transposition of Poole's IS–LM framework to an open economy. In addition, it admits some imperfect substitution between home and foreign bonds, and an official concern with prices as well as quantities. Nevertheless, the model is still quite tractable, and in it Poole's essential conclusions about the choice of instruments generally survive, thus attesting once more to the robustness of these findings. New conclusions, however, also follow. In particular, flexible exchange rates will be seen to add a new argument for monetary control in case the authorities choose also to control their foreign reserves instead of the exchange rate.

* I have benefited greatly from discussions with my colleague Paul Champsaur about sections 1 and 2. He should be totally exonerated from the errors, however. My thanks also to Robert Driscoll and J.L. Ford (University of Birmingham) and Benjamin Friedman (Harvard University) for useful comments.

1. The basis for a general theoretical problem of a choice of policy instruments

Poole begins with a standard IS–LM framework in which the supply of goods is infinitely elastic and, depending upon the decision to control the stock of money, the supply of money is either infinitely inelastic or infinitely elastic. In this model, the demand for goods and the demand for money simultaneously determine money income (Y) and depending on the previous choice, either the stock of money (M) or the interest rate (r). But the authorities cannot arbitrarily set both money and the interest rate. Poole next supposes a target level of money income (Y^*). Thereby he essentially converts the problem into one of optimal control. In the context of this next decision problem, the authorities take Y^* as given, and use the two previous equations simultaneously to determine the values of the two instruments. The same optimal control solution then obtains regardless of whether they decide to control one instrument or the other: the choice has no interest.

Following this, Poole introduces stochastic disturbances in the two equations. This then offers him a basis for a choice of instruments on the ground of a stabilization objective, that is, if the authorities are concerned about the dispersion of income around the mean as well as the mean. To take up his exact model and notation, we have:

$$Y = a_0 + a_1 r + u, \qquad a_0 > 0, \quad a_1 < 0, \tag{1}$$

$$M = b_0 + b_1 Y + b_2 r + v, \quad b_1 > 0, \quad b_2 < 0, \tag{2}$$

where u and v are disturbance terms, which are supposed to be normally distributed, of zero mean, and with respective standard deviations of σ_u^2 and σ_v^2. The variables Y, M and r may be supposed to be in logarithms so that a_1, b_1 and b_2 are elasticities. If we assume that Y cannot be observed except at discrete intervals, then based on the errors u and v, there will necessarily be a variance of income, σ_y^2, around the target level Y^*.[1] If the authorities decide to control r, this variance will be σ_u^2. If they decide to control M, it will be

$$\frac{b_2^2 \sigma_u^2 - 2a_1 b_2 \sigma_{uv} + a_1^2 \sigma_v^2}{(a_1 b_1 + b_2)^2}. \tag{3}$$

σ_u^2 is either greater or less than eq. (3) depending on

$$\frac{\sigma_u^2 (a_1 b_1 + b_2)^2}{b_2^2 \sigma_u^2 - 2a_1 b_2 \sigma_{uv} + a_1^2 \sigma_v^2} \gtrless 1. \tag{4}$$

---

[1]   This variance would also follow even if Y could be continuously observed but eqs. (1) and (2) were only true in discrete time since r still then could not be adjusted so as to keep Y continuously the same.

If only the authorities wish to reduce the variances of income, the previous inequality sign will offer them a criterion of choice of instruments: if greater than, money is preferable; if less than, the interest rate is.

In a subsequent development about which the rest of the literature has never been of a clear mind, Poole shows that, in principle, optimal stabilization implies his so-called "combination policy", which seems to dispose once more of any issue of a choice of instruments. For reasons that will occupy us later, Poole himself minimized the importance of the "combination policy". But what is of immediate interest to us is that the very concept of a "combination policy" is a dubious one. The authorities necessarily cannot simultaneously determine both M and r in Poole's framework. What they can do instead is to modify one instrument based on the observed value of the other. This is precisely what Poole's "combination policy" refers to [and what the "targets, instruments, and indicators" literature also centers upon; cf. Kareken, Muench and Wallace (1973) and Friedman (1975, 1977)]. But then there are clearly two possibilities: either to adapt M on the basis of observed values of r, or to adapt r on the basis of observed values of M. A neglected problem of choice then subsists.

This choice can be interpreted in terms of the following two alternative feedback rules (or official reaction functions):

$$M - M^* = c_1 (r - r^*),$$ (5)

and

$$r - r^* = c_1' (M - M^*).$$ (5a)[2]

M^* and r^* in these two equations refer to the solution values for M and r in the earlier system of eqs. (1) and (2) when Y^* is set equal to the mathematical expectation of Y. The additional presence of (5) and (5a) in the analysis then gives rise to two alternative, new systems of three equations — (1), (2) and (5), and (1), (2) and (5a) — in three unknowns, Y, M, and r (with M^* and r^* supposedly solved beforehand). The reduced-form equation for Y in the first case is

$$Y = Y^* + \frac{(b_2 - c_1) u - a_1 v}{b_2 - c_1 + a_1 b_1},$$ (6)

in the second

$$Y = Y^* + \frac{(1 - c_1' b_2) u - a_1 c_1' v}{1 - c_1' (b_2 + a_1 b_1)}.$$ (6a)

[2] Poole refers strictly to eq. (5) and writes this equation differently, namely, as:

$$M = c_0 + c_1 r$$

However this comes to the same, since he determines the c_0 coefficient residually after solving for c_1 just as we do.

Optimal stabilization then concerns the choice of c_1 or c_1'. The problem is to minimize σ_y^2 with respect to both and to see which of the two yields the lowest value of σ_y^2 (or the lowest loss). Accordingly, we must calculate the variances of the terms on the righthand sides of (6) and (6a) and then minimize them with regard to c_1 and c_1'. Poole solved this problem in the first case, eq. (6), or the only one of the two which he considered. His solution is:

$$c_1 = b_2 - \frac{a_1 (b_1 \sigma_{uv} + \sigma_v^2)}{b_1 \sigma_u^2 + \sigma_{uv}}. \tag{7}$$

In the case of (6a), the solution is instead

$$c_1' = \frac{b_1 \sigma_u^2 + \sigma_{uv}}{b_2 (b_1 \sigma_u^2 + \sigma_{uv}) - a_1 (b_1 \sigma_{uv} + \sigma_v^2)}, \tag{7a}$$

and we get exactly, as expected, $c_1' = 1/c_1$. Whether we substitute eq. (7) for c_1 in (6), or (7a) for c_1' in (6a), we obtain precisely the same value of σ_y^2:

$$\sigma_y^2 = E \left[\frac{b_1 \sigma_{uv} + \sigma_v^2 - (b_1 \sigma_u^2 + \sigma_{uv})v}{(\sigma_v + b_1 \sigma_u^2)^2} \right]^2. \tag{8}$$

Further, if only c_1 and c_1' are non-zero, and eqs. (7) and (7a) are global, not only local, minima, then (8) represents a lower loss than either "pure policy" [i.e. either σ_u^2 or eq. (3)]. Poole (1970) and LeRoy and Waud (1977) have separately shown, in different ways, that (8) does indeed yield a lower σ_y^2 — or at most as low a value of it — than the one resulting from either pure policy. By this chain of reasoning, we then seem to come back again to the previous conclusion that there is no basis for a choice of instruments in case of optimal stabilization, but this time on more solid ground.

It may be shown next, however, that this last conclusion depends on the assumption of instantaneous adjustment in continuous time. If we deviate from this extreme assumption, then an issue of stability may arise, which is likely to permit a clear choice between the instruments.

Let us suppose that the authorities do not respond continuously to the observed values of the uncontrolled instrument but only at intervals, however short. Later we shall insist that the authorities most likely have no choice in this matter since they are probably totally ignorant of the relevant parameters of eqs. (1) and (2) in continuous time. But for the moment we shall let this be mere assumption. Instead of the earlier feedback rules, we than have:

$$M_t - M^* = c_1 (r_{t-1} - r^*), \tag{5'}$$

$$r_t - r^* = c_1' (M_{t-1} - M^*) \quad \text{(see footnote 2).} \tag{5a'}$$

In the case of monetary control, the reduced-form equation for Y_t [based on eqs. (1), (2) and (5′)] is then the difference equation

$$Y_t = \text{constant} + \frac{c_1}{a_1 b_1 + b_2} Y_{t-1} + \frac{b_2}{a_1 b_1 + b_2} u_t$$

$$- \frac{c_1}{a_1 b_1 + b_2} u_{t-1} - \frac{a_1}{a_1 b_1 + b_2} v_t. \tag{6′}$$

In the case of interest rate control, this reduced-form equation is instead the difference equation:

$$Y_t = \text{constant} + c_1' (a_1 b_1 + b_2) Y_{t-1} + u_t - c_1' b_2 u_{t-1} + a_1 c_1' v_{t-1}. \tag{6a′}$$

On the basis of eq. (6′), the necessary and sufficient condition for stability is

$$- 1 < \frac{c_1}{a_1 b_1 + b_2} < 1. \tag{9}$$

On the basis of eq. (6a′), it is instead

$$- 1 < c_1' (a_1 b_1 + b_2) < 1$$

or

$$- 1 < \frac{a_1 b_1 + b_2}{c_1} < 1. \tag{9a}$$

If condition (9) is satisfied, condition (9a) necessarily is not. The stability condition therefore must decide against one alternative or the other, if not both.

We may focus next on condition (9). Since $a_1 b_1 + b_2$ is negative, if c_1 is also negative, this condition requires

$$c_1 > a_1 b_1 + b_2. \tag{10}$$

If c_1 is positive, (9) requires instead

$$- c_1 > a_1 b_1 + b_2. \tag{11}$$

Consider then what happens if the authorities continue to use the correct formula in case of instantaneous action even though they respond with a lag.[3] This we may do by substituting the earlier solution for $c_1 - b_2$, eq. (7), in eqs. (10) and (11); (10) in order to deal with the case of a negative c_1, and (11) in order to deal with the case of a positive c_1. For $c_1 < 0$, we get:

$$-\frac{a_1(b_1\sigma_{uv}+\sigma_v^2)}{b_1\sigma_u^2+\sigma_{uv}}>a_1b_1. \tag{12}$$

This condition will be fulfilled if

$$\frac{\sigma_v^2+b_1\sigma_{uv}}{b_1\sigma_u^2+\sigma_{uv}}>0, \tag{13}$$

and otherwise will be violated. The condition therefore will hold if $\sigma_{uv}\geq0$, *or else* if $\sigma_{uv}<0$ but both numerator and denominator of the ratio on the lefthand side (LHS) of eq. (13) are of the same sign. Under these circumstances therefore, the monetary instrument will be correct, and the interest rate that will lead to instability. If $\sigma_{uv}<0$ and the numerator and denominator of the ratio on the LHS of (13) are of opposite sign, then the monetary instrument is unstable, and the interest rate instrument is the right one to choose.

The case of $\sigma_{uv}<0$ (or $\rho_{uv}<0$) requires further discussion. In this example the condition for both numerator and denominator of the essential ratio term on the LHS of (13) to be positive is

$$-\frac{b_1}{\rho_{uv}}>\frac{\sigma_v^2}{\sigma_u^2}>-b_1\rho_{uv}, \tag{14}$$

and for both of them to be negative the two previous inequality signs in eq. (14) must be the opposite. Such two opposite inequality signs in (14) are impossible since $\rho_{uv}\geq-1$; therefore we can rule out negative values of both numerator and denominator in (13). Condition (14) also cannot be met if $\rho_{uv}=-1$. On the other hand, it is automatically met if $\rho_{uv}=0$. For $0<\rho_{uv}<-1$, there is a bounded range of σ_v^2/σ_u^2 values over which (14) is met. Within this range then, on the basis of the previous paragraph the monetary instrument will be stable. The amplitude of the range will be a positive function of ρ_{uv} (or the smallness of the negative value of ρ_{uv}) and b_1.[4]

This covers the case of $c_1<0$. If c_1 is positive, then the relevant stability condition is (11), not (10), and (11) together with (7) says:

---

[3]   As a result of further work with Paul Champsaur [Champsaur and Melitz (1982)] on a more general treatment of the impact of lagged adjustments in Poole's analysis, I would no longer argue that a stability problem is necessarily implicit with the introduction of lags. But I would still argue that any lags cast up a basis for a choice of instruments. What limits the argument in the text is the assumption that the authorities respond with a lag while the private sector does not do so.

[4]   Because of these bounds on the values of σ_v^2/σ_u^2 that are consistent with a positive variance–covariance ratio term of eq. (13), this term itself has an upper bound. That is, for any ρ_{uv} and b_1, the maximal ratio of σ_v^2/σ_u^2 which is consistent with (14) also yields a maximum positive value of the ratio term on the LHS of (13). While this LHS term then is unbounded with $\rho_{uv}\geq0$, it has a ceiling with $\rho_{uv}<0$. For any b_1, this ceiling approaches zero as ρ_{uv} moves toward -1.

$$\frac{a_1 \left(\sigma_v^2 + b_1 \sigma_{uv}\right)}{b_1 \sigma_u^2 + \sigma_{uv}} > a_1 b_1 + 2 b_2 \tag{15}$$

or

$$\frac{\sigma_v^2 + b_1 \sigma_{uv}}{b_1 \sigma_u^2 + \sigma_{uv}} < b_1 + \frac{2 b_2}{a_1} . \tag{16}$$

With c_1 positive, we know from (7) as such that the LHS of (15) is greater than b_2/a_1, therefore positive. Also b_2/a_1 is necessarily smaller than $2b_2/a_1 + b_1$ on the RHS of (15). Thus it follows that if c_1 is positive, the monetary instrument is essential for stability for values of the LHS of (15) above b_2/a_1 but below $(2b_2 + a_1 b_1)/a_1$. Above that range the interest rate is essential for stability. (Remember from the previous discussion of $c_1 < 0$ that in case of *positive* values below b_2/a_1, the monetary instrument is still essential for stability).

We can get a clearer picture of these conclusions if we focus on the simple case of $\rho_{uv} = 0$. In this case the basic variance–covariance ratio term in (13) or (15) reduces to $\sigma_v^2/b_1 \sigma_u^2$, which is always positive. Further, we can then relate c_1 and c_1' strictly to σ_v^2/σ_u^2, or the relative instability of the two markets. Figure 10.1 illustrates this simple case or considers the situation where the limiting value of c_1 in the adjustment process [based on (7)] is simply

$$c_1 = b_2 - \frac{a_1}{b_1} \frac{\sigma_v^2}{\sigma_u^2} . \tag{7'}$$

In the top panel of the figure, we show this limiting value as a function of σ_v^2/σ_u^2, and in the bottom panel we show correspondingly the limiting value of c_1' as a function of this ratio. The top panel thus concerns the case of monetary control; the bottom panel the one of interest rate control. On the top, the intercept with the vertical axis is b_2 (negative), the slope is $-a_1/b_1$ (positive), and the intercept with the horizontal axis is $b_2 b_1/a_1$. In the bottom panel, since $c_1' = 1/c_1$, the feedback rule breaks up into two hyperbolas, one in positive space, the other in negative space. On the basis of the previous argument, the entire hyperbola in negative space involves instability (since $c_1 < 0$ and (13) holds), while the hyperbola in positive space does too up to a certain point: namely $b_1 (2b_2 + a_1 b_1)/a_1$. Above this point, or once the c_1' values have retreated from extremely high levels and are now below $-1/(b_2 + a_1 b_1)$, we enter the stable range of the hyperbola in positive space. Correspondingly, we then come into the unstable range of the top panel, where c_1 is high: up above $-(b_2 + a_1 b_1)$ and boundless.

The instability in the case of the hyperbola in negative space is easy to intuit. Consider a positive disturbance in the goods market under interest rate control (or in the relevant case). Both income and money rise in the current period. But since $c_1' < 0$ this is a signal to the authorities to lower the interest rate in the next period. The result then is further to raise income, money demand, and money, and so on indefinitely. In the case of positive values of c_1 and c_1', the problem of instability is more difficult to intuit

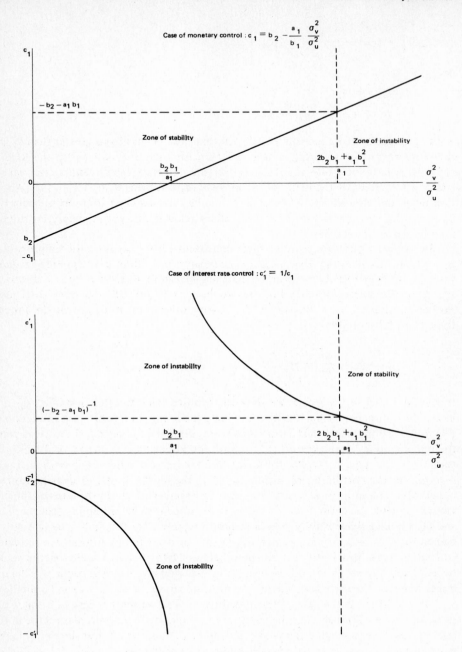

Figure 10.1. The optimal feedback coefficient in the absence of covariance.

because the problem does not lie in the direction of the feedback response as such, but the intensity.

Suppose next we compare the choice of instruments that would result from a pure policy with those resulting from optimal stabilization. The criterion of choice, in the case of a pure policy, is eq. (4). This criterion implies the choice of the monetary instrument if

$$\frac{\sigma_v^2}{\sigma_u^2} < \frac{b_1(2b_2 + a_1 b_1)}{a_1} + \frac{2b_2 \rho_{uv}\sigma_v}{a_1 \sigma_u}, \tag{4a}$$

and the opposite choice of the interest rate instrument in case of the opposite inequality sign. It then emerges that the choice of instruments is exactly the same as under optimal stabilization in case of the positive region of $(\sigma_v^2 + b_1 \sigma_{uv})/(b_1 \sigma_u^2 + \sigma_{uv})$. A mere rearrangement of terms in eq. (15), which defines the relevant condition of choice of the monetary instrument in the instance of a feedback rule of optimal stabilization (or the condition relating to the zone of positive c_1 values), suffices to show that (15) and (4a) are identical. The criterion of choice of pure policies does not apply, however, to the negative region of $(\sigma_v^2 + b_1 \sigma_{uv})/(b_1 \sigma_u^2 + \sigma_{uv})$ (hinging on $\rho_{uv} < 0$), thus it ignores a separate region where the interest rate instrument is preferable based on optimal stabilization, and in this sense is incomplete.[5]

Two fundamental conclusions follow. First, the choice of instruments is even more important in the case of optimal stabilization than in the case of a pure policy, since the authorities may then provoke instability themselves through the wrong choice of instruments. This is, of course, impossible under a "pure" policy, in which case the wrong choice of instruments can only lead to lower performance (higher variance of income). It is therefore clearly mistaken to consider the choice of instruments as immaterial under optimal stabilization, as is sometimes done. Second, at least under our assumptions, the criterion of choice between the two pure policies has very wide ap-

---

[5]   On the basis of the criterion of choice of pure policies, both choices of instruments are equally good if

$$\frac{\sigma_v^2}{\sigma_u^2} = \frac{b_1(2b_2 + a_1 b_1)}{a_1} + \frac{2b_2 \rho_{uv}\sigma_v}{a_1 \sigma_u}.$$

On the basis of the criterion of optimal stabilization, there are two similar critical points. But the problem at these two points is that neither choices of instruments is compatible with stability. One of these two points is the foregoing one in respect of the choice of pure policies (or equivalently

$$\frac{a_1(\sigma_v^2 + b_1 \sigma_{uv})}{b_1 \sigma_u^2 + \sigma_{uv}} = a_1 b_1 + 2b_2).$$ The other is $$\frac{a_1(\sigma_v^2 + b_1 \sigma_{uv})}{b_1 \sigma_u^2 + \sigma_{uv}} = 0.$$

If $\rho_{uv} \geqslant 0$, only the first of these two points is possible; if $-1 < \rho_{uv} < 0$, both may be possible, but only the latter one is sure to be so since, as explained in the preceding footnote, if ρ_{uv} and b_1 are low enough, the basic variance–covariance ratio may never even be able to attain as high a value as $(a_1 b_1 + 2b_2)/a_1$. The whole issue of instability is absent in the case of a pure policy, of course.

plication. Not only does this criterion deal with a general problem, but it deals with it in a nearly general way. If we are willing to consider $\sigma_v^2 + b_1 \sigma_{uv}$ and $b_1 \sigma_u^2 + \sigma_{uv}$ as always positive (which is not very restrictive) then this criterion deals with the problem in a perfectly general way. Thus, under our chosen conditions, the solution to the problem of the choice of pure policies treats a genuine aspect of optimal stabilization.

2. The issue of optimal stabilization

What importance shall we attach to full optimal stabilization, or in other words, the determination of a feedback rule of optimal stabilization as well as the choice of instruments? Poole took a skeptical attitude on this question in the closed economy case. I believe that the grounds for this skepticism are much wider under flexible exchange rates.

The basic problem with a special feedback rule of optimal stabilization is one of information. To quote Poole: "The success of the combination policy depends on knowledge of more parameters than does a pure money stock or pure interest rate policy ... a combination policy based on intuition may be worse than either of the pure policies" (1970, p. 209). In other words, the choice of pure policies does not require us to know anything about the stochastic structure of the system except whether we are on the left or right of a certain dividing line along a σ_v^2/σ_u^2 axis, or more generally, along a $(\sigma_v^2 + b_1 \sigma_{uv})/(b_1 \sigma_u^2 + \sigma_{uv})$ one. But optimal stabilization would require us also to know exactly where we are along the axis. Thus, the ability to choose between pure policies does not imply the ability to discern, even vaguely, the right feedback coefficient.

But this last argument goes much further. In practice, the monetary authorities have a limited horizon. As a basis for discussion, let us assume this horizon to be one year. If so, then so far as the authorities merely wish to decide between a pure interest rate and a pure money stock policy, an annual model of the demand for money and the demand for goods would serve them perfectly well. However, if they wish to engage in optimal stabilization, then they must look for guidance over a fraction of a year. Indeed the number of feedback responses they will be able to make will depend upon the brevity of the period over which they can assign values to all of the relevant parameters, including those of the stochastic structure. What they really need then is a model pertaining to a very short interval of time. It is important, in this connection, that the issue is not the frequency of observations as such. By definition, the authorities can continuously observe their instruments. This hardly means that they can engage in optimal stabilization in continuous time.

It follows that the extra information the authorities require for optimal stabilization is much greater than we indicated before in regard to Poole's statement. Not only do they require knowledge of extra parameters, but all of the parameters they need to know about relate to a much shorter period of time — short enough to mean that *all* of them are much more difficult to know. Indeed the very notion of a stable parametric structure during the relevant interval is tendentious and does not have any empirical support. Even if we can suppose subjective certainty about the parameters in analysing the choice of pure policies, therefore, we do not necessarily have grounds for the same assumption in analysing optimal stabilization. Uncertainty about the parameters, of course, results in smaller absolute values of the feedback coefficients [see Brainard (1967), Driscoll and Ford (1980), and Turnovsky (1975)]. To quote Turnovsky (1977, p. 339): "Any attempts at optimal control may be useless if there is too much parameter uncertainty".[6]

These arguments, however, gain further strength in the context of flexible exchange rates. It is hardly necessary to insist on the low quality of current empirical fits of exchange rate equations, especially in the short run, and especially when official reactions do not enter into the econometric analysis. This is reflected in the emphasis in the current theoretical literature on short-run exchange rates on such factors as expectations, unforeseen events or news, and low and uncertain elasticities of influence. It is then rather surprising that there has emerged, side by side with this literature, another literature on optimal foreign exchange rate intervention in which certain authorities are supposed subjectively to adjust their foreign reserves continuously on the basis of exchange rate observations in the light of knowledge of the parameters of the relevant deterministic and stochastic structure. What do we really know about the parametric structure of the relevant equations? What information are the authorities or anyone else really able to extract from spot, weekly, monthly or even quarterly exchange rates (or official reserves) about the random forces at work? Quite generally, it is arguable that while the problem of the choice of pure policies is now well formulated and clear, the problem of the feedback coefficient of optimal stabilization is not at all so. In the latter case, even the appropriate framework of analysis is very much in doubt. Numerous questions surround the treatment of uncertainty in the parameters, and there are also questions about the appropriate use of the criterion of minimizing the *asymptotic* variance of income.[7] In the following discussion of the optimal exercise of the monetary

---

[6] Since uncertainty about the parameters reduces the absolute values of any feedback coefficient under consideration, it will also upset the reciprocal relation between the two in our analysis. Brunner and Meltzer (1979), and Brunner, Cukierman and Meltzer (1980), have recently emphasized this same type of uncertainty under the title of confusion between the permanent and the transitory.

[7] In regard to this last criterion, suppose that the monetary authorities are concerned about the year 1982, and can see clearly enough ahead to take a dozen or so gambles on feedback responses based on observations of their uncontrolled instruments during the year. Then is minimizing the asymptotic variance of anything a sensible thing to do? Any simple feedback rule like (5') or (5a) will necessarily mean a uniform response to all errors in the uncontrolled instrument (see LeRoy and Lindsey (1975) on this point). In some cases, the use of a feedback rule then will necessarily amplify the movement of Y. The basic example is the case of individual drawings of disturbances that originate exclusively in the money market. In this case all deliberate changes in the interest rate (in either direction) will generate a deviation of income from the target. In the event of monetary control, all negative adjustments of the money stock will do the same (since the fall in M following a rise in r will further contribute to the rise in r, even though associated with a fall in Y). True, over a large enough sample, this risk of moving average income away from the target Y^* tends to vanish, and this is why the argument is erroneous as a general criticism of the asymptotic-variance criterion. But over any limited sample, the criticism makes sense.

policy instruments under flexible exchange rates, we will then focus exclusively on the problem of the choice of pure policies.

3.   A proposed model for examining the choice of instruments under flexible exchange rates

It is an easy matter to transpose the Poole model under flexible exchange rates. Let there be perfect capital mobility and static expectations. Consequently, in the case of a small country, the home interest rate would be exogenously set by the world interest rate. Let the exchange rate also affect the home-currency price of imports relative to the home-currency price of home-produced goods. Then appreciation of the home currency would lower real income. It would also lower the demand for money by reducing the price level. We can then essentially replace the exchange rate, e, for the interest rate, r, in the previous eqs. (1) and (2), bury r in the constant term along with any other exogenous factors, and obtain precisely the same formulas and basic conclusions about optimal monetary management.

This mere transposition of Poole's model, however, has three basic limitations. The first is the assumption of perfect capital mobility, implying continuous identity of expected rates of return on home and foreign bonds. On this assumption, all official changes in the money stock constitute official interventions on the foreign exchange market, and the authorities can only affect the home interest rate by altering the expected rate of appreciation. By admitting imperfect substitution between home and foreign bonds, hence separate markets for the two, we remove these limitations. This can be very important in examining short run monetary-policy management.

The second fundamental problem is the assumed exclusive preoccupation of the authorities with real income. In the previous discussion, we referred to a target level of money income, but this implied a target real income, since we took money and real income to be the same. No matter how short run the short run, however, the assumption of fixed prices is untenable under flexible exchange rates, since exchange rate influence on prices temporally tends to precede those on quantities. Thus, we will now assume that the authorities are interested both in output and the price level. In fact, this will hardly complicate the discussion.

The third basic limitation involves the assumption of static expectations, and needs no discussion since the objections to this assumption are now very much in vogue.

In attempting to meet all three objections, the model we shall propose includes markets for five goods or assets: imports, home output, money, home bonds, and foreign bonds. Implicitly foreign money exists too but nobody at home wishes to hold it. The exchange rate then is the relative price of home and foreign money, and also an index of the home-money price of imports (since the foreign-money price of imports is exogenous). The price level, p, is an aggregate of the home-money prices of imports and home output. Besides e and p, the only other two prices in the analysis are the interest rates on home and foreign bonds, r and r_f. The complete model consists of the thirteen

Table 10.1
The complete model

(17) $a = a(o, r, \bar{p}, p)$.	Desired absorption of home output
(18) $x = x(o, e, p, p_f)$.	Net real exports or the balance of the current account in constant prices
(19) $o = a + x$.	Definition of total output
(20) $m/po = g(r, \bar{p})$.	Demand for money
(21) $b_n = k(r, r_f + \bar{e}, m + eb_{f,n} + b_n)$.	Demand for home bonds by the non-monetary sector
(22) $eb_{f,n} = l(r, r_f + \bar{e}, m + eb_{f,n} + b_n)$.	Demand for foreign bonds by the non-monetary sector
(23) $p = j(o - o_{fe}, e)$.	Price level equation
(24) $m = b_m + eb_{f,m} + exo$	Balance sheet identity of the monetary sector
(25) $b = b_m + b_n$.	Definition of home bonds
(26) $b_f = b_{f,m} + b_{f,n}$.	Definition of home-held foreign bonds
(27) $x = e\Delta b_{f,n} + e\Delta b_{f,m}$.	The balance-of-payments identity
(28) $\bar{e} = \theta(E^* - E), 0 < \theta \leqslant 1$.	Anticipated depreciation of the home currency
(29) $\bar{p} = p - 1 + \mu(p^* - p), 0 < \mu \leqslant 1$.	Anticipated inflation

Symbols: o_{fe} = full employment output; exo = a balance sheet residual resulting from past changes in e or past money-financed fiscal deficits. The m and n subscripts refer to the monetary and non-monetary sectors respectively, thus $b_{f,n}$ for example, equals foreign bonds held by the non-monetary sector. Other symbols are either previously defined or implicit in the definitions of the equations on the right.
Exogenous variables: o_{fe}, exo, b, r_f, p_f.
Other variables: $a, x, o, m, p, r, e, b_n, b_{f,n}, b_m, b_{f,m}, b_f, \bar{e}, \bar{p}$.

eqs. [(17)–(29)] shown in table 10.1. Throughout the rest of this discussion, as in the table, small roman letters refer to ordinary values and upper-case roman letters stand for logarithmic values.

Foreign trade takes place in both goods, but foreigners do not hold bonds or home money. Since there is no distinction between households, firms, and government in the home country — only between the monetary and non-monetary sectors — the only aggregate saving in the discussion is relative to foreigners. It involves a current-account surplus and an accumulation of foreign bonds. b_f thus can change even though b is given. Movements in m take place through trades of b or b_f with the monetary sector, b remaining unaffected. For any set level of net exports, a change in m keeps b_f constant as well. In the Keynesian spirit of the IS–LM analysis, we introduce a simple Phillips curve relation in the price equation rather than anything sophisticated.

According to Walras' law, one of the six behavioral eqs. (17), (18), (20)–(23) is redundant. This is to say that the system is coherent, not only with regard to the aggregate excess demand for goods and assets but also with respect to the sums of the elasticities of the individual variables in the equations. There are however, a few major simplifications in the hypothetical lines of causation. Specifically, anticipated inflation, $\bar{p}$, supposedly induces movements between money and goods only, and the yield on foreign bonds, $r_f + \bar{e}$, affects only the division between desired home and foreign bonds.

Counting all of the variables except those that are always exogenous (that is, regardless of the choice of instruments), we find fourteen of them (see list at the bottom of the table). Fourteen variables in relation to twelve independent equations is two too many, meaning two degrees of freedom for the authorities. The two instruments at their disposal belong to the foursome, m, r, e, and official foreign reserves, $b_{f,m}$. But not all pairs of these four instruments can be simultaneously controlled. Specifically, the simultaneous control of e and $b_{f,m}$ is impossible; so is the simultaneous control of m and r. The first incompatibility is clear; the second may need clarification. If the authorities choose to control their foreign reserves, $b_{f,m}$, their decision to control m necessitates a control of their own home bonds, b_m, which is inconsistent with a control of the price of these bonds, or r. If instead the authorities decide to control e, then the market necessarily determines official reserves, and therefore to control m is just as much to control b_m as before. Any influence of official actions on exchange rate expectations would modify this opposition between control of r and m, but could never deny the basic principle of the inability of the authorities to move one instrument independently of the other.

The derivation of the exchange rate equation, which will occupy us next, could follow equally from (21) or (22). But we find it easier to proceed from (22) or the home demand of the non-monetary sector for foreign bonds. We therefore consider (21) as the equation that drops out on the basis of Walras' law.

Given eqs. (24) and (25), we have

$$b_n = b - m + exo + eb_{f,m}. \tag{30}$$

Accordingly,

$$m + eb_{f,n} + b_n = b + exo + eb_{f,m} + eb_{f,n}. \tag{31}$$

Equation (22) then can be restated as

$$eb_{f,n} = l'\,(r, r_f + \bar{e}, b + exo + eb_{f,m}), \tag{22a}$$

or

$$eb_{f,n} - l'_3\,eb_{f,m} = l'\,(\overset{-}{r}, r_f \overset{+}{+} \bar{e}, b \overset{+}{+} exo), \tag{22b}$$

where $l_3' = \partial e b_{f,n}/\partial (b + exo + e b_{f,m})$.

The signs above the variables in (22b) indicate the direction of the theoretical influences on the demand for foreign bonds. Using (27) and (18), together with (22b), we also have

$$e\,x'(e) - e\,\Delta\,b_{f,m}\,(l + l_3') = \Delta\,l'(r, r_f + \bar{e}, b + exo) - x(o, p, p_f),\tag{32}$$

where $x'(e)$ is the coefficient of e in eq. (18) and $x(o, p, p_f)$ is correspondingly $x(o, e, p, p_f) - e\,x'(e)$. Equation (32) may then be restated simply as

$$e = l''(\overset{-}{r}, \overset{+}{r_f + \bar{e}}, \overset{+}{b} + exo, \overset{+}{o}, \overset{+}{p}, \overset{-}{p_f}, \overset{+}{b_{f,m}}).\tag{33}$$

The signs of o, p, and p_f, in this equation naturally follow from the opposite signs of these three variables in eq. (18). Equation (33) is our basic exchange rate equation.

If we substitute (17) and (18) into (19), we also obtain the aggregate demand for goods. After further altering the form of (17) + (18) and some resort to logarithms, we can now restate eqs. (17)–(27) in the compact form:

$$O = f(r, E, \bar{p}, p, P, P_f),\tag{34}$$

$$M = P + O + g(r, \bar{p}),\tag{35}$$

$$E = h(r, r_f + \bar{e}, B + EXO, F, O, P, P_f),\tag{36}$$

$$P = j(O, O_{fe}, E).\tag{37}$$

where we introduce the more common letter F, for foreign reserves, to designate the logarithm of $b_{f,m}$ in eq. (36).

Attention next focuses on expectations or eqs. (28) and (29). These equations combine elements of regressive and rational expectations, though the rational element is not necessarily complete. The regressive element lies in the positive coefficients θ and μ of possibly less than one. The rational element lies in the anticipated values E^* and p^*, which represent the respective mathematical expectations of the exchange rate and the price level following from the official output and price level targets, O^* and p^*. Equations (28) and (29) would be fully consistent with rational expectations if we supposed a stationary model or supplied some theoretical reason for the market to expect the authorities to maintain the same targets forever. A fully rational market obviously would be concerned with a future stretching beyond the time of the short-run targets of the monetary authorities.

A preliminary part of the authorities' problem of optimal control (which is independent of any concern with stabilization) would be to solve eqs. (34)–(37) for the desired values of their chosen instruments. In doing so, they would first equate E^* with

E and p^* with p in (28) and (29) and then substitute the former equation for $\bar{e}$ in (36) and the latter for $\bar{p}$ in (34) and (35). In other words, they would set $\bar{p}$ at $p-1$ and $r_f + \bar{e}$ at r_f in eqs. (34)–(37). On the assumption that the disturbances in these equations are normally distributed, the rest of this preliminary part of their decision problem would be simple. Using only the deterministic part of eqs. (34)–(37), they would set O at the target O^*, P (and p) at the target P^* (p^*), and proceed to solve for M^*, r^*, E^*, and F^*. With regard to the next, more difficult, problem of a choice of instruments, we can treat E^* then as given on the previous basis, and p^* is necessarily known independently. In this next context, we shall not be able to equate p with p^* and, unless the authorities choose to control E, nor shall we be able to equate E with E^*, since the effects of random disturbances on p and E are very much a part of the problem.

One further simplification may be advisable though, in connection with anticipated inflation. If we suppose that $\mu = 1$, or a complete adjustment of anticipations in the current period, then $\bar{p} = p^* - 1$, and p drops out completely from $\bar{p}$ in eq. (29). The advantage is that we can then proceed from our simplifying assumption of a unitary elasticity of the demand for money with respect to both the price level and output to the conclusion of a common elasticity of influence of the price level and output in this equation. If the coefficient of P partly reflected anticipated inflation, these two elasticities would differ. In the case of anticipated depreciation, the same assumption of a complete adjustment or $\theta = 1$ would bring no similar benefit since E and E^* would remain factors in $\bar{e}$. Therefore we shall not make the assumption. The role of anticipated depreciation in analysing the choice of instruments next requires clarification.

If the authorities choose to control E rather than F, E continuously equals E^*, and therefore eq. (36) can be written as:

$$E = c_1^* r + c_2^* F + c_3^* O + c_4^* P + c_5^* P_f + c_6^* r_f + c_7^* (B + EXO) + c_8^* + w^*. \quad (36a)$$

If instead the authorities choose to control F, we have:

$$E = c_1 r + c_2 F + c_3 O + c_4 P + c_5 P_f + c_6 (r_f + \theta E^*) + c_7 (B + EXO) + c_8 + w,$$

where

$$c_i = \frac{c_i^*}{1 + c_6^* \theta}, \quad i = 1, 2, ..., 8 \text{ and } w = \frac{w^*}{1 + c_6^* \theta}. \quad (36b)$$

The decision to control F therefore implies lower coefficients of all of the influences on E (since $c_6 > 0$). Though this will have no analytical significance subsequently, the point is interesting. If the authorities control F, not E, people will recognize some movements in E as reflecting random disturbances (w^*) rather than any systematic exercise of policy. Hence they will form expectations of opposite movements in the exchange rate. As a result, the disturbances (w^*) will generate smaller movements in the exchange rate than they would if people made no such distinction. By the same token, all other elasticities of influence of the exchange rate are lower than they would otherwise be.

Next we impound all of the exogenous influences, together with the effects of P^* and E^*, in a constant term, and come to the following restatement of the four fundamental equations, which will serve as the basis for the rest of the analysis:

$$O = a_0 + \overset{-}{a_1} r + \overset{+}{a_2} E + \overset{-}{a_3} P + u, \tag{38}$$

$$M = O + P + b_0 + \overset{-}{b_1} r + v, \tag{39}$$

$$\left. \begin{array}{l} E = c_0 + \overset{-}{c_1} r + \overset{+}{c_2} F + \overset{+}{c_3} O + \overset{+}{c_4} P + w, \quad (\text{if } F = F^*) \\[2mm] E = c_0^* + c_1^* r + c_2^* F + c_3^* O + c_4^* P + w^*, \quad (\text{if } E = E^*) \end{array} \right\} \tag{40}$$

$$P = d_0 + \overset{+}{d_1} O + \overset{+}{d_2} E + z, \tag{41}$$

$$\overline{u} = \overline{v} = \overline{w} = \overline{w}^* = \overline{z} = 0, \quad \text{var}(u) = \sigma_u^2, \quad \text{var}(v) = \sigma_v^2,$$

$$\text{var}(w) = \sigma_w^2 = \frac{\sigma_{w^*}^2}{(1 + c_6^* \theta)^2}, \quad (c_6^* \theta > 0), \quad \text{var}(z) = \sigma_z^2.$$

Two points of clarification may be added. First, since the net exports equation is embedded both in the aggregate demand for goods and the home demand for foreign bonds, it helps to suppose that this equation is perfectly stable. Otherwise u and w would be inherently related. On our last assumption, however, we may consider the two disturbances as distinct in eqs. (38) and (40), the former stemming exclusively from instability in desired home absorption, the latter from instability in the home demand for foreign bonds. Second, the u, v, and w disturbances may be uncorrelated with one another, if for no other reason, because they may be correlated with the disturbance in the missing demand for home bonds.[8]

---

[8] It may be useful to situate our discussion in relation to an influential paper by Sargent and Wallace (1975) where they evacuate the possible effect of the authorities on the level and variance of output on the basis of rational expectations, and similarly leave no room for the effect of the interest rate on the level and variance of the price level in the case of such expectations. As they point out themselves, these results depend critically, however, not only on rational expectations, but also on the adoption of a Lucas aggregate supply function. One reason then why fully rational expectations would not have the same implications in our model is that we use a Phillips curve instead of a Lucas supply function in explaining the price level. But a further reason is that we do not restrict the coefficient of E in the price level equation to be equal to one, or in other words, we do not assume perfect purchasing power parity despite our concern with an open economy. This departure from PPP would suffice to yield the basic set of eqs. (38)–(41) and to avoid the Sargent–Wallace results even if we accepted the Lucas aggregate supply hypothesis and fully rational expectations. Sargent and Wallace's conclusions also have recently come under attack on the ground of detailed exegeses of the implications of rational expectations as such. A few relevant, particularly recent references are Dickinson, Driscoll and Ford (1980), Turnovsky (1980) and Woglom (1979).

4. The conclusions about the optimal choice of instruments under flexible exchange rates

In deciding between the alternative instruments, the loss function that the authorities try to minimize will be supposed to be a linear combination of the variance of the price level relative to their target P^* (σ_p^2) and the variance of output relative to their target O^* (σ_o^2). Thus

$$L = \alpha\sigma_p^2 + (1-\alpha)\,\sigma_o^2, \quad 0 < \alpha < 1. \tag{42}$$

On this view, the two variances have totally separable effects on total losses, and since we shall never try to calculate the total loss, the coefficient α will not play an important role in the discussion.[9] Since the exchange rate is a factor in the definition of the price level, the official concern with the price level implies a concern with the exchange rate.

There are four alternative reduced forms of the basic system (38)–(41), depending upon the decision to control E and r, E and M, F and r, or F and M.[10] In all cases the only relevant reduced-form equations are those for output and the price level, eight equations in all. Table 10.2 supplies the coefficients of the error terms of these equations in a certain arrangement. For the moment, we shall disregard this arrangement, or the absolute-value and inequality signs in the table. Moving along any row, we find the elasticities of influence of a particular disturbance for all possible choices of instruments. Moving along any column, then for any given choice of instruments, we find the elasticities of influence of all four disturbances on output, followed by the corresponding elasticities of influence on the price level.

It is immediately clear from the table, as is fairly obvious independently, that the control of r instead of M removes any effect of the disturbance in the demand for money, v, on either output or the price level, and similarly, the control of E instead of F removes any effect of the disturbance in the exchange rate equation, w, on out-

---

[9] Sargent and Wallace (1975) provide a precedent for the simultaneous injection of output and the price level in the official loss function. The official loss function that they propose, we may note, could have served us perfectly well. In one of his related writings, Turnovsky (1978) too uses a dual objective in the loss function (in the context of fixed exchange rates). Further, Fortin (1980, p. 630) refers to an early introduction of such an objective in the Poole model in a working paper by Decaluwe (1972) that I have not seen.

[10] The choice between the control of F or E is sometimes associated in the literature with the difference between fixed and floating exchange rates. In this vein, Roper and Turnovsky (1980) have recently interpreted the presence of a feedback rule of optimal stabilization as a dirty float, at least in the case of a control of F. I find this all very confusing. In the relevant context, at most the control of E can only mean a decision to keep E independent of random disturbances. But the authorities must always be understood to manipulate E in response to changes in exogenous influences on the exchange rate. Since some of these influences, like the foreign interest rate, are highly variable, the movement in E can be frequent, even daily. On this same reasoning, the control of F can have little to do with a clean float. In general, it would require an extraordinarily simple model to leave any scope for anything except a dirty float under optimal control, independently of a control of E or F or the adoption of a feedback rule of optimal stabilization.

put or the price level. Further examination shows that one of the four alternative choices — the control of F and r — is virtually dominated by one of the others — the control of E and r.

In order to show this and throughout the remainder of this section, we shall make the simplifying assumption that the rankings of the elasticities correctly rank the abso-

Table 10.2
The elasticities of influence of the disturbances.

Elasticity	Control of E^a ($E = E^*$)		Control of F^b ($F = F^*$)	
	$r = r^*$ (1)	$M = M^*$ (2)	$r = r^*$ (3)	$M = M^*$ (4)
$O'(u)$	$\left\|\dfrac{1}{1-a_3 d_1}\right\|$	$>\left\|\dfrac{b_1}{\alpha}\right\|$	$\left\|\dfrac{1-c_4 d_2}{\psi}\right\|$	$>\left\|\dfrac{b_1(1-c_4 d_2)+c_1 d_2}{b_1\psi + c_1\lambda + a_1\epsilon}\right\|$
$O'(v)$	0	$<\left\|-\dfrac{a_1}{\alpha}\right\|$	0	$<\left\|-\dfrac{a_1(1-c_4 d_2)+c_1(a_2+a_3 d_2)}{b_1\psi + c_1\lambda + a_1\epsilon}\right\|$
$O'(z)$	$\left\|\dfrac{a_3}{1-a_3 d_1}\right\|$	$<\left\|\dfrac{a_3 b_1 - a_1}{\alpha}\right\|$	$\left\|\dfrac{a_3 + a_2 c_4}{\psi}\right\|$	$<\left\|\dfrac{b_1(a_3+a_2 c_4)-c_1 a_2 - a_1}{b_1\psi + c_1\lambda + a_1\epsilon}\right\|$
	if $a_3 > -1$		if $a_3 > -1$	
$O'(w)$	0	0	$\left\|\dfrac{a_2 + a_3 d_2}{\psi}\right\|$	$>\left\|\dfrac{b_1(a_2+a_3 d_2)-a_1 d_2}{b_1\psi + c_1\lambda + a_1\epsilon}\right\|$
$P'(u)$	$\left\|\dfrac{d_1}{1-a_3 d_1}\right\|$	$>\left\|\dfrac{d_1 b_1}{\alpha}\right\|$	$\left\|\dfrac{d_1 + d_2 c_3}{\psi}\right\|$	$>\left\|\dfrac{b_1(d_1+d_2 c_3)-d_2 c_1}{b_1\psi + c_1\lambda + a_1\epsilon}\right\|$
$P'(v)$	0	$<\left\|\dfrac{-a_1 d_1}{\alpha}\right\|$	0	$<\left\|-\dfrac{d_1(a_1+c_1 a_2)+d_2(c_1+c_3 a_1)}{b_1\psi + c_1\lambda + a_1\epsilon}\right\|$
$P'(z)$	$\left\|\dfrac{1}{1-a_3 d_1}\right\|$	$>\left\|\dfrac{a_1 + b_1}{\alpha}\right\|$	$\left\|\dfrac{1-a_2 c_3}{\psi}\right\|$	$>\left\|\dfrac{a_1+b_1(1-a_2 c_3)+c_1 a_2}{b_1\psi + c_1\lambda + a_1\epsilon}\right\|$
	if $a_3 > -1$		if $a_3 > -1$	
$P'(w)$	0	0	$\left\|\dfrac{d_2 + d_1 a_2}{\psi}\right\|$	$>\left\|\dfrac{d_2(a_1+b_1)+d_1 a_2 b_1}{b_1\psi + c_1\lambda + a_1\epsilon}\right\|$

$\alpha = b_1(1-a_3 d_1) + a_1(1+d_1)$,
$\psi = (1-a_3 d_1) - c_3(a_2+a_3 d_2) - c_4(d_2+a_2 d_1)$,
$\lambda = a_2(1+d_1) + d_2(1+a_3)$,
$\epsilon = 1 + d_1 + d_2(c_3 - c_4)$.

[a] The inequality signs on the left-hand side of the table ($E = E^*$) require no other conditions besides the one indicated for $O'(z)$ and $P'(z)$.

[b] The inequality signs on the right-hand side ($F = F^*$) require further, but trivially true, conditions besides the one mentioned for $O'(z)$ and $P'(z)$.

lute sizes of the influences on the loss function. That is, if the elasticity of influence of a disturbance on the price level is lower in one case than another, we will suppose that the influence of this disturbance on the part of the loss function related to the price level [or the term $\alpha \sigma_p^2$ of (42)] is lower in this case too. This would necessarily be true, of course, if there were no correlations at all between the four relevant disturbances. But it would follow also, in a more general way, if the covariance terms in the loss function were simply too small to upset the rankings.[11]

Let us now come back to the question why the control of E and r is superior to the control of F and r. This is obvious in regard to the disturbance w. It is just as obvious that the two choices are equally preferable with respect to the disturbance v. The question then turns on the cases of u and z. As regards u, calculations show that, subject only to trivial restrictions, the elasticities $O'(u)$ and $P'(u)$ are lower for $E-r$ than $F-r$. The algebra is a bit tedious, but the underlying economic reasons are clear. Under interest rate control, a positive disturbance in the demand for goods (u) will raise O, which in turn will raise P. If E then is free to move – i.e. in the case of a control of $F - E$ will rise since the increases in O and P will both contribute to this effect. The rise in E, however, will only aggravate the rise in O and P. It follows that it would be better to combine the control of r with a control of E. The case of a positive price level disturbance, z, under interest rate control, yields a more complicated result. P rises and therefore O falls. On the reasonable assumption that the positive effect of the rise in P on E is greater than the negative effect of the P-induced fall in O on E $(c_4 > a_3 c_3)$, E would rise if it could, that is, under control of F. This rise in E then would amplify the rise in the price level, but dampen the fall in output. This last dampened fall in output then is the only advantage of $F-r$ over $E-r$. In light of all of the other advantages of $E-r$, we may safely consider this latter choice as the dominant one.[12]

If we then ignore the third column in table 10.2, we need only examine the choices between columns (1) and (2), (1) and (4), and (2) and (4). The comparison between columns (2) and (4) yields many uncertainties. Thus we may focus on the other two choices, about which clear conclusions follow. In fact, table 10.2 places the focus on the choices between columns (1) and (2), and (3) and (4), instead of (1) and (2) and (1) and (4), thus it focuses on the choice between r and M regardless of the control of E or F. This facilitates the exposition, and will lead to no particular difficulties since transitivities in the rankings, together with other information we shall provide, will permit us to rank columns (1) and (4) unambiguously.

---

[11]   The u term in the part of the loss function related to the price level is

$$\alpha \, [P'(u)^2 \, \sigma_u^2 + \overset{i}{\Sigma} \, 2 \sigma_{ui} P'(u) \, P'(i)],$$

where $i = v, w, z$. Thus our required assumption with respect to u, for example, is that the element $\Sigma^i \, 2 \sigma_{ui} P'(u) \, P'(i)$ of this expression fail to interfere with the rankings of $\partial \alpha \sigma_p^2 / \partial \sigma_u^2$ in the four alternative cases.

[12]   The further restrictions necessary in order to derive the rankings of the elasticities for $E-r$ relative to $F-r$ all stem from the negative influence of the price level on output (a_3). All the inequalities follow if $a_2 + a_3 d_2 > 0$ and $a_3 < -1$.

In examining table 10.2, if we first look at the respective effects of u and v on output, we find exactly Poole's results. Control of the interest rate is superior to monetary control in avoiding any effect of v on output, but monetary control has an advantage in attenuating the effect of u on output. (By setting all of the individual terms in our expressions for the elasticities at zero except those that were also present in Poole, we even fall back exactly upon his coefficients for the disturbances, which is precisely as it should be.) The advantage of monetary control in the case of u may be spelled out in the instance where F, not E, is under control, involving an extra consideration. Let us first suppose interest rate control along with the control of F. Then a positive u would raise output not only directly (since u is a factor in the demand for goods) but indirectly by raising E (since both the rises in O and P would raise E). If then we compare with the opposite case of monetary control, the difference is that r would go up under the impact of the rise in the demand for money, and this would then attenuate the rise in output directly (via a_1) and indirectly, by restraining the rise in E (via $c_1 a_2$). It follows then that monetary control is preferable.

Analysis of the effects of u and v on the price level yields essentially similar results. Interest rate control avoids any effect of v on P, while monetary control attenuates the positive effect of u on P. In the example of a control of E instead of F, the advantage of monetary control in regard to u depends entirely on the preceding tendency of such control to lower the rise in output (and therefore comes through d_1). In the case of F control, the stabilizing effect of monetary control also comes through the restraining effect of the rise in the interest rate on the depreciation of the exchange rate (therefore partly through d_2).

What about the effect of z, the disturbance in the price-level equation? Here we get a mixed result: interest rate control is better with respect to output, but worse with respect to prices. The reasons are clear. A positive disturbance in the price level has a negative effect on the demand for output, but also raises the demand for money (since the positive effect of the rise in P can be supposed to outweigh the negative effect of the P-induced fall in output on this demand). Thus, if the quantity of money is under control, the interest rate will go up, which will amplify the negative effect on output on the one side, but by this very token, limit the rise in the price level on the other. So far the analysis ignores any change in E. In the event of control of F, not E, the results are much the same. A positive z still raises P and lowers O (the rise in P stemming partly from induced depreciation in the case of interest rate control). If r can move, it still rises because of higher demand for money. This rise in r then heightens the fall in output directly (a_1) and indirectly by lowering $E(c_1 a_2)$, and the heightened fall in output and lessened depreciation both check the rise in P. In this way we come to the same conclusion as before that interest rate control is superior with respect to $O'(z)$, but inferior with respect to $P'(z)$.

The impact of the disturbance w in the exchange rate equation may be considered a central issue since it touches intimately on the system of flexible exchange rates. In fact, if F instead of E is under control, then the w disturbance adds an unambiguous argument for monetary control. Why? A positive w, implying depreciation, will raise both output and the price level. But if there is monetary control, the concomitant increase in the demand for money will also raise the interest rate, which in turn will check the depreciation of the currency. Both the rise in r and the diminished rise in E will dampen the increase in output and, likewise, dampen the increase in the price level.

It remains now to explain the ambiguity mentioned above in the case of the comparison between columns (2) and (4), or concerning the choice between E and F under monetary control. The problem is an inability to determine the direction of change of the exchange rate in the case of F control. This problem relates to u and z, not v. Positive values of u and z raise the interest rate under monetary control, thus tending toward appreciation. But such positive values also raise O or P or both, which goes the other way, toward depreciation. The degree of international capital mobility is then obviously important in deciding whether the effect of r on E will be the dominant one.[13] In the case of v, there is no similar ambiguity about the direction of change of E because a positive v raises the interest rate, lowers output and thereby lowers the price level, all of which tend toward appreciation. With F control, this appreciation heightens the fall in P and O. Consequently, control of E is clearly superior to control of F in case of monetary control with respect to v.

Table 10.3, which summarizes the rank orders of the four alternative choices based on the analysis, requires no further discussion. Table 10.4 involves an attempt to shed light on the orders of magnitude under consideration. The table shows the numerical values of the elasticities in table 10.2 based on a set of hypothetical, but seemingly plausible, numbers. The three highest elasticities in the example, 0.5, relate to the effects of the interest rate on the two financial asset demands in the analysis (b_1 and c_1) and the impact of the price level on the exchange rate (c_4). The only other notable elasticities, 0.25, concern the effects of output and the exchange rate on the price level. Otherwise the relevant elasticities are 0.10. It should be remembered, however, that we have preset the price level and output elasticities of the demand for money at unity. Below each of the elasticities in the table, we show in parentheses the squared value of the elasticity. Except for any covariance term, this squared value is the coefficient of the variance of the relevant error term in the loss function.

If we judge strictly from the elasticities in the table, the differences resulting from

[13]   Compare Parkin (1978). Parkin generally reaches the same conclusions as I do so far as our focuses converge. However, there are some notable differences in emphasis between us which can mostly be traced to his allegiance to the Sargent–Wallace position (about which I have already commented in footnote 8). Parkin's paper also provides an occasion to recognize a problem I have neglected in this paper: namely, imperfect monetary control. Like many others, Parkin properly includes a money supply with a disturbance term, and views the monetary base, rather than the stock of money, as the instrument of control. The upshot of this precaution, however, is simply to show that money-supply and money-demand errors have perfectly symmetrical effects. Both errors also obviously argue against reserve-base control. The distinction thus has a practical, rather than a theoretical interest. Moreover, so far as this practical interest is concerned – that is, so far as money-supply disturbances argue against an attempt to control money – it should not be forgotten that a similar stochastic error may argue against interest-rate control, since the interest rate under official control is not the same in practice as the one in the demand for goods. For such reasons, I see no inherent distortion involved in the simple level of analysis in this paper.

the choice of M and r seem generally important. Comparing highs and lows, these differences range from 8.5 to 31 percentage points from row to row. If we judge in terms of the squares of the elasticities (or in a manner more closely related to the hypothetical loss function), then the differences in many of the elasticities tend to dwindle (along with the elasticities themselves), and the differences in a few of them tend to grow. Basically, the differences that are related to v and w cease to amount to much; and the differences that really loom large are those related to the effect of u on output, and in case of F control, the effect of z on the price level. With regard to these last effects,

Table 10.3
The rankings of the alternative choices of instruments.

| | $E = E^*$ | | $F = F^*$ | | | $E = E^*$ | | $F = F^*$ | |
	$r = r^*$	$M = M^*$	$r = r^*$	$M = M^*$		$r = r^*$	$M = M^*$	$r = r^*$	$M = M^*$
$O'(u)$	3	½	4	½	$P'(u)$	3	½	4	½
$O'(v)$	1	3	1	4	$P'(v)$	1	3	1	4
$O'(z)$	2	¾	1	¾	$P'(z)$	3	½	4	½
$O'(w)$	1	1	4	3	$P'(w)$	1	1	4	3

Table 10.4
The elasticities and coefficients of the variances in a numerical example.

$a_1 = a_3 = -0.10$ $a_2 = c_3 = 0.10$ $b_1 = c_1 = -0.50$ $c_4 = 0.50$ $d_1 = d_2 = 0.25$

| | $E = E^*$ | | $F = F^*$ | |
	$r = r^*$	$M = M^*$	$r = r^*$	$M = M^*$
$O'(u)$	0.976	0.784	0.994	0.771
$[O'(u)]^2$	(0.952)	(0.615)	(0.988)	(0.594)
$O'(v)$	0	−0,157	0	−0.171
$[O'(v)]^2$		(0.0246)		(0.029)
$O'(z)$	−0.0976	−0.235	−0.057	−0.240
$[O'(z)]^2$	(0.0095)	(0.055)	(0.003)	(0.057)
$O'(w)$	0	0	0.085	0.0171
$[O'(w)]^2$			(0.007)	(0.0003)
$P'(u)$	0.2439	0.1961	0.3125	0.0171
$[P'(u)]^2$	(0.055)	(0.0385)	(0.098)	(0.0003)
$P'(v)$	0	−0.039	0	−0.226
$[P'(v)]^2$		(0.0015)		(0.051)
$P'(z)$	0.976	0.941	1.125	0.884
$[P'(z)]^2$	(0.952)	(0.886)	(1.266)	(0.781)
$P'(w)$	0	0	0.3125	0.223
$[P'(w)]^2$			(0.098)	(0.0497)

there is a huge benefit from monetary control. Of course, these comments disregard the sizes of the individual variances as such. In this connection, one notable hypothesis is that instability in the exchange rate equation is a capital feature of the current exchange rate arrangements. If so, then in the instance of a control of official reserves, the argument for monetary control may still be quite important as regards the price level. The numerical example tends to show that the $F-M$ option is generally an important one (as is not evident from table 10.3). In fact the general impression from table 10.4 is that, as regards the price level, the basic choice is really between $F-M$, on the one hand, and either $E-r$ or $E-M$ on the other, but, as regards output, the basic choice is between $E-r$ on the one hand, and either $F-M$ or $E-M$ on the other. It certainly seems that the choice between the three fundamental pairs of instruments in the analysis is important.

References

Boyer, Russell, 1978, Optimal foreign exchange interventions, Journal of Political Economy 86, Dec., 1045–52.

Brainard, William, 1967, Uncertainty and the effect of monetary policy, American Economic Review, Paper and Proceedings 57, May, 411–25.

Brunner, Karl and Allan Meltzer, 1979, Guiding principles for monetary policy, paper presented at June 1979 Konstanz Seminar on Monetary Theory and Monetary Policy.

Brunner, Karl, Alex Cukierman and Allan Meltzer, 1980, Money and economic activity, inventories and business cycles, paper prepared for June 1980 Konstanz Seminar on Monetary Theory and Monetary Policy.

Champsaur, Paul and Jacques Mélitz, 1982, The optimal choice of monetary-policy instruments: A generalisation, CORE Discussion Paper no. 8202.

Decaluwe, Bernard, 1972, Variables instrumentales optimales dans un modèle stochastique: Une généralisation, Working Paper 7208, Institut des Sciences Economiques (Louvain).

Dickinson, D.G., M.J. Driscoll and J.L. Ford, 1980, Rational expectations, the non-neutrality of money and choice of monetary policy, University of Birmingham, Discussion Paper, no. 246, Sept.

Driscoll, M.J. and J.L. Ford, 1979, Optimal choice of monetary policy instruments, monetary versus fiscal policy, in a simple macro-model with instable parameters, University of Birmingham, Discussion Paper, no. 236, Nov.

Fortin, Pierre, 1979, Monetary targets and monetary policy in Canada: a critical assessment, Canadian Journal of Economics 12, Nov., 625–46.

Friedman, Benjamin, 1975, Targets, instruments, and indicators of monetary policy, Journal of Monetary Economics 1, Oct. 443–74.

Friedman, Benjamin, 1977, The inefficiency of short-run monetary targets for monetary policy, Brookings Papers on Economic Activity, no. 2, 293–335.

Henderson, Dale, 1979, Financial policies in open economies, American Economic Review, May, 232–39.

Kareken, John, Thomas Muench and Neil Wallace, 1973, Optimal open market strategy: The use of information variables, American Economic Review 63, March, 156–72.

LeRoy, Stephen and Roger Waud, 1977, Applications of the Kalman filter in short-run monetary control, International Economic Review 18, Feb., 195–207.

LeRoy, Stephen and David Lindsey, 1978, Determining the monetary instrument: A diagrammatic exposition, American Economic Review, no. 68, Dec., 929–34.

Mélitz, Jacques, 1979, Usage optimal des instruments monétaires en régime de changes flexibles, Revue Economique 30, Sept., 780–806.

Parkin, Michael, 1978, A comparison of alternative techniques of monetary control under rational expectations, The Manchester School, Sept., 252–87.

Poole, William, 1970, Optimal choice of monetary policy instruments in a simple stochastic macro model, Quarterly Journal of Economics 84, May, 197–210.

Roper, Don and Stephen Turnovsky, 1980, Optimal exchange market intervention in a simple stochastic macro model, Canadian Journal of Economics 13, May, 296–309.

Sargent, Thomas and Neil Wallace, 1975, Rational expectations, the optimal monetary instrument, and the optimal money supply rule, Journal of Political Economy 83, April, 241–54.

Sparks, Gordon, 1979, The choice of monetary policy instruments in Canada, Canadian Journal of Economics 12, Nov., 615–24.

Turnovsky, Stephen, 1975, Optimal choice of monetary instrument in a linear economic model with stochastic coefficients, Journal of Money, Credit, and Banking 7, Feb., 51–80.

Turnovsky, Stephen, 1977, Macroeconomic analysis and stabilization policy, (Cambridge University Press, Cambridge).

Turnovsky, Stephen, 1978, Stabilization policies and the choice of monetary instrument in a small, open economy, Bergstrom, Catt, Peston, and Silverstone (eds.), Stability and inflation (John Wiley and Sons, New York).

Turnovsky, Stephen, 1980, The choice of monetary policy under alternative forms of price expectations, The Manchester School, March, 39–62.

Woglom, Geoffrey, 1979, Rational expectations and monetary policy in a simple macroeconomic model, Quarterly Journal of Economics 93, Feb., 91–105.

Recent Issues in the Theory of Flexible Exchange Rates, edited by E. Claassen and P. Salin
© *North-Holland Publishing Company, 1983*

Chapter 10.2

COMMENT ON MELITZ

Stanley FISCHER

This paper extends the Poole analysis of closed economy optimal choice of monetary instrument — as between the interest rate and the quantity of money — to the open economy. Now the choice is more complicated, in that there are four potential monetary instruments, the interest and exchange rates, and the quantity of money and central bank holdings of foreign assets. The results are therefore likely to need more explanation than Poole was required to give.

Melitz's results are of the same general type as Poole's: namely, if disturbances originate in the asset markets, the optimal policies are to fix the prices of the corresponding assets. In Poole's case, this says that when money demand causes the major disturbances, appropriate policy is to fix the interest rate. For Melitz, when disturbances to the demand for money function and/or the exchange rate equation — of which more below — predominate, then the exchange rate and the interest rate should be fixed.

For Poole, when the demand for goods, the IS curve, is the main source of disturbances, asset prices should be allowed to perform their stabilizing role, so the quantity of money should be fixed. In Melitz's analysis, if the predominant disturbances are in the demand for goods, then fixing the money supply is the better policy than fixing the interest rate. There is a mild preference that this decision be accompanied by the fixing of the central bank's holdings of foreign reserves rather than the exchange rate, indicating that the exchange rate plays a stabilizing role. Finally, when disturbances arise in the Phillips curve, the results are quite ambiguous.

So much for the results. I want now:

(1) to take up the interesting discussion at the beginning of the paper, which is reasonably separable from the rest, about what Poole's combination policy might be, and Melitz' discussion of stability in sections 1 and 2 of his paper;

(2) to describe the model Melitz uses, drawing attention particularly to the expectations assumptions; and

(3) to discuss the issues of the usefulness of this type of analysis, and also the question of how a central bank should operate in an uncertain environment.

1. The Combination Policy

The problem with which Poole is dealing should be understood as one in which there are no observations on target variables (such as the level of GNP or price level) during an interval, but there are observations on the instrument variables, like the money supply and the interest rate. During the course of, say, a month, the Fed does not get new information on output and prices, and has to set the money supply or interest rates in a way that it hopes will bring the economy close to target levels for output and for prices. As soon as the new data come in, the Fed can change its desired setting of the instrument variables.

An alternative interpretation is that we are dealing with a situation in which authority has to be delegated to the trading desk, and the desire is to give them instructions they can follow and be held accountable for. Thus although new information is indeed coming in, it is not efficient for administrative or other reasons, to issue new sets of instructions more than once a week, or once every three weeks. And the question is, how should those instructions be framed?

The basic analysis asks which decision produces a better outcome: fixing interest rates, or fixing money. But it is formally possible to write down a "combination policy" setting the interest rate as a function of the money stock or *vice versa*. Then one has to ask what this means. The answer is that it should be thought of as the limit in continuous time of a process in which there is feedback from the money stock to the desired interest rate, or from the interest rate to the desired money stock, within the period in which either there are no observations on target variables, or there are no new instructions issued. And this is indeed the interpretation offered by Melitz.

However, his view that this way of posing the problem will show that setting one variable is destabilizing, while setting the other is stabilizing, is difficult to understand. The issue of stability here is tricky in two ways. First, as one goes to the continuous time limit, the variances of the stochastic term have to be shrinking in some way. Thus it is highly unlikely that the variance is increasing, per unit time, in a well-posed problem, as the controller is given the option of changing the frequency and amount of his interventions. Second, even if the variance were increasing per unit time, the target variables get reset at fixed intervals. In Melitz's equation $(5')$, the full dynamics has to take into account the behavior of M^* and r^* over time if stability is being considered.

In this connection, it should be noted that it may well not be a good idea for the Fed to intervene continuously. If there is some discrete cost of taking action or an error in setting the money supply or interest rate that is independent of the size of the Fed's intervention, but a function of the fact of intervention, then it will probably not be optimal to take action frequently.

2. The Melitz model

This is an open economy model with goods market clearing condition, money market clearing, a Phillips curve, and markets for foreign and domestic bonds. The exchange rate may on one interpretation be determined in the market for assets, though this is not the interpretation used in the paper. Expectations enter the model; Melitz's expectation formation could be rational for some money supply processes, but expectations are not explicitly set up to be rational. There is a direct effect of the exchange rate in the Phillips curve.

The key equations are eqs. (37)–(40), derived from the more structural equations set out earlier. Aside from the exchange rate equation, these are quite standard. The exchange rate equation is more difficult to understand. First, the coefficients in that equation differ depending on whether the exchange rate is held constant or not. If the exchange rate is kept constant, expectations are that it will be kept constant. If the stock of foreign bonds held by the central bank is kept fixed, the exchange rate will vary, and expectations will reflect those movements. Since expectations in turn enter the equation, the reduced form expression (39) will differ depending on whether the exchange rate is held fixed or not. Given the generally regressive nature of Melitz's expectations, allowing expectations to move exerts a stabilizing effect on the exchange rate, and hence the non-asterisked coefficients in eq. (39) are smaller when F is fixed than when E is fixed.

Here we should once again be asking about the length of time for which variables are being kept fixed. It will not in general be optimal to keep the exchange rate fixed forever – only during the decision period – so that it is not obvious that expectations should disappear under the exchange rate option, unless Melitz is thinking about much longer-run strategies, in which case we can throw out the interest rate fixing rule anyway.

I would like to raise a question about the derivation of the exchange rate equation. As I look at the underlying structure, it seems that the exchange rate can perfectly well be viewed as being determined on the basis of existing stocks of assets by either of equations (21) or (22), which would give a relationship between the exchange rate, stock of foreign reserves and interest rate. Melitz chooses to integrate this equation with the current account, apparently defining an end-of-period equilibrium. In any event, the question is why it is necessary to bring the current account in; equivalently is there any reason for O and P to enter eq. (39)?

Now, where do the results come from? First, observe that in the money market and the "exchange market" – eq. (39) – there are equations in which appear a disturbance and a variable that each do not appear elsewhere in the system. In (38) M appears, in (39) it is F. Given their non-appearance elsewhere, they can freely be manipulated to eliminate the disturbances without having adverse consequences elsewhere. But how reasonable is it that these restrictions apply?

Melitz extends the Poole analysis by looking at policies to control or reduce the variance of both output and prices, but as he notes, this fortunately does not complicate matters much.

The results that are definite come from the exclusion restrictions described above. If every variable entered every equation, there would be no way, short of working through the parameters of the system, of reaching the type of conclusion described in the introduction.

3. What does this type of analysis tell us?

How useful is this type of analysis? It is becoming increasingly possible to identify sources of disturbances to the economy, so that part of the problem is less serious than it used to be.

However, the other question is how useful the models being used to generate policy conclusions are. For instance, the ability to manipulate the exchange rate in this model turns on the monetary authority's ability to affect the domestic interest rate relative to the foreign by conducting open market purchases in foreign bonds. I doubt such a policy can do much other than stabilize short term swings in exchange rates. Ultimately, the central bank cannot stand alone at the bridge, fighting the barbarians. Further, it is essential to get the time relationships here right. I do not doubt that the type of semi-rational expectations used by Melitz are appropriate for short periods, which is probably what this paper is about. But then one cannot go on to assume things like the exchange rate being fixed in perpetuity.

Within such short periods, not a great deal can be riding on whether an interest rate or quantity is held fixed. Over longer periods, a nominal quantity has to be held as the target for domestic policy (I incline to the view that it should be a price level rather than money supply). In the long run, there is no way of setting the exchange rate independently through monetary policy. The choice is not there. There may well be an issue of whether the exchange rate should be smoothed during short periods, and here the answer is undoubtedly yes, as long as you explain how you know you are smoothing. Indeed, the only truly plausible story about intervening to fix the exchange rate in the short run is that it is a way of showing what your true long-run intentions are.

Recent Issues in the Theory of Flexible Exchange Rates, edited by E. Claassen and P. Salin
© *North-Holland Publishing Company, 1983*

Chapter 11.1

THE FRENCH MONETARY AND EXCHANGE RATE EXPERIENCE IN THE 1920s*

Abdessatar GRISSA

The French experience of the 1920s with freely fluctuating exchange rates has been, and continues to be, often cited as an example of the inherent instability of floating rates. Nurkse, who had an important influence on subsequent thinking in this area, argued that the persistent external depreciation of the franc became "self-aggravating" as a result of the effect it had on the growth of the money supply.

> When the decline in the exchange value of the franc began to create anticipations of further decline causing a strong desire to transfer capital abroad, the refusing owners obtained the necessary liquid funds by refusing to renew the short-run treasury bills. It was this, rather than the current budget deficit, that forced the Treasury to borrow from the Bank of France.[1]

This argument makes the chain of causality run from the depreciation of the exchange rate to the growth of the supply of money, and this inflationary process is supposed to continue as long as there is an easy access to the central bank that makes the money supply elastic with respect to the deterioration of the currency's covered interest rate differential, due in particular to the widening of its forward discount. In this case, the exchange rate of the currency will depreciate whenever the net yield of foreign assets rises above the corresponding domestic yield, and should appreciate whenever the covered differential turns in favor of the domestic assets.

S.C. Tsiang, on the other hand, argued that the French money supply was rendered highly elastic by the existence of an important volume of "bons de la Défense Nationale", a government security that had a pegged rate of interest and a maturity of one, three, six and twelve months. The outstanding volume of these "bons" at the end of

* This paper is based on research done at Brown University in 1966, in the fulfillment of Ph.D. requirements. Other activities prevented the author from continuing working on the subject, and he owes his renewed interest in it to the kind encouragement of Professors E. Claassen of the Université Paris–IX–Dauphine, M. Connolly of the University of South Carolina, and J.L. Stein of Brown University.
[1] Nurkse (1944, p. 122).

1922 amounted to 57 billion francs, against the volume of note issue of 36.4, and a total money supply of 50.3 billions. This meant that there was an important monthly flow of "bons" requiring refunding or redemption into cash, and according to Tsiang the money supply was a function of the differential between the pegged rate of this security and other yields. But it should be noted that he insisted on the point that this would have been the case regardless of whether the exchange rate was free or pegged. His argument is that the "bons" holders would cash them whenever their pegged rate of interest fell below the yields of other domestic or foreign assets, while their sales would expand with the fall of other yields, in relation to their rate, in order to prevent their price from rising above their par values.

Consequently, a rise or fall of other yields in relation to the basic pegged rate of interest, should set in motion an inflationary, or deflationary, development that would force the depreciation, or appreciation, of the exchange rate, or the withdrawal of the peg from the security. Pegging both, the rate of interest and the exchange rate, would be out of the question. One or the other must give way.

1. Main features of the situation

The argument of Tsiang will be valid, however, only in the case that the government is not willing to borrow through the issue of non-pegged securities. But in reality the holders of "bons" had the choice, in addition to non-government assets, to hold non-pegged government bonds.

Their decisions therefore were based on the comparison of three types of yields: the pegged yield $\bar{i}$, the yield on non-pegged government securities i_n, and the yield on non-government assets i_o, and, supposing that the last two carry an element of risk and loss of liquidity equal to α and β respectively, three cases can be considered:

Case a: $i_n - \alpha > i_o - \beta > \bar{i}$. In such a case the supply of money will not increase, despite the existence of pegged securities, as the government can borrow from the public by the issue of non-pegged bonds to finance its budget deficit and refund whatever amount of the pegged part of its debt presented for redemption.

Case b: $i_o - \beta > i_n - \alpha > \bar{i}$. The supply of money will increase not because there are pegged securities outstanding, but as a result of the government refusal to borrow from the public at rates of interest that could compete with private yields. Moreover, the supply of money would increase in this case even if there were no pegged bonds or other maturing government securities, provided that the budget was in deficit.

Case c: $\bar{i} > i_o - \beta > i_n - \alpha$. The sale of pegged securities should expand and the money supply decrease in order to prevent the pegged rate from falling. This case constitutes the inverse of the Keynesian liquidity trap, and it is the only case where the existence of interest pegged securities can have a direct effect on the supply of money.

In order, however, to verify Tsiang's hypotheses, the following equations were tested.

A supply of money equation given by

$$\Delta M_t = a - b \, \Delta B_t, \tag{1}$$

where ΔM is the monthly change in the money supply and ΔB is the monthly change in the volume of outstanding "bons", and a "bons" equation given by:

$$\Delta B_t = a_1 X_{1t} - a_2 X_2 t - a_3 (r - i_b) + a_4 \Delta P_t \tag{2}$$

In this equation, the volume of outstanding "bons" is made a function of yields of foreign as well as of domestic assets. The effect of foreign asset yields on the demand for "bons" is supposed to take place through:

(1) the "bons" minus the foreign short-term rate of interest, represented by the British Treasury bill rate, this differential being X_1;
(2) the premium (−), or discount (+), on the forward franc, X_2;
(3) the fluctuations in the spot exchange rate, ΔP; and
(4) the differential between the "bon" rate and the long-term, "rente" rate.

As to the effect of the yield of domestic assets, it is presented by the differential between the "bons" rate, i_b, and the yield of perpetual bonds, the "rente", r. The variables X_1, X_2 and ΔP would indicate to us whether the holders of "bons" were sufficiently sensitive, both as hedgers and speculators, to what was taking place on the foreign exchange market. However, in case that the relationship between ΔB and $(r - i_b)$ is significant while that between ΔM and ΔB is not, we would conclude that the change in "bons" outstanding was being refunded. The results of these correlations are the following.[2]

January, 1921–February, 1924

$$\Delta M_t = 0.13 - 0.026 \, \Delta B_t, \tag{3}$$
$$(0.006)$$
$$r = 0.06.$$

---

[2] The study covered the French experience for the period January, 1921–July, 1926, but due to government intervention in the foreign exchange market in March and April, 1924, these two months, plus May, are eliminated from the analysis. However, the Bank of France did not have, during the period under consideration, 1921–1926, the right to buy or sell gold and foreign currencies, except at the pre-war parities. Consequently the intervention in support of the franc that took place in March–April, 1924 was made by the Treasury with the help of two loans raised in New York and London.

June, 1924–July, 1926

$$\Delta M_t = 0.93 + 0.035\ \Delta B_t,$$
$$\qquad\qquad (0.134)$$
$$r = 0.05.$$

(4)

January, 1921–February, 1924

$$\Delta B_t = 0.595\ X_{1t} + 0.09\ X_2 t + 1.38(r - i_b) - 0.075\ \Delta P_t - 1.4,$$
$$\quad (0.275) \qquad (0.16) \qquad\qquad (1.24) \qquad (0.073)$$
$$R^2 = 0.22.$$

(5)

June, 1924–July, 1926

$$\Delta B_t = 1.121\ X_{1t} + 0.004\ X_2 t - 1.762\ (r - i_b) - 0.045\ \Delta P_t + 3.5,$$
$$\quad (0.498) \qquad (0.049) \qquad\quad (0.692) \qquad\qquad (0.053)$$
$$R^2 = 0.35.$$

(6)

The coefficients of ΔB are not significant in both eqs. (3) and (4) which leads us to reject Tsiang's assertion that the reduction in the volume of "bons" was responsible for the French monetary inflation. In fact we find that the supply of money changed in the same direction as the volume of "bons" in 18 out of the 38 observations of the period 1921–1924, and in 13 out of the 26 observations of the period 1924–1926. This explains the positive, though non-significant, relationship between ΔM and ΔB in the latter period.

In the case of the equation explaining changes in the volume of "bons" held by investors, we find that the only significant regression coefficient in the period 1921–1924 is that of X_1 but it has the wrong sign, which indicates that the volume of "bons" outstanding rose when the interest rate differential was in favor of the British Treasury bills and declined when this differential turned in favor of "bons".

The coefficients of X_2 and $(r - i_b)$, though not significant, have also the wrong signs. As to the coefficient of ΔP, though it has the right sign, it is far from being significant. We can safely say therefore that neither hedged arbitrage nor speculative activity had a significant effect on the attitude of "bons" holders during the period 1921–1924.

In the second period, however, we find the coefficients of X_1 and $(r - i_b)$ to be statistically significant and to have the correct signs. But since the coefficients of X_2 and ΔP are not significant, it is doubtful that the small differential between the "bons" rate and the Treasury bill yield could have exerted a notable influence on "bons". This differential was markedly in favor of the three months "bons" from July, 1924 to February, 1925 and during the months September–November, 1925, at par in March, 1925, and in favor of the bill rate by less than 1 percent for the rest of the period.

When eq. (2) is tested for the period January, 1921–July, 1926 as a whole, only the coefficient of $(r - i_b)$ turned out to be significant. These results plus the non-significant relationship between ΔM and ΔB confirm my contention that the "bons" were replaced by non-pegged government securities and not by cash. This point can also be supported by the data of tables 11.1 and 11.2.

A comparison of the "bons" figures of tables 11.1 and 11.2 reveals that the government succeeded in reselling half of the amounts of "bons" refunded by the issue of non-pegged securities. The sum of "bons" reduction of table 11.1 amounted to 24,936 million francs, while the net decrease of table 11.2 was limited in 1922—1925 to 12,680 millions, 69.4 percent of which took place in 1925, mostly in exchange for the gold guaranteed "rente".

Moreover, the French money supply rose between the end of 1920 and the end of July, 1926 from 50.1 to 79.3 billion francs. 53.4 percent of this increase took place in 1925 under the effect of the expansion of Bank of France advances to the government. But as can be seen from the data of table 11.2, the redemption of "bons" was far from being the determining factor of this expansion. The volume of "bons" outstanding decreased in 1925 by 8,800 million francs, of which 6,011 million were refunded by the guaranteed "rente". Consequently, of the 15,100 million francs increase in Bank of France advances, deposits with the Treasury, and the net sale of Treasury bills: 2,790 million were used to pay off "bons" holders, 4,700 million to finance the current budget deficit, 7,100 million to redeem maturing medium term bonds, and the remaining 430 million went to help reduce the external debt.

The continued renewal of "bons" was considered an enigma, and a reporter of *The Economist* wrote:

> It is common knowledge that the French Treasury is fed daily by the sale of National Defense bonds of three, six and twelve months maturity. The total amount of these bonds in circulation is about 56 milliards (billions), and they are continually renewed. I have heard this renewal described by a financial specialist as a miracle.[3]

This miracle, however, was the consequence of the fact that these bonds were primarily held be small savers who bought and sold them at their local post offices. They constituted for them, therefore, a perfect substitute for cash with the advantage that they earned interest. This explains the relatively limited subscription for gold guaranteed "rente" issued in October 1925, which was expected to refund 30 billion francs worth of "bons". The acceptable alternative to these investors was to put their funds in the post office saving accounts, with the disadvantage of getting a lower rate of interest for practically the same degree of liquidity and risk of depreciation. The "bons" holders, therefore, were not so sophisticated as to understand the mechanism of the foreign exchange market and did not have sufficient funds with which they could take part in its operations. Rather, it was the holders of medium and long-term bonds who should have been more responsive to the influence of the foreign exchange variables.

---

[3] *The Economist* (1925, p. 710).

Table 11.1
Reduction in volume of "bons" outstanding and the issue of non-pegged securities[a].

Date	Reduction in "bons" (billion francs)	Amount raised by new issues of non-pegged securities (billion francs)	Yield (%) of new issues
June–July, 1922	1.284	3.290	6.2
October–November, 1922	5.456	8.237	6.4
January–February, 1923	2.291	2.991	6.0
March–April, 1923	5.740	10.090	7.1
October–November, 1923	2.740	6.189	7.3
January–February, 1924	0.339	1.633	6.3
November–December, 1924	2.509	4.912	8.6
October, 1925	4.579	6.011	(b)

[a] The rank correlation between the new issues and the amount of "bons" reduction is 0.95.
[b] 4 percent gold guaranteed "rente" issued exclusively in exchange for "bons" [Haig (1925, table 20, pp. 264–9)].

Table 11.2
Changes in the French internal public debt, 1921–26, at the end of each year (millions of current francs).

Type	1921	1922	1923	1924	1925	1926
Bank advances	−2,000	−1,000	−300	−700	13,350	1,500[a]
Deposits with the Treasury	−380	2,920	−600	2,540	1,230	490
Treasury bills	−20	700	360	−1,130	520	70[a]
Bons de la Défense Nationale	9,480	−2,000	−1,700	−180	−8,800	1,500[a]
Medium Term bonds[b]	14,580	19,160	13,130	6,660	−7,180	660
Perpetual and long-term[c]	7,070	3,470	9,730	3,700	6,010	3,630
Net foreign borrowing (over reimbursement)	−1,520	−1,240	−850	−1,000	−900	−1,150
Total	27,210	22,010	19,770	9,890	4,230	
Revenue from coinage	90	210	290	200	110	
Reparation receipts[d]					550	2,850
Total	27,300	22,420	20,060	10,090	4,880	
Budget deficit[e]	−28,000	−24,700	−18,100	−9,100	−4,700	+200
Notes in circulation	36,490	36,360	37,900	40,600	51,080	56,020[a]

Source: Haig(1925, chapters X to XIV and XX).

[a] Outstanding at the end of July, 1926.
[b] Includes borrowing by the Credit National and bonds issued in compensation of war damages which were included in recoverable expenditure.
[c] The gold guaranteed "rentes" issued in exchange for bons.
[d] Only the reparations received under Dawes Plan are included. Almost no reparations were received before 1925.
[e] The change in the debt and the state of the budget do not match each other, particularly in the years 1921–23. This may be explained by not including reparation receipts. However, data on the debt and the budget are not highly accurate, but the results are quite close.

2. The money supply and the cost of government borrowing

The point here is that the French money supply became elastic in 1925–26 simply as a result of the government's incapacity to continue borrowing from the public at rising rates of interest. The situation became such that:

$$i_0 - \beta > i_n - \alpha > \bar{i}$$

Consequently, the explanation of this increased elasticity must be sought in the factors that determined, on the one side, the government's net borrowing needs and, on the other, the rise of interest rates.

The borrowing needs of the government were mainly the consequence of:

(1) Heavy government expenditures of which an average of 66% was spent in 1921–24 on reconstruction and the payment of interest on the national debt. This debt rose in 1923 to 310 billion francs compared to a government income of only 19.8 billions.

(2) The main growing item of government expenditure was the cost of the debt. The ratio of the interest payment to total government expenditure rose from 27.6 percent in 1921 to 56.7 percent in 1925.

(3) The tax payment base of the economy was still weak as a result of the damages it suffered during the war.

(4) The hope that the flow of reparation receipts would spare the government the necessity of resorting to the imposition of higher taxes in order to finance its reconstruction expenditure proved to be illusory.

(5) The incapacity of successive government coalitions on the left to take the unpopular step of imposing higher tax rates. In fact some members of these coalitions went to the extent of calling overtly for the acceleration of monetary inflation in order to reduce the real burden of the internal national debt.[4]

This attitude was supported by Keynes:

> The level of the franc exchange will continue to fall until the commodity-value of the franc due to the "rentier" has fallen to a proportion of the national income which accords with the habits and mentality of the country.[5]

The combined effect of these factors was to exclude the possibility for the government to raise, at 1921–24 incomes and prices, a tax revenue that would have permitted the covering of its expenditure needs.

As to the rise of interest rates, it began at the end of 1922, and its pace of increase was accelerated after August, 1923. This development was mainly the consequence of

---

[4] *The Economist* (1922).
[5] Keynes (1924, p. 80).

the growth of the national debt itself. The accumulated budget deficits of the three years 1921–1923 amounted to 70.8 billion francs, while government reconstruction expenditure rose to 41.1 billions. This resulted in a very rapid recovery of the French economy, to the point that its industrial production, including utilities, mining, and construction, returned to its pre-war level by the end of 1923. But while industrial production increased between the end of 1920 and the end of 1923 by 46.3 percent, retail prices rose by 5.3 percent and the supply of money by 5.4 percent.

This must have put an increasing pressure on the velocity of circulation and the cost of holding money. This pressure was aggravated in 1924, as the index of industrial production rose by another 15.3 percent and that of retail prices by 10.9 percent, while the increase in money supply was limited to 4.9 percent. *The Economist* described the monetary situation at the beginning of 1925 in the following terms:

> The efforts of the Finance Minister to solve the problem of getting rid of the present shortage of paper currency as compared to the business of the nation, without increasing the (note) issue, which is perilously near the maximum of 41 milliard (billion) francs allowed by the law, are continuing. Instructions have now been issued to the effect that in the future all public servants, including military and naval officers, whose pay is over 12,000 francs a year are to be paid by check.[6]

It was in January–February, 1924, that the government encountered its first serious difficulty with the effect of the rise in interest rates.

A long-term bond issue, of which the interest rate was set at 6.29 percent, produced only 1,633 million francs. This failure discouraged the government from organizing other long-term issues, and apart from the limited issues of November–December, 1924, yielding 8.6 percent, and the gold-guaranteed "rente" issued in exchange of "bons" in July–October, 1925, it withdrew from the medium and long-term side of the market until the end of 1926, when the franc became stable.

Moreover, and as can be seen from table 11.3, the effect of this shortage of money

Table 11.3
Corporate capital issues (billion francs).

Date	Bonds	Stocks	Total
1922	5.139	1.378	6.517
1923	6.055	2.277	8.332
1924	4.311	3.694	8.005
1925	2.550	2.705	5.255
1926	4.206	3.020	7.226

Source: Rogers (1929, tables 75 and 76).

---

[6]   *The Economist* (1925, p. 140–141). It was of course naive to think that the payment by check would not lead to an increase in the note issue.

on interest rates was also felt by the private borrowers and the level of industrial activity.

Industrial production sharply declined between October, 1924 and August, 1925, while French enterprises, after having shifted their capital-raising from bonds to shares, were forced in 1925 to reduce their issues of both.

The surprising thing, therefore, was not that there was a sharp increase in the French money supply in 1925, but that this increase did not take place before. The government was inflating on one hand, through the massive deficit spending on the reconstruction of the devastated areas, and deflating on the other through its attempts to prevent the money supply from rising. In fact the government even tried to lower effectively the note issue by formally agreeing in December 1920 to reduce the Bank of France advances to the Treasury by 2 billion francs a year.

The data of table 11.2 show that these advances were in effect reduced by 2 billion francs in 1921, despite a budget deficit of 28 billions. But the sums reimbursed in the following years declined to 1 billion in 1922, 300 millions in 1923 and to 700 millions in 1924. As a consequence of this reimbursement, the volume of note circulation declined from 37.9 billion francs at the end of 1920 to 35.5 billion in March, 1922, but it rose steadily afterwards to the point of exceeding the legal limit of 41 billion francs in April 1925. The reason for this was a subterfuge employed by the government which consisted of borrowing from the commercial banks with the understanding that they get larger access to the discounting facilities of the Bank of France. Consequently the monthly average of commercial bills discounted by the Bank rose from a monthly average of 3.5 billion francs in 1923 to 5.5 billion in February–April, 1925.

The news that the note issue had exceeded its legal limit broke into a scandal, and legislation was soon passed raising the ceiling on both the advances to the Treasury and the note issue. This meant the opening of the floodgates, and before the end of the year, the legal limit was raised again; twice on the note issue and three times on the advances to the Treasury. What had been a suppressed inflation suddenly became an open one. The note issue rose between March and December, 1925 by 25 percent

Table 11.4
French government expenditures (billion francs).

| Year | Total expenditures | of which | | Deficit or surplus |
		Interest on the debt	Reconstruction expenditures	
1920	52.409	12.026	21.252	−38.0
1921	43.778	12.086	16.259	−28.0
1922	37.428	13.195	11.055	−24.7
1923	37.944	12.810	13.782	−18.1
1924	41.214	13.074	11.780	− 9.1
1925	34.186	19.481	1.062	− 4.7

Source: Einzig (1934, Appendix 1).

and the advances to the Treasury increased by 64 percent, while throughout the period December, 1920–March 1925 the note issue had risen by a mere 8.2 percent. Moreover, the monetary expansion of 1925 had an immediate effect on the recovery of industrial production, on the acceleration of the internal and external depreciation of the franc, and resulted in a slight decline of interest rates.

3. The French money supply and the foreign exchange rate of the franc

One of the points insisted upon in the previous analysis is that the supply of money grew in France during the period 1921–1924 by a lower rate than the demand, as indicated by the country's expansion of real output and the rise of its price level. This had the inevitable effect of accelerating the velocity of circulation and of raising markedly the level of interest rates, a development that should be particularly clear from the comparison of the following growth rates covering the period December, 1920–December, 1924:

Money supply	10.6%
of which notes in circulation	7.1%
Retail prices	16.8%
Industrial production	72.7%
Franc–dollar exchange rate	9.5%
Franc–pound exchange rate	43.0%

The higher depreciation of the franc–pound rate was mainly due to the appreciation of the pound with respect to gold. The dollar–pound rate rose by 32.5 percent between the end of 1920 and the end of 1924. Moreover the United Kingdom had already begun in 1920 its deflationary policy with the firm intention of restoring the pound to its pre-war gold parity. The cost of this policy, in terms of unemployment and loss of production was terribly high. For, while the British industrial production remained throughout the period 1921–1926 at its 1920–1921 average, with the evident effect of repeated strikes, particularly in 1921 and 1926, and an unemployment rate that fell below 10% only for a brief interval in 1924; the French industrial production was practically doubled by the end of 1924. In addition, unemployment soon disappeared in France, so that the unfilled vacancies exceeded those seeking work continually in 1922–1926, and this despite a net gain to the labor force of 736,000 migrant workers.[7]

Developments of this kind, characterized by considerable changes in relative absorption should have been associated with marked movements in the equilibrium rates of exchange. It was this displacement of the equilibrium rate and not destabilizing speculation that was responsible for the depreciation of the franc in this period. The sporadic speculative attacks that took place in these years were of short duration and

---

[7] *Bulletin de la statistique générale de la France* (1920 to 1927).

associated exclusively with events relating to the reparation problem, such as the Ruhr occupation. These speculative attacks were limited simply because they could not be supported by an elastic money supply. The rising cost of funds was in fact an effective obstacle to the growth of this activity.

The foreign exchange rate of the franc experienced, on the other hand, marked seasonal fluctuations in this period, but they were due primarily to changes in the foreign trade balance of France which tended to improve in the first and to deteriorate in the second half of the year. This balance was in the whole in deficit in the years 1921–1923 and in surplus in 1924–1926.

Moreover, we find that the level of economic activity, as indicated by the index of industrial production, began rising first in the period 1921–1924, followed by the price level and the franc–dollar exchange rate, and later the increase in the money supply. Albert Aftalion remarked in analysing this period that:

> From 1920 to 1924 the change in the note circulation followed and did not precede those of prices. The lag of the changes in monetary circulation was of about five months in the first two years and of one month in the last three. Moreover, this lag was longer during the periods of contraction than it was in the periods of expansion.[8]

This simply confirms the stickiness of the money supply to the extent that:

> It was only in 1924, and under the very pressure of the rise in prices and of industrial and commercial needs that the note issue rose at a pace a little more accentuated.[9]

As we have seen, it was the persistent growth of the demand for money and the government's attempt to continue borrowing at rates of interest unacceptable to the financial market that forced the note issue to rise above the legal limit in April, 1925. But it should be noted that this event, which resulted in an immediate raising of the legal ceiling on the note issue and on the advances of the central bank to the Treasury, took place at a time when the foreign exchange rate of the franc was rather stable. The franc–dollar rate averaged for the months February–May of this year 19.22 francs, with a maximum deviation of 18 centimes, or 0.9 percent. This relative stability was realized despite the fact that it was in this period that the pound returned to its pre-war gold parity.

The franc–dollar rate rose to 21.20 francs in June, 1925, a level at which it was maintained for the following months of July–September, after which it embarked, with the exception of a short lull in January–February, on a rapidly depreciating course until July, 1926. This depreciation became particularly accelerated between March and July 21. During this period the franc–dollar rate rose from 27.2 to 50.5 francs.

[8]   Aftalion (1933, p. 63).
[9]   Aftalion (1933, p. 52).

But what distinguishes this depreciation from the preceding ones is that it was far out of proportion with regard to the growth of money supply, the price level and real output. This point is clearly demonstrated by the following and the previous percentage increases in these variables.

	March—September 1925	October, 1925 July, 1926
Money supply	16%	21.7%
Retail prices	6%	30.0%
Franc—dollar rate	12%	138.0%

However, if the increase in the French money supply that happened in April, 1925, was an overdue development rendered inevitable by the growth of the transaction demand for money, whatever effect the depreciation of the franc might have on monetary creation should have taken place after this date. But it may also be reasonable to suppose that the government was forced to raise again the ceiling on the note issue before the end of 1925 simply because the amount added to the supply of money in April proved to be insufficient in the light of the accumulated thirst for money. It was mainly for this reason that the depreciation of the franc remained up to October within reasonable proportions, given the continued budget deficit and the incapacity of the government to finance its current and debt refunding needs through the issue of longer-term securities.

The franc became, therefore, subject to an increase destabilizing speculation only during the months October, 1925—July, 1926. Its depreciation in this period took an exaggerated form that could not be justified by the concomitant growth of money supply and the rise in prices. This depreciation was also accompanied by a considerable widening in its forward discount, the three month rate of which rose during the third week of July to 30 percent per annum.

But why this intense speculative activity against the franc?[11] During this period the inherent problem of the budget deficit and the refunding of the national debt were aggravated by government instability and a loss of control over the money supply. The government was changed six times during the period October, 1925—July, 1926 and each time the cause of its defeat was the financial question. These governments were generally composed of the same personalities, and four of them were headed by the same man, Briand, but each one of them had a different Finance minister. Their dilemma was that they had to face a left majority in the House of Deputies and a

---

[11]   The Belgian franc, the Italian lira, and the Norwegian krone were the only other European currencies still floating freely in this period. But while the Belgian franc followed very closely the course of the French franc, depreciating against the dollar by 87.3 percent between September, 1925 and July, 1926, the Italian lira depreciated relatively moderately, by 25 percent. As to the krone, it appreciated under the impact of a deflationary policy to its pre-war parity with the pound to which it was finally attached at the end of 1927. The Belgian franc was suffering from inherent difficulties similar to those of the French franc.

conservative majority in the Senate, with the result that what was acceptable to one Chamber was not acceptable to the other. This meant that the end of the country's political confusion and the deterioration of its financial situation were not yet in sight – a prospect that could not possibly leave the speculators indifferent.

The attitude of the market as regards the capacity of these successive coalition governments to solve the financial problems of the country is easily demonstrated by what happened during the last three days of this period. The franc–pound rate stood at 199 francs on the eve of the fall of Briand's last government, and it rose to 235 francs when it became known that Herriot, an old timer who took part in the previous coalition government, including the presidency of one, was called upon to form a new government. The rate rose to a record of 245.5 francs by the time Herriot went before Parliament seeking a vote of confidence. But as soon as the news came out that he had failed in his initiative, the franc–pound rate fell to 223 francs. This recovery of the franc was reinforced by the agreement of Poincaré to form a "national government", the primary function of which was to apply the stabilization measures recommended by a committee of experts appointed three months earlier. These measures consisted of the following main points:

(1) the imposition of higher taxes;
(2) the creation of a "Caisse d'Amortissement" for the management and the refunding of the national debt with certain taxes being allocated to it to enable it to assure the payment of the debt's interest and the creation of a sinking fund;
(3) with inflation being stopped, the franc should be allowed to continue floating freely until its *de facto* stabilization was realized, which would be followed by *de jure* stabilization.

The appreciation of the franc, following the failure of Herriot's government to obtain its vote of confidence, points to the root of the problem, which was not destabilizing speculation, but the absence of a government that was strong enough to impose solutions to the country's financial difficulties.

Once this government was established, the rate was automatically stabilized, and neither foreign loans, nor a massive intervention from the Bank of France proved to be necessary for this stabilization. The reversal of capital movements, was quite sufficient to lower the franc–dollar rate by the end of 1926 to its level of November, 1925, a level at which it was finally pegged to gold three months later.

However, statistical tests can be employed in order to determine whether a significant relationship existed between the French money supply and the foreign exchange rate of the franc. The implication of Nurkse's assertion that the growth of the money stock in France was "sometimes a consequence of the violent and uncontrolled exchange fluctuations", is that a freely floating exchange system would be fundamentally unstable in the case where a functional relationship exists between the exchange rate and the money supply. In order to verify the validity of this assumption, the following equation is tested:

$$\Delta M_t = b_1 \Delta M_{(t-1)} + b_2 \Delta P_t + b_3 \Delta P_{(t-1)} - b_4 X_{1t} \tag{7}$$

Where M is the French money stock, P_t the spot franc–pound rate, and X_1 the interest rate differential, given by the "bons" minus the British Treasury bill rate. The variable $\Delta M_{(t-1)}$ is included in this equation in order to see whether the creation of money in France was self-aggravating, a possibility that would render the situation explosive.

The statistical results of this equation are the following:

January, 1921–February, 1924

$$\Delta M_t = \; - \; 0.071 \; \Delta M_{(t-1)} + \; 0.05 \; \Delta P_t + \; 0.088 \; \Delta P_{(t-1)} - \; 0.01 \; X_{1t} - 0.007,$$
$$\quad\quad (0.160) \quad\quad\quad (0.04) \quad\quad (0.037) \quad\quad\quad (-0.06)$$
$$R^2 = 0.25, \quad F = 2.79, \quad \text{D.W.} = 2.26. \tag{8}$$

May, 1924–July, 1926

$$\Delta M_t = \; 0.228 \; \Delta M_{(t-1)} - \; 0.005 \; \Delta P_t + \; 0.149 \; \Delta P_{(t-1)} + \; 0.007 \; X_{1t} + 0.24,$$
$$\quad\quad (0.173) \quad\quad\quad (0.049) \quad\quad (0.054) \quad\quad\quad (0.040)$$
$$R^2 = 0.44, \quad F = 4.1, \quad \text{D.W.} = 2.01. \tag{9}$$

The only significant regression coefficient in the two equations is that of $\Delta P_{(t-1)}$, a result that would seem to confirm Nurkse's hypotheses, especially as the same equation is also tested for the United Kingdom using the dollar–pound rate and discount rate differentials, but with none of the coefficients being significant.

Moreover, when this equation is reversed to an equation explaining the fluctuations of the spot exchange rate:

$$\Delta P_t = \; B_1 \Delta P_{(t-1)} + B_2 \Delta M_{(t-1)} - B_4 X_{1t}, \tag{10}$$

the following results are obtained:

France

January, 1921–February, 1924

$$\Delta P_t = \; 0.311 \; \Delta P_{(t-1)} - \; 59.7 \; \Delta M_{(t-1)} - \; 2.2 \; X_{1t} + 0.9, \tag{11}$$
$$\quad\quad (0.158) \quad\quad\quad (46.7) \quad\quad\quad (1.4)$$
$$R^2 = 0.23, \quad F = 3.31, \quad \text{D.W.} = 1.85.$$

May, 1924–July, 1926

$$\Delta P_t = \; 1.084 \; \Delta P_{(t-1)} + \; 55.54 \; \Delta M_{(t-1)} + \; 3.25 \; X_{1t} + 0.21, \tag{12}$$
$$\quad\quad (0.236) \quad\quad\quad (78.40) \quad\quad\quad (2.73)$$
$$R^2 = 0.49, \quad F = 7.11, \quad \text{D.W.} = 1.62.$$

U.K.

January, 1921—April, 1925

$$\Delta P_t = \underset{(0.110)}{0.419} \Delta P_{(t-1)} + \underset{(0.041)}{0.031} \Delta M_{(t-1)} - \underset{(0.0013)}{0.0003} X_{1t} + 0, \qquad (13)$$

$$R^2 = 0.26, \quad F = 5.60, \quad \text{D.W.} = 1.80.$$

In these regressions only the coefficients of $P_{(t-1)}$ are statistically significant. Neither the changes in the lagged money supply nor the interest rate differentials had a significant relationship with the changes in the spot exchange rate. Moreover, the coefficient of $M_{(t-1)}$ has a wrong sign in regression (11) and that of X_1 has the wrong sign in (12). This should be explained by the fact that the franc depreciated in the period 1921—1924 when the government was attempting to reduce the money supply, and that the interest rate differential was submerged in the second period by the forward discount on the franc which rendered it totally ineffective, with the consequence that the franc was depreciating rapidly when this differential was markedly in its favor.

Moreover, the relation between M_t and $M_{(t-1)}$ is not significant in the case of both the franc and the pound which indicates the absence of explosive tendencies in the growth of money supply, especially in the case of the franc in 1921—1924 where this relationship was negative.

But what should be of particular interest is that, while the relation between changes in the lagged exchange rate and changes in M_t is statistically significant, the results of the reversed situation are not. Does this mean that the chain of causality ran, in the case of the French experience, from the exchange rate to the supply of money as supposed by Nurkse, or was it due to other factors? We have seen that during 1921—1924, and due to the government effort to repay the advances of the Bank of France to the Treasury, the rise in the exchange rate and in the price level preceded that of the money supply. Aftalion found the lag of the change in money supply with respect to the change in the price level to have been from one to five months, while a monthly lag is used in these regressions.

The acceptable explanation, therefore, is that the exchange rate and the price level rose under the impact of the inflationary deficit spending of the government, while the increase in the supply of money lagged behind due to the repayment of the Bank of France advances.

In the case of the second period, however, the relation between the lagged change in the exchange rate and the change in money supply is markedly stronger and should have a different explanation from that of the first period. But the fact that the supply of money became more elastic in this period does not necessarily mean that its rate of growth was accelerated by the rapid depreciation of the franc.

The case could be the other way around in the sense that the change in the supply of money had its effect on the exchange rate by anticipation, in particular due to the fact that the raising of the legal limit on the note issue took place only some time after the previous legal margin was exhausted and following heated parliamentary debates.

The impact of fear of inflation and of actual inflation, however, often overlap and their respective effects become difficult to distinguish. In France, in particular, their simultaneous psychological consequence had been very great because of such superstitious fear of inflation and because also of our system of fixing a legal maximum on note issue, a system which tended to lead to a fall in the value of the franc not only when the actual increase in the supply of money took place, but also prior to that when Parliament was considering the authorization of raising the legal maximum amid heated public discussion which intensified the prevalent harmful impression.[12]

The effect of public debates, associated with changes in the legal limit on the note issue, on speculative anticipation against the franc, should be similar to a parliamentary debate on a government proposal to devalue a pegged exchange rate. Any uncertainty that may exist about the future course of the rate is removed, and the speculative outflow of capital would result in the immediate rise of a flexible exchange rate. In such a case, therefore, changes in the exchange rate would precede, as Aftalion indicated, changes in the supply of money. This should be the result of a normal and expected reaction by speculators who, as they anticipate the increase in the supply of money, discount its effects on relative absorption and prices and consequently cause the foreign exchange rate to rise even before actual monetary increase. The relatively high regression coefficient of $P_{(t-1)}$ in eq. (12) indicates also that the foreign exchange rate of the franc became unstable in the period May, 1924–July, 1926. But this instability could not have been prevented by a mere pegging of the rate, as this would have required, as a necessary condition, the stabilization of the underlying monetary situation. In fact, it was clearly demonstrated by the French experience, that given a government that was able to limit its deficit spending and apply effective measures of monetary control, the exchange rate would become stable by itself, without the need of a supporting intervention from the central bank.[13] As Keynes put it three years earlier

In short, any deliberate or artificial scheme of stabilization is attacking the problem at the wrong end. It is the regulation of the currency by means of sound budgetary and bank-rate policies that needs attention. The proclamation of convertibility will be the last and crowning stage of the precedings and will amount to little more than the announcement of a *fait accompli.*[14]

[12]   Aftalion (1933, pp. 317–318).
[13]   The Bank of France began to intervene in the foreign exchange market only in March, 1927, or some months after the franc became *de facto* stable.
[14]   Keynes (1924, p. 117).

4. Conclusion

The French experience of the 1920s with freely floating exchange rates remains one of the most interesting episodes we have had so far with these rates. Product and factor prices were still flexible downward as well as upward, there were no legal restrictions on capital movements, and foreign trade was rather free. Moreover, the central bank observed a strict neutrality with regard to the market fluctuations of the foreign exchange rate of the franc. This bank was not allowed to buy or sell gold and foreign exchange except at their pre-war parities, with the result that their effective market prices made the cost of its intervention prohibitive.

However, the Bank of France had, during the period of this experience, practically no control over the money supply. Its assets consisted mainly of frozen gold reserves, calculated at their pre-war prices, and of non-commercializable book advances to the Treasury. Its discounting facilities were limited however, to commercial bills. Further, it had neither the right nor the means of intervening actively in the financial market through open market operations. Consequently, its discount rate was of little attraction to short-term capital movements, and had practically no effect as an instrument of monetary control.

The money supply was in fact determined by the financial needs of the government. But as the budget was overcharged with a substantial deficit, and the rising cost of the national debt became the predominant item of its expenditure, the government progressively found itself unable to continue borrowing from the public at rising rates of interest. It was this that made the government resort to borrowing from the banking system, and in particular the central bank, and thus lose control over the supply of money between March, 1925 and July 1926. And it was as a result of this loss of control over the money supply that the rate of depreciation of the franc accelerated in this period. The acceleration in the depreciation of the franc began in the second half of May, 1925, whereas the raising of the ceiling on the note issue took place in April. Nurkse recognized the inflationary consequences of the way the government was financing its budget deficit, and its effect on the foreign exchange value of the franc:

> Government inflation due to inadequate taxation, administrative weakness, political upheavals, etc. was, of course, the main general influence tending to depress the exchange.[15]

and,

> Government inflation drove up domestic prices and costs with increasing speed. As people began to realize the one-way character of the movement, anticipations of further depreciation became a dominant influence on the exchange market.[16]

---

[15] Nurkse (1944, p. 113).
[16] Nurkse (1944, p. 114).

Yet he insisted on attributing the depreciation of the franc to destabilizing speculation. It seems that he wanted speculators to act irrationally, in the sense that they should
not try to profit from an opportunity when they see one. He did not consider the
capital imports into France before 1922 to be destabilizing, though they "proved
largely a gift" to this country. These gifts were the result of errors of calculations on
the part of the speculators, but after correcting their position they became, from his
point of view, destabilizers.

It is evident from what he wrote that Nurkse considered capital movements to be
stabilizing only if they flowed from the surplus to the deficit countries. In this case
a transfer of capital in the opposite direction in anticipation of a shift in the equilibrium rate would be considered, from his point of view, as destabilizing, even though
it accelerates the movement of the rate to its new equilibrium position. This, however, should be considered as contrary to rationality which views all obstacles that
hinder a movement to a new equilibrium situation as being destabilizing.

It should be noted, on the other hand, that Keynes, a very keen observer of this
period, wrote:

> The wide fluctuations in the leading exchanges over the past three years (1921–
> 1923) as distinct from their persisting depreciation (which he attributed to
> fundamental causes) have been due, not to the presence of speculation, but to
> the absence of sufficient volume of it relative to the volume of trade.[17]

Moreover, as the French money supply remained relatively stable in the period
1921–1924, with the consequence that the internal price level did not rise as fast as
the exchange rate, the purchasing power parity of the franc did not fall to the extent
of its external value, which is taken by Tsiang as an evidence of the existence of
destabilizing speculation, whereas, it should be considered as the effect of the lagging
growth of money supply.

References

Aftalion, Albert, 1933, Monnaie, prix et change (Sirey, Paris).
Aliber, A.Z., 1962, Speculation in the foreign exchange; The European experience, 1919–1926,
    Yale Economic Essays.
Baumol, W., 1957, Speculation, profitability, and stability, Review of Economics and Statistics,
    Aug.
Bergman, Karl, 1927, The history of reparations (Houghton Mifflin and Co., Edinburgh).
Brown, W.A. Jr., 1940, The international gold standard reinterpreted, 1914–1934, Vol. I & II
    (NBER, New York).
Bulletin de la Statistique Générale de la France, issues 1920 to 1927.
Dulles, Eleanor, 1929, The French franc, 1914–1928 (MacMillan, New York).
Eastman, H.C., 1958, Aspects of speculation in the Canadian market for foreign exchange, Canadian
    Journal of Economics and Political Science, Aug.
Edgar-Bonnet, Georges, 1937, Les expériences monétaires contemporaines (Armand Colin, Paris).

---

[17]   Keynes (1924, p. 148).

Einzig, P., 1934, France's crisis (MacMillan, London).

Einzig, P., 1935, World finance, 1914–1935 (MacMillan, New York).

Einzig, P., 1937, The theory of forward exchange (MacMillan, London).

Einzig, P., 1962, A dynamic theory of forward exchange (MacMillan, London).

Federal Reserve System, Monthly Bulletin.

Friedman, M., 1953, The case for flexible exchange rates, Essays in positive economics (Chicago).

Friedman, M., 1963, Statement, Hearings, Joint Economic Committee U.S. Congress, 88th Congress, 1st Session, Part 3 (Washington).

Friedman, M. and Anna Schwartz, 1963, A monetary history of the United States, 1867–1960 (Princeton University Press, Princeton).

Gides, Charles and W. Oualid, 1931, Bilan de la guerre pour la France (Les Presses Universitaires, Paris).

Graham, F., 1930, Exchange, prices, and production in hyper-inflation, Germany, 1920–23 (Princeton University Press, Princeton).

Graham, Frank D., 1949, The cause and cure of "dollar shortage", Essays in international finance, no. 10, January (Princeton University Press, Princeton).

Haberler, G., 1943, The choice of exchange rates after the war, American Economic Review, June.

Harris, E.S., 1931, Monetary problems of the British Empire (MacMillan, New York).

Hawtrey, Ralph, 1932, Art of central banking (Longmans, Green, London).

Hicks, J.R., 1953, An inaugural lecture, Oxford Economic Papers, June.

Jack, D.T., 1927, The restoration of European currencies (P.S. King, London).

Johnson, H.G., 1961, International trade and economic growth, chapters III and IV (Harvard University Press, Cambridge, Mass.).

Kemp, M.C., 1964, The pure theory of international trade (Prentice–Hall Englewood Cliffs).

Keynes, J.M., 1924, Monetary reform (Harcourt, Brace & Co., New York).

Keynes, J.M., 1925, The economic consequences of sterling parity (Harcourt, Brace & Co., New York).

Keynes, J.M., 1927, The British balance of trade, 1925–27, Economic Journal, Dec.

Keynes, J.M., 1958, Treatise on money, Vol. I & II (MacMillan, London).

Laursen, S. and L. Metzler, 1950, Flexible exchange rates and the theory of employment, Review of Economics and Statistics, Nov.

League of Nations, 1924, Memorandum on currency and central banking, 1913–24, Monthly Bulletin of Statistics (Geneva).

League of Nations, 1929, Memorandum on public finance, Monthly Bulletin of Statistics (Geneva).

Lewis, W.A., 1949, Economic survey, 1919–1939 (Allen and Unwin, London).

Lutz, F.A., 1965, World inflation and domestic monetary policy, Banca Nationale del Lavoro, June.

MacDonald, W., 1922, Reconstruction in France (MacMillan, London).

MacGuire, Constantine E., 1926, Italy's international economic position (MacMillan, New York).

Marion, Marcel, 1931, Histoire financière de la France, Vol. VI (Rousseau et Cie, Paris).

Meade, J.E., 1955, The case for flexible exchange rates, Three Bank Review, September.

Metzler, L., 1947, Exchange rates and international monetary fund, Board of Governors, Federal Reserve System, Post-war economic studies, no. 7.

Morgen, E.V., 1952, Studies in British finance (MacMillan, London).

Myers, Margaret G., 1936, Paris as a financial centre (P.S. King and Son, London).

Nurkse, R., 1944, International currency experience, League of Nations, United Nations reprint, 1947.

Nurkse, R., 1945, Conditions of international monetary equilibrium, Essays in international finance, Princeton University, no. 4. Reprinted in the Readings in the theory of international trade.

Ogburn, W.F. and W. Jaffe, 1929, The economic development of post-war France (Columbia University Press, New York).

Orcutt, G.H., 1950, Measurement of price elasticities in international trade, Review of Economics and Statistics, May.

Peel, George, 1937, The economic policy of France (MacMillan, London).

Pigou, A.C., 1948, Aspects of British economy history, 1918–1925 (MacMillan, London).

Polak, J.J., 1943, European exchange depreciation in the early twenties, Econometrica, April.

Report, 1931, MacMillan Committee on finance and industry (HMSO, London).

Rogers, J.H., 1929, The process of inflation in France, 1914–1927 (Columbia University Press, New York).

Rhomberg, R.R., 1960, Canada's foreign exchange market, IMF, Staff Papers.

Rhomberg, R.R., 1964, A model of the Canadian economy, Journal of Political Economy.

Rowe, J.W., 1927, An index of physical volume of production, Economic Journal, June.

Shepherd, H.L., 1936, The monetary experience of Belgium, 1914–1936 (Princeton University Press, Princeton).

Sohmen, Egon, 1961, Flexible exchange rates (Chicago University Press, Chicago).

Stein, J.L., 1962, The nature and efficiency of the foreign exchange market, Essays in international finance, no. 40, October (Princeton University Press, Princeton).

Stein, J.L., 1963, The optimum foreign exchange market, American Economic Review, June.

Stein, J.L. and E. Fower, The short-term stability of the foreign exchange market, Review of Economics and Statistics.

Stolper, W.F., 1950, Note on multiple flexible exchange rates and the dollar shortage, Economia Internazionale, August.

Telser, L.G., 1959, A theory of speculation relating profitability and stability, Review of Economics and Statistics, August.

Tsiang, S.C., 1957, An experiment with flexible exchange rate system, IMF, Staff Papers, Feb.

Tsiang, S.C., 1958, A theory of foreign exchange speculation under a floating exchange system, Journal of Political Economy.

Tsiang, S.C., 1959, Fluctuating exchange rates in countries with relatively stable economies, IMF, Staff Papers.

Vanek, J., 1965, International trade theory and economic policy (Richard D. Irwin, Homewood Ill.).

Young, J.P., 1925, European currency and finance (Government Printing Press, Washington).

Recent Issues in the Theory of Flexible Exchange Rates, edited by E. Claassen and P. Salin
© North-Holland Publishing Company, 1983

Chapter 11.2

COMMENT ON GRISSA

Michael CONNOLLY

The richness of the historical details on France in the 1920s provided by Abdessatar Grissa makes for exciting reading, and there is no doubting the originality of his analysis which was done in the mid-1960s. We are thus doubly fortunate to have an opportunity to revisit this especially interesting period. In the essay, the following points are stressed:

(1) The importance of expectations in explaining the movement of the exchange rate, and in particular, expectations regarding the future supply of money.
(2) The role of high and unsteady inflation in crippling both private and public bond markets so that the state increasingly resorted to finance by the printing press.
(3) The phenomenon of overshooting in the rate of inflation and the exchange rate in the later stages of the inflationary process.
(4) The importance of confidence in the implementation of a stabilization program.

These points are well-documented and leave little room for quarrel. They also have a distinctly modern ring.

As Grissa points out, the French franc experience of the 1920s led Ragnar Nurkse to conclude that speculation was destabilizing, a point disputed by Milton Friedman in his case for flexible exchange rates. What appears to be the case is that from late 1925 through mid-1926, there was a collapse of confidence in the franc and its value depreciated substantially more than warranted by the increase in the money stock. This overshooting in the exchange rate came to an end with Poincaré's stabilization program in 1926. Nowadays, the phenomenon of overshooting is a commonplace theoretical and empirical finding. Further, recent expectations theories suggest that movements in the exchange rate can be very volatile. For these reasons, it is difficult to conclude that the exchange market was unstable, so that the focus of the debate has shifted away from this consideration.

Grissa seems to have put his finger on the source of the problem: high and unstable monetary growth to finance government deficits. Contrary to Tsiang, the existence of pegged "bons du Trésor" was not the source of monetary growth. Grissa appears to be right on this point. What is quite extraordinary is that during this very inflationary period in France, England had been undergoing a deflation in order to return to the gold standard at the pre-war parity. The early twenties was thus a period of deflation and umemployment in Britain, quite a contrast with the French experience.

Britain returned to the gold standard in 1925, somewhat earlier than the French in 1927, but experienced great unemployment problems in 1926, as Keynes had predicted. His criticism was that the pre-war parity could not be maintained without severe deflation, so it was a quarrel with the rate rather than the fact of returning to the gold standard. It is thus interesting to note that the quotation Grissa takes from Keynes' *Monetary Reform* suggests that sound economic policies should precede a return to convertibility, and that the latter would be the announcement of a "fait accompli."

In short, this essay is a very rich one indeed, in terms of historical insight, attention to detail, and thoroughness of analysis. It is a pity that it was not published at the time it was completed. It was certainly pioneering work then, but is a bit dated here and there. In particular, it would have been useful to incorporate developments of the 1970s such as rational expectations and tests for causality of the Sims and Granger variety. Nevertheless, it is still today a remarkable essay that significantly adds to our understanding of the French experience of the 1920s.

AUTHOR INDEX